Patrick Heron

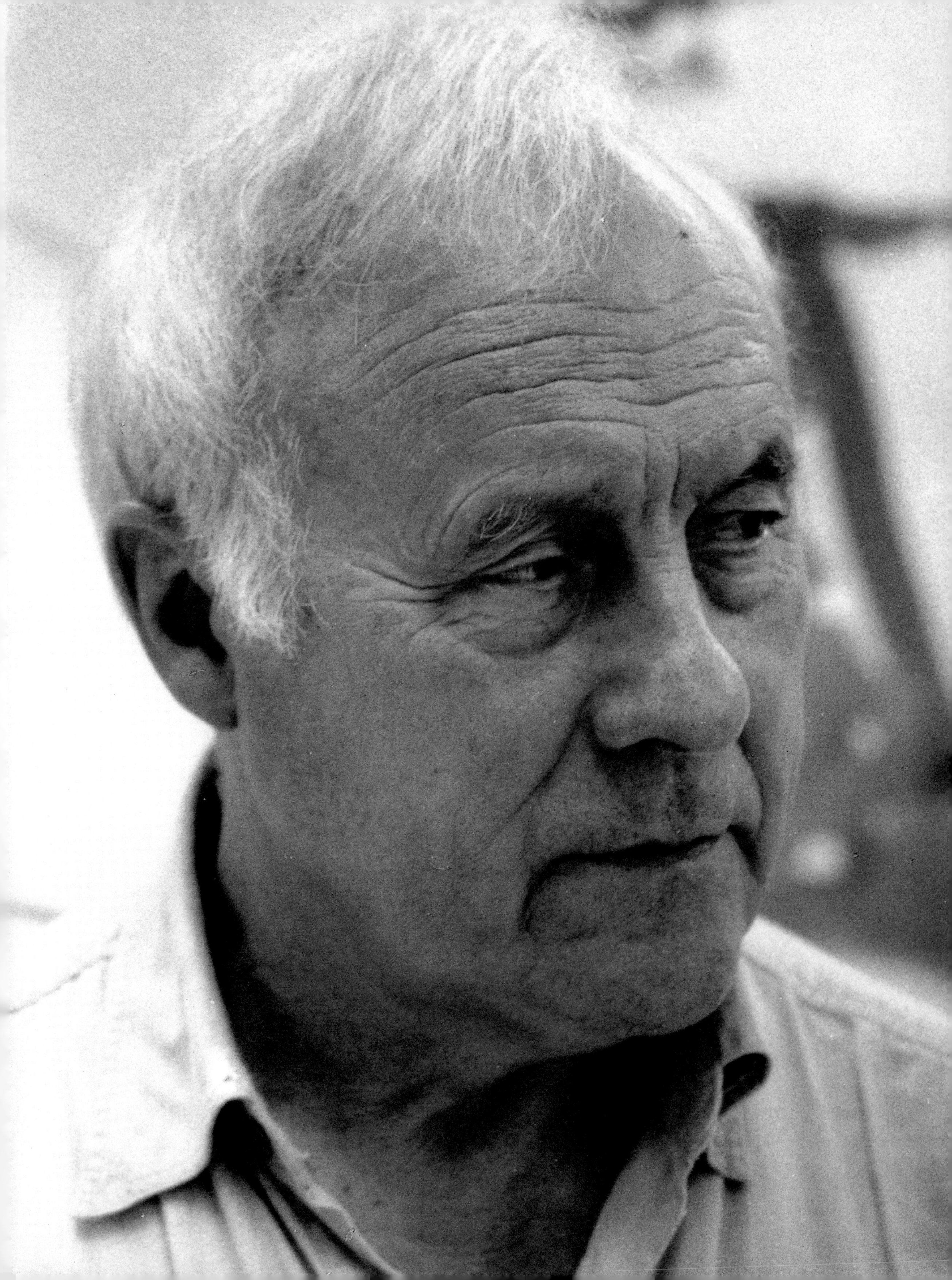

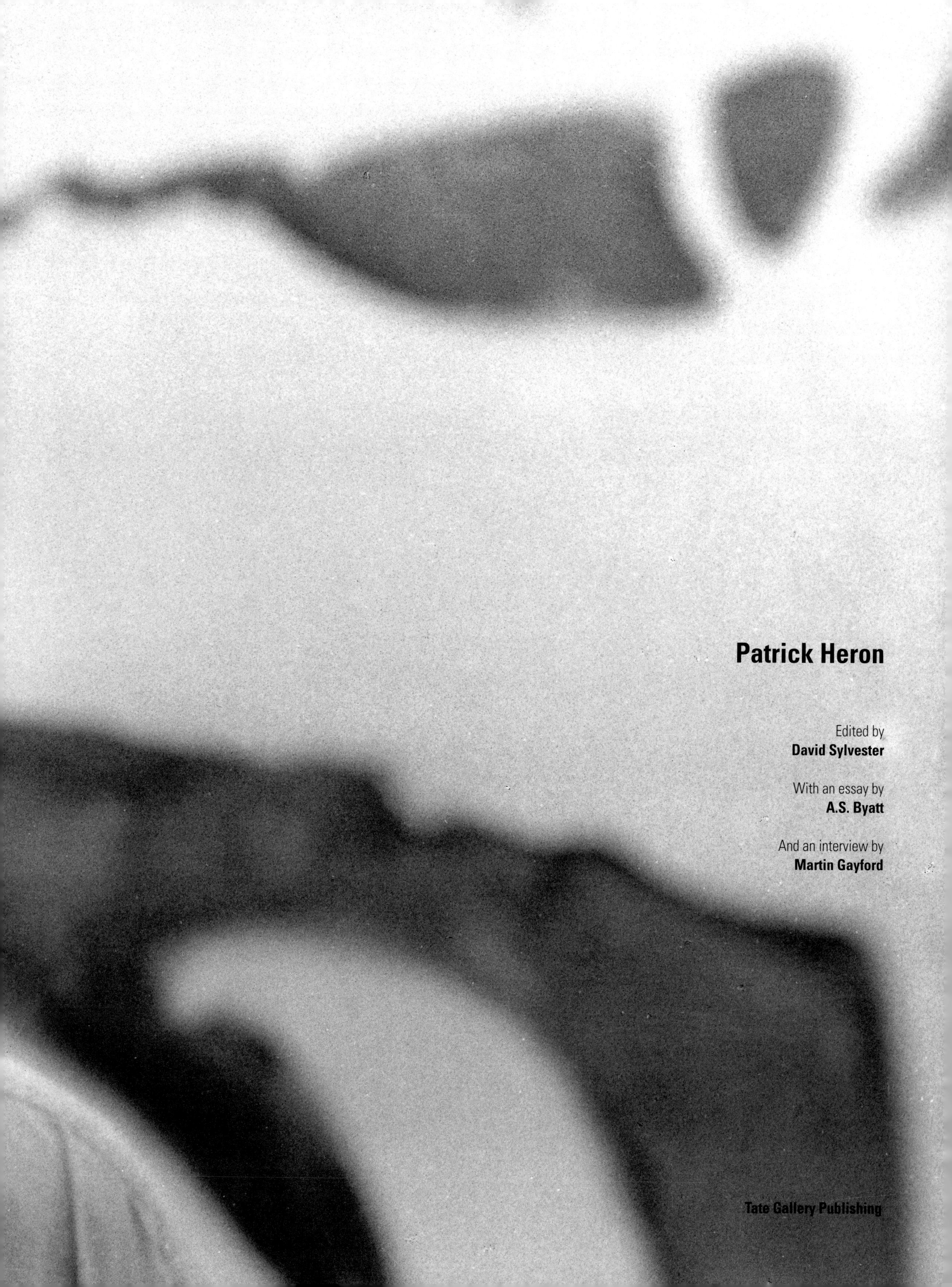

Patrick Heron

Edited by
David Sylvester

With an essay by
A.S. Byatt

And an interview by
Martin Gayford

Tate Gallery Publishing

The exhibition at the Tate Gallery is supported by Tate Friends

TateFriends

Cover
Vertical Light: March 1957 (no.20)

Title page
Patrick Heron in his studio 1995
Photograph by Julian Feary

Published by order of the Trustees of the Tate Gallery 1998
on the occasion of the exhibition at the Tate Gallery 25 June – 6 September 1998

ISBN 1 85437 250 5

A catalogue record for this publication is available from the British Library

Published by Tate Gallery Publishing Limited
Millbank, London SW1P 4RG

Designed and typeset by Isambard Thomas

Printed in Great Britain by Westerham Press, Edenbridge, Kent

Contents

Foreword

Nicholas Serota, Director

It is with great pleasure and anticipation that we are presenting this exhibition of Patrick Heron's paintings at the Tate Gallery. Heron is one of the leading figures in twentieth-century British art and he has played the role of a catalyst in the development of post-war abstract art. However, he has lived and worked in Cornwall since the 1950s and his work also reflects a passion for the landscape of West Penwith, with its extraordinary light, colour, shapes and texture. These elements are apparent in the work with a vitality that has been maintained throughout his career. Heron has an ability to work on very divergent scales, from small canvases to large-scale, seventeen-foot paintings. The power of the image is sustained in whatever scale he chooses to work with.

David Sylvester, who has had a long association with Heron's work, has selected this exhibition and edited the catalogue. We are enormously grateful to him. He has been rigorous in his choice of works and the decision to make this an exhibition of just paintings was not an easy one, but it seemed very important to allow the works space to breathe. The synthesis of sixty years work has produced a show that we are sure will not only be very exciting but a revelation.

We are indebted to the lenders to this exhibition, both public and private. Their support cannot be underestimated and we would be unable to present such a comprehensive exhibition without them. Special thanks must also be extended to the artist's daughters, Katharine and Susanna, who have been unstinting in their support. They, together with Julian Feary, have given over much of their time and we cannot thank them enough. Leslie Waddington and Tom Lighton of the Waddington Galleries have given often and freely their advice. Janet Axten, the artist's assistant has also been a great source of information. We owe a special debt to Sarah Tinsley who has guided the preparations of this exhibition with her customary skill and insight.

I should like to thank Martin Gayford for his illuminating interview with the artist and A.S. Byatt for her vivid personal response to the art of Patrick Heron. Thanks are also due to Sir Alan Bowness, James Faure Walker, Alan Gouk, and the estate of the late Peter Fuller for allowing earlier writings on Heron to be reproduced. An anthology of writings by the artist himself has been selected by Mel Gooding and is being published to coincide with this exhibition. This is entirely appropriate for an artist whose critical reflections on the art of the past as well as the present and comments on art education have been so influential over a period of more than half a century.

David Thomson and Mr and Mrs D.M. Shalit have generously supported the catalogue and their involvement has enabled us to pay particular attention to the colour plate section and ensure that the reproductions are of the highest quality.

This is the first time in its history that the Tate Friends have supported an exhibition and we are truly delighted that they have chosen to do so, in celebration of their fortieth anniversary. Their continuing commitment to the Tate and all its activities is warmly welcome.

Finally and most particularly, my thanks go to Patrick Heron, who has approached this exhibition and the inevitable invasion into his life and work with a warmth and openness that has been truly magnificent. Throughout this time he has continued to paint and we are pleased to be including a new work completed earlier this year. My colleagues at the Tate, from many departments, have thoroughly enjoyed working with him and his commitment to this project has ensured a remarkable exhibition and catalogue.

Supporter's Foreword

Wilf Weeks, Chairman
Friends of the Tate Gallery

I am delighted that we are able to make the Patrick Heron show the first exhibition at the Tate to be supported exclusively by the Friends. It is wholly appropriate that the Friends should be closely associated with this exhibition, as Patrick Heron has been both a Trustee of the Tate Gallery and a leading supporter of the Gallery in St Ives.

Since the Friends of the Tate Gallery was founded in 1958, we have traditionally helped the Tate with its acquisitions policy. More recently, we have been able to allocate our funds to the broader work of the Gallery, helping with education, conservation and other activities, whilst continuing to support new purchases. I can think of no more fitting way to celebrate our fortieth anniversary than by supporting our first exhibition. I very much hope it will be greatly enjoyed by all who visit it.

Curator's Preface

David Sylvester

This exhibition has been a product of real teamwork. Patrick Heron has been an inspiring source of constructive suggestions. His daughters, Katharine and Susanna, have responded with unstinting generosity to requests for advice and information, as has his son-in-law, Julian Feary. And his assistant, Janet Axten, has provided crucial adminstrative support.

I am extremely indebted to David Thomson, the artist's most devoted and expert collector, for his guidance, and am similarly indebted to Heron's dealer, Leslie Waddington. At the Tate, Nick Serota has been closely and rewardingly involved in every aspect and at every stage of the planning and realisation of the show. Ruth Rattenbury, the Head of Exhibitions, made a substantial contribution to the initial planning. Celia Clear, Judith Severne and Tim Holton of Tate Gallery Publishing have been most helpful and perspicacious in the realisation of the catalogue. Sarah Tinsley, the exhibition officer, ably assisted by Ben Tufnell, has made the adminstrative wheels run with impeccable smoothness. Besides that, she has been jointly responsible for virtually every decision in the selection of the works, the design of the exhibition and the editing of the catalogue.

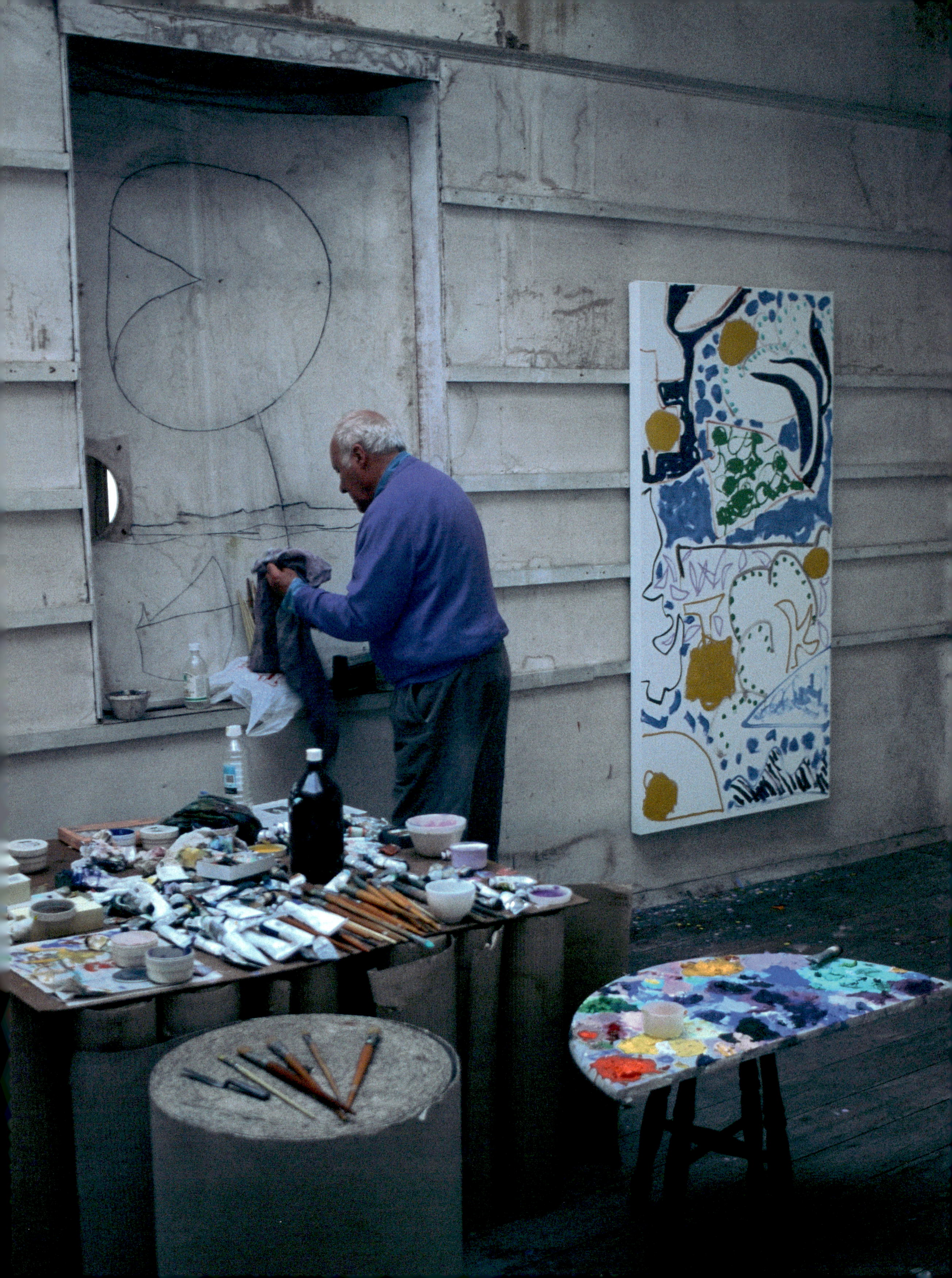

Patrick Heron in his studio
Photograph by Susanna Heron

'The most damning thing you could say'

David Sylvester

Patrick Heron is nothing if not politically incorrect. He tells Martin Gayford that 'the height of art' is the decorative, defining this as 'the flawless organisation of the surface into terms that are instantly pleasurable to the eye', tells him too that 'Tintoretto, Velázquez, Constable and all the great French are fantastically decorative in that sense', even when they are painting 'horrendous subject matter'. And he derides and denounces the English for their habitual use of 'decorative' as 'a term of the utmost contempt and dismissal'.

It is odd that he sees disdain for the 'decorative' as a peculiarly English vice – and even as the reason why English art was 'not much good for so long' – given that a scathing attitude to the 'decorative' goes far beyond this country and the kinds of artist it specialises in producing. It is not just the Francis Bacons of this world who deem 'decoration' to be beyond the pale; a leading American abstract sculptor such as Carl Andre thinks of 'decoration' as unworthy. Not wishing to take the positions of two artists, however distinguished and divergent, as conclusive, I thought I should take a poll on the subject among art-world people who were not artists and males, and chose a random sample of one woman. 'What do you think "decoration" means nowadays?', I asked. '"Decoration"? I suppose that's the most damning thing you could say about a piece of art.' So Heron is politically incorrect all the way across the board.

Heron's aesthetic creed affirms, then, that it suffices for art to be joyful – to be permeated by joy, to provoke joy, to be made with joy. With reference to the latter, he has said that he knows no greater pleasure than putting paint on canvas: 'there's nothing to match it.' But there's another matchless pleasure about which he spoke to Gayford: 'Looking at something – anything – is more interesting than doing anything else, ever, as a matter of fact.' On the subject of this delight he also said: 'The greater the intensity of your consciousness and visual concentration, the greater the pleasure. Any data can supply that. Even if you were in a prison cell, you could sit there and become aware of the shape of colour and the colour of shape. To the extent that you become aware, you will be transported.'

What delights me primarily in Heron's paintings is precisely the feeling of transport they convey. They look as if they'd been painted by someone who was intoxicated – intoxicated by the air he breathed so long as his eyes were open.

But it doesn't stop there. Bacon, to quote him again, used to say that painting was good in so far as it returned the spectator to reality. Painting doesn't have to be realistic to do that: there are 'realist' painters the sight of whose literal representations doesn't at all return me to the reality of the subjects they depict but only makes me ask myself why they painted them. Heron's dances of colour and line immediately summon up, vividly and electrically, all sorts of floating sensations of the world, gloriously mixed and melting and colliding and entwining – leaves and flowers and pots and tables and breasts and arms and faces and skies, all moving and growing, all breathing.

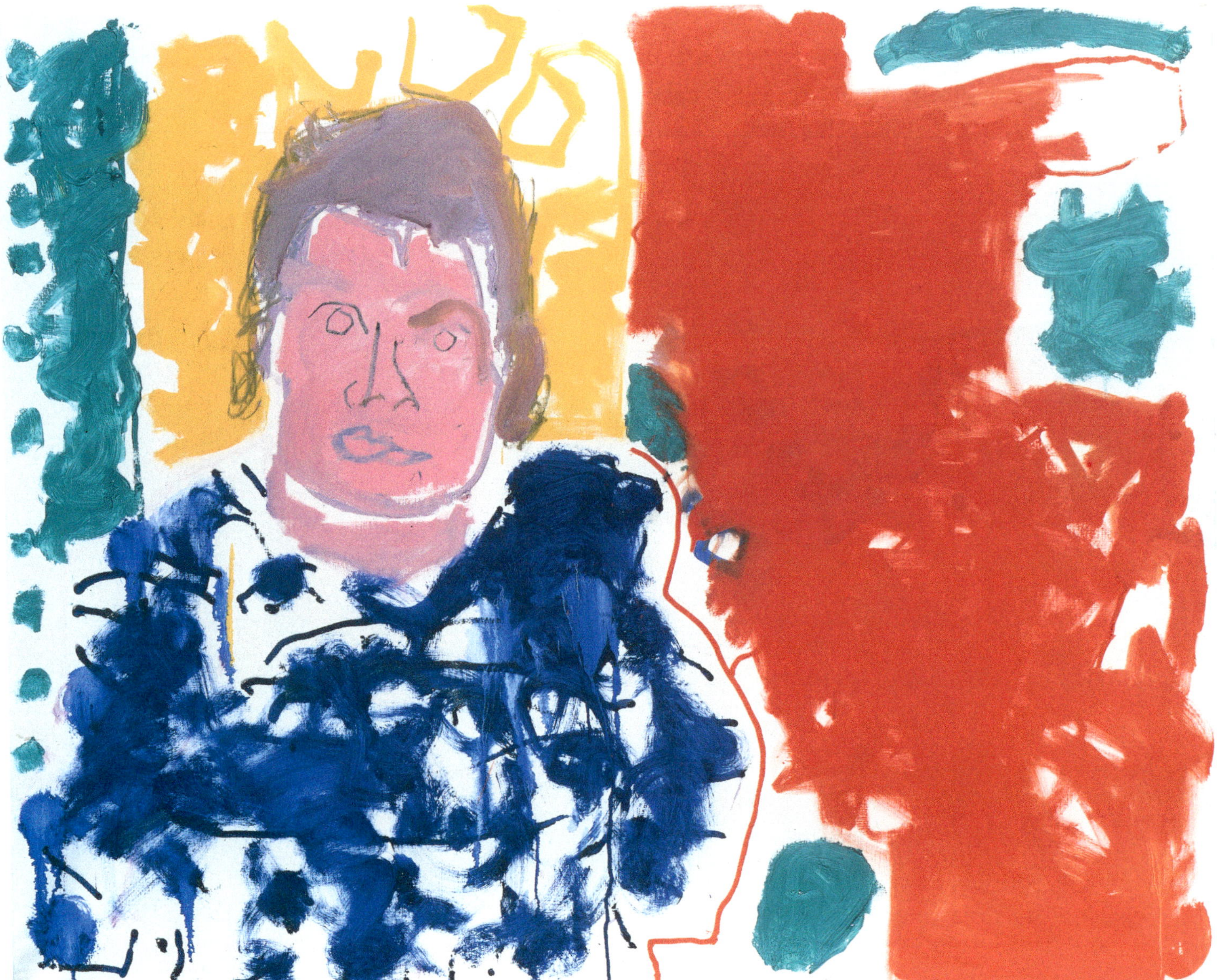

A Riddle around the Edges of Vision

A.S. Byatt

fig.1 **Portrait of A.S. Byatt: Red, Yellow, Green and Blue: 24 September 1997** Oil on canvas 96.5 × 121.9 cm National Portrait Gallery, London

The English are timid – reticent may be a better word – about colour. Our light is muted through our watery air; we incline naturally to soft greys and greens and faded blues. It is not in our nature or our tradition to assent eagerly to van Gogh's assertion that the painter of the future will be above all a great colourist, or to Patrick Heron's claim in 1962 that 'colour is now the *only* direction in which painting can travel. Painting still has a continent left to explore, in the direction of colour, and in no other direction.' Colour is notoriously difficult to write about, partly for linguistic reasons explored by Wittgenstein in his *Remarks on Colour* where he worries away at the problem of how two people know that they share a sensation they call 'red', and partly for reasons that Heron himself gave when he wrote that he wished his words about paintings to 'militate against mere verbal consciousness. Too much painting today arises out of verbal consciousness; too much painting springs out of and is dictated by a conceptual consciousness which is verbal in origin and utterly unintuitive.' Writers tend to like paintings with concepts, meanings and narratives attached, and this inclination has become more fierce and intense during Heron's painting life. What I love about Heron's work is the visual and intellectual delight of the colours and forms which are *other* than language, and cannot be reduced to it, or involved in it. This makes him hard to write about. It is as though there is something inappropriate about metaphor and analogy, in the context of this pure abstraction.

My first acquaintance with him came from the series of clear, brilliant, complex prints he made in the 1970s. Seen in galleries, across art fairs, standing out in a wall of other images, glimpsed out of the corner of the eye across a large space, these works had an authority, and a coherence, which gave a pleasure both immediate and lasting, both simple and enduringly complicated. Colour to the innocent eye is a personal matter; everyone has a range of colours they naturally respond to. We bought a clear buttercup yellow print, with a canary yellow disc on it, and an interlocking corner of dark shadowy blue and a paler green-blue. There is a small red form on the left edge, and a dark brown form, both with jigsaw holes round the predominant yellow. These words are completely inadequate. Buttercups and canaries vary, and those are the evocative words. Then we bought a light speedwell-blue print with strong dark pink on scarlet at one edge, a small, bright yellow at another, and a dark blue vanishing at the bottom right-hand corner. Then a dark green with swimming pinks and scarlets, then a dark purple with reds and greens and blues, then a quite different purple, then, finally, a predominantly orange print, with a sharp and a rich yellow, a dark red and a khaki. Orange is a colour I don't like, in the abstract, a colour I don't choose for pots or clothes or furnishings. Yet I *needed* the orange print because of the existing presence on the wall of the yellow and the blue, the pinks and the green and the purples. Now I look at it every day, and it shines simply and intensely, and I contemplate orange, and how I do not know what it is, how it is quite another experience, surrounding a three-quarter circle of soft khaki, or surrounded by a very slightly acid harbour or necklace of yellow, or interlocking with dark red.

I wrote that these images had both authority and coherence. The authority is to do with the onlooker's sense of rightness and unexpectedness of the relation between the elements in the paintings, the choice and juxtaposition of colours, the relative sizes of the forms.

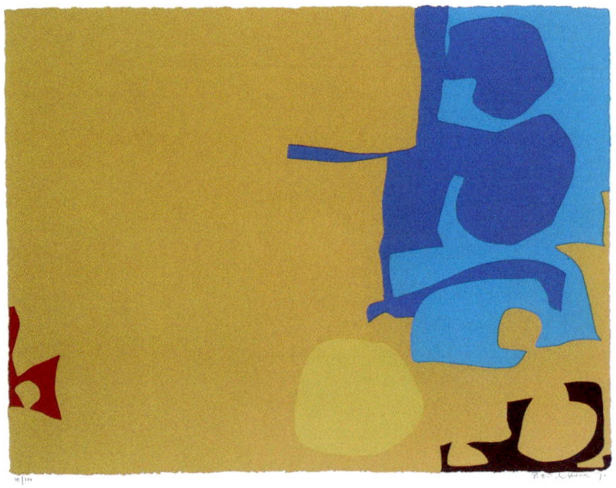

Coleridge often spelled the word 'coherence' 'co-haerence', in order to recall its Latin root, with the meaning of things clinging, or holding together. The forms in the fields of Heron's wobbly hard-edged paintings of the 1970s cohere in the arbitrary and necessary limits of the frame, giving both the impression of being in their only possible and proper places, and, simultaneously, of an attempt to shift, or escape, to change relations in the much larger field of one's whole visual experience. Heron's paintings are paintings about vision – not visionary experiences, but contemplations, illustrations, makings strange, of the way our eyes and brains put the world together, from moment to moment. They need to be contemplated over time with a steady stare, so that the eye, and the mind's eye, are saturated with rich expenses of red, or depths of purple purple, and they need also the attention of the flickering, travelling movement of the eye that catches forms at the edge of vision (or the edge of the frame) and shifts to put these forms in focus, a movement which transforms what had been the deep, still centre of the gaze to a shimmer at the edge of the vision. The travelling movements teach us that we do not know what colours are, and cannot hold them steady. Concentration on the hooks and eyes of red in blue, or blue in red (it is both simultaneously) makes the blue and red both more uncertain, and more themselves. These paintings both create and are about after-images. Staring at a Heron, like staring at the sun, can fill a white wall with moving discs and strips of visible mind-made colours, called up by looking. 'Harbours', or wandering sunspots, protrude from the straight edge of the frame, or run along it, as though they are parts of moving things that are going on elsewhere, just out of sight. Patrick Heron's simultaneous emphasis of, and questioning of, the frame is a quite different matter from the conceptual idea that framing something is a cultural statement that it is a work of art. Heron's frames are a riddle about the edges of vision and the edges of forms and paintings. Indeed, what I profoundly love and admire about his work is its lack of *self*-assertion. His proceedings are, as he says, instinctive and intuitive, but his brush-strokes do not say 'This is mine. I, Patrick Heron made this. Look at me.' They create autonomous shapes which are colours, colours which define and construct forms. He wrote in 1969 'When you open your eyes, the entire visual field (which opening them reveals to you) consists of one thing; and that thing is colour.' His paintings are about opening your eyes, moving your gaze through the fields of light. He is as T.S. Eliot said the artist should be, impersonal, one who 'nothing himself, lets all things be through him.'

fig.2 (above) **January 1973: 18** Screenprint 58.6 × 79.4 cm A.S. Byatt

fig.3 (below) **Blues Dovetailed in Yellow 1970** Screenprint 59.7 × 78.7 cm A.S. Byatt

fig.4 **10–11 July: 1992** 198.1 × 274.3 cm Tate Gallery

I have said that it feels inappropriate, or reductive, to insert metaphors or analogies into descriptions of the colour paintings of the 1970s. This is not true of the recent series of garden paintings and gouaches, inspired by the light and flora of Sydney Harbour and the Sydney botanical garden. What was an elegant contemplation of divisions, edges, and stains has become a Monet-like record of what William James called the blooming buzzing confusion of innocent, unordered sensory experience. The surfaces are not lacquered and fine but alive with zig-zags, scribbles, hatchings, paleness scuffed and overlaid, with pure white trails of paint on pure white canvas making material patches of light. The reds and sharp yellows and blues of the earlier paintings have given way to candy pinks, and opaque mauves, with light in the paint, to bluish greens that remind one that (English) grass green

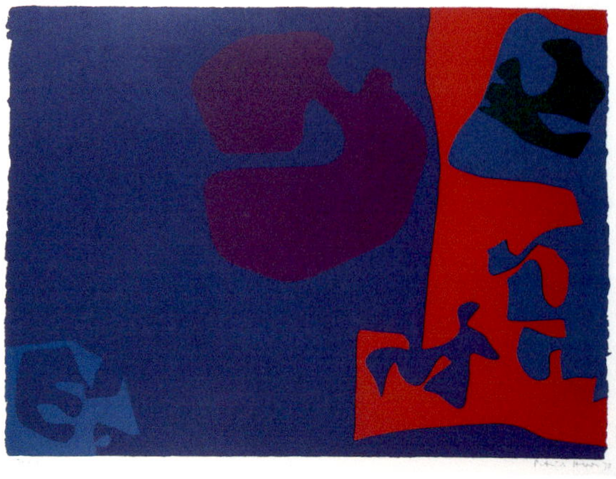

looks unnatural in Australia amongst the gums and eucalyptuses. One has to learn to look at them all over again; the eye has to be busy, weaving and disentangling, standing back and seeing the coherent forms of all the activity in the whole painting; they are forms that are designed to reveal their coherence only slowly and only momentarily, and sometimes more easily in small colour reproductions than in the vast wandering spaces, with their paths and flower-beds and pools and fences crazily intersecting on the canvases. These, too are colours I had to learn to love, and to see for themselves. Mel Gooding has rightly said that they are related to the mauves and pinks of Matisse's late paintings, which also carry associations of prettiness, slightness, that people are anxious about. Associations we make to colours are a mystery, and not constant, either within or beyond cultures. One critic felt it necessary to defend Heron against a charge of using 'toy-box colours' – which was simply to say that we now have toys in brilliant primary-coloured plastic in a way that was never technically possible in earlier times.

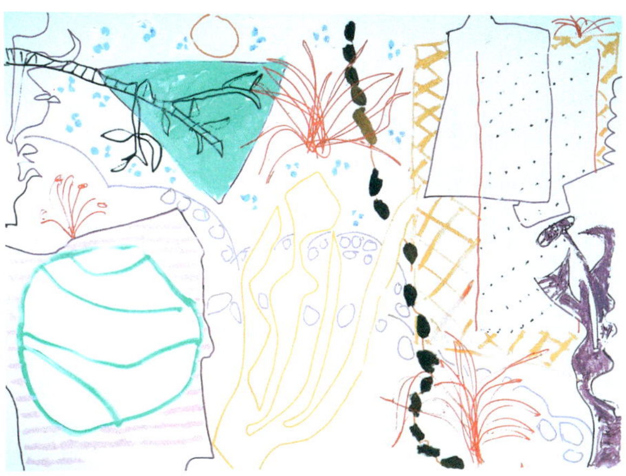

Having been drawn to Heron's work by the intensity of the non-verbal experience of it, I was disconcerted to find how easily and well he himself writes about paint, his own, and even more, that of other painters. He has a particular grace in describing the relations of the abstract form to the real forms in the world of things, from which the paintings are abstracted. His essay on Bonnard is masterly, both in his precise description of the characteristic abstract rhythm or pattern of Bonnard's surfaces, and in his equally precise analysis of the painting and depiction of the objects in depth which are present. Bonnard, he says, can be seen through the metaphor of 'a piece of large-scale fish-net drawn over the surface of the canvas: it is through an imaginary structure of loose, connected squares – sometimes pulled into oblongs and sometimes into diamond shapes – that Bonnard seems to look at his subject'. He remarks, en passant, that 'Velasquez is *concealing* purely abstract shapes – egg-forms and fish-forms just under the surface of his subjects, whether human or inanimate'. Both these observations reveal something, teach a way of looking. Or take his description of Ivon Hitchens at work:

> *The passionate sideways stabbing of a large blunt brush, loaded with a dull yet luminous olive mixture, registers the near (so near, it is almost out of focus) curved, lower branch of a pine tree in terms of a broad, fuzzy arc of olive paint. A second stab, and there we see a second branch, exactly ten feet behind the first, but less fuzzy, more in focus; and greener, perhaps, because of some play of the light, as it filters down through the furry, blue-green layers of the pine-tree. The point is: the stabbed arc of greeny-olive paint is the pine branch.*

Or his comparison of the rhythms ('slow, precise, immaculate') of Tintoretto and Braque, his analytic description of the 'dark marble lozenges' of Tintoretto's painting of the floor in *Mars and Venus* which reveal the Venetian as 'a master of allover design', his perception of the solid forms of the paintings as 'silhouettes', flat outlines bounded by continuous outlines. And in parenthesis an unforgettable description of the Susanna of Tintoretto's *Susanna and the*

Elders. 'Her immensely luminous body *floats* in the dark-green of the garden.' Heron's exact curiosity, looking at other painters' work, is a form of generosity which is related to the calm curiosity (which is a passion) of his painting of vision, which is not self-assertion but feeling and understanding.

Heron has said repeatedly that his work is a materialist art, dealing with images not symbols. it is a profoundly intelligent art, a thinking art as well as an expressive art, but it is no more conceptual than it is symbolist. It deals with the endlessly changing, endlessly beautiful, endlessly interesting relations between the finite human body and the world it perceives and constructs. I havc thought that the colours, and the fine surfaces of the 1970s paintings, are a response to the complete changes in the colours in our environment in our lifetime. I remember reading Norman Cohn's *The Pursuit of the Millennium* in the 1960s and realising that the medieval experience of man-made colour was rich and rare – bright cloths

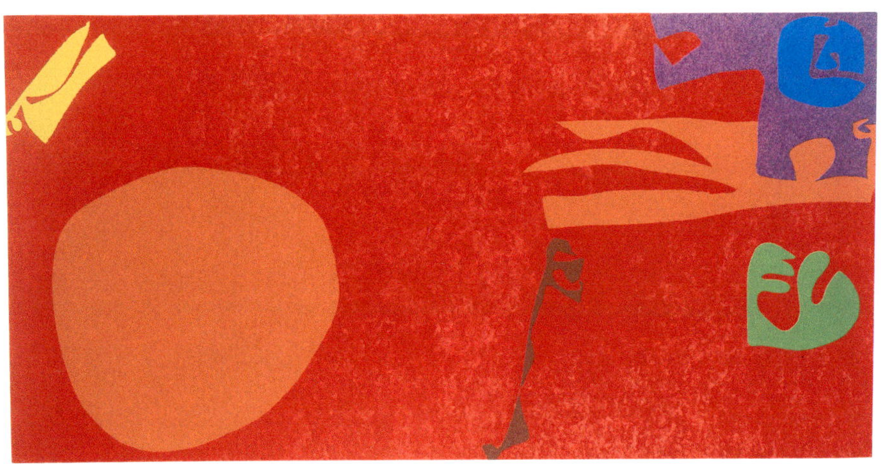

fig.5 **Long Cadmium with Ceruleum in Violet (Boycott): July–November 1977** Oil on canvas 198 × 396.2 cm Waddington Galleries, London

fig.6 **Window for Tate Gallery St Ives: 1992–3** Coloured glass 460 × 420 cm Fabrication in coloured glass by W. Derix Studio

for the aristocracy, miniatures in private libraries, the transparent coloured glass in the great cathedrals. I remember the absence of colour in the khaki utility world of the Second World War. Colour television arrived in 1968, and I sat transfixed in front of this blaze of transparent, coloured light which was a completely new way of seeing. At the same time I was teaching literature to art students, one of whom explained to me that there was a common experience, in students who had learned to see Matisse or Monet, Titian or Vermeer, through the medium of the projected slide, with its *light through colour*, its capacity to expand details like a vision, of slight disappointment when presented with the painted surface itself, less bright, more limited and solid. The student was worried that his fellows were being deprived of, or given a distorted vision of, painted surfaces. But I felt all that was a new vision of things unknown before then. Alan Gouk has expressed doubts about Heron's refusal in those 1970s paintings, made with hours of work with a very fine brush, of the 'painterly' working of the surface of

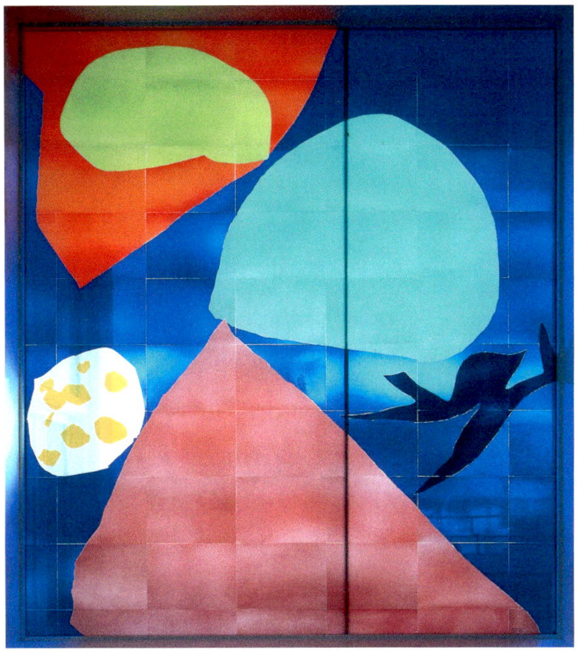

the paint. Heron himself, like all the painters I know, feels that the activity of arm and brush, hand and eye, is an essential part of the experience of colour in the body. But I feel that those great floods of cadmium, cerulean, violet, those bright meetings and juxtapositions, are a response to the new colours in our world, which often come to us as stains, or coloured light, colours never before seen. Matisse hoped that his colours would make his paintings sources of light in their surroundings, and I find myself staring into the Heron prints in winter as I stare into the full-spectrum light-box I bought as an antidote to SAD (seasonal affective disorder). It is amusing, in the context of light-boxes, to discover that Patrick Heron keeps an old television set in a shadowed room next to a painting with floating round-cornered lozenges that echo its shape, for that reason. Its lightless, brownish glass surface is part of the whole act of vision.

Early intense colours were made of glass, in mosaic, and in stained glass in windows. Heron's own window, in Tate Gallery St Ives, is a most wonderful wall of coloured glass, a completely modern experience of transparent light, where colour meets colour, without the lead surrounds of earlier windows. The lop-sided, vaguely triangular forms, rosy below, scarlet above, rise and descend in a dark blue space, in which a pale blue form, neither rounded nor pointed floats, balanced by a smaller white form, splashed with bright yellow, which contrasts with the sharp yellow which sits in the scarlet. There is a Matisse-like bird or sea form, ultramarine, swimming or flying, and the two reds are the reds of eyelids opening on the sky. The combination of these clear colours fills the space inside the window with a wonderfully uniform violet light, like a tank of violet liquid, which nevertheless changes as, in the outside world of sea and sky, and the Atlantic light beyond clouds stream across the sun, or swirl round it, dimming the brightness which then strikes again and changes the nature of the indoor violet. The colours are constant and constantly changing.

fig.7 (opposite) **Wicca Cove (from Eagles Nest): 1928**
Pastel on paper 22.8 × 30.5 cm
Private Collection

'Looking is more interesting than doing anything else, ever'

An Interview with Patrick Heron

Martin Gayford

MG *You came in a way from a very artistic background, didn't you?*

PH My father, Tom Heron, had many sides to him, and one of the strongest things about him was his purely visual aesthetic sense, which was amazing. He was a businessman, who set up his own firm when he was nineteen, manufacturing silk blouses in Leeds. But he was also a Fabian and a pacifist. In Leeds, he knew painters who were very aware of what was happening in Cubist Paris. In London he would go to the Café Royal to meet Ginner, and Gore, and Epstein, whom he knew well before the First World War. He had a good time meeting the avant garde. On several occasions he bought chairs and pottery and other things from Roger Fry's Omega Workshop. Herbert Read once actually said to me that my father had 'introduced him to modern art'. As far as painting was concerned, Britain then was totally benighted; my father's interests were utterly unusual. You know the saying 'my father knew Lloyd George', well, I used to say 'my father knew Gaudier-Brzeska'. So I was born into that kind of setting.

MG *And your mother?*

PH Her visual sense was extremely acute, but not painterly; her family were intensely orientated in a literary direction. They were also passionate about landscape, all her sisters and her brother adored the Lake District and the Yorkshire Dales. My mother's reaction to anything seen that was beautiful was extraordinary – frequently it was to flowers and landscape. Her whole face would go still and her eyes would open slightly wider, and you knew she was simply absorbing visually. It created a kind of silence.

MG *How did you come to St Ives?*

PH My father had a Yorkshire friend, called Alec Walker, who popped down here and bought a house, intending to become a painter. But instead he started a small firm called Crysede Silks Limited, for which he did the designs, which were very original, in Newlyn. In 1925 Alec asked my father to come down to Cornwall and run Crysede, abandoning his own firm in Leeds. So my father came down to Newlyn, and took over. The family moved to Newlyn, then Lelant, and finally St Ives. In my father's hands, in the next few years, Crysede flowered into a huge success. We lived in a big double-fronted house in St Ives for a while, just above where the Tate is now, and I went to two schools in St Ives. First St Ia's, where my greatest friend was Teddy Cothey. He lived at no.1 Harry's Court, which was entered from Back Road West exactly six inches from Alfred Wallis's front door. But in 1929 Walker suddenly told my father he was fed up with Crysede and wanted 'to close it down or give it away', as he told my mother. So my father left St Ives in the summer of 1929, and in the autumn he founded Cresta Silks at Welwyn Garden City, a firm which made history in British textiles. The first designs were by Paul Nash, Cedric Morris and Bruce Turner. The firm's stationery and the boxes for the dresses to be packed in were by E. McKnight Kauffer – wonderfully Cubist. But for the chain of Cresta shops and the factory at Welwyn Garden City, my father commissioned Wells Coates, who had had no previous architectural training, and made his name as a foremost architect of the modern movement in Britain with the Cresta shops.

MG *But to return to Alfred Wallis … this must have been before Wallis had taken up art as a pastime.*

PH He was unheard of; I must have seen him hundreds of times, but I don't remember him. In any case, Wallis had not yet started to paint. Then I was sent to a school, higher up the hill, where, among the other pupils were Mark Arnold-Forster, Peter and Mary Lanyon and Eleanor and Jessamine Leach – my parents were great friends of the Leachs. Peter was nearly two years older than me. We formed a club – The Golden Harp Club, with the sub-title 'for the preservation of culture in England' with Peter, my brother Michael and myself the sole members. At that stage, Peter wanted to be a sculptor, whereas I was already in full flood as a painter. I never had any doubt whatever, from the age of two or three, that I was going to be one, and my parents encouraged this greatly. They kept all my drawing books.

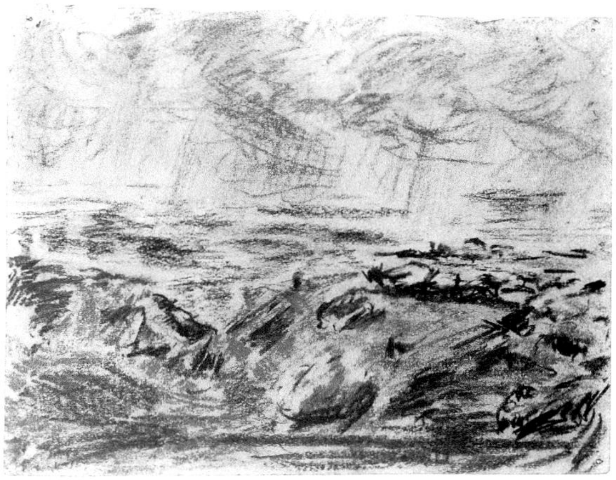

MG *So you were drawing St Ives subjects from the age of five. This house where you live now, Eagles Nest, always seems to me to have been your childhood paradise.*

PH Absolutely. I was still very attached to Yorkshire and the Dales, but there was no doubt about it that this house and this piece of coast and St Ives were amazingly important. When I was seven we moved here to Eagles Nest for five winter months, invited by the owners, Will and Ka Arnold-Forster. I spent my eighth birthday here at Eagles Nest. This landscape made the most tremendous impact on me as a child, especially living in this house. There's a gouache I painted in 1928 of some rocks on the sea-shore, with the waves breaking over them, and they are just the same shapes you find throughout my work, twenty years later.

MG *What was it about them that cast such a spell?*

PH Well, this landscape is remarkably wild, carved out by the elements. All these rocks around here that look as if they've been dropped or moved around are the residual core of stratified rock that has been carved by the rain and the wind. It's terrific stuff, sculpturally. I drew it all at the time, as a child. It was a great blow when my father's friend Alec went bananas and insisted on kicking my father out of Crysede, and we had to leave, in 1929. I remember my father saying, it won't be fishing boats and harbours any more, it'll probably be trams and buses again. In fact we moved to Welwyn Garden City. That was some change of scene – from Zennor to Welwyn. I went to Welwyn Garden City High School, and I met my wife Delia Reiss there. She was in the class the first morning. And that was that.

MG *Did you carry on painting at school?*

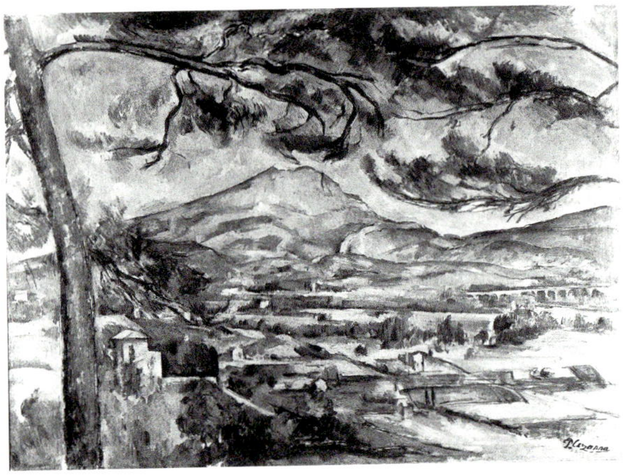

fig.8 Paul Cézanne **Mont Sainte Victoire** *c.*1886–8
Oil on canvas 66.8 × 92.3 cm Courtauld Institute of Art, London

fig.9 **Melon: 1934** Silk crepe de Chine 96.5 × 96.5 cm Private Collection

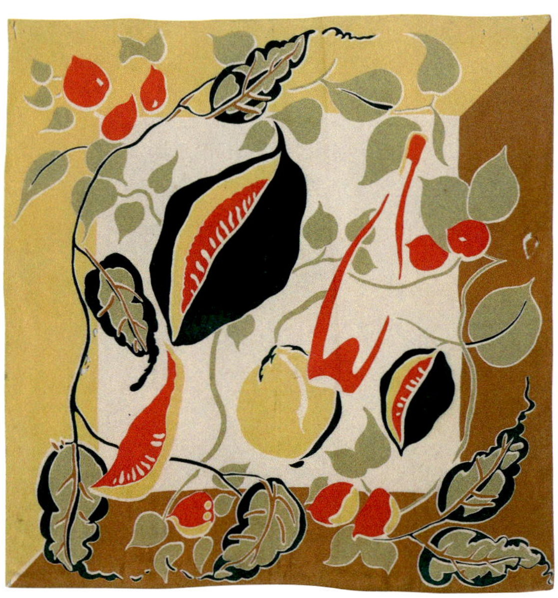

PH After a while, in 1932, my parents sent me to St George's School, Harpenden, where, because of asthma – which I rather cultivated – I was able to get out of games to go every afternoon to the art room. This was presided over by the art master, Ludwig van der Straeten – Vandy – who was amazing. He was very important in my life. One day, since we had a whole afternoon without games, he said 'Jump into the car, Heron'. And he leapt into his Ford V-8 and went at ninety miles an hour from Harpenden to Trafalgar Square, parked at the bottom of the steps on the Pall Mall side, didn't bother to lock the car, said 'Follow me, Heron', and led the way through the National Gallery to a room of the Courtauld pictures. He said not a word, just pointed at Cézanne's *Mont Sainte Victoire*. I went straight back and started painting Cézannes.

MG *Do you see connections between these boyhood works and your later painting?*

PH I maintain, really, that one never changes. The line in my childhood drawings, of the 1920s, emerges again in my paintings of the 1970s, and 1980s. They have the same wobbliness. I have never drawn a straight line, still less taken a ruler. In my case there really is very serious continuity between my childhood shapes and drawings and lines and my mature ones. Another example is *Bogey's Bar* [no.3], which was done at Welwyn a month or two after I left St Georges School, in early 1937, and it was a memory of a small café in Woburn Place. Years later, when I joined the Waddington Gallery, Victor Waddington said 'I notice you've pinned your future horizontal stripe paintings to the facade opposite'. I thought that was fantastically perceptive. It's absolutely right.

MG *Meanwhile, you were doing designs for your father's new firm, Cresta Silks.*

PH Yes, the first one was done in 1934, when I was fourteen. It was a large square called *Melon* [fig.9]. He was always tremendously supportive. Later, after the war, when I got married, I became as it were chief designer for Cresta, and he paid me a retainer, which we lived on really as I wasn't selling anything to speak of. I actually had a studio in the factory.

MG *So you had really a great deal of experience as a textile designer. Do you think that had an effect on your painting? That very early design from 1934 is much more like your later work than your paintings of the same date.*

PH I think it was. The paintings bowed down to Cézanne, and in some cases Sickert, but the Cresta design of 1934 is much more related to Matisse. But throughout my early life I had this tremendous battle against the total English contempt for anything they could call decorative. The word 'decorative' in English discussion of painting was always a term of the utmost contempt and dismissal, and I had the utmost contempt for *that* attitude. To me that just showed that England was puritanically excluding itself from understanding great painting. When one had shows after the war, *The Times* critic, for example, would write

'Mr Heron's paintings are effortlessly decorative' then, in brackets, 'he designs for Cresta silks'. That was how they got rid of me.

MG *Decorative meaning non-serious, whereas in your view …*

PH It's the height of art really. I defined decorative as the flawless organisation of the surface into terms which are instantly pleasurable to the eye. As far as I'm concerned Tintoretto, Velázquez, Constable, and all the great French are fantastically decorative in that sense. It doesn't matter if they are paintings of horrendous subject matter, I don't care a fig about that. The perfectly ordered surface gives very great pleasure. That pleasure used to be run away from by the English, that's why they were not much good for so long. We're heading for that condition again with all these chopped-up sheep.

MG *After a period of surprising precociousness, after 1937 when you went to the Slade, you seem to have entered a fallow period.*

PH That's absolutely true. The Slade was a complete wash-out. I should never have agreed to go. It was complete and utter rubbish from one end of the building to the other. Almost nobody there was aware of twentieth-century painting. That's why I only went for two days a week, and very arrogantly refused to take any course. There wasn't a single member of the Slade staff at that date who didn't assert that Cézanne suffered from astigmatic vision. Picasso they hadn't heard of. I cannot tell you how benighted England was then.

MG *When the war came you registered as a conscientious objector.*

PH Rather too conscientiously, because if I'd gone into the army I'd have been kicked out in a week because of asthma. Pacifism was a serious thing in my family: my mother's brother, Tal Davies, spent three and a half years in prison during the First World War. I worked near Welwyn Garden City for two very energetic women running a chicken farm, then dug ditches in the fens near Cambridge for 18s. 6d a week. As a result I got pneumonia, and then my life was saved by an invitation from Bernard Leach to go and join the tiny gang of four or five assistants he had helping him at the Pottery in St Ives – who were all conscientious objectors, incidentally.

MG *Did you paint through the war?*

PH It put rather a stopper on things, there are barely a dozen very small pictures from that period that I've kept.

MG *But it was then that you painted* The Piano *– the first mature painting you produced [no.4].*

PH Yes, that was painted in the middle of the war in Welwyn, in 1943. It's the view down my parents' drawing room towards the piano end. There was a big window at the end, and a grand piano up against it. The window is open and you can see over the sill – which comes right out of Bonnard and Matisse – those lines of orange, blue and orange – into the bushes and trees. Through those trees was the house of the Reiss family, where Delia was brought up. So I was looking, without intending to, slap at Delia's end of her house where she occupied a large bedroom. She had become a close friend by this time, and she used to pop across the road. She watched that painting grow, and later told me she was fascinated watching the process; with the result that on her twenty-first birthday, I made her a present of it. One of my brothers said, you had to marry Delia to get *The Piano* back.

I didn't say it was my first mature work until thirty years later, but I actually knew that that picture was a fantastic step forward at the time. It's oil paint on a piece of paper, which began with a pencil drawing, and was then filled in with area-shapes – a method which survived until the 1970s in my work, and a very unpainterly thing, you might think. Delia said that she was amazed that I filled in patches, like a mosaic, leaving bits where I hadn't decided on the colour bare – quite different from the way since Impressionism people had painted the whole surface together.

Delia and her brother Stephen Reiss were the only people I knew in those days who were totally fascinated by French painting, Matisse and Bonnard in particular, and modern music. At that time, to meet anyone in Britain who knew who Matisse and Bonnard were was a bloody miracle.

fig.10 Henri Matisse **The Red Studio 1911**
Oil on canvas 181 × 219.1 cm The Museum of Modern Art, New York. Mrs Simon Guggenheim Fund

MG *What do you think led you to take an interest in those artists, when practically nobody else did?*

PH God knows. Bloody good taste, I suppose! Round about 1938 there were a couple of very important one-man exhibitions at Rosenberg and Helft, one of Picasso and one of Braque (their very latest paintings in each case) which I saw and was utterly fascinated by. And Delia had a wonderful Derain in reproduction. My mother had a cousin, Geoffrey Barlow, who bought an amazing little Bonnard head of a girl, which I had seen at the Redfern Gallery, and lent it to us for the duration of the war – a sort of reward for my having persuaded him to buy it. It hung in my parents' drawing room. But my main acquaintance with Matisse was largely through reproductions. There was a marvellous series by Braun et cie which I carried around – twenty-four full-page excellent colour-plates – and the Matisse was the first to come out. Others on Braque, Picasso and Bonnard followed. I can remember the day at the Slade, in 1937, when I suddenly saw the point of Matisse. I thought, 'God, this actually supersedes Cézanne'. This is why it was so staggering to find Matisse's *The Red Studio* in a downstairs room at the Redfern Gallery, filling one wall.

MG *When was that?*

PH It was in 1943. I went back to look at it throughout 1944 and half of 1945, repeatedly, just to gaze at it. Later on, I met Erica Brausen (who was helping Rex Nan Kivell at the Redfern Gallery during the war), showed her some of my work, and had my own first show at the Redfern. She was mad about *The Red Studio*, and she was very, very disdainful about the English and their utter philistinism, which she never ceased to rail against. One day in 1945 I went back to the Redfern and said 'Where's *The Red Studio*?' And she said, 'Oh darling, didn't you know, Rex was broke and sold it to an American for £600, and the bloody Tate never even came to look at it'.

MG *So that was a seminar in depth with Matisse. What were the lessons you learnt?*

PH Realities I absorbed, I would say – its flatness, and the linearity of its definition, those wonderful wandering lines. The planes parallel to the picture surface – my whole experience of painting is summed up in that phrase actually. If you look at any of the greatest painters, all their paintings break down into a series of silhouetted planes. Out of that flatness, the flatness of those planes, volume is evoked, and it's evoked much more strongly than if you'd actually – like de Kooning or someone – tried to model it with your brush in a sculptural fashion.

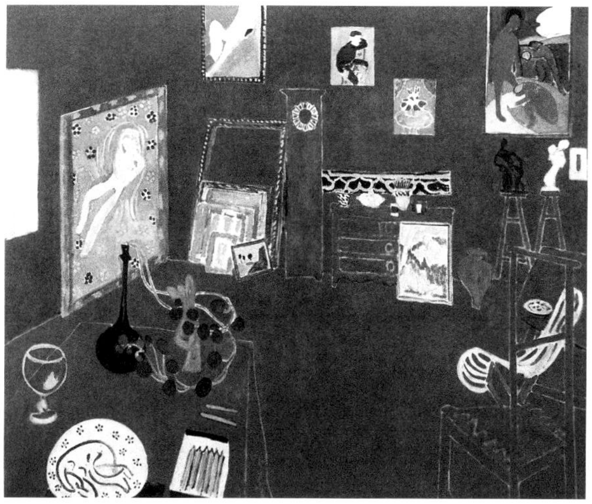

Everything is to do with flatness in painting, everything. Painting is illusionistic in its evocation. Sculpture creates volumes literally; painting creates them illusionistically out of essentially flat surfaces. That's the great antithesis between painting and sculpture. Henry Moore accused Ben Nicholson and Ivon Hitchens and all these people of not being able to draw. He had come to lunch at 53 Addison Avenue with Delia and me; this must have been in 1950 or so. He suddenly said rather ferociously, 'The trouble with Ivon is that he can't draw. None of the English artists can draw. They can't get form.' I said, 'What do you mean by "form" and "draw"?' He replied, 'If you look at a Rembrandt, you feel you could put your arm, right up to the elbow, right into the canvas, behind the head, and feel the back of the skull. You would get enough information to cast it in bronze'. I said, 'Oh, and how far do you think you could get your hand into the apples in a Cézanne still life? I reckon they're just about as thick as a digestive biscuit'. And I tried to explain to him that form in painting is illusionistic, and is conveyed in planes parallel to the picture-surface, and not in anything that you feel you could get a handful of three-dimensional form out of. It revealed his limitations, and his own drawings are strangely awkward, I think.

MG *Then in 1944, you went to work at the Leach Pottery. Did going back to St Ives feel like coming home?*

PH It was just magic. I'd been back once before in 1943 for a ten-day holiday, and met Bernard again – for the first time, really, since I was ten or eleven. It was quite sublime to come down for the last fifteen months of the war. I made the jam pots, then I made the mustard pots, and so on. Bernard was allowed to run the Pottery during the war on condition

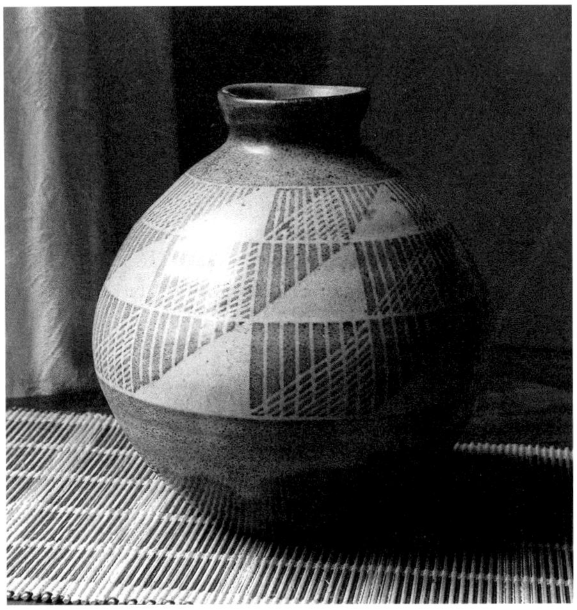

fig.11 Bernard Leach **Stoneware vase 1952** Collection of Patrick Heron

fig.12 Georges Braque **Studio V (Atelier V) 1949–50** Oil on canvas 145 × 175 cm Private Collection

he made things for domestic use, not just 'arty stuff'. There was a very big range, which he had designed, but we modified to some extent. He encouraged that, very decently I thought. Then the war ended and I immediately got married to Delia. And started living in London for the first time in my life.

MG *Do you think working for Leach had any effect on your work? Later you wrote a piece, 'Submerged Rhythm', which links the forms in Leach pots, and in Braque and Bonnard.*

PH Well, I do think there are terrific formal cohesions and sympathy between the blunt rhythms of a Braque and the blunt rhythms of a Leach. A Leach coffee jug is exactly like the jugs in Braque's war-time paintings, but Bernard had never seen a Braque; I know that.

MG *Do you think there's also a connection with the blunt rhythms one often finds in a Patrick Heron?*

PH Yes, absolutely. There's a Leach pot in a later painting of mine, *The Long Table with Fruit: 1949* [no.7]. There is also a Leach jug and a Hamada bowl in another still life, called *Black Bananas: 1948* [no.6]. I like to think of that unity between the Leach pots you find in this house, and my paintings. I was very moved by the pottery experience, although I never thought for an instant that I might become a potter, and hardly ever consciously made a pot of my own rather than basically of Bernard's design.

MG *So in 1945 your life changed dramatically.*

PH Yes, I got married, went to live in the top half of a house my father-in-law owned in Addison Avenue, Holland Park, and set about being a painter. The first morning Delia went out to teach, I thought 'Now, my God, I've got to start painting. Terrible.' So I got three eggs and put them on a plate, à la Derain, and painted that.

MG *When was it that you first came across the work of Braque? Was it at the Tate show in 1946?*

PH I had previously bought a book on him, but the exhibition in 1946 was absolutely overwhelming. Nobody knew anything about Braque. There was no thought or mention of him really until in 1946 a wall and a half of the Tate was devoted to him. The other half of the room was given to a painter that everyone thought was probably greater – you'll laugh – Rouault. But the Braques were the great amazing war-time ones of the Grand Piano and Billiard Table, and so on. It was fantastic. I was so bowled over I wrote a long article about it for *The New English Weekly*.

Braque was a huge influence. The sight of those Braques altered my own paintings just like that, when I discovered the space-creating nature of those flat surfaces. I went in to see the show at about eleven o'clock on the day it opened to the public, and noticed that a major painting, *La Gueridon Rouge*, was hung upside down. I pointed it out to the attendant, then eventually John Rothenstein arrived with a group of dignitaries, and was hugely embarrassed. 'You'll realise', he said, 'the British Council were responsible for hanging this exhibition?' – and immediately fled the room, leaving his guests faintly smiling at me. But all the critics and the VIPs had already seen it, and not noticed, at the opening.

MG *You started to paint interiors and still lifes in a Braquean mode, but there are unBraquean qualities to them as well.*

PH My own handling, my own colour sense were infinitely more Matissian and always had been – and at times, Bonnardian. My paintings never looked *like* Braque; Braque is full of straight lines, ruled lines, and submerged, indeed, not very submerged, cubist geometry, of a very severe nature. There is nothing like that in my paintings. My paintings are always fluid in a Matissian way.

But my devotion to Braque registered very much with people because of my being the first person in Britain to write about him, really. This is a complication in my case, because of my having once for a time been a part-time writer about painting as well as being a painter. If I became identified with an artist through writing with enthusiasm about his work, people became totally convinced that my work was entirely indebted to that painter's! There are two paintings of mine which possibly show the influence of Rothko, but in reviews for twenty years it was Rothko, Rothko, Rothko – because I opened people's eyes to Rothko in my writing.

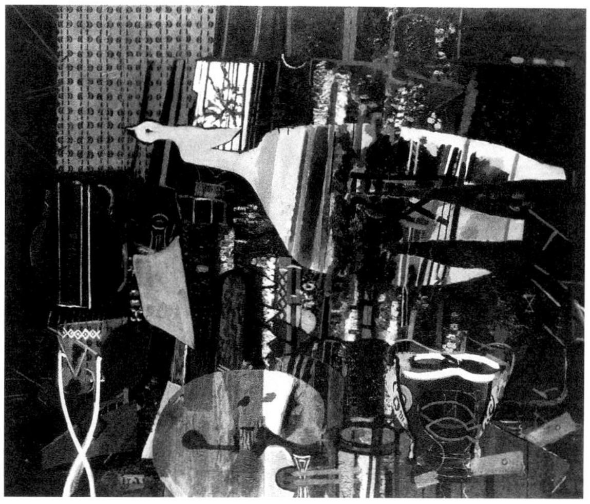

MG *How did you start writing?*

PH I had gone back to Welwyn from the Pottery at St Ives for a weekend with my parents, and I was talking to Philip Mairet, the editor of *The New English Weekly*, about Ben Nicholson, whom I had just met in St Ives. Mairet was very intrigued and we talked about Nicholson for an hour or two. You see I actually didn't like, at that point, Nicholson's literal preciseness. I liked a more painterly style. It took me a long time to feel that Ben's idiom produced a formal fullness in spite of that literalness. After a while Philip Mairet said, with his amazing stutter, 'If you c–c–care to put down something of what you've been telling me about B–B–Ben Nicholson, I'd p–p–publish it, you know'. For someone who'd never published a word in his life, that was quite flattering, because *The New English Weekly* had more prestige than any other weekly in the land at that time. T.S. Eliot and Ezra Pound were contributors.

MG So your Nicholson piece was critical?

PH Devastating really. I was really critical of the whole Constructivist development.

You see, at St Ives, I was exposed not just to Ben, but to Naum Gabo too, who was a very powerful personage, and I liked him very much. He was very warm and very intellectually passionate. I remember him coming over to the Leach Pottery one afternoon for tea. He got on very well with Bernard – Leach didn't get on with Ben at all, and vice versa. But nevertheless, you can see, if you were submerged in Braque, Bonnard and Matisse, you wouldn't go much for Gabo. I liked Gabo very much, and had great respect for him. But he had absolutely no influence on my painting practice. Nor had Ben really. But Ben had gone out of his way to be friendly to me. Not only had he borrowed a little painting, and invited me to his studio, which was then a bedroom in an Edwardian villa at Carbis Bay (Barbara Hepworth's studio was the dining room). He was being fantastically supportive. I bumped into him one day, fairly soon after this short article had come out, in New Bond Street and at once I felt guilty. So I said, 'By the way, I've written something about you and the movement which was slightly critical'. His grey eyes looked very sharply at me underneath that yachting cap, and he said, 'Oh, I didn't know you … wrote things'. 'I don't', I said. 'It's the first thing I've written.' 'I should very much like to see that', Ben said. I sent it to him, but he never mentioned it again. I used to write critically of Barbara too, I'm afraid to say. I wrote the introduction to her exhibition at Wakefield, and oh boy was that critical, and I didn't show it to her, which was beastly.

MG *Were you in awe of them?*

PH No, because I was very much in awe of artists I thought were infinitely greater. I was not in awe of anyone in England. The only English artist I went overboard in support of, at that time, was Henry Moore. I thought he was a great sculptor. But I did praise Ben to the skies years later.

MG *Did you feel isolated in Britain in the 1940s, with this interest in Bonnard, Matisse, Braque and Picasso?*

PH Rather. Absolutely. The result was when I did finally have the show at the Redfern, in October 1947, it was full of French influences, one after another, which I felt no need to hide.

MG *In 1946, you wrote about the Braque exhibition, then visited him in his studio in Paris.*

PH Yes, I went to see Braque in 1949, when he was at work on some of the late *Atelier* paintings, among other things [fig.12]. I gave him a copy of *The New English Weekly* article and he told me it was the first serious article on him in English. I only wrote very occasionally, but everyone in London somehow or other saw that Braque article. Later, in 1947, I got a letter from Raymond Mortimer, asking me if I would like to try my hand as art critic of *The New Statesman and Nation*, because he had seen the Braque piece. Everyone remembered the bloody Braque article.

Herbert Read, much later, warned me that my big mistake had been to *write* about painting; for a painter he said, it is just not done in this country. They all want any painter they write about to be a dumb ox – it's quite true actually. I didn't need Herbert to tell me that. I knew it was a risk. But it seemed to me that a lot of things desperately needed saying because of this country's almost still-Victorian culture, which was dismal to a degree.

MG *You find a lack of feeling for the sensuous in the British sensibility, you wrote.*

PH I just feel that great European painting, with total ease, with immense invisible manipulative power, evokes forms in space very, very powerfully through the sensuous handling of materials. The terrible British weakness was the illustrative talent for doing little drawings and colouring them in. That was why I was a champion of Matthew Smith, and later Ivon Hitchens. They were more European in that respect – virtually French.

MG *You personally remained a figurative painter until 1955.*

PH It didn't feel like that, you know. It felt terribly abstract. Figuration is various things, it's Constable or Vermeer, Monet or Corot. It's dissolving into non-figuration with Cézanne. As far as the British public was concerned, my work was insanely abstract. They thought it was wilfully distorted. But they didn't know anything about the whole tradition. It hadn't been exposed here really, except by Roger Fry in those early shows, in 1910 and 1912, which of course most people had never seen. The issue of figuration or not wasn't uppermost in one's mind at that time. That was just how paintings happened. An element of the painting could be read and could not be read as having an overlay of reference to certain factors in the external world.

In 1953 I put on an exhibition called *Space in Colour*, with an introduction to the catalogue that really stated my position. It took me three weeks to hit on the phrase 'Space in Colour', which totally expresses, I think, the most profound of totally pictorial experiences. I still think that. It was like hitting a gong when I thought of it.

MG *Why most profound?*

PH Because it's what it's made up of. What painting is about, and what it consists of, and what it manipulates, and what it explores, and what it can't get away from doing and being is space in colour, and illusion. It is impossible to mark a surface without that mark being a colour immediately in juxtaposition to whatever colour the rest of the surface is, and it immediately jumps out in front of it or sits behind it, or both simultaneously. You can't take a white canvas and make a mark on it without that happening. You have two feelings. You know physically that there is a flat surface with something called paint smudged on it. But at the same time everything that is on that surface is creating the illusion of space, a pictorial illusion of depth.

It was perfectly natural to me from the word go to discuss painting in terms of spatial sensation. But in 1950 I was actually sacked by *The New Statesman* for writing too much about 'space'. The literary editor, T.C. Worsley, wrote to say that the general reader must at last have some respite from having to consider abstruse matters of *space*, as a matter of course, week after week. Of course, I don't think it's abstruse at all, it's the heart of the matter.

MG *Let me put something to you. Other people might say, no, it's the emotions of the artist, or the artist's personality, or vision, that count, or the artist's sense of reality. Any number of other things might be thought the most profound.*

PH There you are. The great English blasphemy used to be that painting must have a subject, which is something outside the painting, and that subject used to be of far more importance to 99 per cent of the English critical establishment than the material reality of the painting itself. They were always off into meanings, and significances, and symbols. I once said I hate all symbols, I love all images. There was a determination to escape from having to put into words something about the exclusively pictorial experience. It was too strong for the English. They raced off into absolutely anything to escape, they were just dying to discuss anything that the painting can suggest – and a painting can suggest a million things. Bloody English critics would dash off and discuss all of them, because they couldn't accept the amazing pictorial reality.

fig.13 **Scarlet Verticals: March 1957** Oil on canvas 102 × 127 cm
Private Collection

MG *How would you reply to someone who said, why are these colours and shapes so important? What's so profound about them, about the purely visual?*

PH Well, I would say that as far as I'm concerned, my consciousness is flooded by the imagery of the seen. Wherever I look there is fantastic significance, about the whole of the physical setting in which we exist on this planet, night and day. What I shall never understand is why people think that that is not enough. Mere visual reality is so fantastically interesting. And that is the realm of painting. Because that is what painting, which deals with the visual, is about. Why we should insist on buckling on to it some idiotic symbolism or illustrational thing is just to my mind the hallmark of a totally, hopelessly provincial Anglo-Saxon culture. Except that the Angles and the Saxons have produced some great painting. No landscape painter is greater than Constable, he was much better than Turner.

MG *You were exploring Braquean space in your work of the late 1940s and early 1950s. Could you explain the way that worked in for example this splendid painting* The Room at St Ives: 1952–3 *[no.10], which you have here?*

PH It shows the studio room at 3 St Andrew's Street, a cottage on the sea wall at St Ives. The harbour window there featured in a lot of the paintings of that period. In this one, the biggest one, the harbour window is on the left, with the balcony outside. You are looking straight out at that, but the door – with my younger daughter, Susanna, coming through it, and my elder daughter Katharine just behind her – is 180 degrees removed from the view through the window. To the left of them is the nude figure of Delia in blue. This is a big room with the window at one end and the little door at the other, so your eyes are swivelling through space. It is complicated isn't it? It's possible that having been briefed by the late Braque ateliers in the Royal Academy exhibition people's eyes might be more attuned to this.

MG *Did becoming an abstract artist ever present itself to you as a crunch question?*

PH Well, in 1951 there was a de Stäel exhibition at Mathiesen's in New Bond Street of his, so to speak, great period, the middle period when everything was put on with a spatula in great blocks half an inch thick, bricks of paint. After that I immediately started painting some de Staël-type paintings. In 1952 I suddenly had a little period of about three months of painting de Staël-ish abstracts, even exhibited some, then I went back again to the flat-colour interiors, tables, still lifes and windows. No, these were two very deliberate moves, first to start then to stop. It was a false start, although there were some good pictures painted.

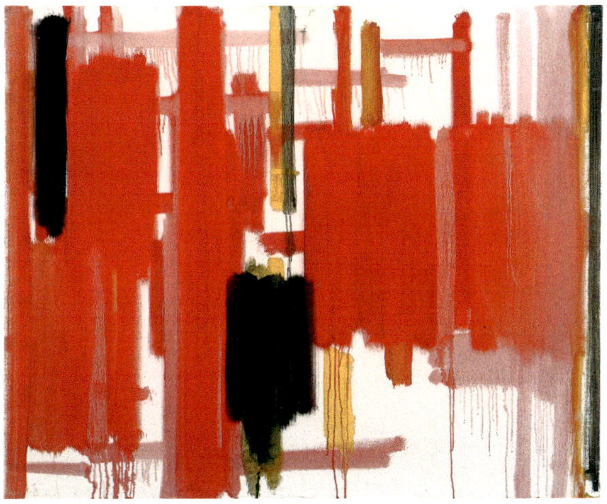

MG *Once Robert Melville predicted that you would just transform into a purely abstract painter. He wrote that one day the object will just 'float out of sight, behind an exquisite cloud of paint and Patrick Heron won't even notice that it has gone'. Did that prediction come true in 1955, when you moved into abstraction?*

PH Even those in a funny sort of way have another subject. Although I was conscious of painting the most abstract paintings that anyone was painting, I didn't call them abstract, I called them Garden paintings. That rather foxed people in a way. Of course the so-called 'Tachisme' from France was a word that was used in relation to my work. The vertical touch in these tachiste or garden paintings became longer and longer, until in one painting in early 1957 they became so long that the strokes touched top and bottom. Suddenly there were actually seven vertical stripes in one painting, which at the time I actually called *Scarlet Verticals: March 1957.*

MG *So in your case there was a much more gradual evolution than in the case of say Victor Pasmore, who very famously and drastically 'went abstract' in the late 1940s?*

PH Oh no. When I analysed for you just how the stripes emerged from the vertical brush-strokes of the previous garden painting or tachiste phase it's an analysis which only occurred to me many years after the event. At the time the rapid development of the stripes was profoundly shocking and surprising, both to me and to everybody else. An American critic who stayed at Eagles Nest in December 1957 told me a decade later that they were the first stripe paintings he had ever seen. The reception the stripe exhibition got was quite violently hostile. You can tell this from the reviews. *The Sunday Times* reviewer said (I've got the cutting here)

'There is much to rejoice at in the fact that the tyranny of illusionism in painting no longer exists; but it is undesirable, all the same, that a tyranny of fatuity should take its place. We know from his writings that there is nothing fatuous about Mr Patrick Heron, whose new paintings are on view at the Redfern Gallery; and no one could deny, I think, the charm and originality of the isolated chords of colour which he has struck in his new canvases. But the fact that many of the canvases contain nothing but these bands of colour seems to me to poise them on the very edge of the absurd'.

But the BBC 'Tonight' television programme came on the Saturday morning, just two days after the opening, and interviewed all the visitors to the show, and recorded Winifred Nicholson and William Scott saying a lot of terribly nice things, with great emphasis on my colour. I hid in the next room listening, and heard Scott say something I had never heard said before. He said Patrick Heron is a great colourist. Colour is everything to him. I thought, really? Both those statements were complete news to me. I'd never actually heard anyone else say that to me. In fact, I'd never consciously thought of myself as a 'colourist'. Yet out of the whole of our group, of course, I was the one who was using bright colours. That's why every review I had had the word 'colour' in the headline. Colour, colour, colour, colour, colour, said the reviewers. Nowadays, everyone's mad about colour, but then all my friends – William Scott, Roger Hilton, Peter Lanyon, Terry Frost, Alan Davie, everybody – were painting in beautiful greys and mud-colours and blacks and whites and lovely dirty greens.

fig.14 **Delia: 1945** Oil on canvas 55.8 × 43.1 cm Private Collection

fig.15 **Portrait of T.S. Eliot O.M.: 1949** Oil on canvas 76.2 × 63.5 cm National Portrait Gallery, London

MG *It's quite bleak, early 1950s St Ives painting.*

PH Well … I was the only one using strong colours – clear, unmixed, primary colours. The stripes show, of course, wasn't entirely stripes. The first squares followed the first stripes very closely indeed – almost the same week, actually. I always thought that the squares arose from stripes in two directions crossing over.

MG *I gather the stripe show was a spectacular fiasco? What happened exactly?*

PH Despite immediate notoriety, the exhibition was fated to be publicly insulted by the Redfern Gallery. They closed it down after a mere three days, turned the lights out, removed the paintings from two of the walls and stacked them face inwards against the paintings remaining, face outwards, on the other two walls. They hired a decorator to repaint the entire room, walls and ceiling, in his spare time! So visitors were confronted by a huge tarpaulin on the floor, covered with pots of white paint, and a ladder up the middle of the room. A number of the paintings were actually splattered with tiny spots of white decorator's paint.

Bryan Wynter, who was also a Redfern artist, phoned me from London describing the appalling scene. He said he'd immediately cancelled his own show and resigned from the gallery. But the result of this disaster was that Bryan walked across Cork Street and joined the brand-new gallery just recently opened by Victor and Leslie Waddington. I followed him.

You have to realise that for my generation of English painters, by which I mean painters

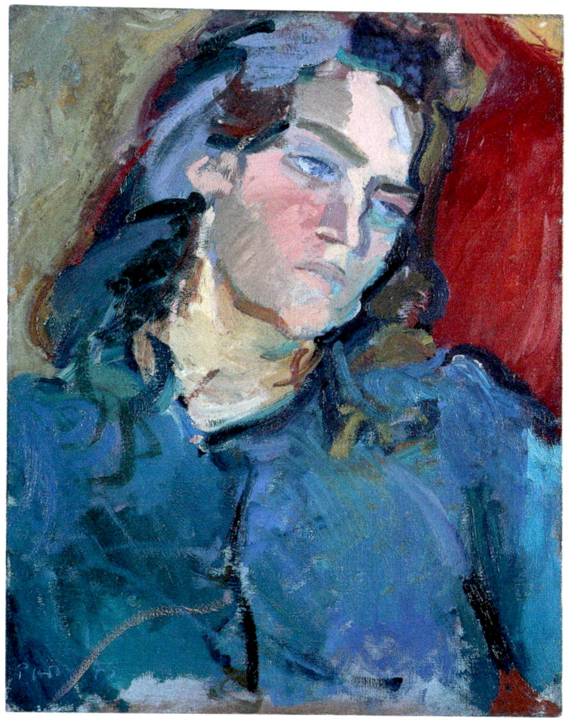

older than myself as well, such as Victor Pasmore, there was a very dramatic moment. It felt like an awful risk, too, financial as well. When I left the Redfern the director, Rex Nan Kivell, wrote a fake tear-stained letter in which he said that, just as he was getting 'an interest in the still lifes, you go and do this'.

MG *This was obviously a very critical moment for you?*

PH Yes. But in retrospect the drama of 'going abstract' seems exaggerated. There was a time in my life when I maintained that all figurative art is abstract and all abstract art is figurative. I actually profoundly believe that. There is no great figurative painting in which, when we look at it, we are not in fact savouring a sort of abstract visual harmony, or music of interacting form and colour. That is what we are looking at. That is what is occupying not just the back of our minds, but the front of our minds.

The objective world does not look like any painting ever painted on God's earth. It looks completely different. All painting is made up of elements which are in fact operative on our senses pleasurably by reason of purely abstract proportional relationships. I maintain that when you look at a Renoir breast or a Cézanne apple, the pleasure that you get from those great paintings has hardly anything to do with apples or breasts. It's to do with the shapes and forms and their spatial and harmonic relationship.

MG *In the early 1950s you wrote about the difficulty of portraiture in the twentieth century, going so far as to say that after Picasso's portrait of Gertrude Stein, there were no portraits. Yet you yourself have produced a few, including a portrait of T.S. Eliot which is one of the favourites at the National Portrait Gallery [fig.15].*

PH I have, also the Herbert Read one [no.8] and several of Jo Grimond; and quite a few, early on, of Delia, of course [fig.14], and the children. How do I explain it? Well, they are the exception, aren't they, in one's work? Just here and there is dotted a thing called a portrait. I did feel the absence of portraits in modern painting was a challenge. But I must say actually I would go back to a certain extent on what I said. I would include Matisse as a portrait painter, the endless women in Matisse's paintings are all portraits, don't you think? Everything about the figures in his paintings is obviously terribly particular to a given woman.

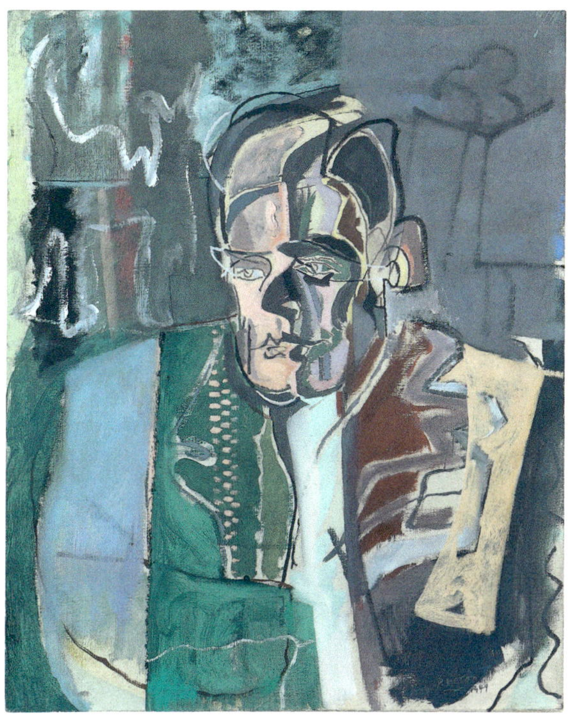

MG *So to some extent it is possible to reconcile …*

PH … A figurative function? Oh yes. You can paint a portrait which is also a painting. All generalisations are false, including this one – who said that? It's one of my favourite sayings, especially when I'm charged with an inconsistency.

MG *Still, something changed in your work in 1955, when you became a fully abstract painter.*

PH The linear network of the Braquean paintings falls away, leaving only the dabs between.

MG *You can see it in the process of happening in* Winter Harbour: 1955 *[fig.16], and* Girl in Harbour Room: 1955 *[no.15], where the dabs overlay a Braquean painting. What were you thinking at that time?*

PH Well, it is certainly true that one was anxious to get away from under the umbrella of the overwhelming greatness of the French. In fact, the whole impulse of the so-called tachiste garden paintings, and the stripe paintings, was to get away from those great masters. I had absolutely venerated them, both in words and in my work. In fact Braque at last did go clean out of my mind, after having been on it a lot. The disappearance of the Braquean influence really coincides with the disappearance of figuration. I don't think Braque is an influence once I'd 'gone abstract', although I think that Bonnard and Matisse have never really been out of my mind. But I then wanted desperately to leave them behind, too. Now was the moment to break free.

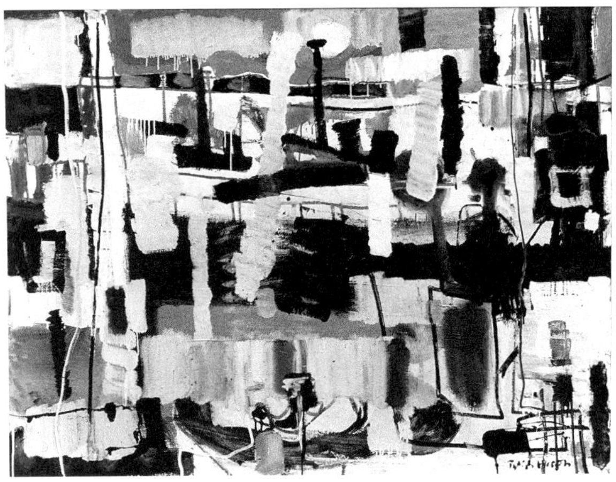

MG *Was the first English exhibition of Rothko, Pollock and the American Abstract Expressionists, at the Tate in January 1956, an important revelation?*

PH What, when one finally came upon it, was interesting about the Americans was that they were doing just that – breaking with Paris – with a crudity that was the essence of the escape, so to speak. In fact, what I really championed them for was their innovatory boldness – boldness to the point of crudity.

MG *Was that what triggered your development towards total abstraction?*

PH No. I was very articulate at the time about the qualities I admired – the shallow space, as I put it, the emptiness, and the brashness of paint application, the scale, the size. But I was also very conscious of developments in France. When I went to Paris in 1949 I visited the Salon de Mai, and saw the young French painters, Soulages in particular, and immediately wrote about him.

MG *How did the stripe paintings come about?*

PH They did not come about conceptually. Such a concept didn't exist *anywhere*. I was trying to find a way of making more than one colour present on the canvas – with no *shapes* to diminish or distract from that sensation of colour – and the most economical way and the purest way in which you can restrict the painting to chromatic differentiation and intensity was by laying those colours side by side in a stripe-format. But this way of putting it only occurred years after the event, you know. Stripes I later justified as being the compositional form which one arrived at if one's main interest or only interest, virtually, was in colour-sensation – which it now was.

MG *You have pointed out that you employed the device of stripes, which was to become one of the most common formal features of the art of the following four decades, well before the Americans of the hard-edge and colour-field schools.*

PH Yes. And over four-and-a-half years before Morris Louis's first stripes. It's an illustration of how frightfully self-deprecating we are in this country. If an American had come up with something like that, it would have been trumpeted round the world. As it is I'm regarded as obsessive on the subject, although I did not once raise it until nearly ten years after I'd painted and exhibited the stripes, and then only in an American art magazine.

MG *Some people have read your stripe paintings as disguised Turnerian landscapes. But personally I think it rather spoils looking at a picture like,say,* Red Layers (with Blue and Yellow): 14 December 1957 *[no.25] to think of it as a sunset.*

PH Yes. That's ridiculous. In any case, the first stripe paintings were of vertical not horizontal stripes. The idea of the horizontal stripe paintings being sunsets horrified me more than I can possibly say. The point is, the entire natural scene, everything which is available to you through your eyes is chaotic, until you, from inside your head, start to project formal imagery, to differentiate one section of a surface from another. In so doing, you begin to make shapes. You can't have more than one colour on a plane without making some sort of formal shape-arrangement.

I think this is a very profound point. Strictly speaking, everything that we see in this three-dimensional world is so subtle, and so complex, that it's got a million different readings. My thesis is that painting's prime function for mankind is to provide us with a vocabulary of formal shapes to see things with. Because you can't see anything unless you have a formal shape to project into it.

If you lose a hammer, unless you concentrate mentally on the image of that hammer, you won't see it among the rubbish. That's because you're not projecting the hammer-shape. But suddenly, when you do, the projection overlaps with the real hammer. I think we see out there what we have previously seen and understood in painting, and we don't see anything out there that we haven't seen in painting. The illusion is that it's the other way round. People think that the landscape is like a Constable or a Ben Nicholson. It's not that at all. You are projecting Constable-abstraction or Nicholson-abstraction into the amorphous data of the visual scene until you find bits that overlap with it. So painters are inventing what we think nature looks like. And it's changing all the time. Nobody would have seen stripes out there unless they had seen these paintings.

fig.16 **Winter Harbour: 1955** Oil on canvas 101.6 × 127 cm
Vancouver Art Gallery (Gift of the Contemporary Art Society, London, 1959)

_MG_ _So through purely formal investigations you can sometimes hit on a way of seeing that flux outside the window._

PH What we think we see – is that a projection or is it an extraction? In other words, are we abstracting or superimposing? The answer is that we are doing both, and we can't do one without the other.

_MG_ _How do you react to the idea that your work is abstraction related to landscape?_

PH Well, I don't think it is related to landscape. I think it's related to stuff in this landscape like rocks. But I think that the underlying spatial structure of my paintings is far more related to interiors with still lifes, and windows.

_MG_ _Like the work of your figurative phase, in fact?_

PH Exactly, yes I do think that.

_MG_ _The other big change of the period was your move back down to Cornwall, and to this house which you bought in 1955, and moved into permanently in spring 1956, just as the azaleas and camellias were coming out in this amazing garden you have. In moving to Eagles Nest, of course, you were moving to a place stuck out into the sea on this knob of rock surrounded by light. You look down on a turquoise and purple sea, surrounded by this unique garden. That must have had an effect._

PH A tremendous effect. Of course, the light of St Ives is now universally spoken of. I put that in words in a little essay fifty years ago. I coined the following explanation for the quality of light in St Ives. Even now, at this moment, it's growing late but it's still dazzling, isn't it? It's almost enough to make you want to shut your eyes. I hit on the idea that at the end of this peninsula, which is the longest tongue of land in Europe, you are miles out into a huge ocean. This ocean is a mirror all round. There are only 8 degrees from this house where land is continuous, otherwise you are out into the sea in no time. All that plane of water is reflecting light upwards into, most of the time, a very humid atmosphere. So the light is then being refracted in all directions.I called this 'multi-directional reflected light', which causes everything in the landscape to be illuminated from all sides. When you look at anything in this landscape, you feel very strongly that light is going round the corners. All objects in this landscape are being approached by light from every side, from every direction. It's the very opposite of light in the middle of a great land-mass, light in the centre of France, for example, which crashes down from one side, with dark shadows on the other. There aren't any dark shadows ever here at all. Even when the light is full blast the dark shadows are themselves almost ceruleum blue. All profiles, whether of hills, houses or headlands rise up towards you, but the light also flattens them, they aren't like a sculpted form.

The fact that the profiles of houses, hills and headlands come nearer to you than the forms they contain is an amazing thing from painting's point of view, because I've always maintained that all the best painting exists in terms of flat areas, interleaved and overlapped. Bad painting to my mind has always been painting of the kind that is literally modelled.

MG *So you found yourself in a place not only with extraordinary visual qualities, but also your childhood paradise. This house has a lot of very specific qualities which you either sought out, or it produced in you. This extraordinary Zennor landscape is the constant background to everyday life.*

PH It's strong stuff, isn't it? It is *the* constant background to everyday life. What it looks like, and feels like, and is, is why one's here. I mean, one wouldn't hide oneself away at the end of nowhere for nothing, for no reason, would one? There is no question about it, I came down here because of this landscape. I would never have painted the way I have if I'd stayed in London. But then a very strong feeling and knowledge of this landscape has followed me around, even before we bought this house, when we were living in London, it was there.

MG *So this house and its environment seem related in a deep and complicated way to your work?*

PH Yes, here's another example. In my paintings there are certain shapes that crop up a lot, jigsaw shapes. Walking along that path opposite the gate, up the moor, an American friend once said, 'Oh, I see where you get your shapes, Patrick'. We were walking over a rock that surfaces through the grit with exactly that shape that evolved so much in my paintings (a sort of 'harbour shape'). I was absolutely staggered.

But I said to him, 'Listen, I haven't got my shape from that, you're seeing my shape in that because you've seen my work'. People say that they see my shapes everywhere around here, as in this rock. But I reply 'You would never see that rock like that if you hadn't seen these shapes on this canvas. If I were Mr Seurat, not Mr Heron, you would be saying, "My goodness, look at all these separated blobs of violet and green all over the bloody sky."'

MG *Are the shapes that return insistently in certain painters – like the Heron shapes – generated internally, or are they slowly abstracted from unconscious contemplation of the world around them?*

PH It's impossible to answer. For instance, a late twentieth-century painter of my generation, or even of Ben Nicholson's generation, could never see anything in Hertfordshire that would stimulate his visual imagination. You can't imagine Christopher Wood landing up at Welwyn Garden City, or Harpenden, or somewhere, and getting cracking. You just can't imagine it. There are certain landscapes that are immensely potent in their relationship to certain periods of art. The reason why any number of people congregated near St Ives at a certain point was because late twentieth-century abstract and semi-abstract painting had certain underlying rhythmic alliances with this kind of terrain.

MG *That explains why there seems to be a sudden burst of creativity the moment you arrived here in 1956.*

PH When I took the plunge. That's true, absolutely. I would be desolated if I had to move from this house. I always thought that my future ideas for paintings are as it were stacked up around me invisibly in the air in this house and in that studio down there in St Ives. I couldn't just go to somebody else's studio, even if it was empty, and produce something. Because the ideas that have generated in my own studio for forty years are hanging in the air waiting to be tapped. That's what I feel.

The disadvantage of being based here, of course, has been that one has been away from all the meetings and decision-making. On the other hand, I used to make rather a convincing claim for regarding St Ives as the metropolitan centre. There was a chart of all the British one-man shows in New York compiled by the National Gallery in Washington in the 1970s, and you would be amazed how St Ives wipes the board in the 1950s and 1960s. We must have had about twenty or thirty important one-man shows in New York in that period. Far more than the artists from London. They followed us into New York a decade later. The last time I saw Rothko, he opened his arms wide and said, 'Come to dinner, what goes on in St Ives?' Larry Rivers turned up once here to have breakfast. The whole of New York was focused on St Ives – American critics and dealers in particular.

fig.17 **Big Green with Reds and Violet: December 1962**
Oil on canvas 152.4 × 213.4 cm Private Collection

MG *To what extent was there a rubbing of minds, a community, between you and the other artists around? Was there a social unit of artists in St Ives? Or is that a myth?*

PH It's an illusion largely, I think. I personally am very conscious of never having really joined in. I don't know why, it wasn't a protest or anything.

MG *How did you actually paint the stripe pictures?*

PH Each one was painted very, very quickly. *Red Layers (with Blue and Yellow): 14 December 1957* would have been painted in half an hour or less.

MG *Did you ponder for a long time in advance what you were going to do?*

PH No, it was all done on instinct, very rapidly. Stroked and brushed in. You can see. I painted the whole show very quickly. The very big work, the one Peter Gregory commissioned for the office at Lund Humphries designed by Trevor Dannatt, *Horizontal Stripe Painting: November 1957 – January 1958* [no.24], on the other hand, took some time. That had a specific purpose; to be an architectural object. And *Lux Eterna: May–June 1958* [no.30], the last of the stripes, went on and on and on. It's very rich and overpainted. Incidentally it has that religious title only for a bogus mundane reason – I wanted the Contemporary Art Society to include it in a mixed show called *The Religious Theme.*

MG *In some of the stripe paintings there are stripes of different thicknesses, too, virtually oblongs.*

PH All the stripe paintings were done by brushing top to bottom or from side to side of the canvas quickly, flatly. Then slowly things became quite different. Then, following the stripe period, slowly one was returning to a scribbled texture within area-shapes that were delineated.

MG *In the period that followed, your work took the form of soft-edged discs and oblongs. If I've understood it correctly, you arrived at the shape through the colour, getting it the right size for the weight of the colour.*

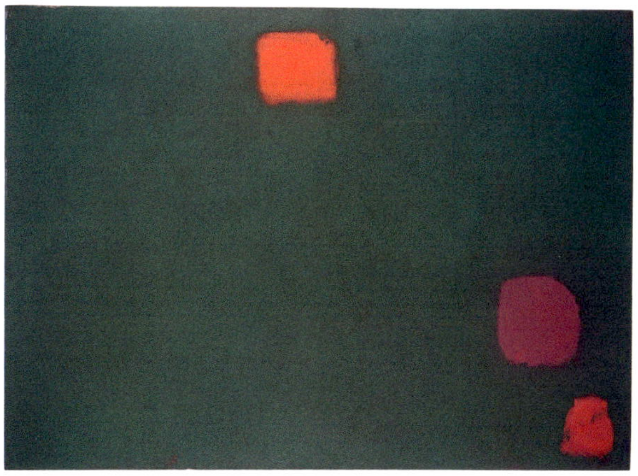

PH That's right, I didn't draw an outline. Or I might have drawn one with a soft brush. But nevertheless a colour-area-shape became a colour-area-shape by expanding a scribbled area – or mass. The pressures from within and without operated on that. I mean, one shape would be partly defined by the scarlet going outwards, and a little bit by the green coming in, in the case of a painting such as *Big Green with Reds and Violets: December 1962* [fig.17]. In some places the red spread onto the green, and in others the green spread onto the red.

MG *Therefore, from time to time, you might take a patch out.*

PH Oh yes, there are all sorts of submerged discs and submerged forms. In fact the word 'submerged' occurs in some of the titles. And the word 'suppressed'. Often an entire square or rectangle of one colour would be painted over by the surrounding 'ground' colour expanding into it.

MG *And you carried on until it worked visually?*

PH Yes, of course they were painted very quickly sometimes. In a case like *Big Green with Reds and Violets: 1962* I probably waited until the green was dry before starting the invading or superimposed reds.

MG *You were very close to monochrome painting at times.*

PH I was very close to that here. One was tempted in a funny kind of way to paint an all-green painting, but I didn't think Yves Klein was justified. I thought that just to have an all-one-coloured rectangle removed the picture from the realm of painting. It simply became an architectural panel – which you could fit into a position on the wall, but it wouldn't have any internal organisational life.

MG *So* Big Green *is an absolute limit as far as you are concerned?*

PH Well, there are one or two paintings like *One Form: September 1959* [fig.18] or *Red in Red: September 1961* which are even more pared-down – just one soft-cornered square on a so-called ground. Also I remember other canvases where everything was pushed to one side for a long time. That was quite a novelty. It was the right-hand edge usually. I cleared the whole picture space, emptied it entirely, and then clustered forms down the right-hand edge of the canvas. I'd written about Bonnard in 1947, just after he'd died, and described his habit of concentrating detailed forms along the four edges of his canvases while leaving the middle of pictures comparatively empty. The *importance of the edge*, and the greater intensity of the pictorial composition and incident the nearer to the edge it comes. Empty in the middle. Concentrated around the edges. The edges – this is a Heronian dictum – are the first four formal statements of any painting.

Right through this period one is enclosing colour-area-shapes within a larger colour-area-shape which some people would call the 'ground'. But to call it the ground implies that it has less integrity and positiveness as a shape than the others, that it is just a background.

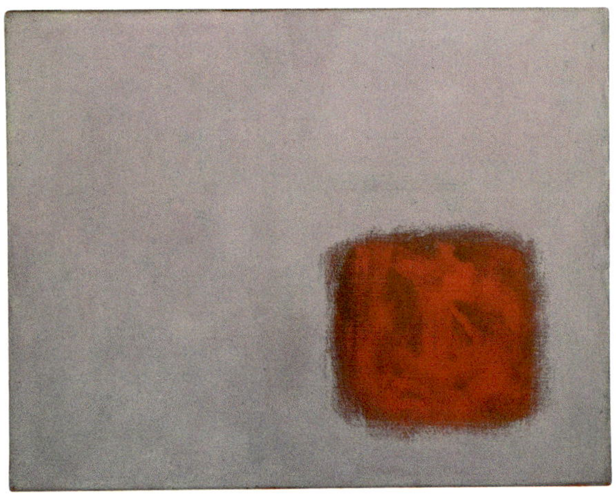

MG *As if the picture were like stones on a table or something.*

PH Yes. And that is completely untrue of my work. Nevertheless this entire period consisted of individual colour-area-shapes set in a so-called ground. As I say, I've always eschewed that word because if you say that's the ground and that's the shape, you mean that the first is negative compared to the second – as if it didn't exist in its own right formally with exactly the same intensity as an individual shape. That's why I say that all frontiers defining colour areas must define equally, with equal defining power, in both directions simultaneously. Nothing in the canvas is not a shape. Every square inch of the canvas belongs to a colour-area-shape.

Of course those frontiers aren't outlines, because an outline suggests a profile, suggests something of which the relevance, so to speak, faces one way only. For instance, if I talked about your profile, everybody would think that the line defined inwards, towards you, not that it defined outwards too. Bad painting is painting which presents collections of single forms against a 'background', which is actually a vacuity; like Augustus John. Now Cézanne is the absolute antithesis of that. In Cézanne every part is equally solid and in the same instant equally spacious. Cézanne's space is *solid*.

MG *Would it be true to say that while you had written and thought about Braque, Bonnard, and Picasso, you had thought much less consciously about your own work?*

PH I don't know about that. It's true I never wrote about my own work seriously until I gave the Power Lectures in Australia in 1973 called 'The Shape of Colour', which was entirely about my own work. But that's the first time I did that. I had a kind of rather scrupulous attitude that I shouldn't write about my own work, shouldn't use my powers as a writer to explain and further my own work. I felt very strongly I should let my paintings make their own way, quite independently of my writing. If people thought of me as a kind of intellectual word-man, that's because the printed word races round the world a million times faster and further than the painted canvas. Everything I did, in writing, was destined to be anti my own interests as a painter, everything. Except the painting itself.

MG *You seem to find your new departures as a painter quite disconcerting when they happen. The articulating comes at the very end.*

PH There's no absolute statement, verbally, which remains exclusively valid. The moment you put it to yourself in words, or to an audience, at that moment you are aware of a need to modify, and restate. So the talk about the paintings really goes on changing all the time.

MG *Which is why the critic's role is a doomed one, never quite to get it right.*

PH That's true, actually. It can't be got quite right.

MG *How did you move towards the next phase, which you came to call the 'wobbly hard-edge paintings'?*

PH The previous period was made up of soft discs and rectangles which could be likened to islands in a sea. Then I began to draw, and draw right up to the edges of the canvas. The painting that started it was *Rectilinear Reds and Blues* from 1963. I drew it on with soft charcoal, and then I rubbed it off, so if you got a pair of specs on you could probably see traces of a drawn line. Then I painted right up to that line with big soft brushes.

MG *In fact, it was shortly after you had made a declaration that you didn't draw, and weren't interested in drawing.*

PH Exactly. That's right. Then suddenly I drew! I picked up a stick of charcoal and drew.

MG *Almost as if saying that hadn't finished off your interest. Often you have explored a certain area to the absolute limit – it might take two years, it might take ten – then find yourself rebounding back in an opposite direction.*

PH That's right. Alan Bowness put that very neatly, that I was an explorer in a certain direction up to the limit, and would then go off in an opposite direction.

fig.18 **One Form: September 1959** Oil on canvas 35.6 × 45.7 cm
Private Collection

MG *That's why you've never developed a signature style.*

PH That's right, I'm glad you think so. The other thing about *Rectilinear Reds* was that there was a Nicholsonian influence. I never had been influenced by Ben, but I now was. It's a Nicholson repertoire of shapes: squares and rectangles, and rectiliniarity, discs and verticals. Infinitely looser in drawing than Ben – and utterly different in brushstroke and paint textures.

MG *In a more wobbly mode.*

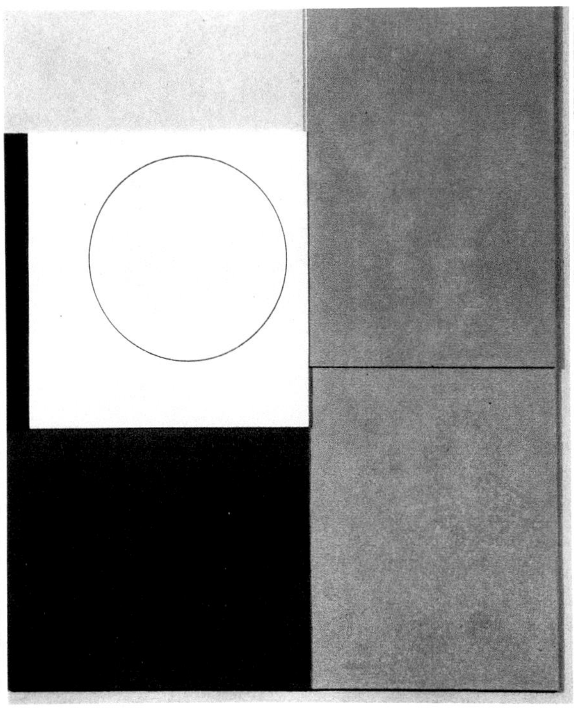

PH The discs which I have made use of throughout my life are very close to Ben's very earliest discs which were irregular, actually. But of course he sheered off into pure geometry, getting out his schoolboy compasses and drawing circles, ruling lines, it was a very daring and strange thing to do. But still it worked in his case. (I found the school-boy compasses in his studio when I took it over.)

It strikes me that my main object at this point was to get the colours at the frontiers harder and sharper. So in order to get straight on to that aspect, one perhaps seized on a known format. The main feature of it was the tightness of the relationships. Very soon I departed from that Nicholsonian format and various irregularities crept in.

In the painting called *Two Vermilions, Orange and Red: September 1964* [no.43], the Nicholsonian format suddenly wobbles as if you were looking at it through water. What had been semi-rigid vertical and horizontal lines begin to waver. That happened and I never returned to Nicholson. Totally remote from the Nicholson geometry was, of course, an earlier painting called *Fourteen Discs* of 1963 [no.42], which I didn't exhibit for many years. It would have been impossible to have shown *Fourteen Discs* with the other pictures of the same period: by contrast, they all have exactly the same degree of flatness, and go out to the frontiers of the picture. *Fourteen Discs* is much more plastic in a sense. Therefore I never showed it for twenty years. It stayed in the store in my St Ives studio.

MG *You write that the tighter the line between two colours the sharper the contrast and the more intense the colour. And your work until 1978 …*

PH … consisted of it getting tighter and tighter and tighter.

MG *And the colours more and more brilliant.*

PH That was the effect of it. In fact the colours already were unmixed, neat. All the colours in this long period until the late 1970s I used to use absolutely neat out of the tubes, unmixed, because I felt that the chromatic intensity was greatest if the colours were not mixed, diluted by other colours. So throughout this whole twenty year period all colours are as they came out of the tube.

Colour, two colours in juxtaposition, is one of the conscious fascinations. A colour doesn't really exist until it's in juxtaposition with another. And it changes constantly. For example, that painting over there, *Two Vermilions, Orange and Red* from 1964, looks quite new to me today. The colours look quite different to anything I've thought about them before. There's a flush in that red at the top that I've never seen before. I know that the painting consists of paint from four tubes of colour, and they're used neat. But you wouldn't believe it, would you? That shape there doesn't look orange, it looks yellow. But it wasn't, it was cadmium orange. And do you see this disc here which looks almost like dark chocolate? Well, that actually is vermilion. Chinese vermilion. So is the big area over to the right.

MG *You said that the actual contour, the line, the frontier as you put it, between two areas of colour, alters the intensity of the colour.*

PH The colour of the colour. It alters the apparent colour of the colour.

MG *So that if it is a more jagged line, dividing two reds, the colour will be hotter, is that the way it works?*

PH Because each little jag has got another colour working on it optically. As it zooms down to nothing the power of that is much greater than it is in a bigger mass of a colour.

MG *At that point did you begin that extraordinary method of work, whereby you painted these huge pictures with tiny Japanese watercolour brushes?*

PH Well I needed that small brush to get up to this drawn line and sort of make it irregular, but the irregularities of it had to be a mirror-image of the irregularities coming from the other side. They had to fit exactly. It was fatal for them to overlap, because if they overlapped, one colour on top of another, that created a third colour, a line. So I used to edge this up with pointed little brushes.

MG *But why did you use the small brushes for the whole area? Why not just fill in in the middle?*

PH Because then I wanted to develop those large areas in a rhythmic way into the broad surface. I wanted the texture with which I covered these huge areas to develop a certain rhythm which would be visible in relief. The absolute antithesis, in other words of the hideous sprayed and rollered painting which came from America and is totally mechanical, totally flat. I would simply squirt about £50 worth of, say, cadmium red into a pudding basin, add some turps and some linseed oil and get it to a certain consistency.

I took immense pleasure in weaving a certain texture with these small brushes. In none of those paintings of that period is there a double application of paint. All those paintings, all of

fig.19 Ben Nicholson **1940 (Painted Relief, Version 1)** Oil on carved board 52.5 × 50 cm Private Collection them, consist of one skin of colour over the white ground only. If you took the same colour and put it on again on top of itself, it would be twice as dark for one thing, and totally different chromatically. So the luminosity of the flat areas of colour was dependent on there only being one layer over the white, so that the white was reflecting light back through the paint from behind.

MG *Had you done studies before?*

PH I used to fill up sheets of paper with things like postage stamps – miniature drawings – endlessly composing with these kind of elements with a Biro. I've got masses of them somewhere. So I drew a lot, then I thought, 'Oh, I'll do that one'. So that was it. I would re-do it, very quickly, not trying to copy it, but taking that as an arrangement of the elements that it was going to be.

MG *In fact you operate by impulse?*

PH Entirely. Just feeling. Just pleasure, nothing was 'thought out' in inverted commas. Nothing. What was so strange about these big paintings in the 1970s was that I seemed to be dictated to by the nature of the work that I was being led into making. I was slowly forced into this amazing procedure. One feature of the process was that, because I didn't paint any area-shape twice (and all colours were all in one layer only), before they were completed these big paintings would have huge shapes that were white still.

MG *So you didn't really know whether it was all going to work until you finished?*

PH Yes. You'd get a big painting, and there would be one shape that was white, and you thought, Christ, there's time now to bugger this painting up completely right at the last hoop. You couldn't just put a bit on and see what it looked like and then smudge it off. That would show through. There was an amazing discipline. The moment the last bit of white was filling in ... zoom! It was as if a great hot flood had come on. Because as long as there was a white piece still there the colours meant nothing. The moment you filled in the last bit of white the whole world would suddenly pulse, as if you'd turned on the electric current onto the whole thing. One came to relish the last moments of those paintings, knowing that that would happen.

Also, if one was confronted with a very large area, as in the painting *Long Cadmium, with Ceruleum in Violet (Boycott)* from 1977 [fig.5], one knew that two-thirds or three-quarters of this thirteen foot canvas had to be covered at a go. It took all day. I went up and down like a ploughman ploughing a field, because as this stuff dried, if it dried too much, then you would see a water-line between one application and another, and you didn't want that, you wanted it to merge invisibly. So it took about fourteen hours non-stop to paint the ground colour in *Boycott*.

MG *Were you listening to the cricket commentary while you were doing it?*

PH Yes, I was. But I couldn't go away and have lunch or anything, because when I came back where I'd got to would have become minimally drier and wouldn't merge. All that should be visible were the endless brush-weavings, in which I took great pleasure. The scribble of paint application is one of the greatest pleasures of the eye, I think. I once said that the application of paint with a brush is just about the greatest pleasure I can think of.

When I went to visit Braque in his studio in Paris in 1949, he had five easels arranged in an arc. On two of them were large late *Ateliers*, one almost finished, and another only just begun. These were painted in thin, turpsified paint. But also there were small landscapes and still lifes which were painted in very thick paint indeed. When I pointed out the difference in paint-texture between the big *Ateliers* and the little landscapes he said, referring to the thickness of the pigment of the brushstrokes and knife strokes on the little paintings, 'Naturellement, ils existent pour exprimer l'émotion directe'. The implication being that the bigger paintings don't express emotion *directly*, but after prolonged contemplation. One felt everything, in those late *Ateliers*, was being forced through various restraining grills or sieves.

Those two modes, so to speak – *l'émotion directe*, uncontemplated and unforeseeable, and the very controlled mode – existed in all my wobbly hard-edge paintings, because they were brought into existence by a line being rapidly drawn. Those huge thirteen foot compositions were drawn in every case in less than thirty seconds, under great emotional pressure because they're bloody expensive, those great big canvases, and you don't mess them up lightly.

So that's *l'émotion directe*, and then began this incredible business with the Japanese brushes. But if you analyse what's going on on a more minute scale the emotion direct is there too because those brushstrokes are not being thought about, or consciously directed. Your whole arm and body are registering the dance which is productive of this scribble.

MG *That calligraphy is very evident in the 1980s paintings. There's an impetuousness about them. After this very long period of wobbly hard-edge paintings, painted meticulously with very small brushes, everything suddenly reverses.*

PH The wobbly hard-edge period came to a sort of crescendo in the paintings that were painted especially for the big retrospective in Austin, Texas, in 1978, of which there were quite a few. Unfortunately Austin is the worst place for an asthmatic like myself. It's the asthma capital of the USA; in the morning the cars look as if they've been sprayed yellow because of the pollen, and I was also under a lot of pressure. I fell ill with pneumonia, never recovered, and when we got home after driving right across the USA to Los Angeles, collapsed completely and totally. Then there was another terrible crisis because my wife dropped dead the next spring. Every conceivable crisis.

These crises coincided with having pushed the wobbly hard-edge to extremes. So when

I started painting again, I suddenly felt, I'm through with all this. I hadn't taken up a big brush for fifteen years. Except in the gouaches, which are another story, I hadn't made gestures larger than ones possible with the Japanese watercolour brushes. So for every reason one felt free to bugger things up and try something crazy. That's when the new big brush, free paint things started. It happened slowly by degrees. There was a painting where the free application was restricted to only one disc and one other area.

MG *You felt a physical desire for release, especially after you went to Australia.*

PH There was a very big show with Leslie Waddington before that. It's easy to think now that it was all the Australian impulse, which of course I loved. I had a wonderful time there in 1989–90. In the four months in the artist's studio in the Art Gallery of New South Wales, which hangs above the Woolloomoolloo creek of Sydney Harbour, I did forty-six large gouaches and six large canvases. It wasn't so much the landscape as the vegetation that got into the work. The flora of Australia I simply adore, but of course I was already in love with that sort of thing through this garden, with its Australian and New Zealand shrubs. Those big broad-leaved things in this garden were the first ever grown north of the equator, pioneered of course by my predecessor here, Arnold-Forster. It's a New Zealand tree, but it grows all over the south-west of England now.

MG *What is the relation in those pictures of the 1980s and 1990s to the garden?*

PH There's a strange factor. I have not, since I came to live here forty odd years ago, gone into this garden with a pencil and a pad and done a drawing. I did start to draw again, figuratively, when I was on holiday with Leslie Waddington in the Dordogne, soon after Delia's death. I suddenly drew some line drawings. And thereafter I made drawings very frequently of places that I liked very much, like the Dordogne, Japan, the Lake District and the Scilly Isles. The motive was excitement with things seen – with a landscape. But I never actually drew this garden direct!

MG *But the paintings are often permeated with a sense of the garden – an outdoor feel, unlike the interior space you noted in most of your work. Some of them clearly have plant forms in them, as well as Heron discs and so forth. Is it something to do with the remarkable combination of vegetation you have here with …*

PH … the rocks, and horizon and light.

MG *The vegetation and rocks mimic each other in the garden, don't they? The rocks have been eroded into softly rounded forms, and the shrubs and trees sculpted into similar rotund shapes by the wind. Also there are tremendous, brilliant Heron colours coming from the camellias and the azaleas.*

PH You're taking the elements with which you are building, to some extent, from a direct visual experience of rocks and trees. And not only visual. I mean, the rhythmic realities of a landscape where you live permeate your awareness and your mind, and your consciousness through the soles of your feet, upwards.

The garden dictates the rhythmic outlines which one deploys; but the way one deploys them springs from the paintings one has done in the past. Without representing given rocks or given trees, you have invented a vocabulary out of the rhythms of these outlines. All one's present painting is a direct, on-going outcome of what one has done before. There is no such thing as a complete breach, you see, in any important respect. My heavy pencil drawings of these rocks, and this garden – done at the age of six, seven and eight – the rhythmic nature of those drawings is exactly like what's happening now in my work.

MG *But clearly you don't go into the studio and think to yourself, now I'm going to paint some rhythms derived from rocks in the garden. So is it unconscious?*

PH It is not unconscious, I'm aware of what I'm doing. It's super-consciousness. But I can't do anything else. If I say, I'm going to have a disc here, I suppose the order goes out to put a disc down. But you leave it to every muscle and nerve in your arm to do it. I frequently look in the opposite direction when I'm actually drawing the thing, so one is not interfering with any stupid conscious interruption or control. The control is coming from a rhythmic feeling, I was almost going to say a musical feeling. Rhythm is a word that is vastly used, and overused, but it's very hard to find anything else.

MG *I think it's the basis of everything, certainly of good writing. Painters have told me it's the basis of good painting too.*

PH I think it is. Finding new ways of making divisions of the canvas's surface, new relationships, new ways of producing a new harmonious dividing-up of a canvas rectangle. So that you are avoiding everything that you've ever done before.

MG *You seem to enter a different world with the change of medium to gouache. These watery effects with spreading pigment are all completely different to the oil paintings, those tendrils of paint suspended in water.*

PH It is completely different. That's because it's their nature to enable you to do that. That flooding was an accident which I welcomed with both arms, if you see what I mean?

MG *So you are very much following the medium.*

PH Oh, God, yes. The medium is the message, or rather, the medium is the image. I mean, bad painting is painting in which the shapes and colours that the painter is apparently trying to state are totally detachable from the matter of the paint, the material of the paint, and the brush-strokes which render it onto the surface. These things should be indissolubly united. People think of drawing first, then colouring. Nothing is more ridiculous than that. The colour is the shape. In fact 'The Shape of Colour' was the title of the Power Lectures I gave in Australia in 1973.

After the early 1980s, there's a great deal of white ground left as such in my work, but it's not left in a state in which you feel that the painting is just the coloured stuff stuck here and there onto the white and that the white ground is a separate spatial generator. It is still obeying the Heronian principle of being equal in its spatial pressure. The colour areas and the white areas are identical in their operation.

MG *It is interesting that in addition to oil paint, your other medium is gouache, which has specific qualities different from watercolour. It is not transparent.*

PH It's opaque. It's essential that it should be opaque. I've never used watercolour since I was fourteen. The fact that all the colour areas are flat in themselves from frontier to frontier, is important to me. But that flatness is opaque, it's not transparent. On the other hand, it's a one-layer application. The unity of that painting [pointing to a gouache on the kitchen wall] would be shattered if I painted the same colour twice on top of itself. That's just as true as it is of the oil painting, the unity is generated by the fact that all the colour areas are only one skin, so that the white of the ground is actually illuminating them from behind.

MG *Do you think your temperament is more calm, and contemplative, less filled with say violence and aggression than say that of many other artists, whose work is filled with violence, sexuality and qualities one does not associate with a Heron?*

PH In the twentieth century everybody thinks that sexual intercourse is the be-all and end-all in the pleasure scale, don't they? Well, I don't really agree about that. Perhaps I'm very limited. But I think that's asking for trouble.

MG *It's not your subject as a painter, is it? You once said that you know no greater pleasure than putting paint on canvas. You find the actual physical act of painting deeply satisfying. Oil paint on canvas, you wrote, there's nothing to match it.*

PH It's really tremendous. I'm perfectly capable of enjoying looking at nude women, and photographs of them, but it's totally different. It's certainly not anything to do with the superior kind of consciousness that I'm enjoying now, at this moment, looking out of this window at the garden and the sky, and this amazing plant.

Mind you, I think one is full of the most terribly disturbingly violent thoughts and feelings all the time. I am very passionately interested in politics and the political fate of this nation, so I read the papers and never any books. I'm quite capable of shouting about some organisational idiocy. But the point is that the expression of these strong feelings, that I have all the time, is not through painting.

MG *You've fought a number of passionate campaigns in defence of this landscape.*

PH Delia totted up from the letters and diaries just before she died, and announced that I had actually spent five and a quarter years of my life on campaigns, all of which I'd won hands down. But my God, when you've got a landscape like this, you can't possibly just sit by and let it go.

MG *But this activism seems to belong in a different mental compartment from your work.*

PH That's perfectly true. In pure visual awareness there's a terrific intense passivity, or receptivity, isn't there. You are receptive to the extent that you actually look, and to the extent to which you are capable of receiving. You don't project, you don't look at something and think 'Oh, I'll make something of that'. Painting should be calmness itself. But that calmness is there because it's the product of the containment of tremendous pressures.

MG *What kind of emotional pressures do you mean?*

PH Well, the perception of anything, the contemplation of anything, develops the most fantastic emotional excitement, terrific excitement. It's reality you're looking at. Whatever you look at is real.

MG *So the kind of emotion you mean is not the kind of passion that might be generated by politics, say, but a kind of elation that you get from a landscape or a colour.*

PH It's the elation of perceiving what is.

MG *Do you get intense pleasure from just looking at colour itself?*

PH There is no such thing as colour itself. All colour is shape and all shape is colour. There is no shape that is not conveyed to you by colour, and there is no colour that can present itself to you without involving shape. If there is no shape then the colour would be right across your retina. If you stuck your head inside a blue globe so that the only thing you saw as you opened your two eyes was blueness, actually the blueness of the blue you would cease to be aware of in a matter of seconds, because colour awareness depends on colour opposition – on *two* colours being present.

But I do believe that one's awareness is saturated with visual pleasure. The greater the intensity of your consciousness and visual concentration, the greater the pleasure. Any data can supply that. Even if you were in a prison cell, you could sit there and become aware of the shape of colour and the colour of shape. To the extent that you become aware, you will be transported.

It's very strong. It's the central experience of my life, really. Everything is completely different all the time, just as any good painting looks different every time you see it. Because the disposition of your mental state is changing all the time, and what's outside is changing all the time. I could just sit in this chair for the rest of my life and be totally entertained.

MG *So if there's an emotion being expressed in your picture, it's a sort of joy.*

PH Yes, it certainly is. I get it again and again. What you see, your visual field, consists of one thing only, colour. Colour is light and sight. That is what sight makes available to you. And that colour has a million varieties and variations. So looking at something – anything – is more interesting than doing anything else, ever, as a matter of fact.

Catalogue

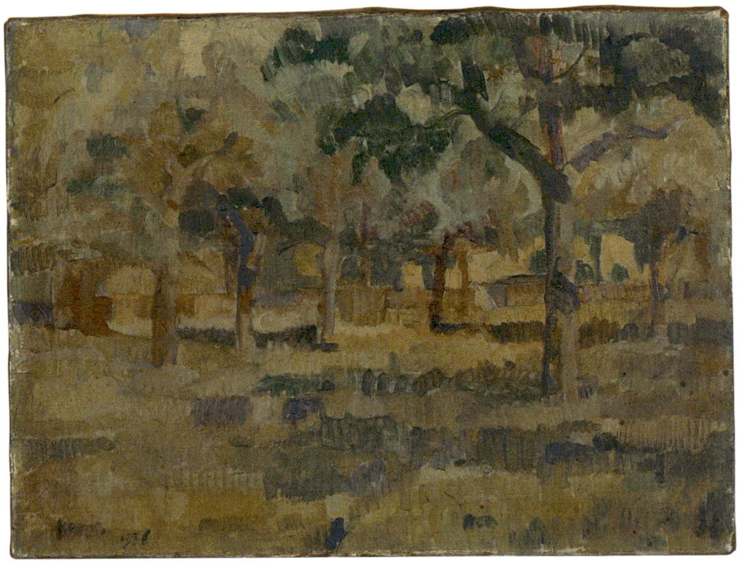

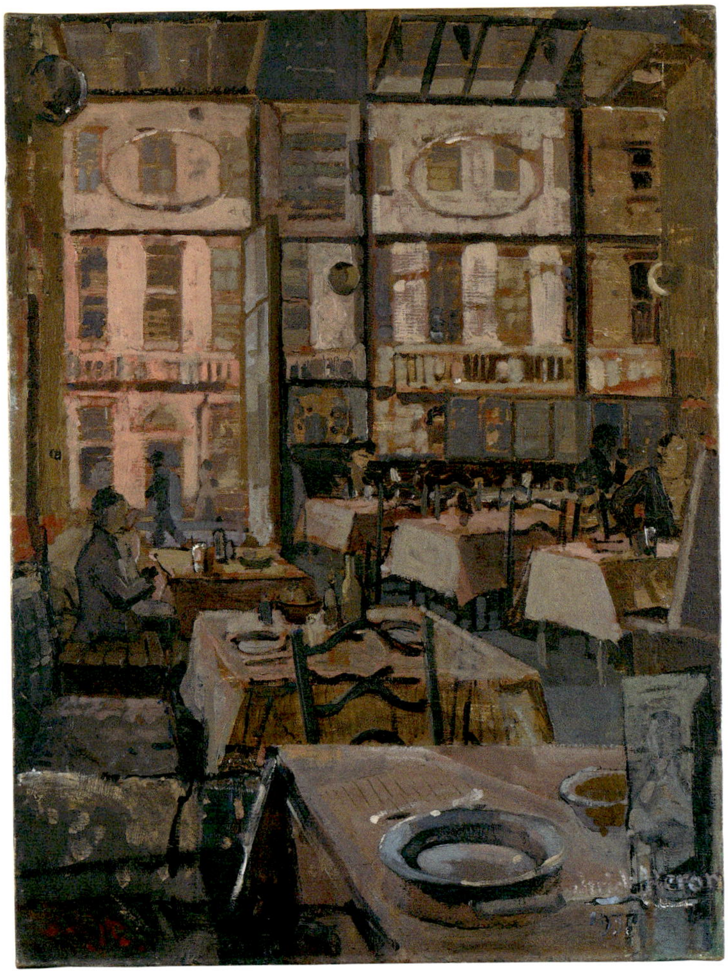

1 Orchard, Lower Slaughter: 1936 41.3 × 55.2

3 Bogey's Bar (Woburn Place): February 1937 91.4 × 71.1

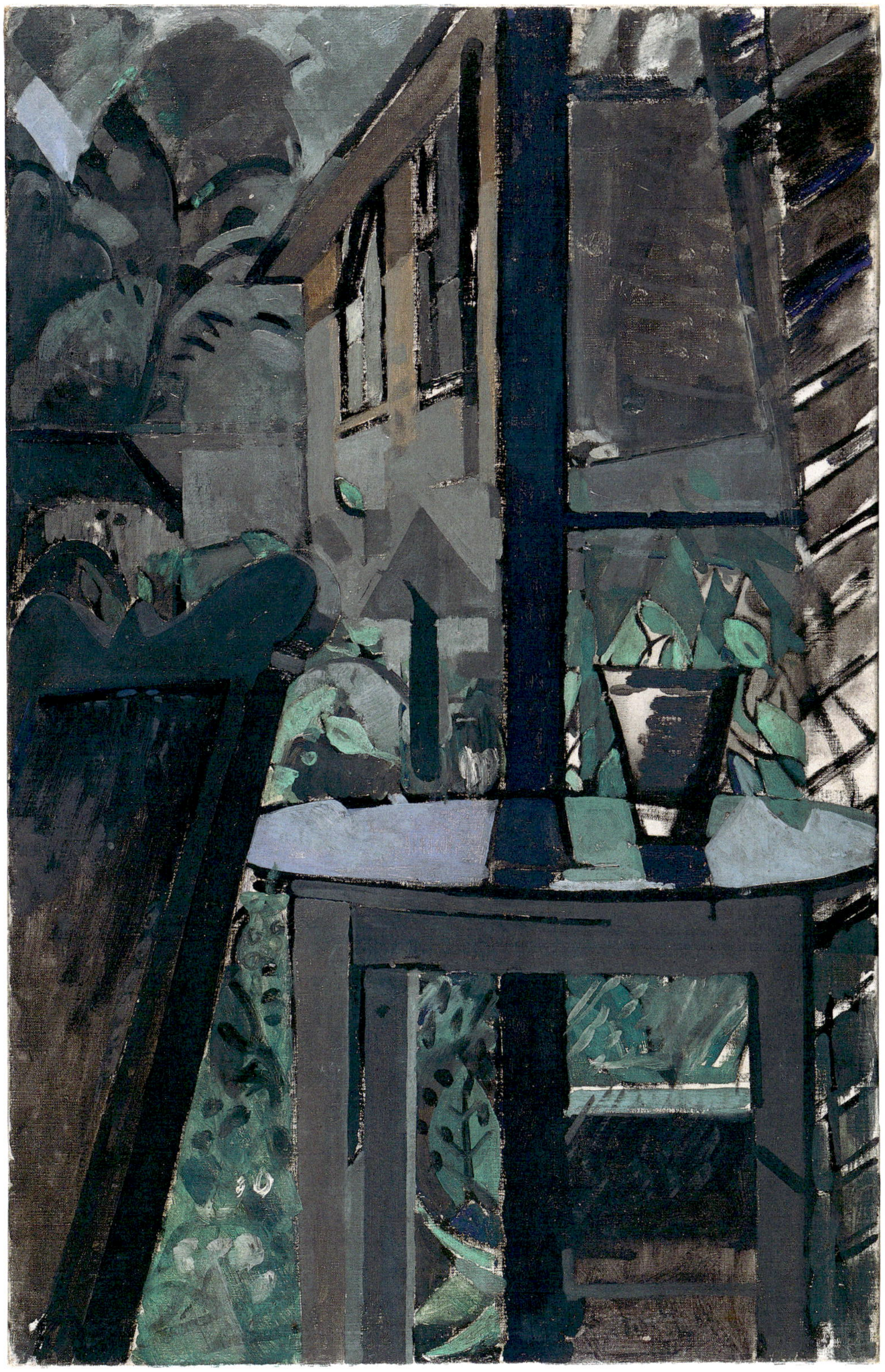

2 Table, Window and Chair: 1937 76.2 × 50.8

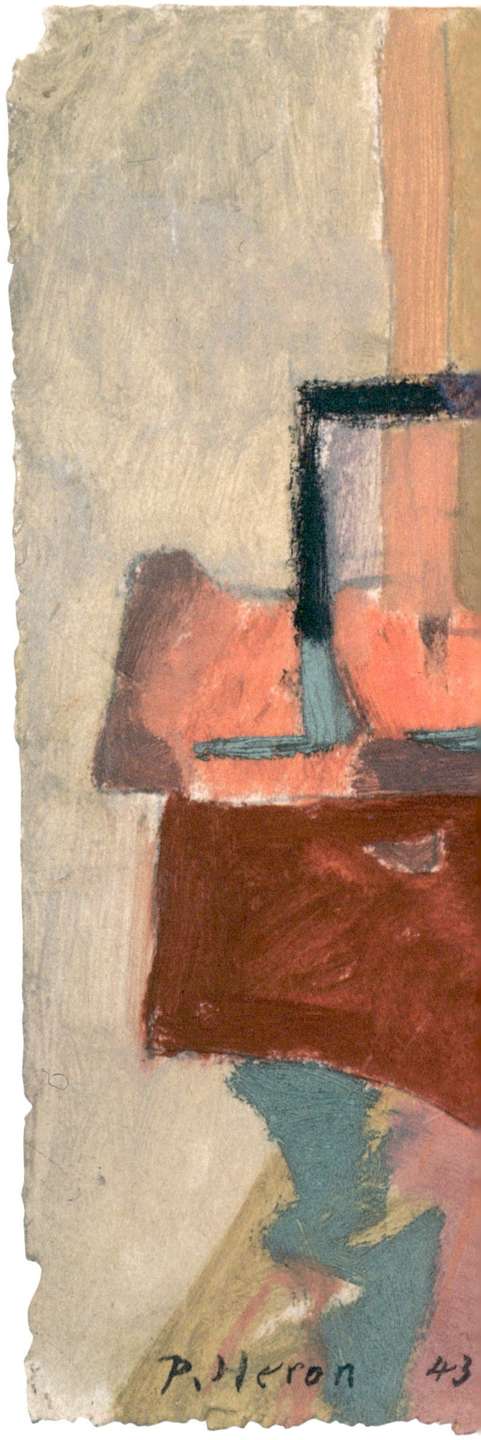

4 The Piano: 1943 19 × 27.3

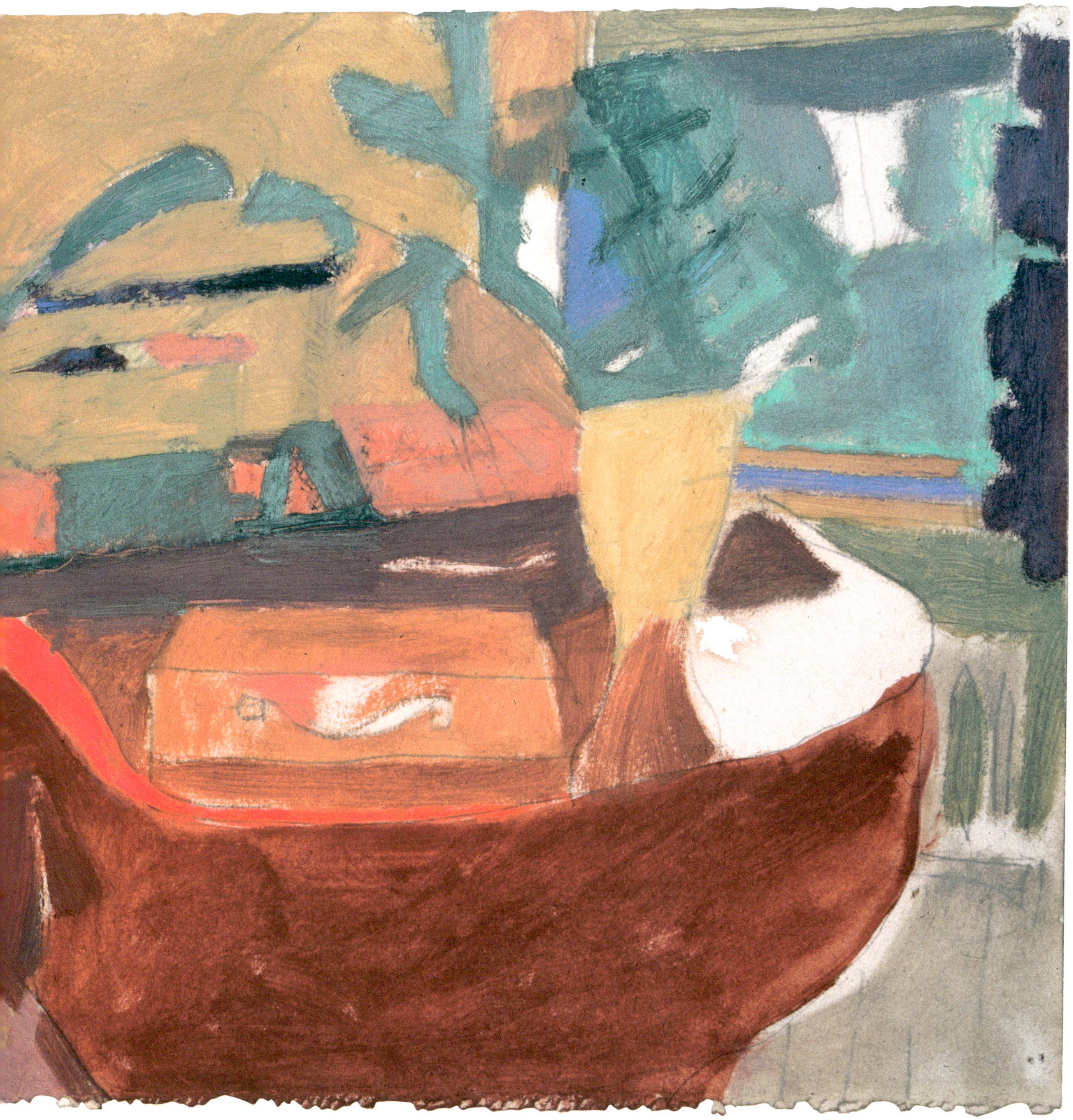

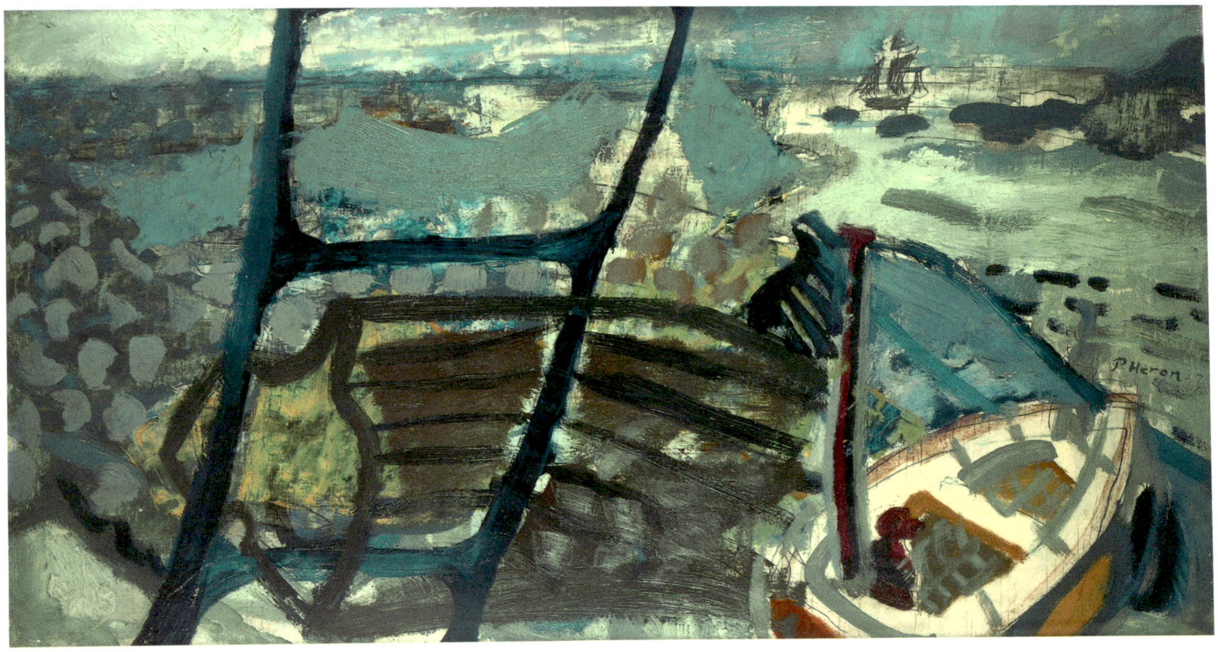

5 The Boats and the Iron Ladder: **1947** 30.4 × 60.9

11 Indigo Bay: **1952** 45.1 × 121.9

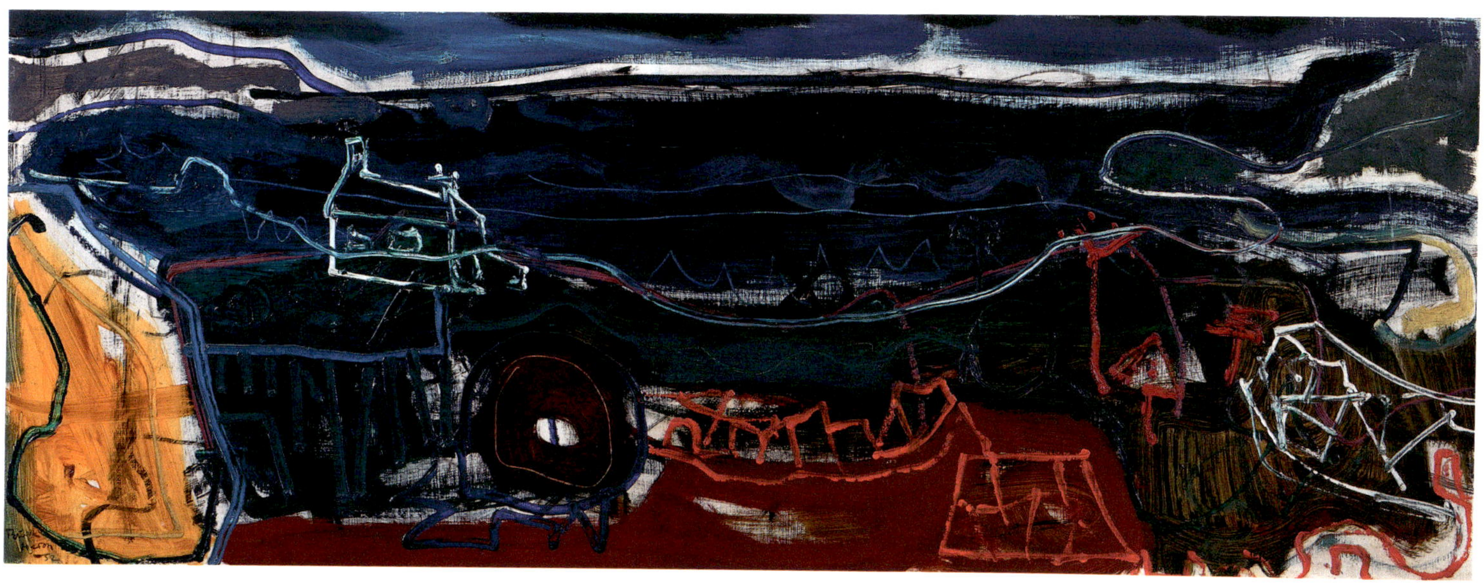

6 Still Life with Black Bananas: **1948** 45.8 × 91

7 The Long Table with Fruit: **1949** 45.8 × 91.4

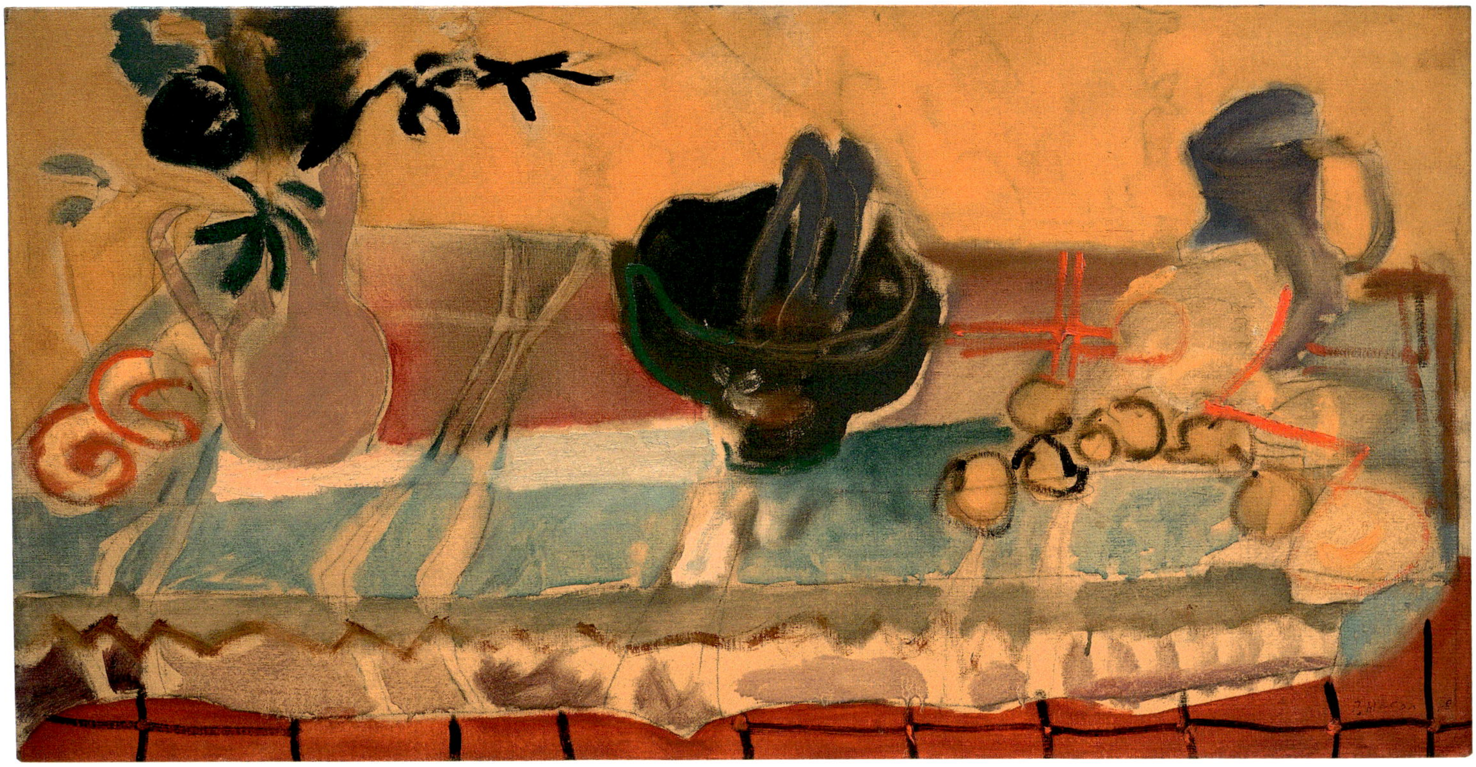

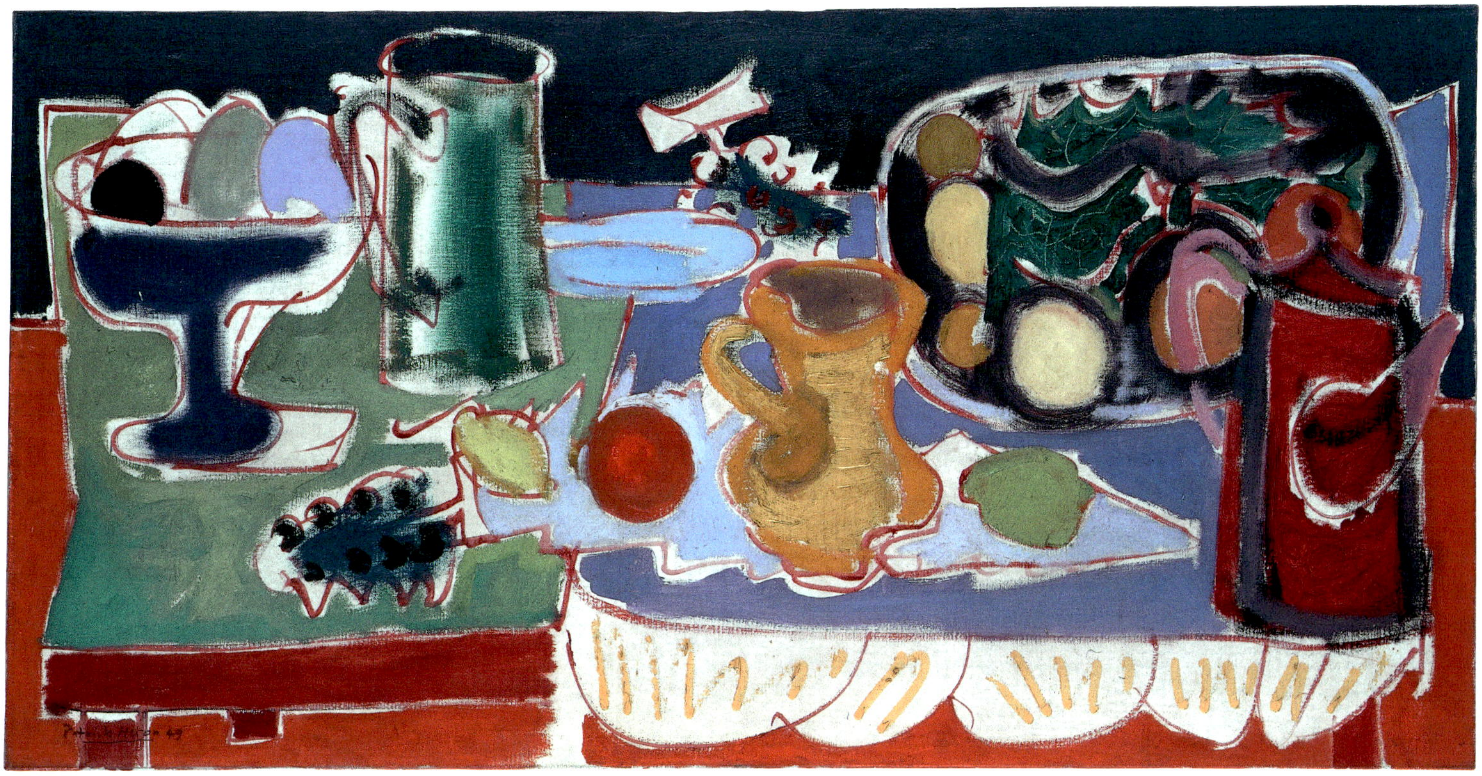

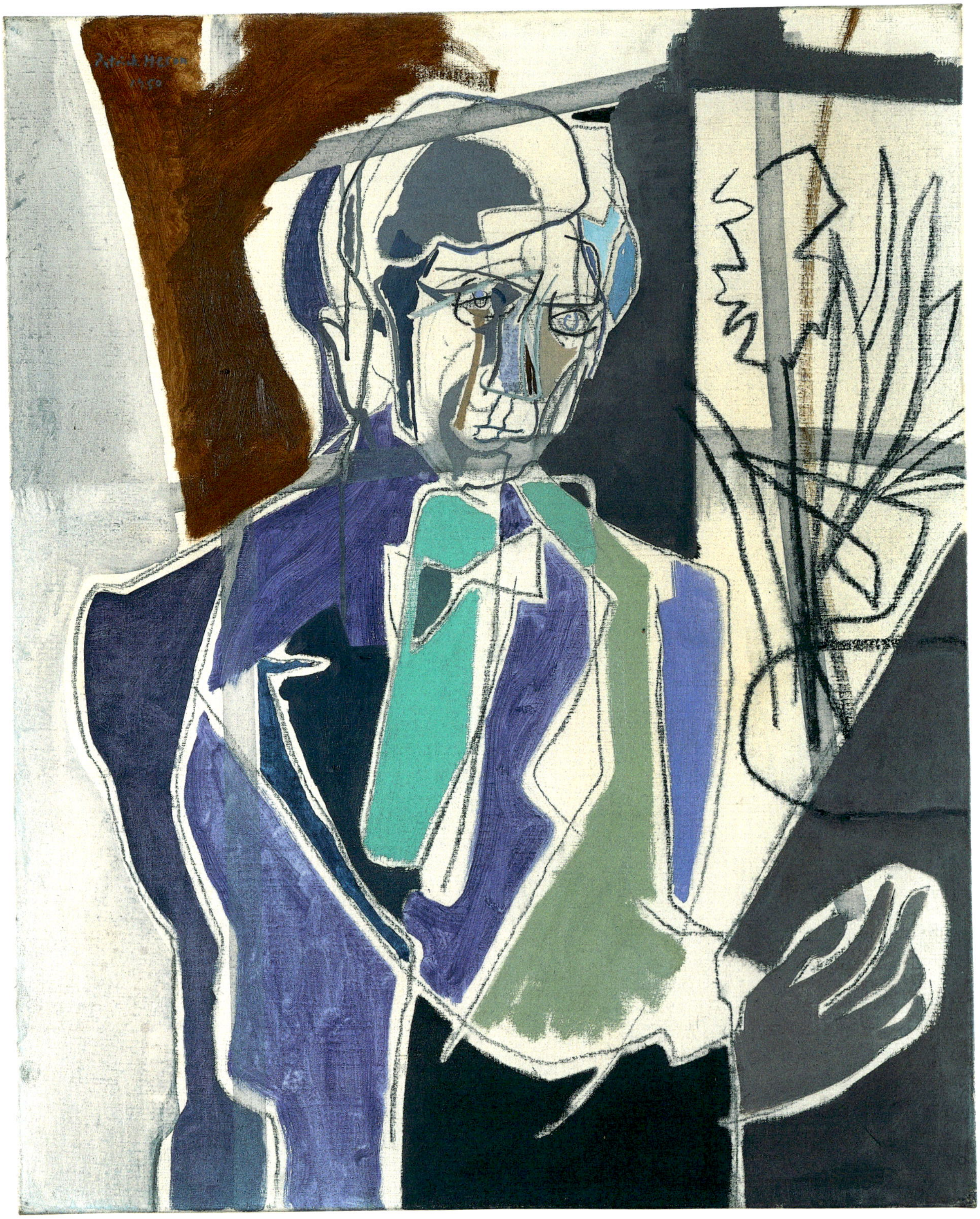

8 Portrait of Herbert Read: 1950 76.2 × 63.5

10 The Room at St Ives: 1952–1953 121.9 × 182.8

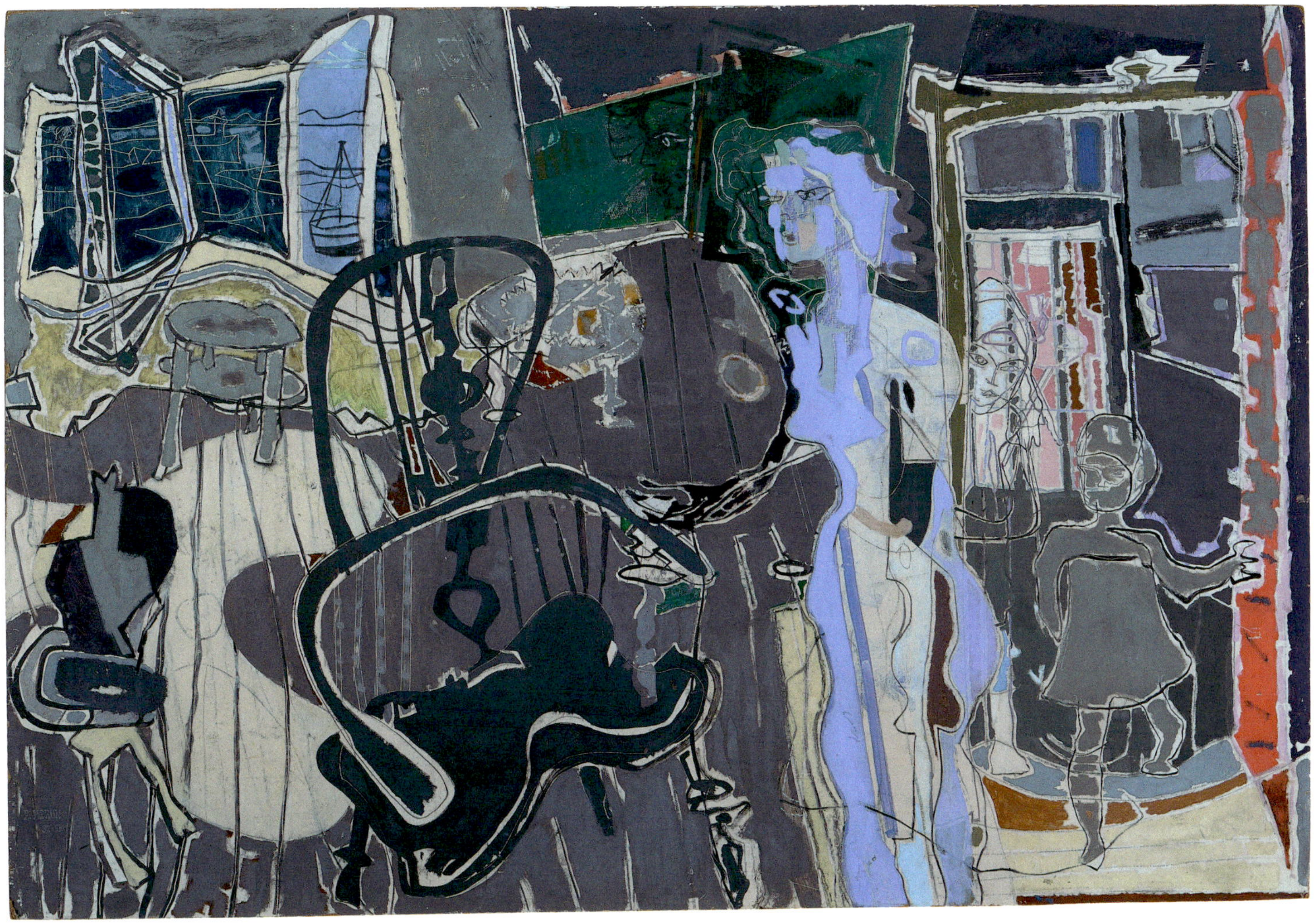

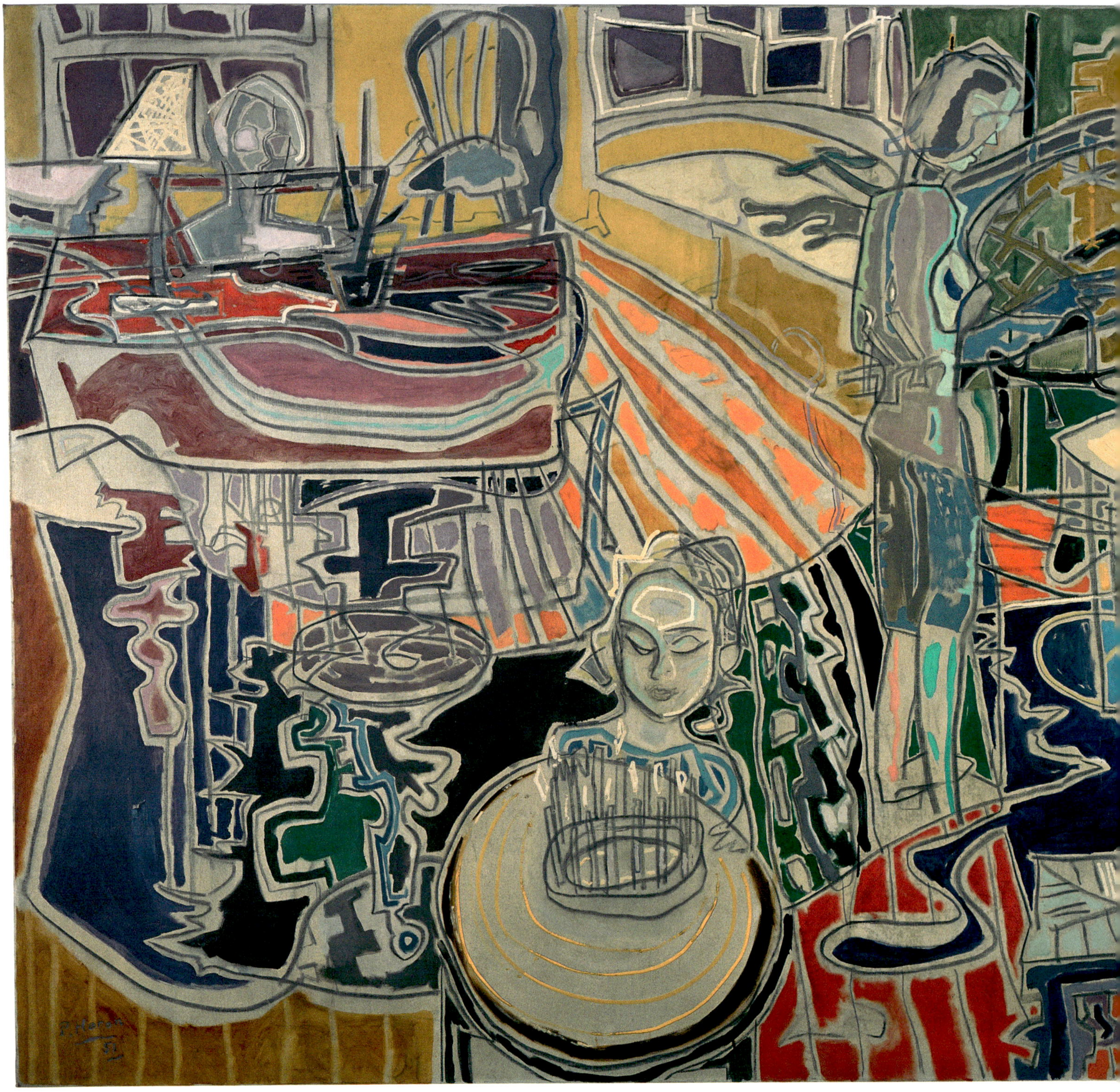

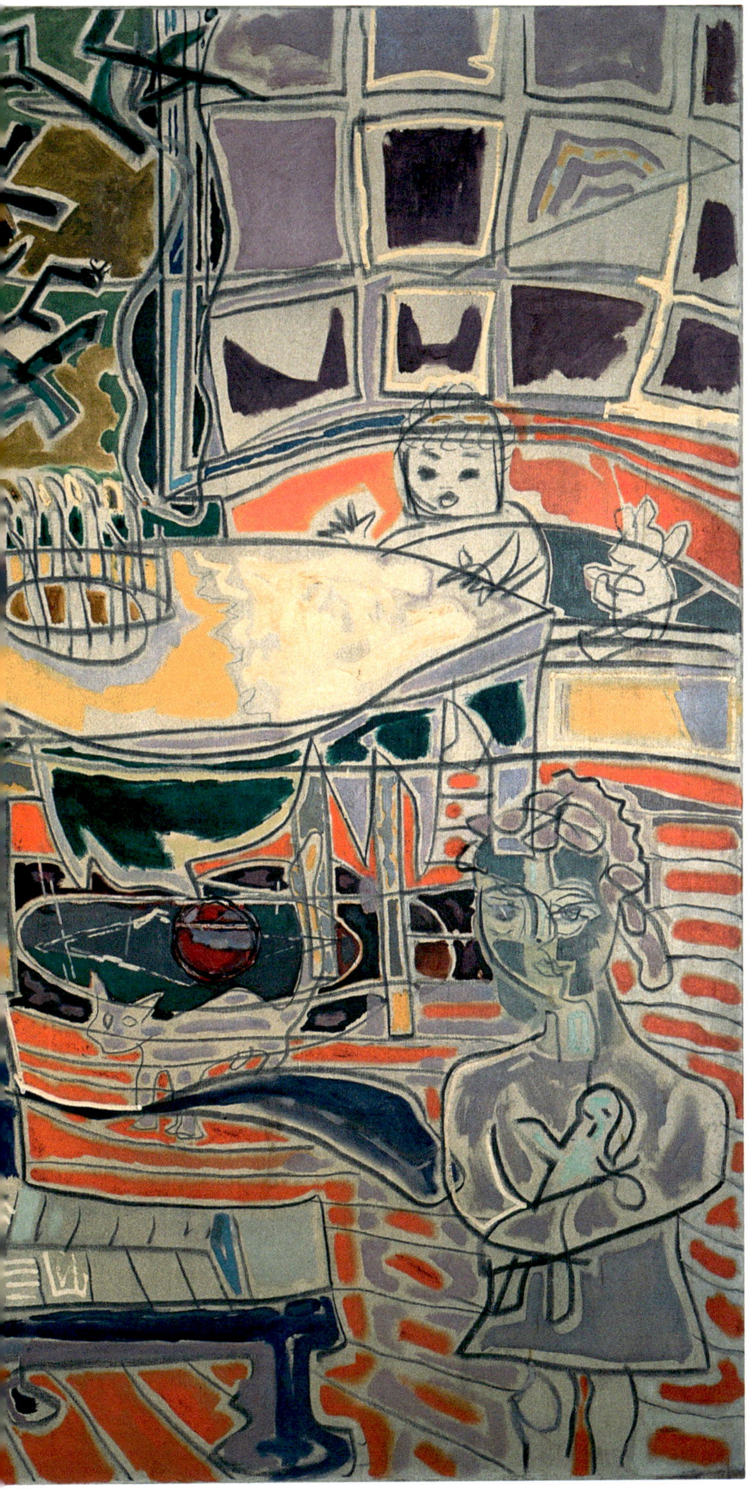

9 Christmas Eve: 1951 182.9 × 304.8

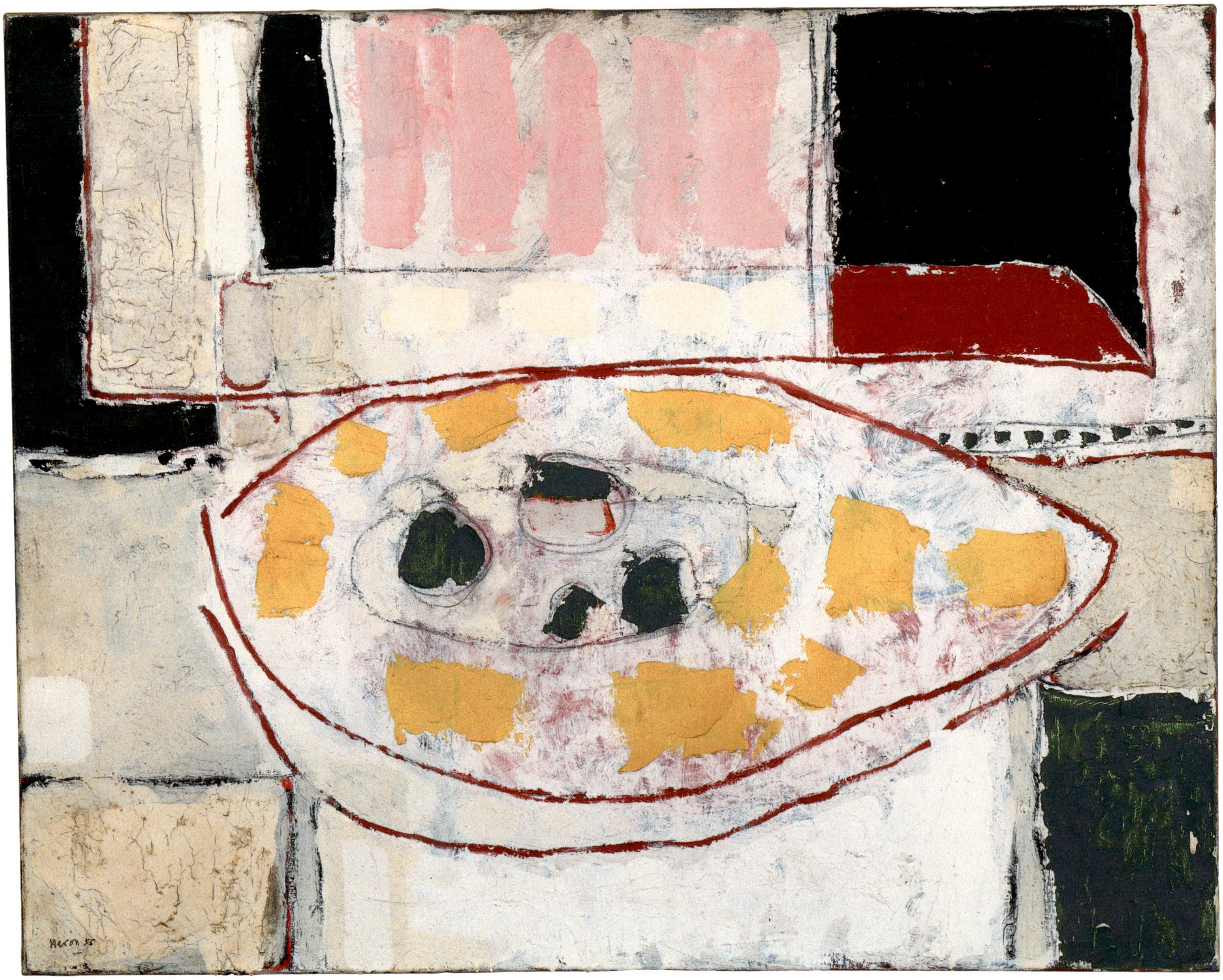

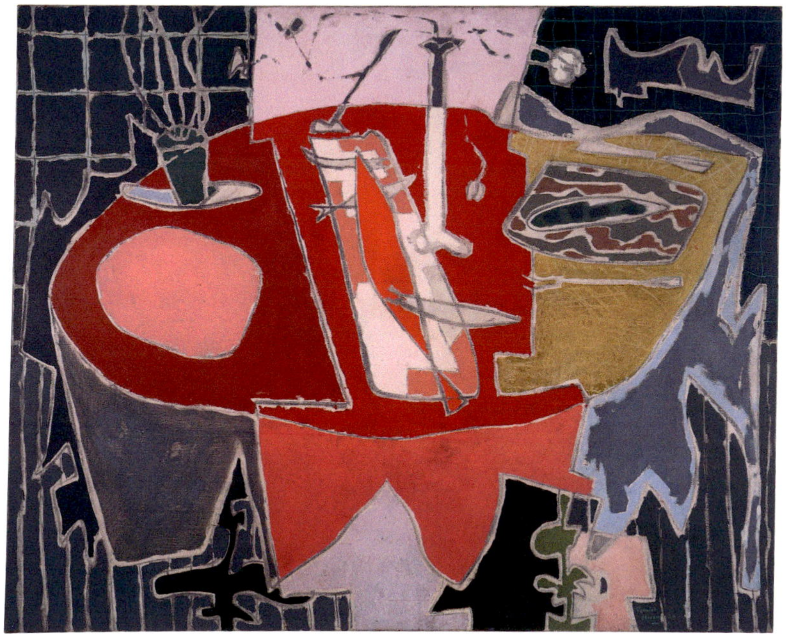

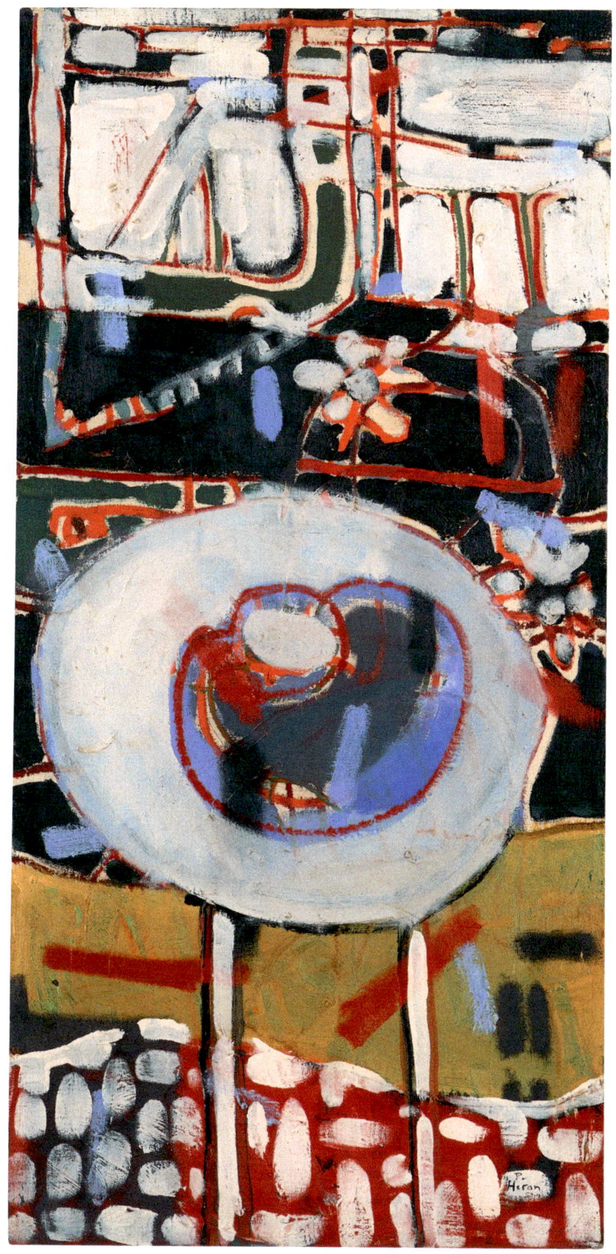

14 [L] The White Table: 1955 71.1 × 91.4

13 [A] The Red Table: 1954 101.6 × 127.6

12 [R] Round White Table: St Ives: 1953–1954 91.4 × 45.8

15 Girl in Harbour Room: 1955
121.9 × 182.8

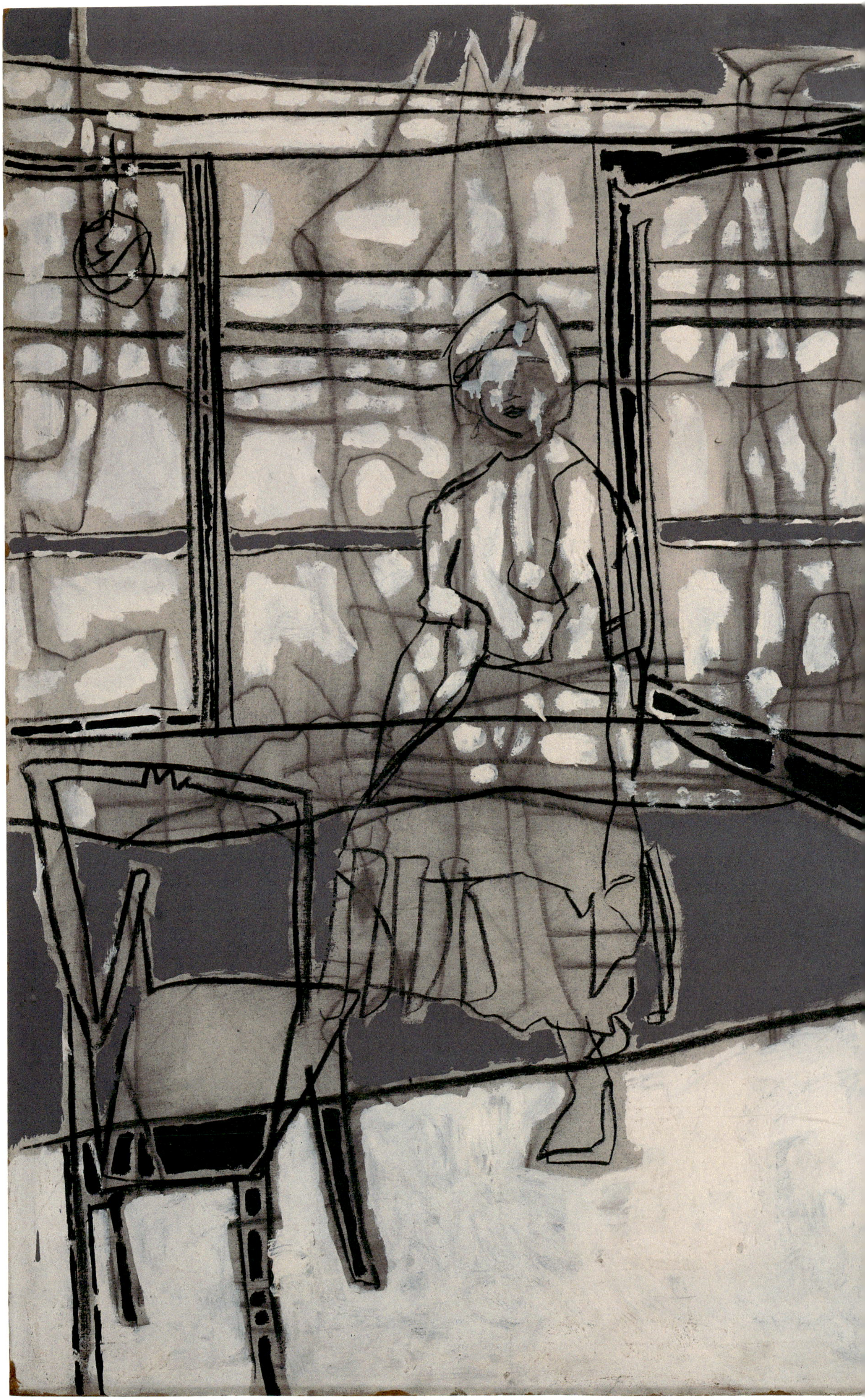

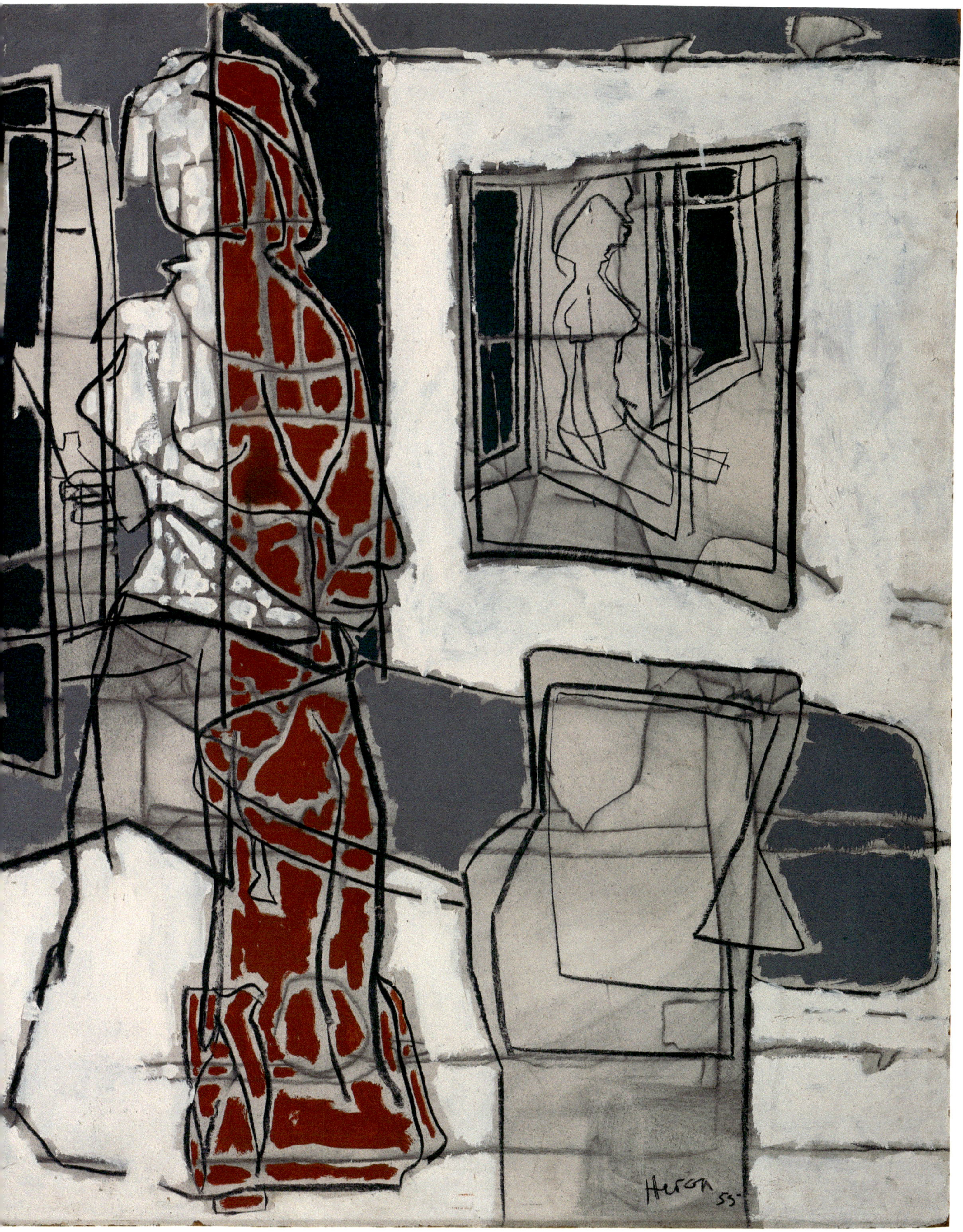
Heron 53

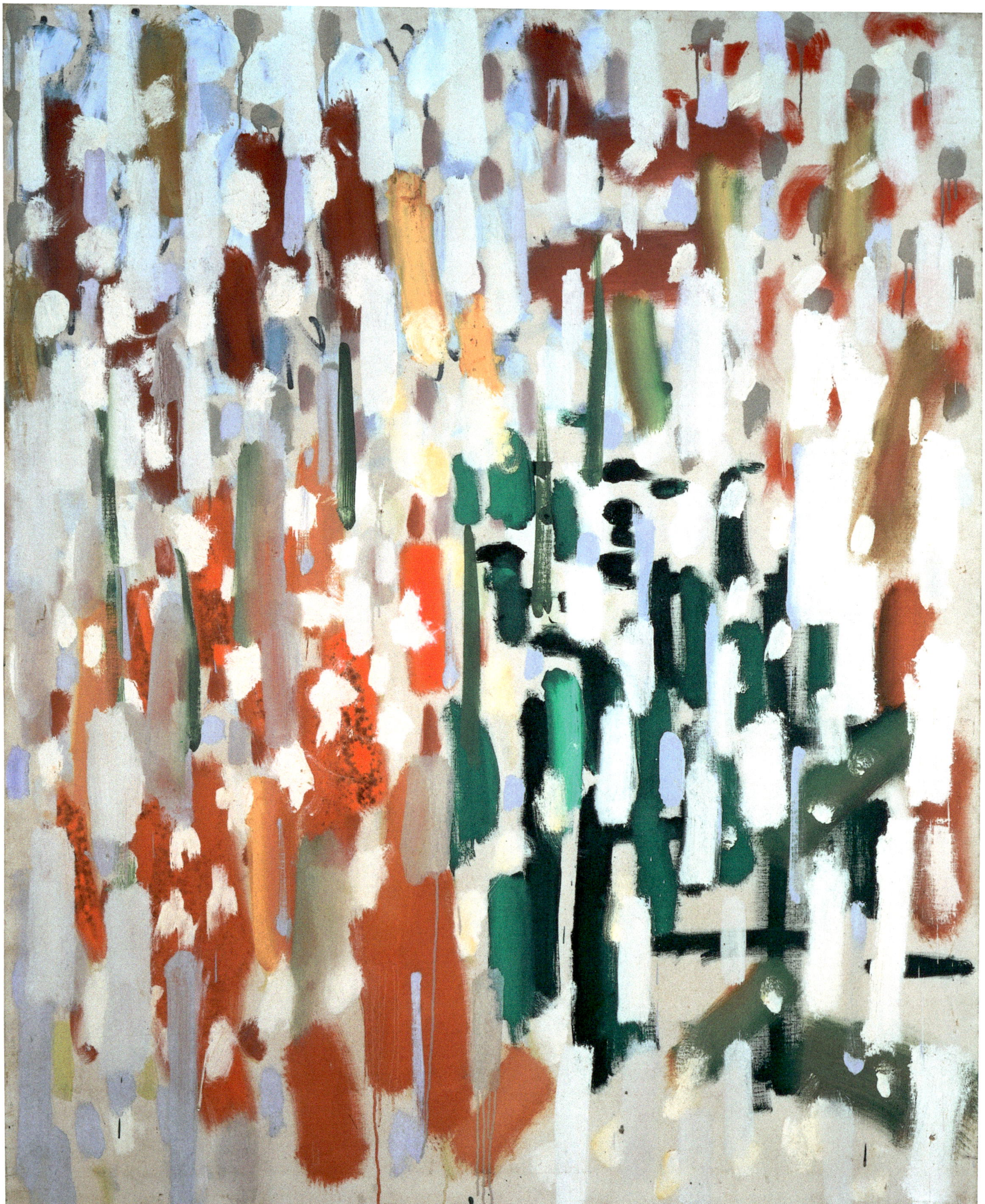

16 Azalea Garden: May 1956 152.4 × 127.6

17 Garden Painting: August 1956 127.6 × 91.5

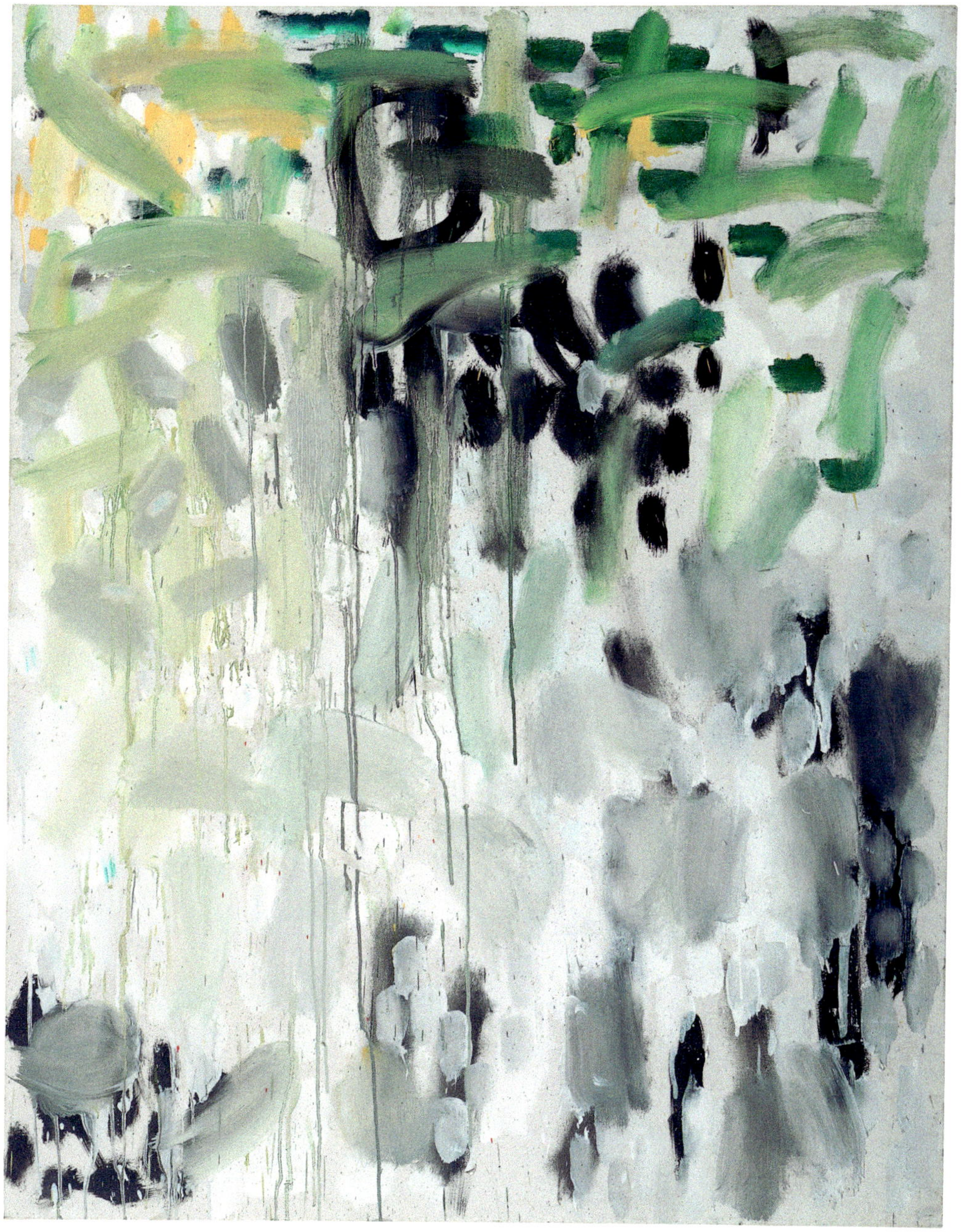

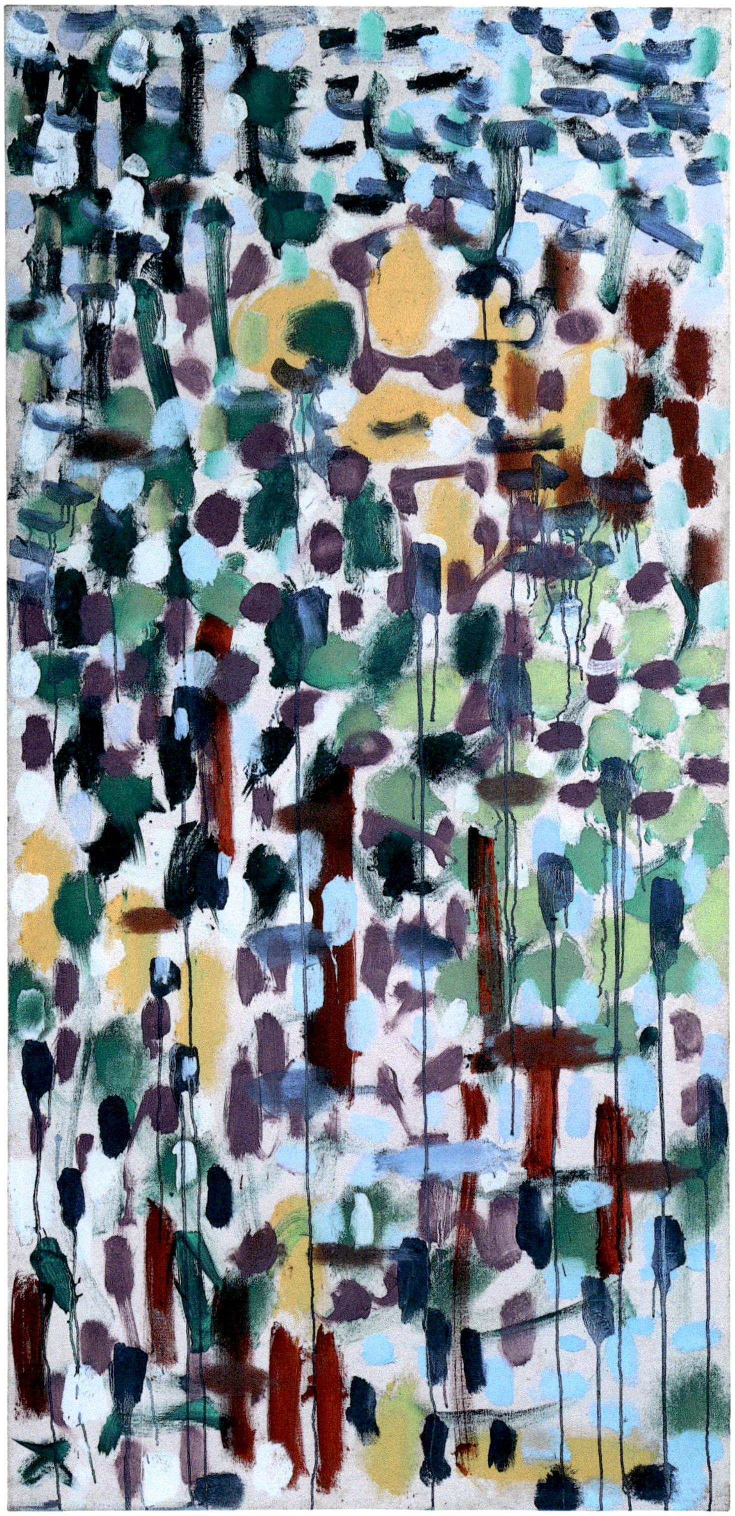

18 Autumn Garden: 1956 182.9 × 91.5

19 Summer Painting: 1956 182.9 × 91.5

Overleaf

20 Vertical Light: March 1957 55.9 × 121.9

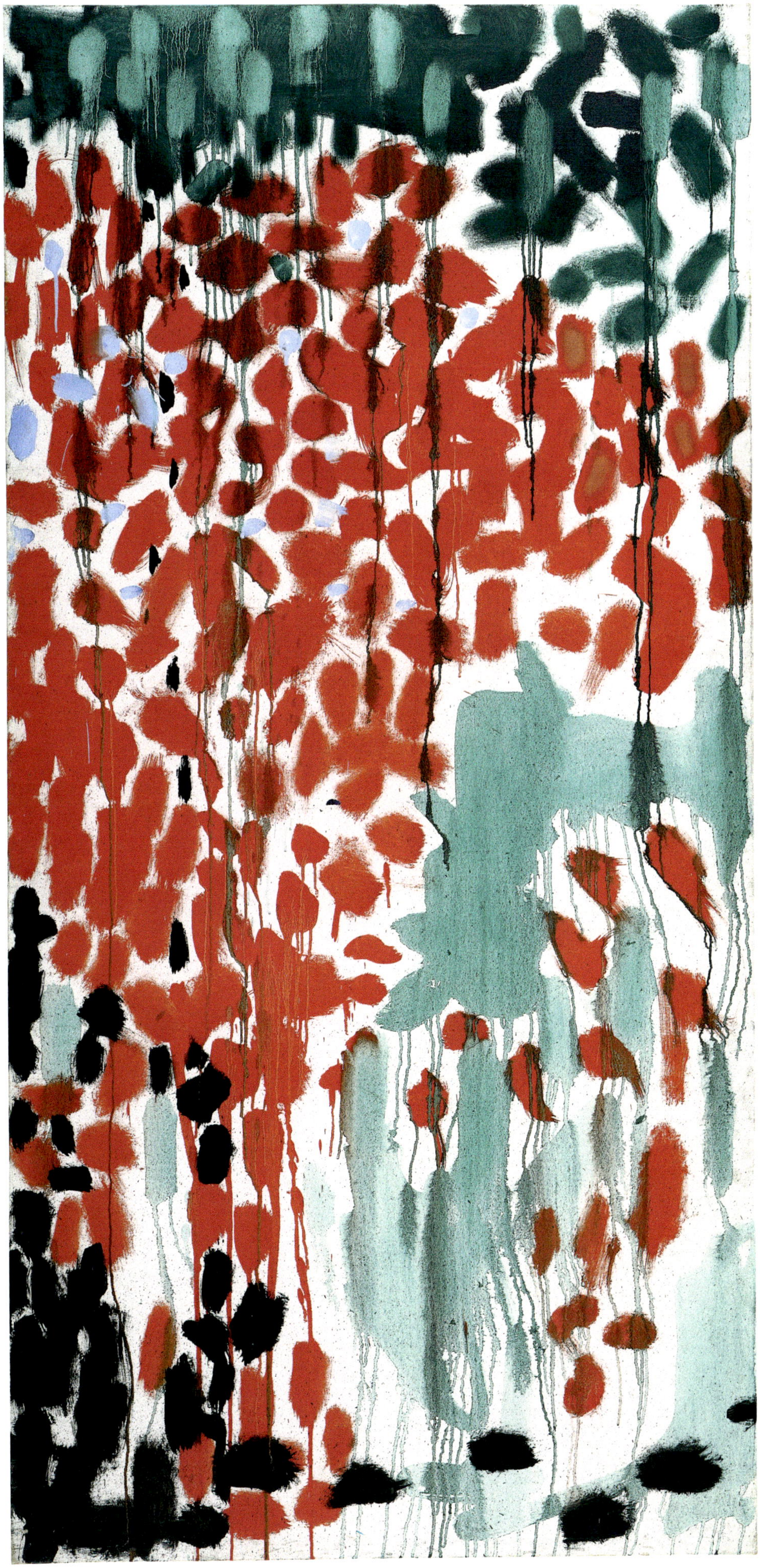

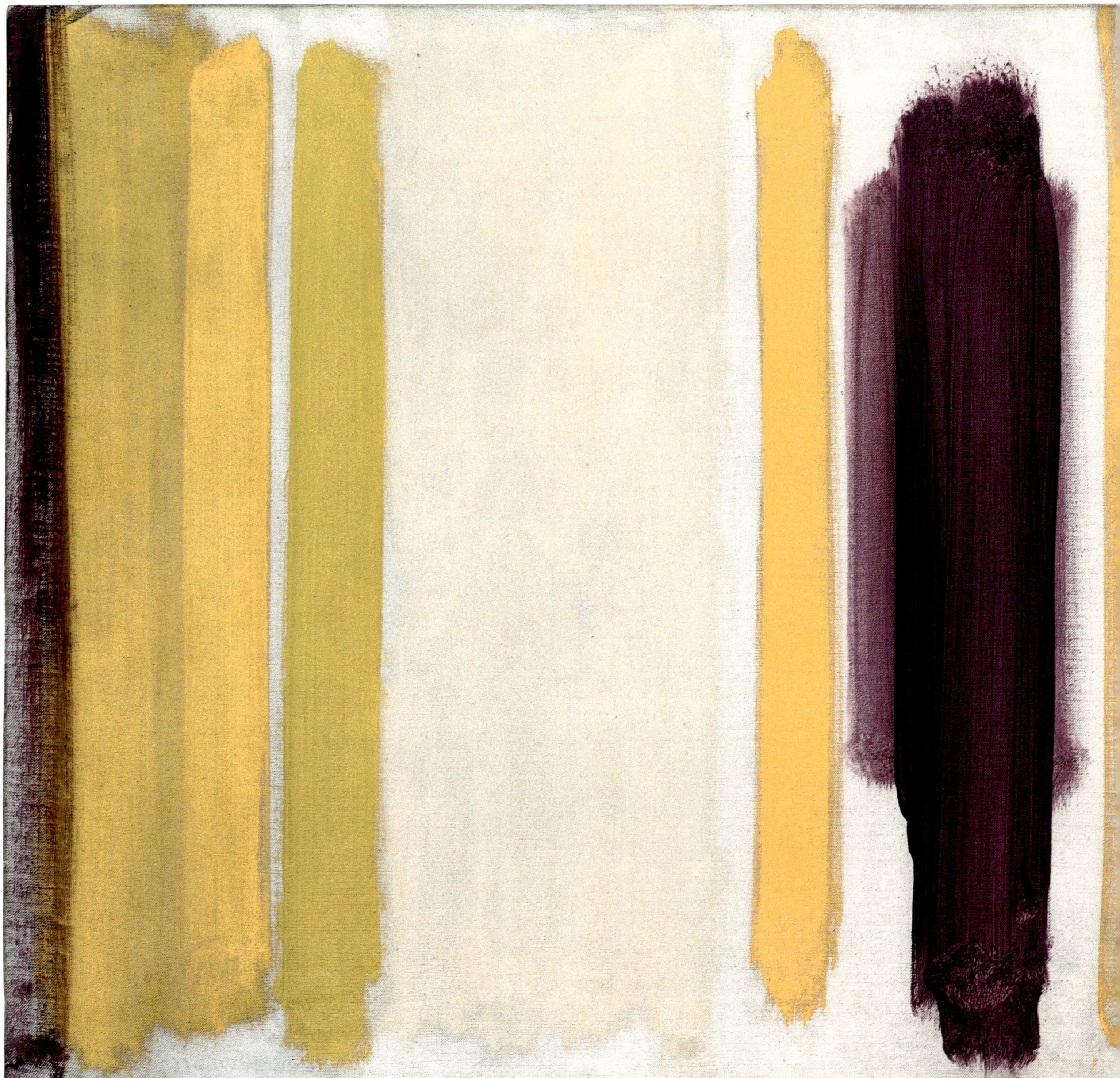

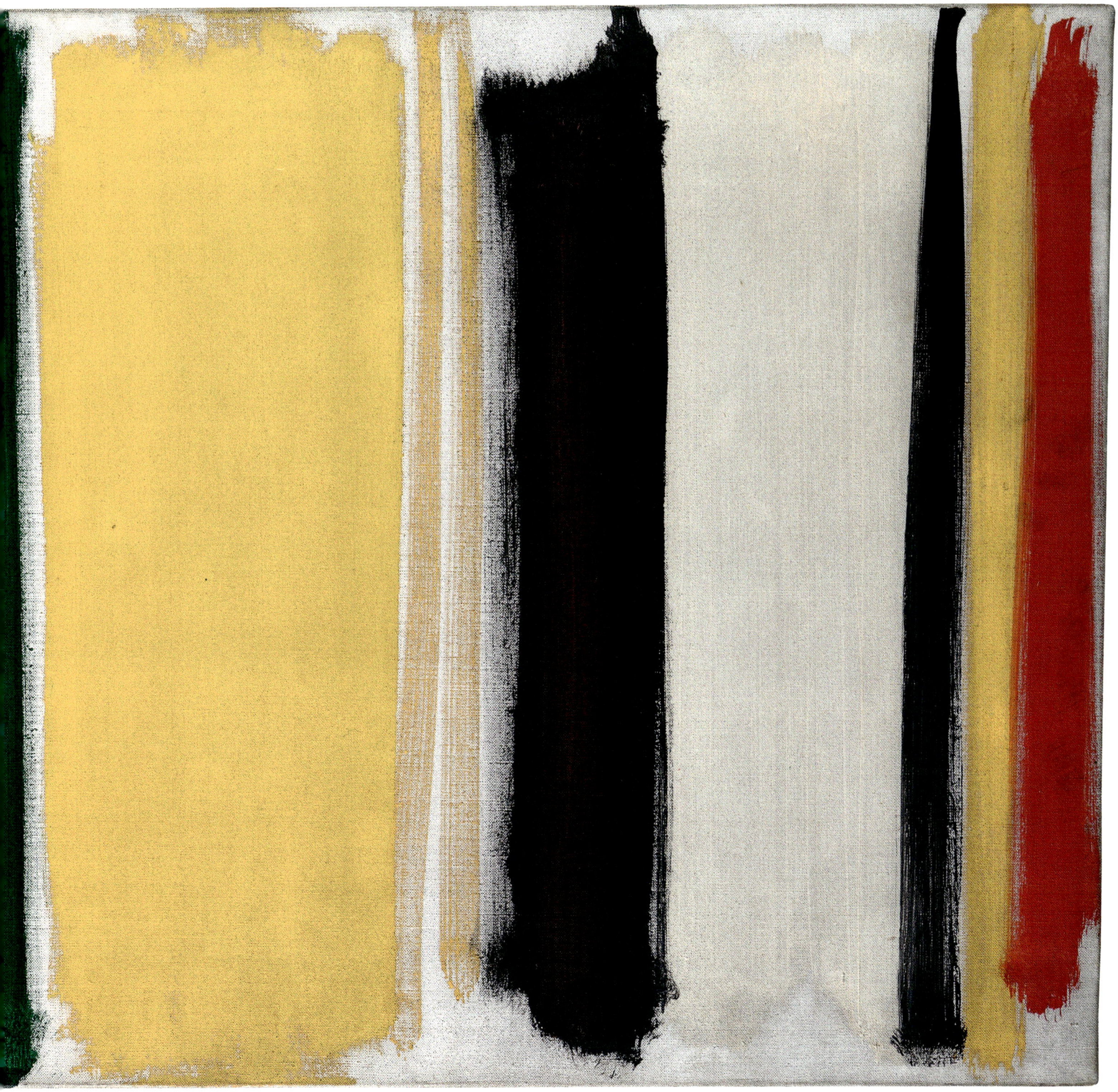

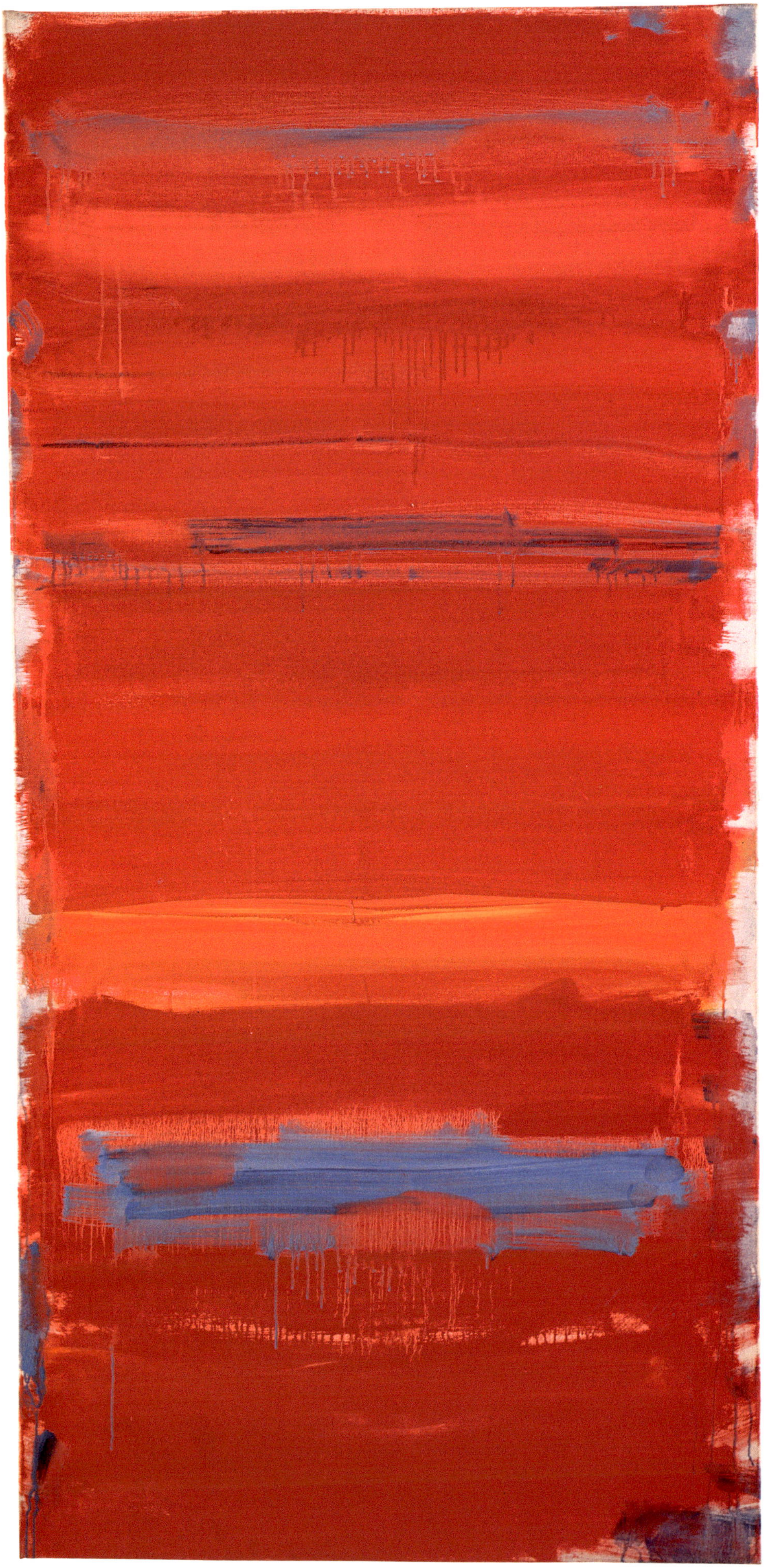

25 Red Layers (with Blue and Yellow): 14 December 1957 182.9 × 91.5

21 Scarlet, Lemon and Ultramarine: March 1957 61 × 182.9

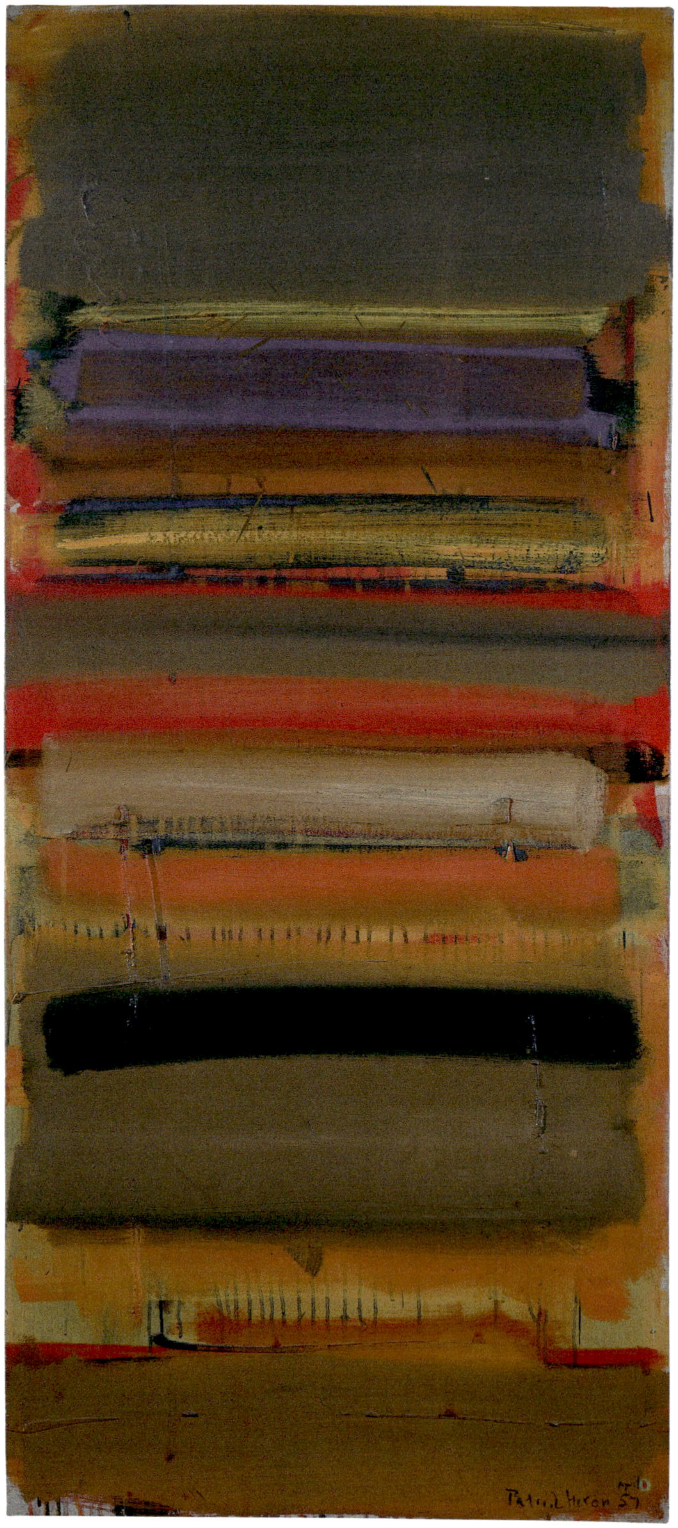

27 Green and Mauve Horizontals: January 1958 121.9 × 55.9

22 Ochre Skies: April 1957 121.9 × 55.8

29 Atmospheric Strata: February 1958 121.9 × 55.8

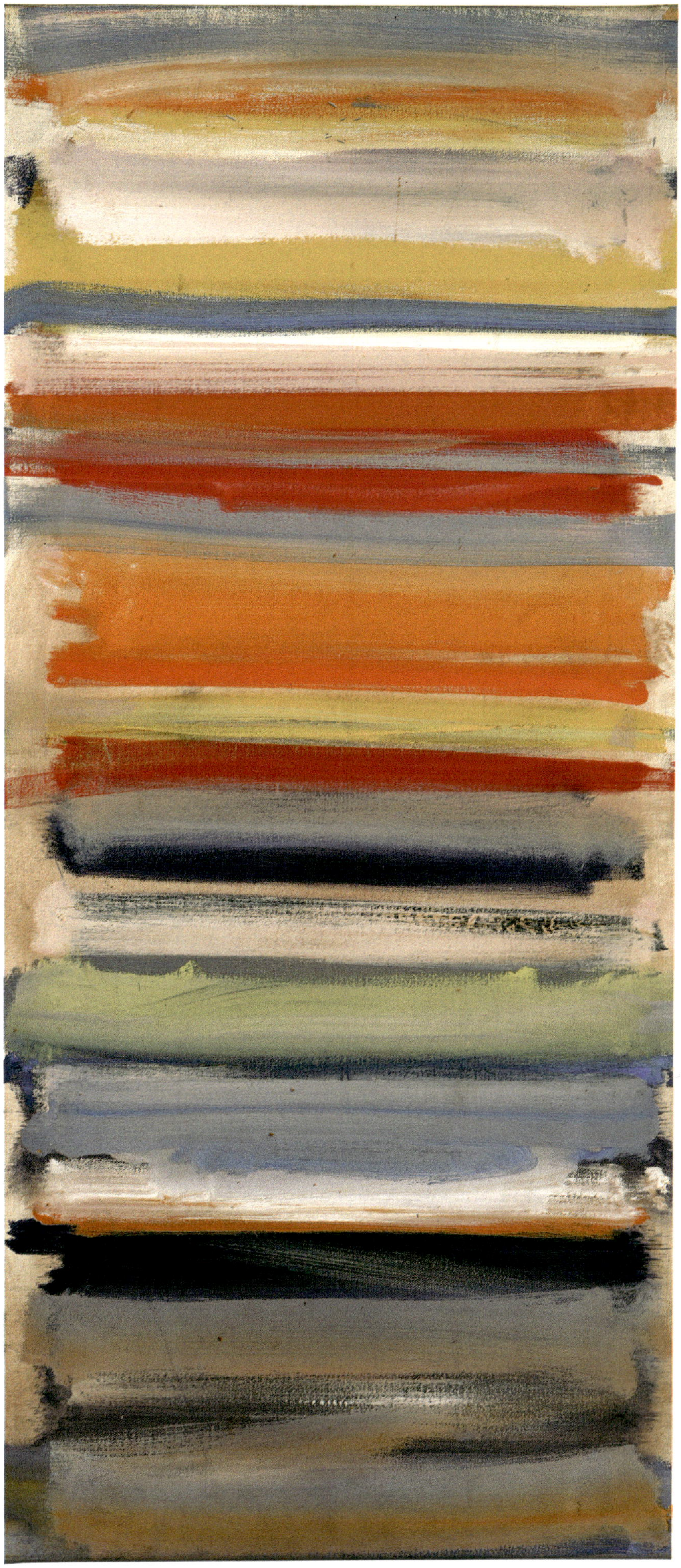

30 Lux Eterna: May – June 1958 182.9 × 91.4

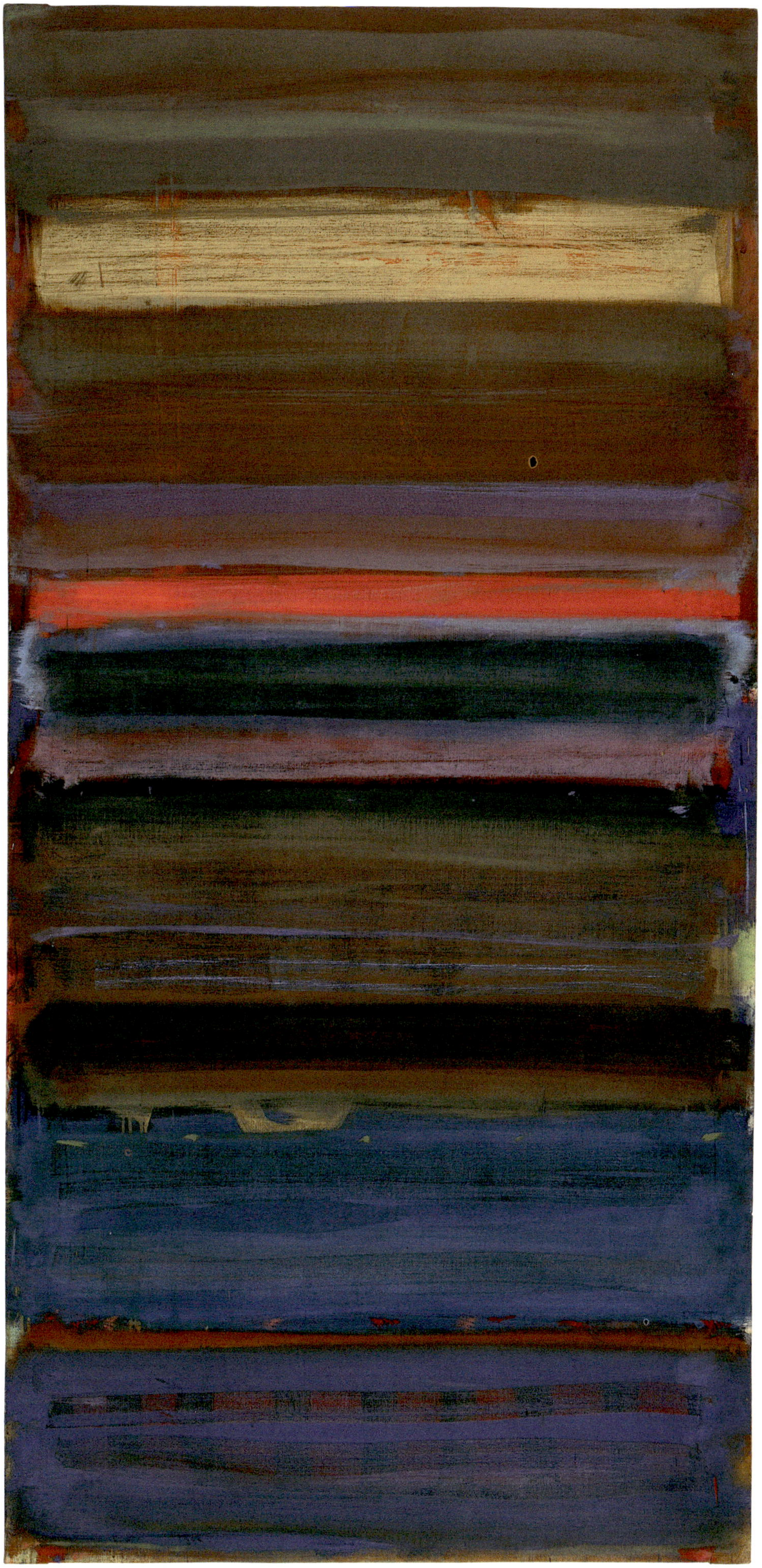

24 Horizontal Stripe Painting: November 1957 – January 1958 274.3 × 152.4

23 Yellow and Black: May 1957 91.4 × 121.9

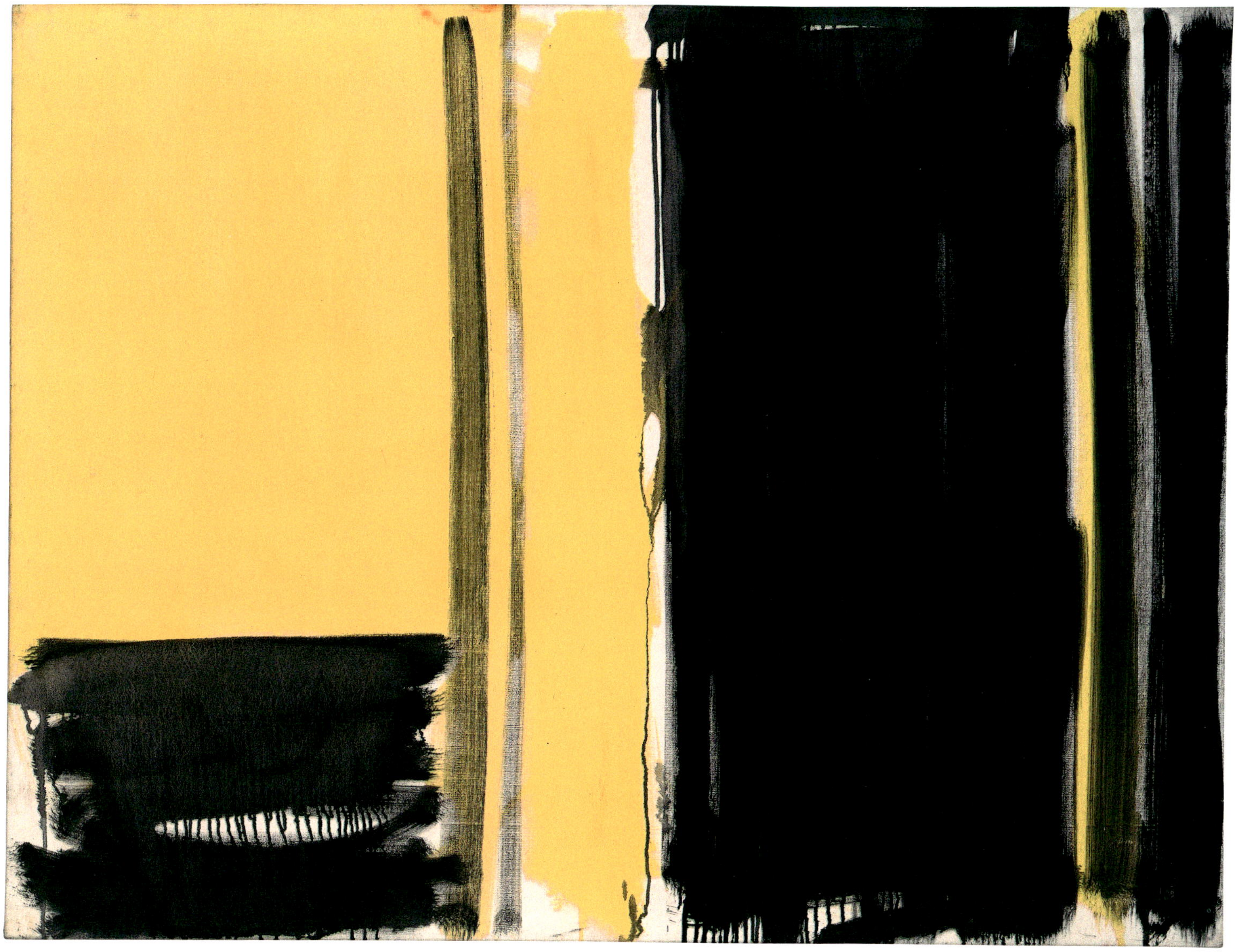

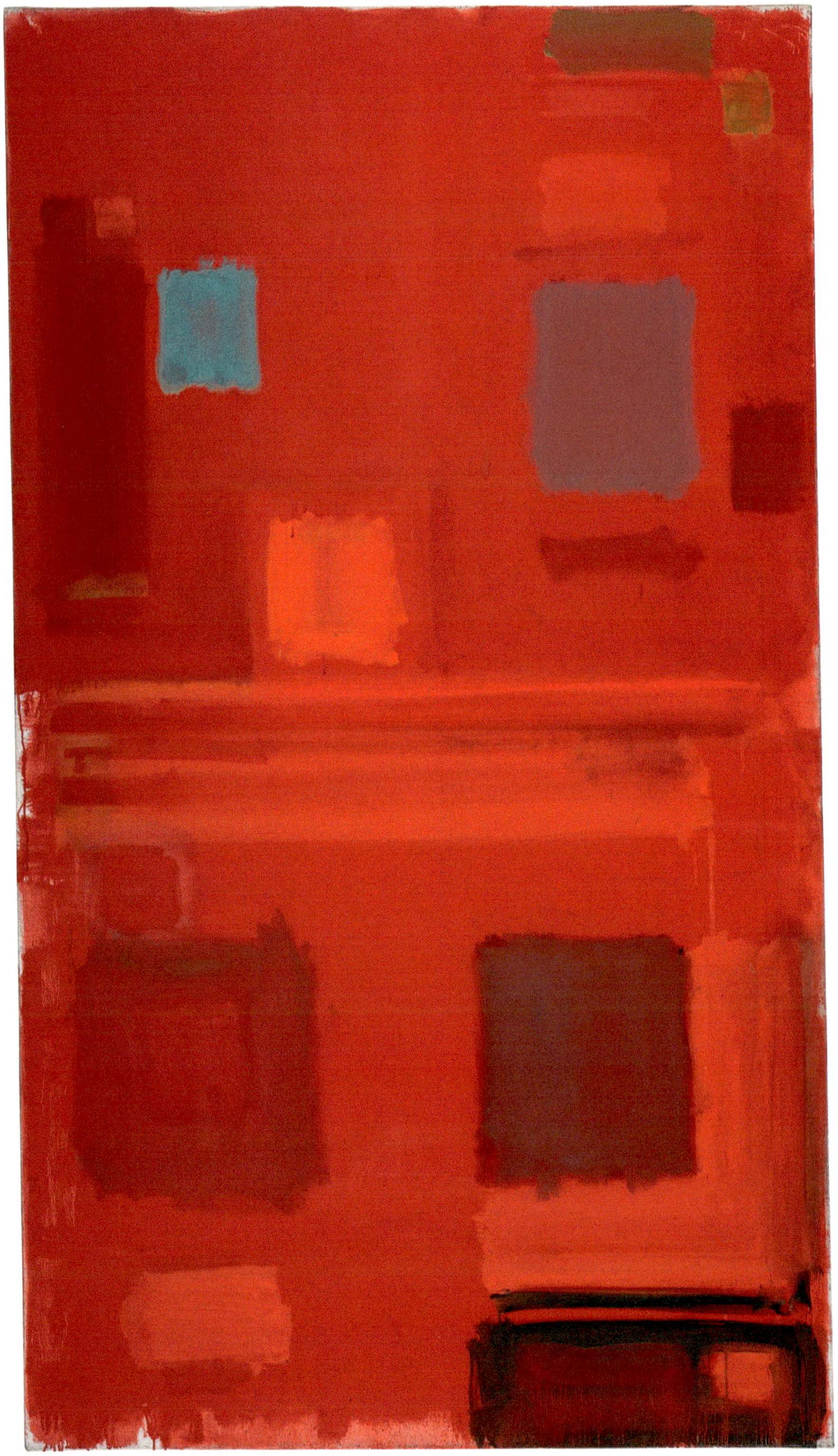

28 Squares in Deep Cadmium: January 1958 182.9 × 106.6

26 Cadmium Scarlet: January 1958 182.9 × 106.6

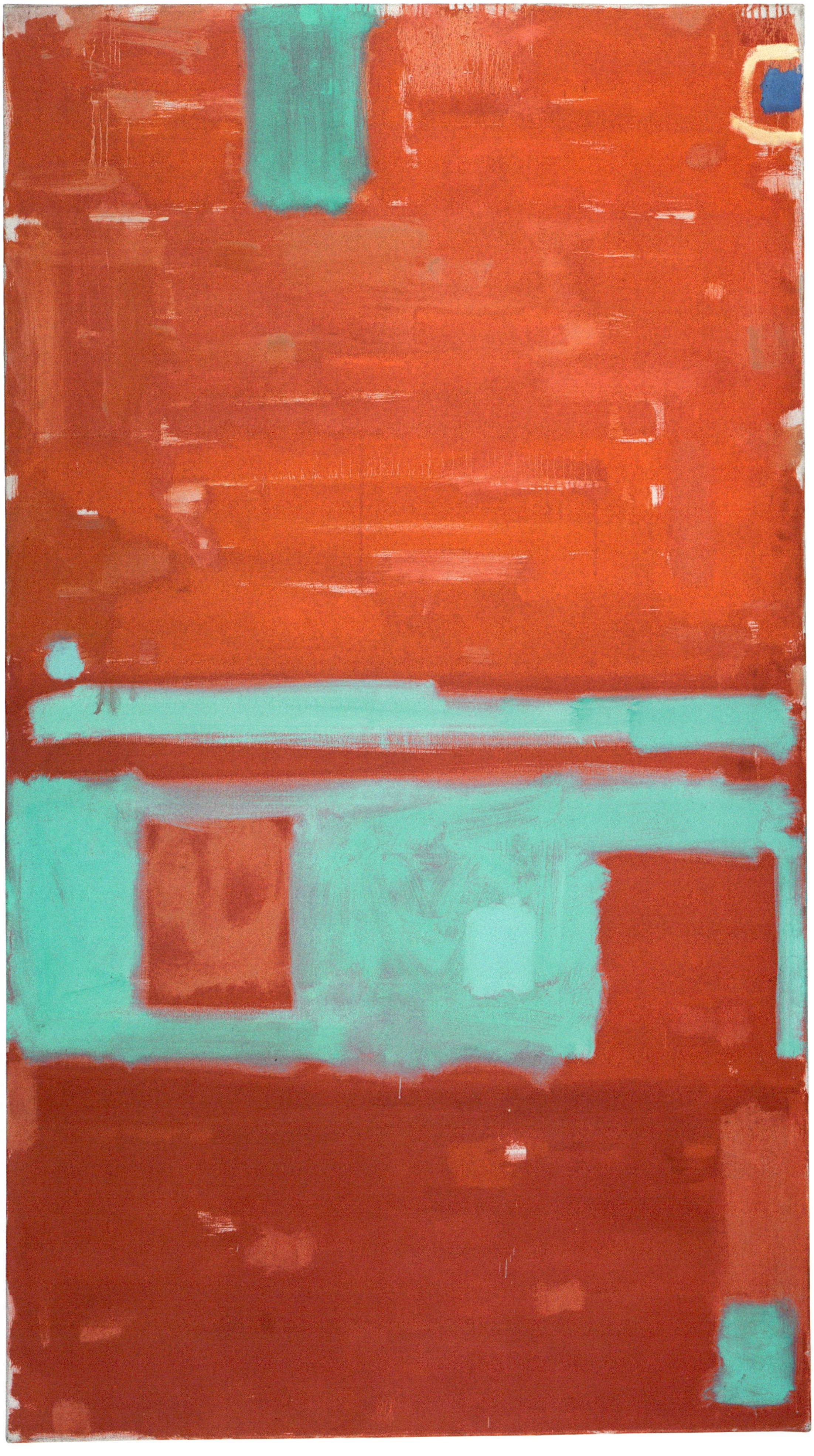

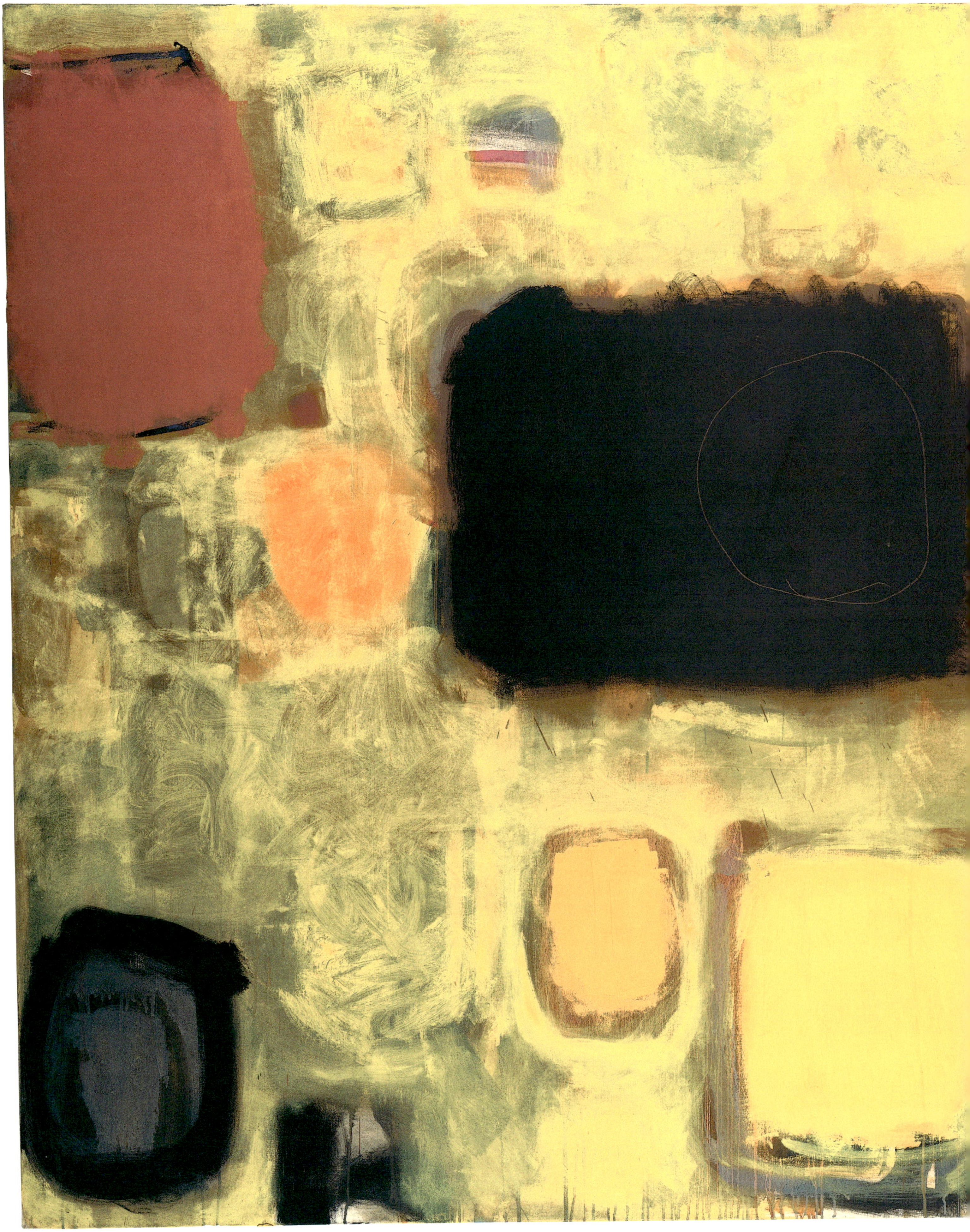

33 Yellow Painting: October 1958 – May/June 1959
152.4 × 213.4

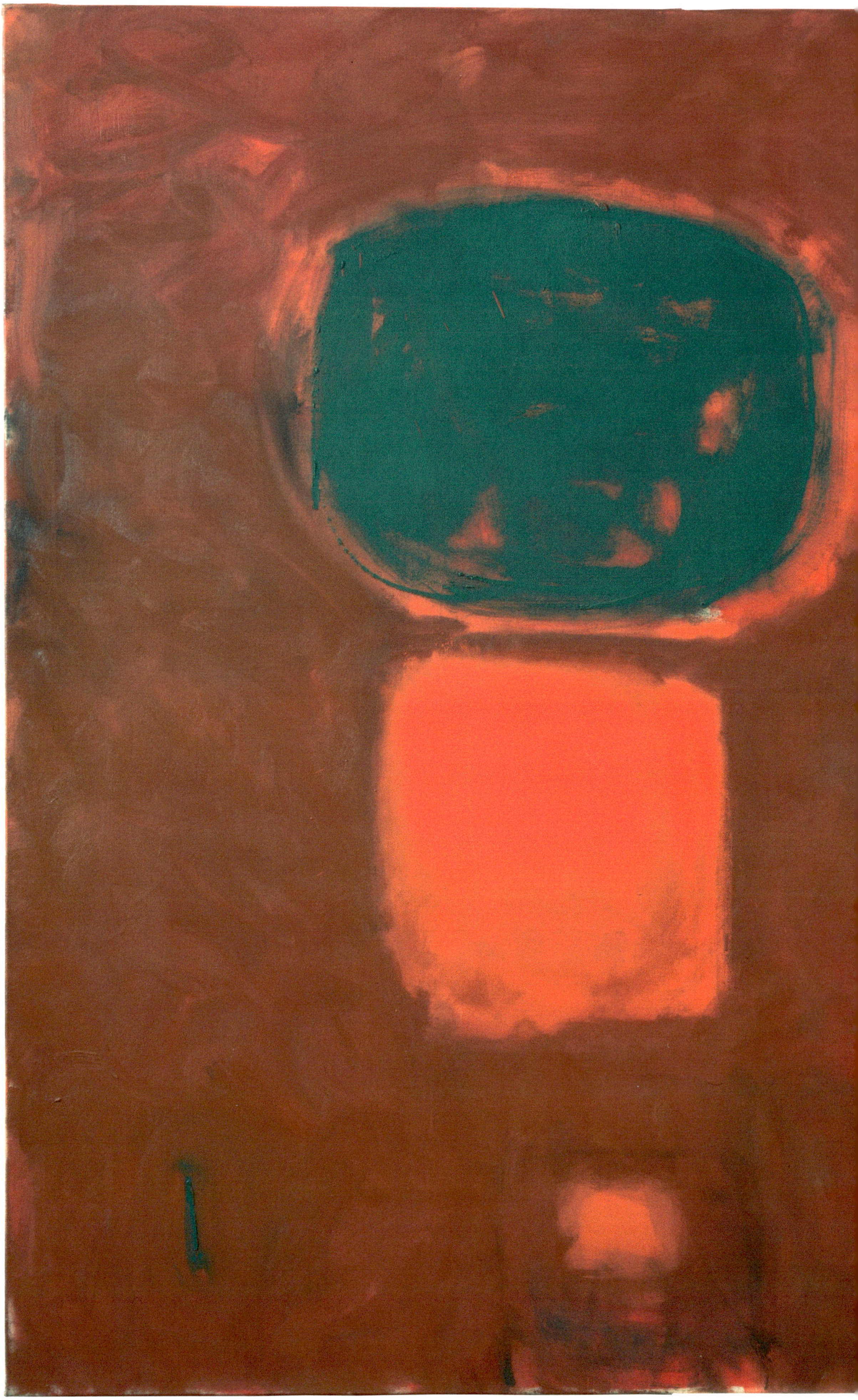

31 Brown Ground with Soft Red and Green: August 1958 – July 1959
152.4 × 213.4

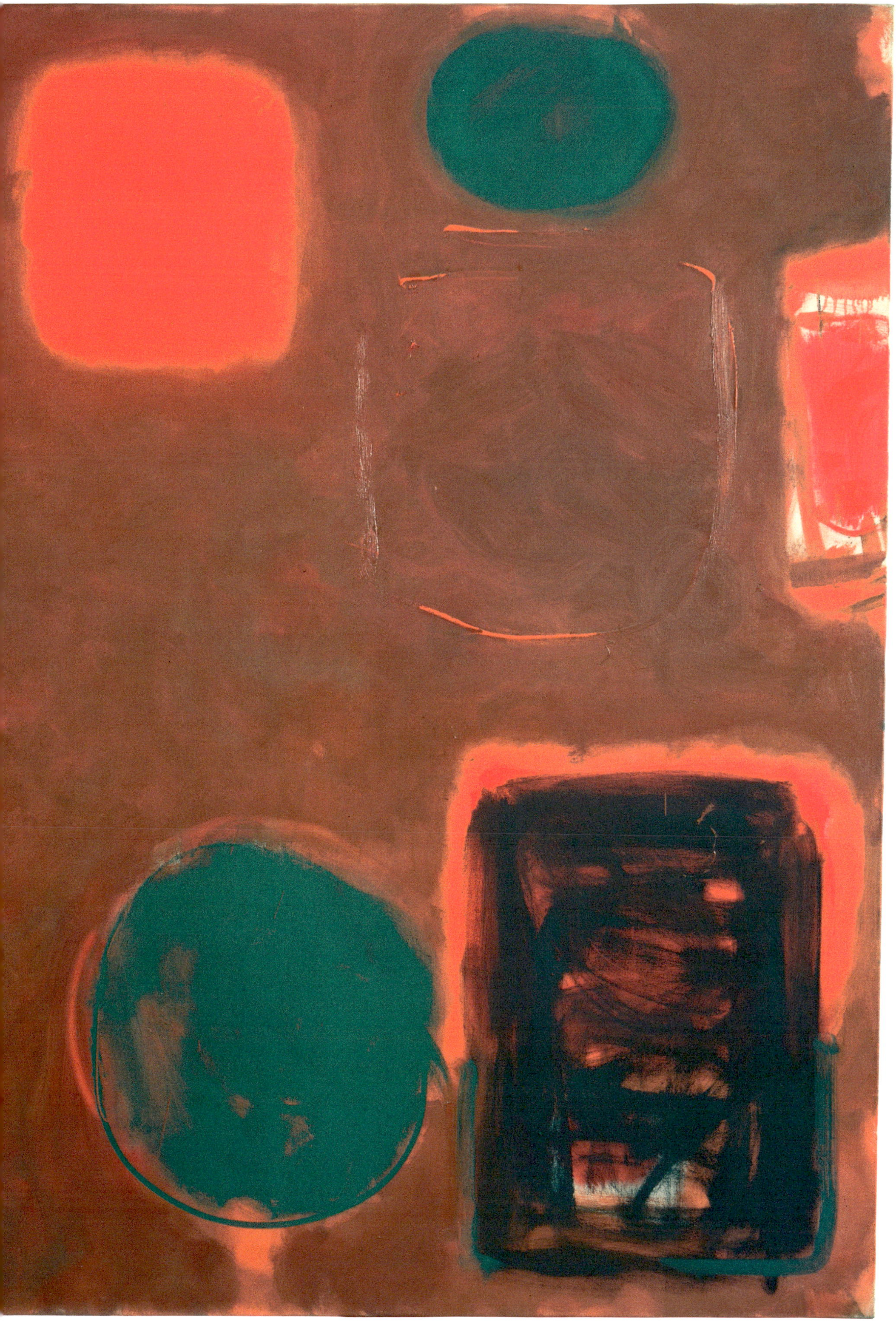

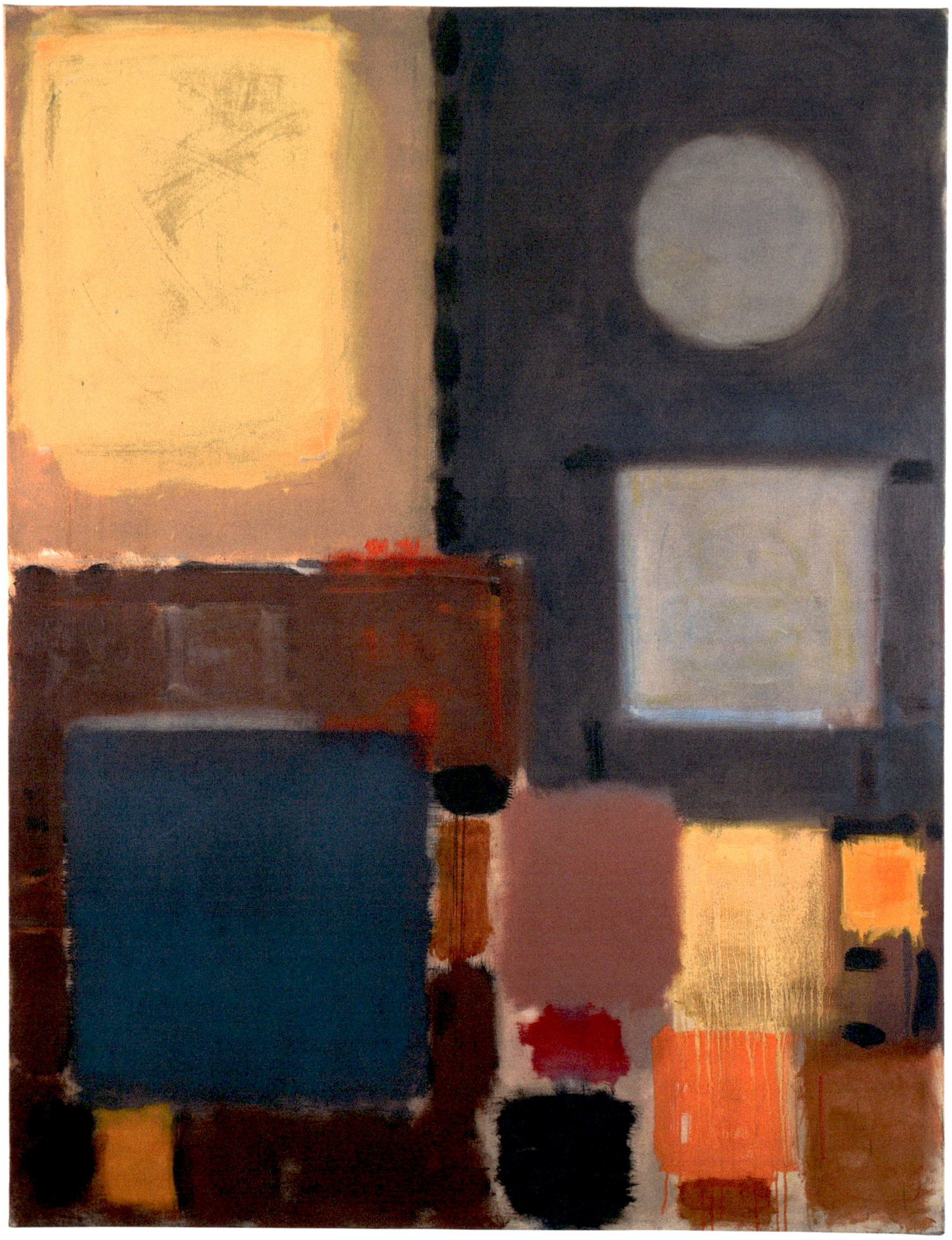

32 Grey and Yellow (with Circle): October 1958 – February 1959 152.4 × 121.9

34 Big Grey with Disc: June – September 1959 213.4 × 152.4

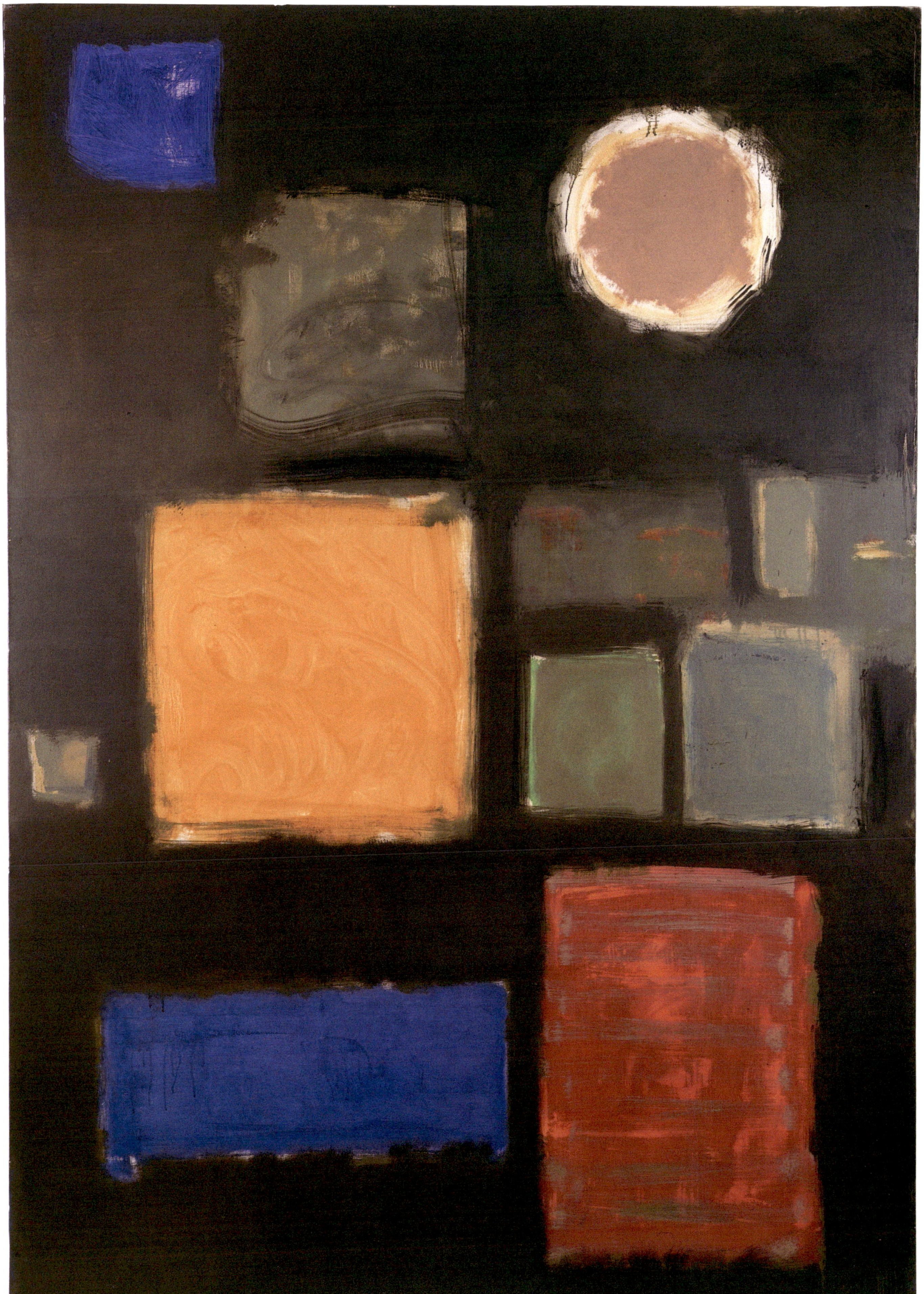

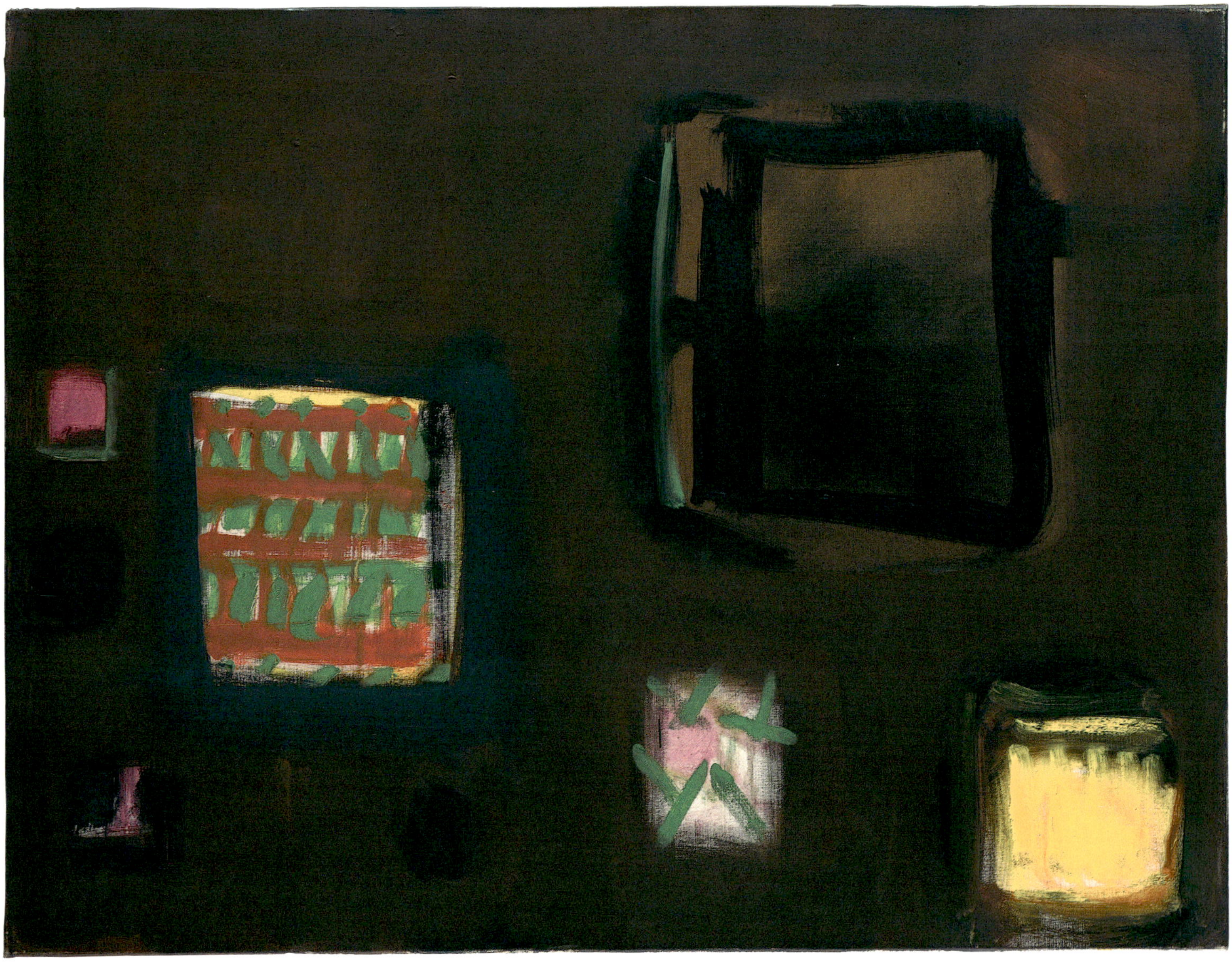

36 Squares Floating in Brown (Emerald, Lemon, Violet): January 1960 76.2 × 101.6

35 Cadmium Painting with Soft Lemon Oblong: August 1959 213.4 × 152.4

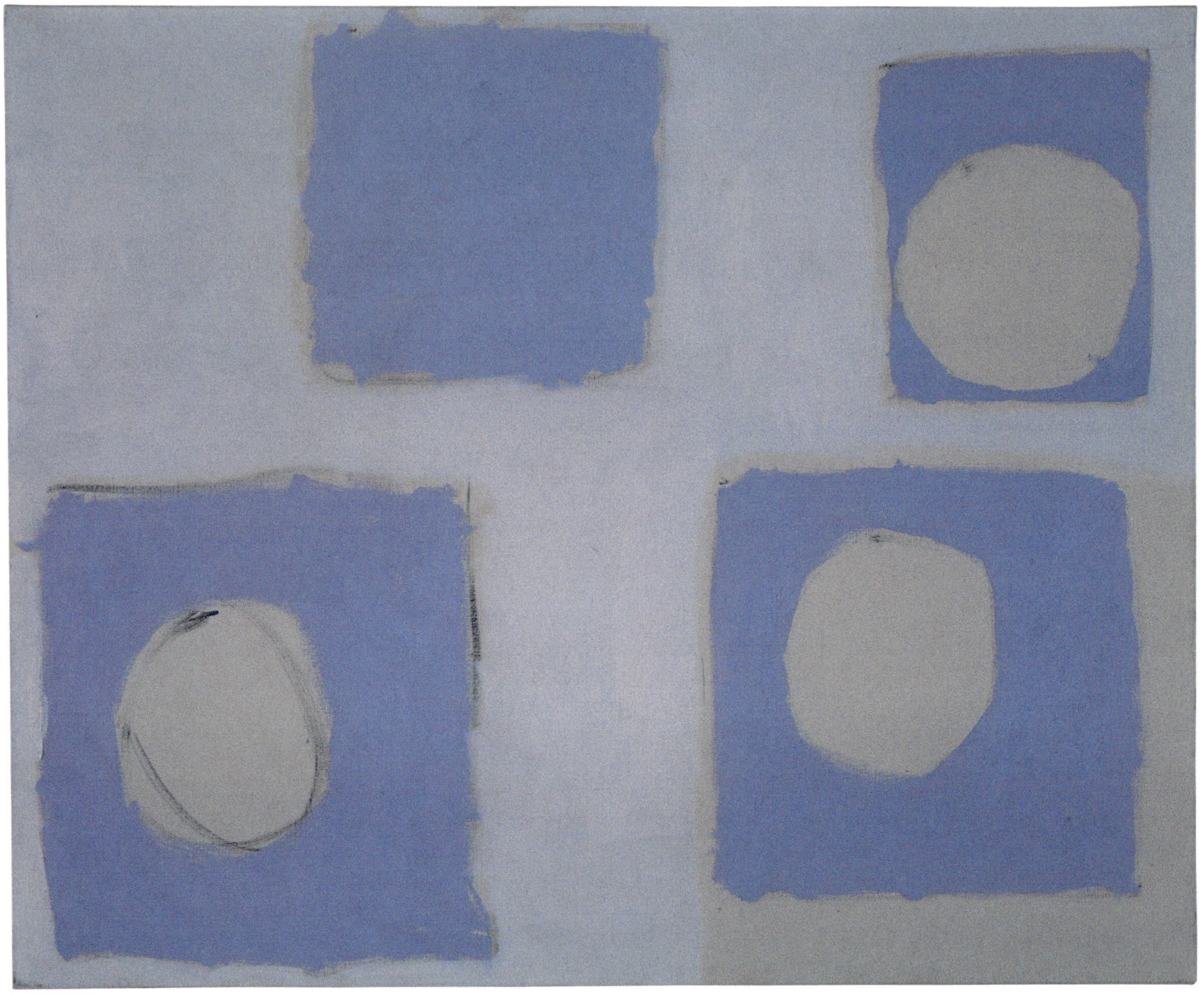

37 White Painting (Pale Squares): 1961
96.5 × 121.9

38 Blue Painting: September 1961 – September 1962
121.9 × 182.9

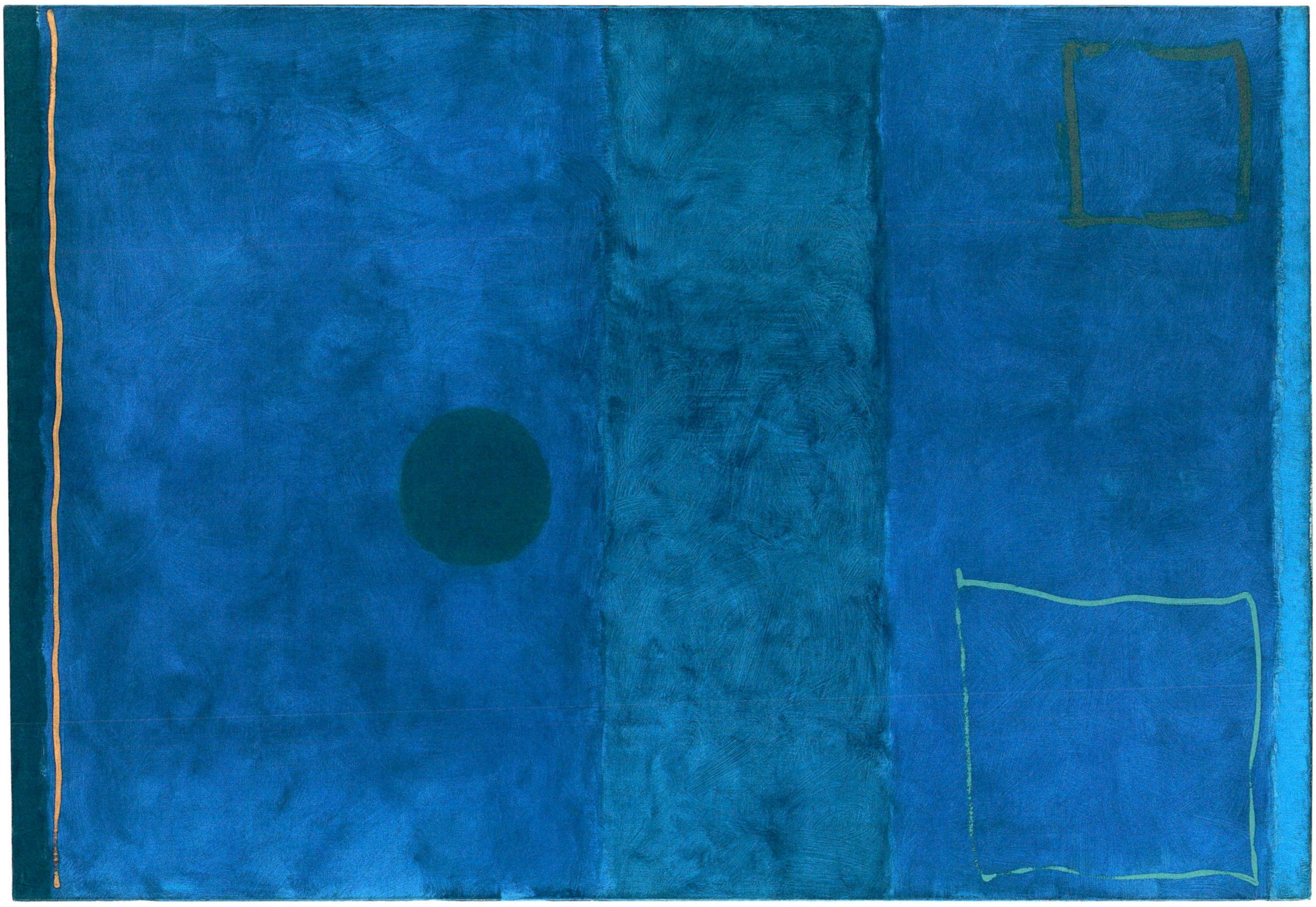

39 Dull Green with White: December 1961 182.9 × 91.5

40 Orange (with Five): September 18 1962 121.9 × 152.4

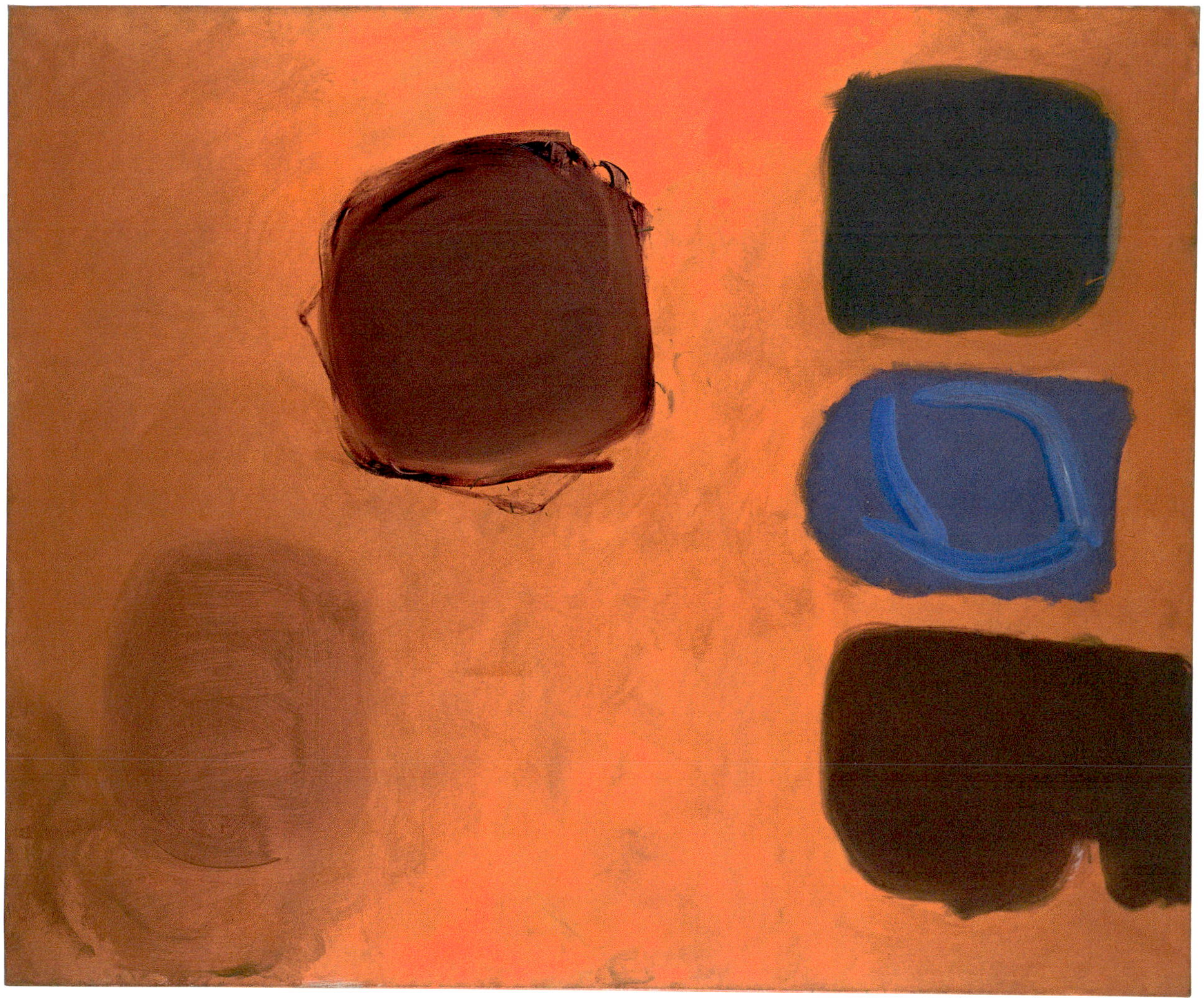

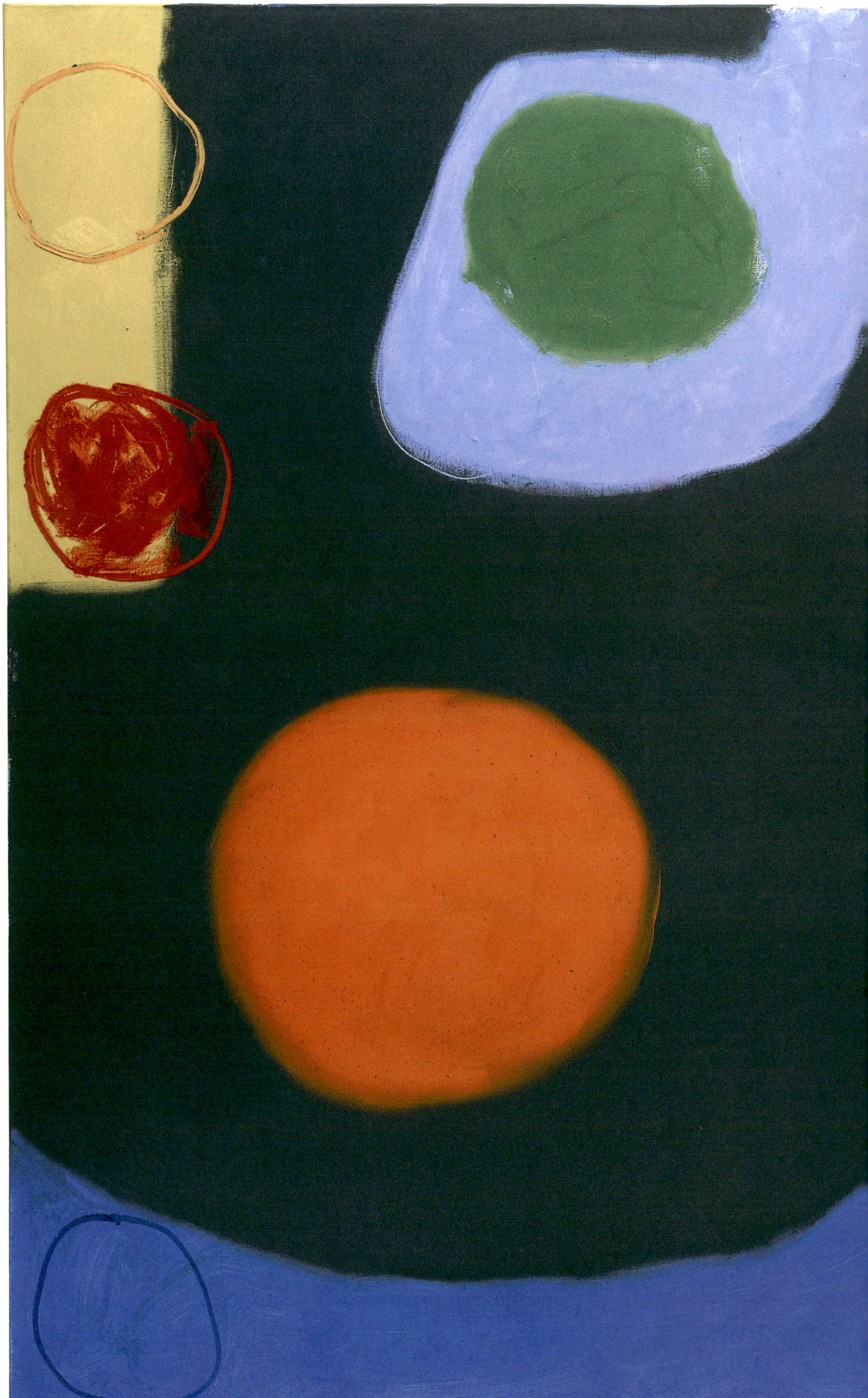

42 Fourteen Discs: July 20: 1963
152.4 × 121.9

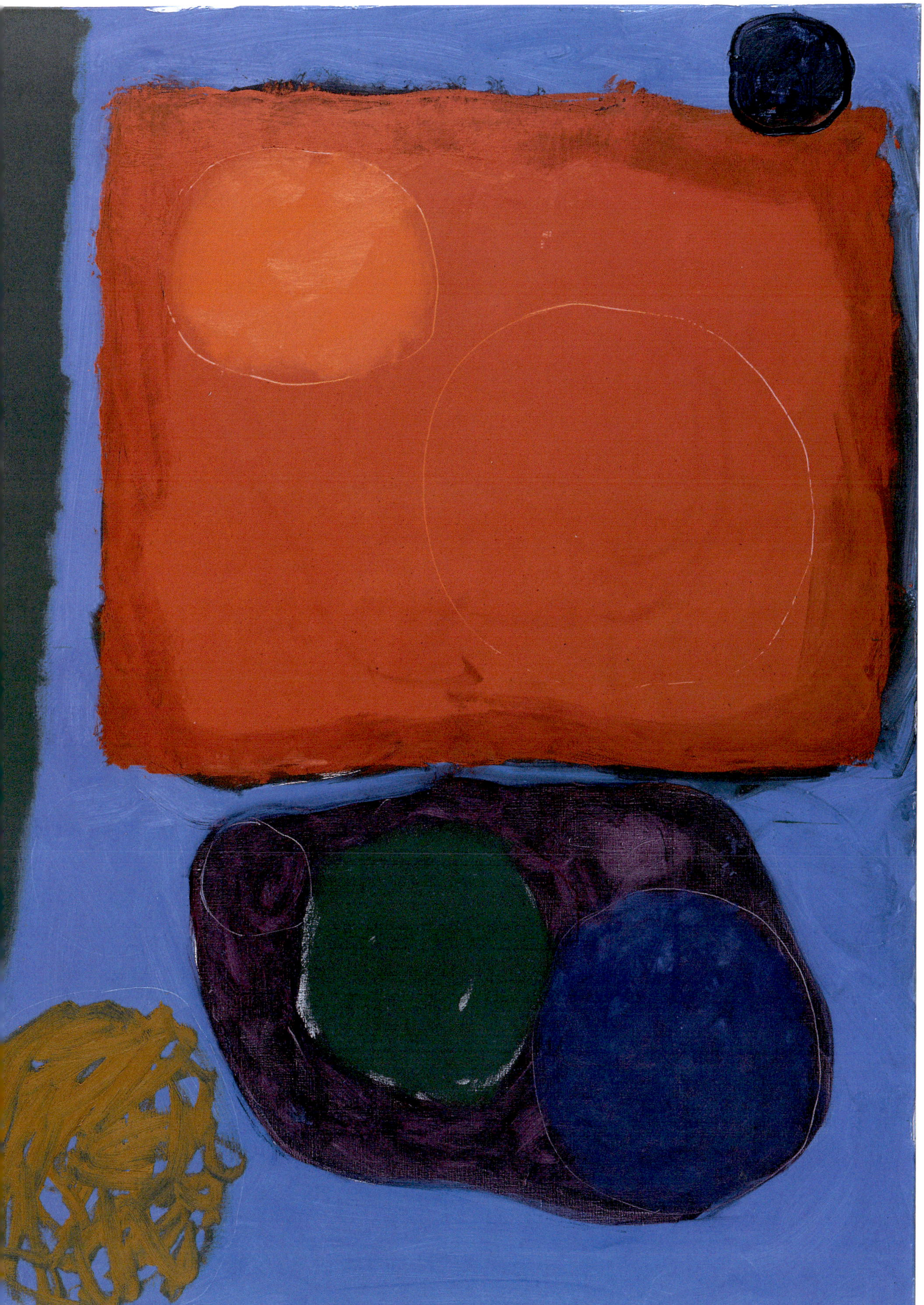

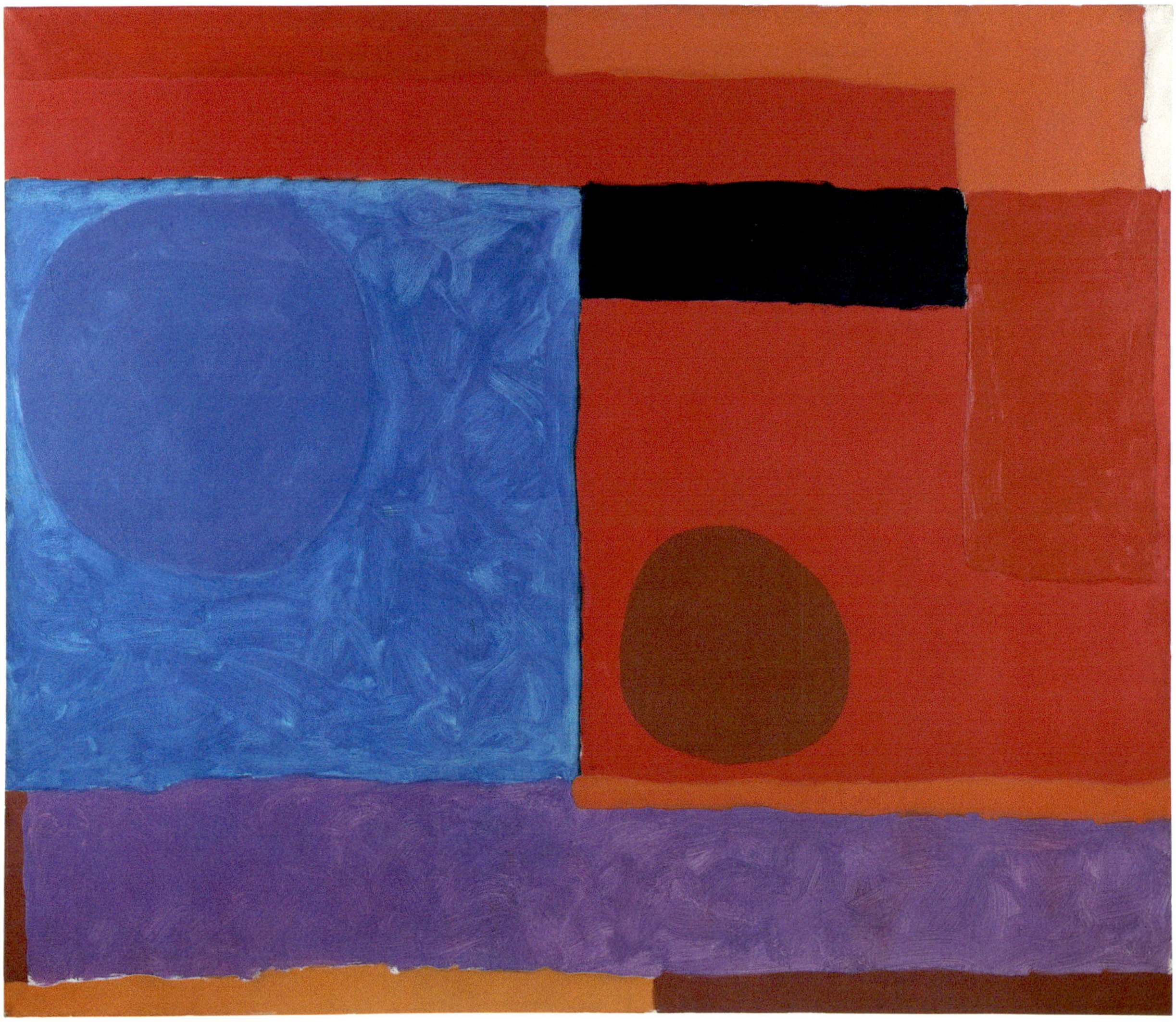

41 Rectilinear Reds and Blues: **1963** 152.4 × 182.9

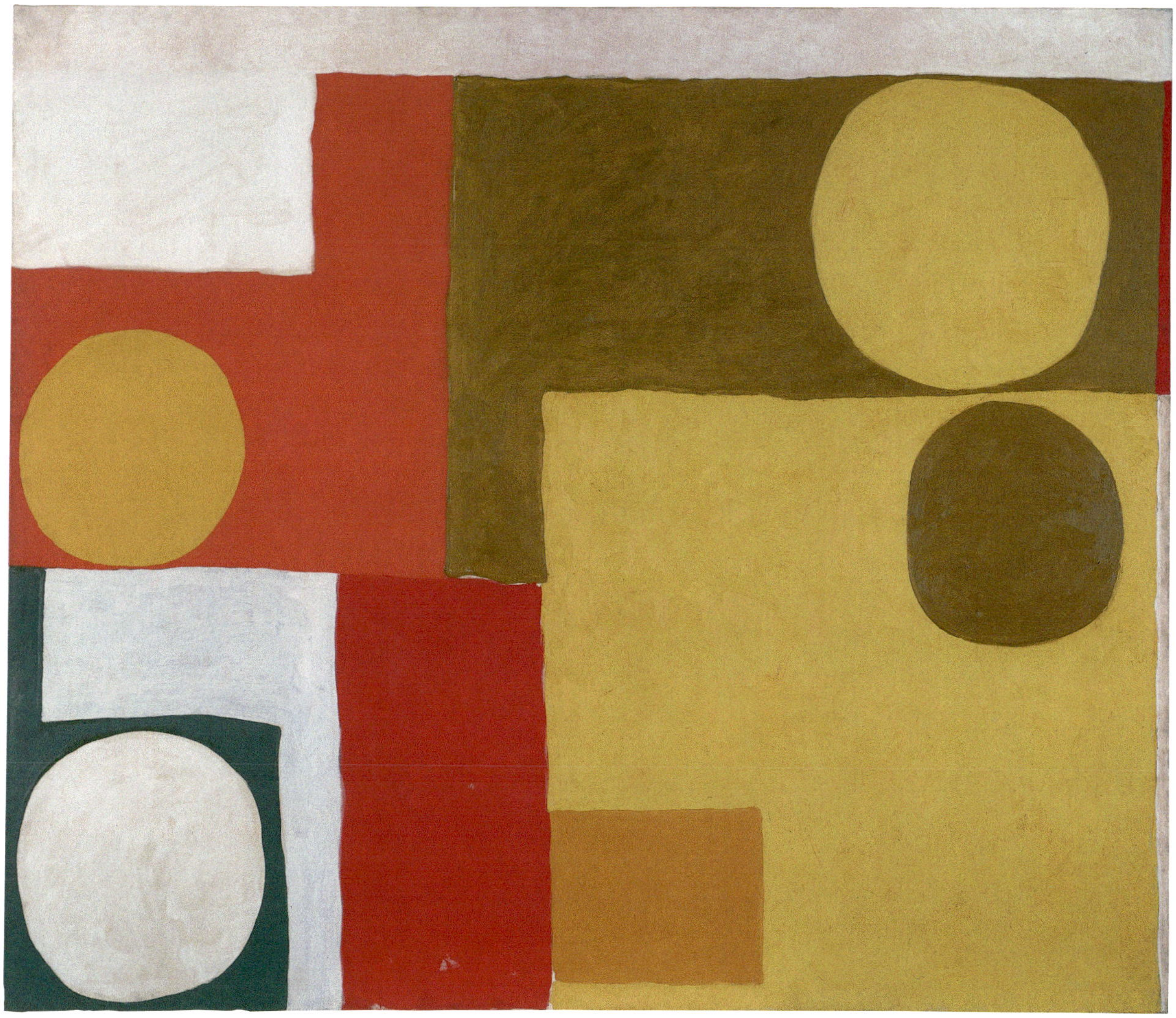

44 Yellow Painting with Four Discs: 1964
152.4 × 182.9

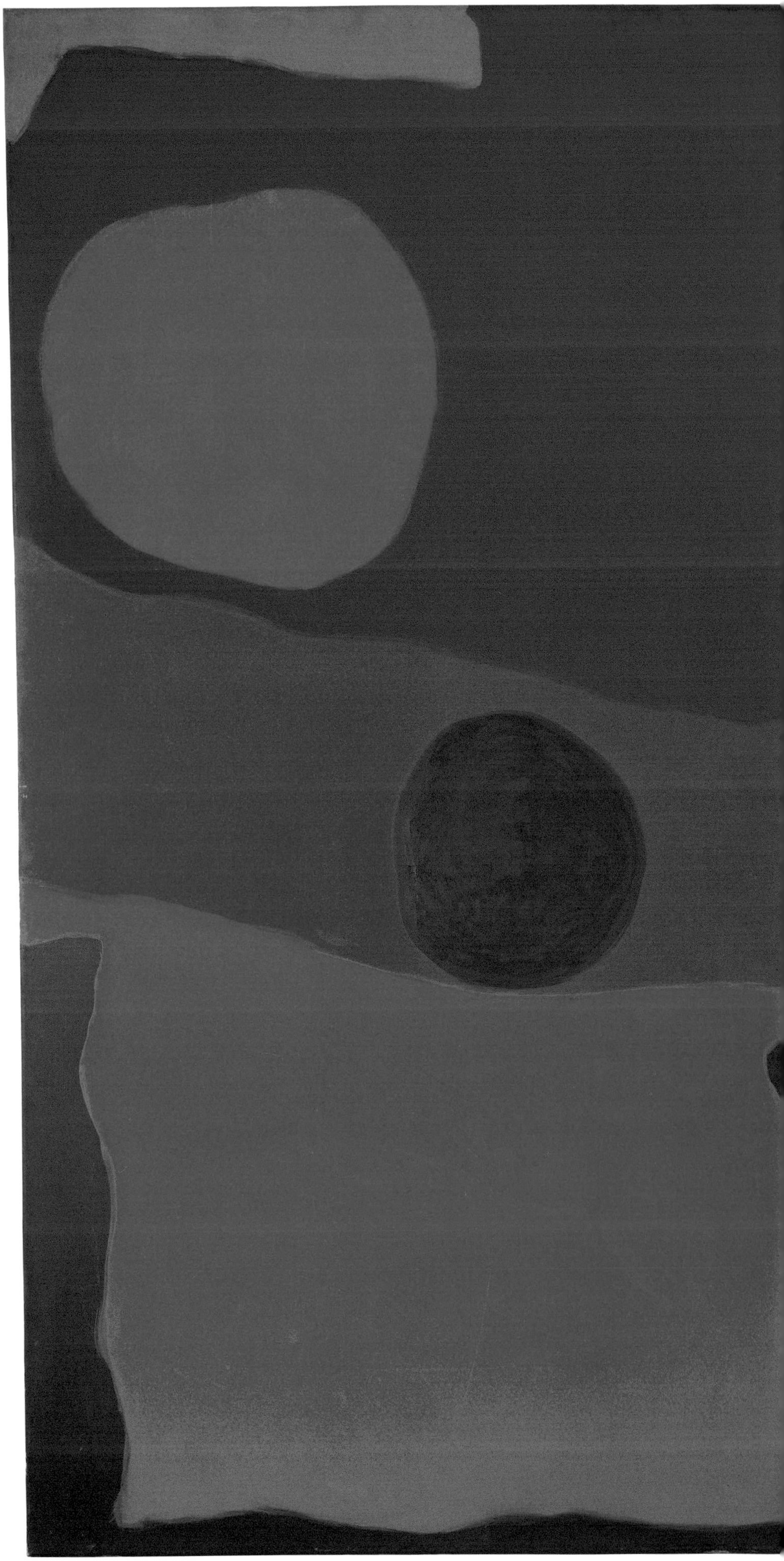

43 Two Vermilions, Orange and Red: September 1964
152.4 × 213.4

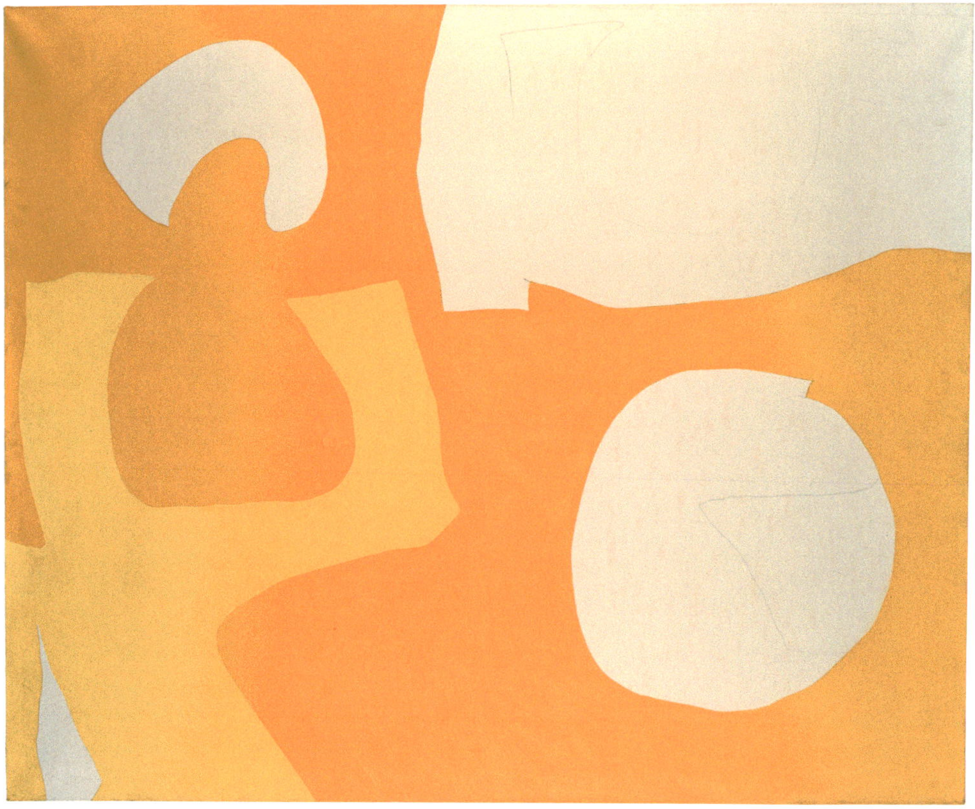

47 Two Yellows and White: July 1966 121.9 × 152.9

45 Complicated Reds (Five Discs): March 1965
121.9 × 132.2

46 [R] Yellows and Reds with Violet Edge: April 1965
152.4 × 167.6

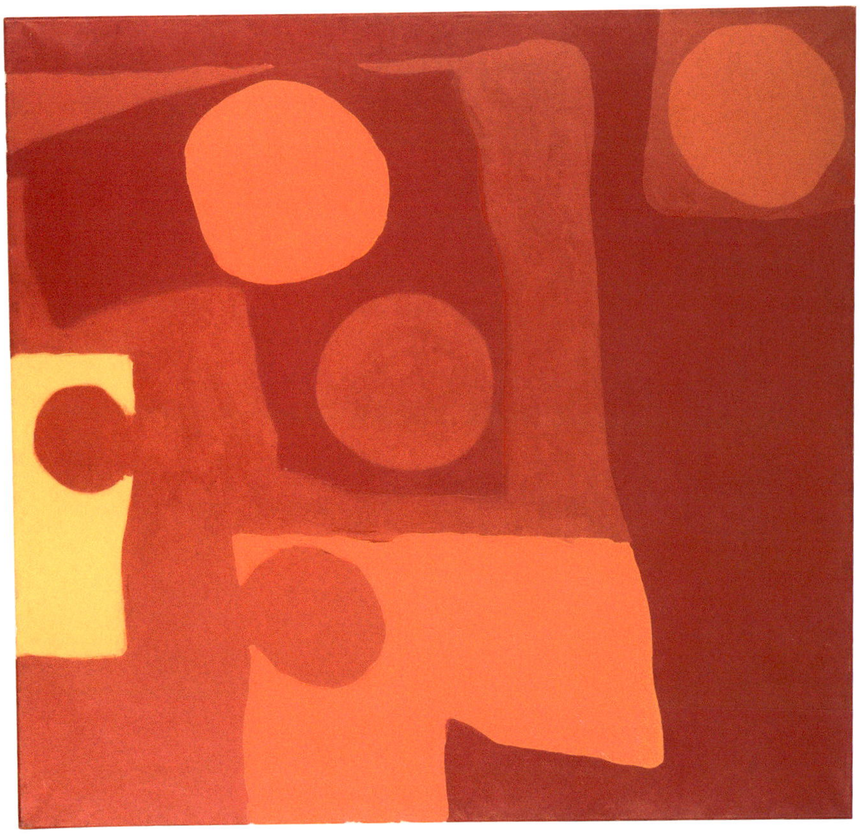

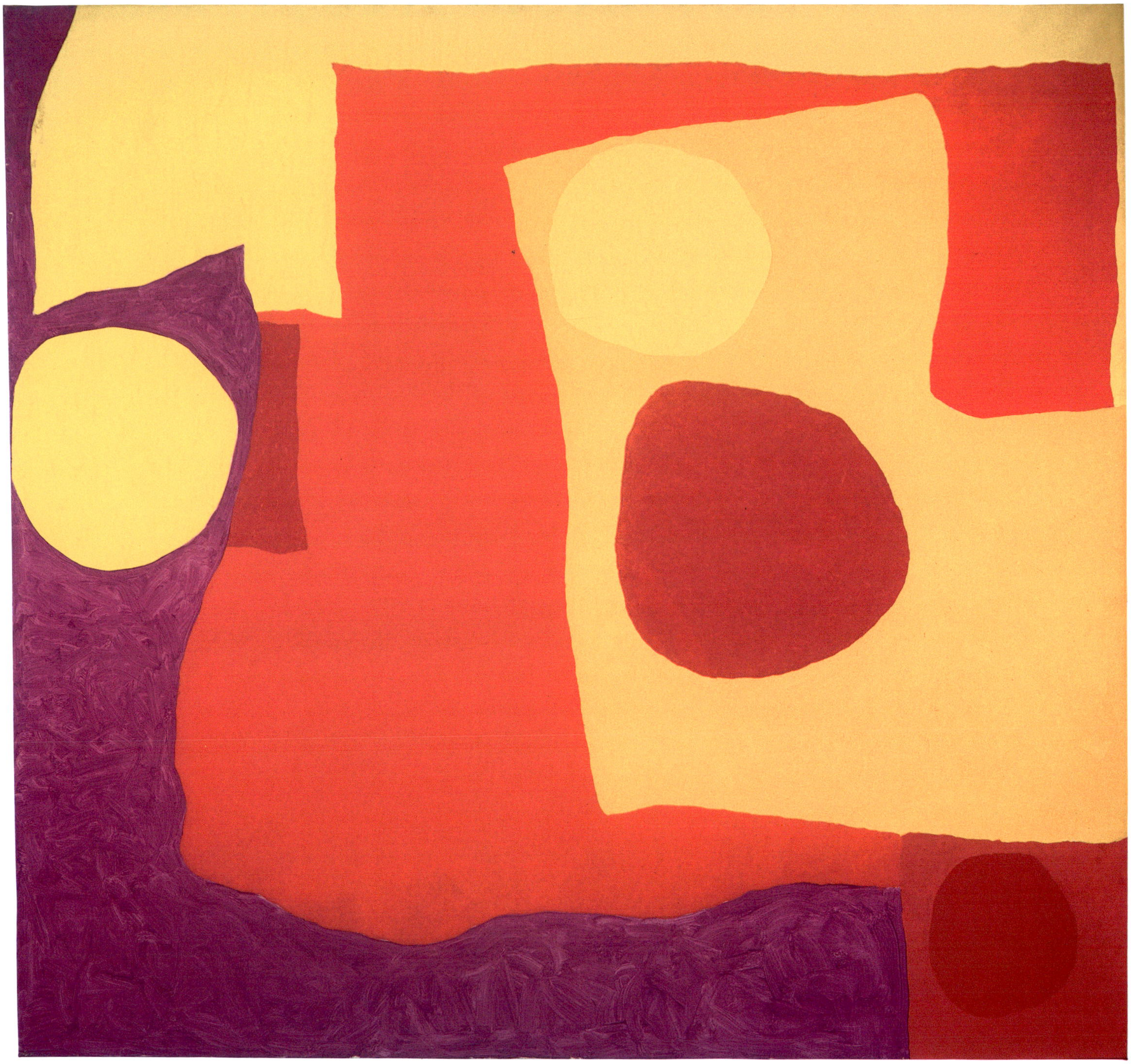

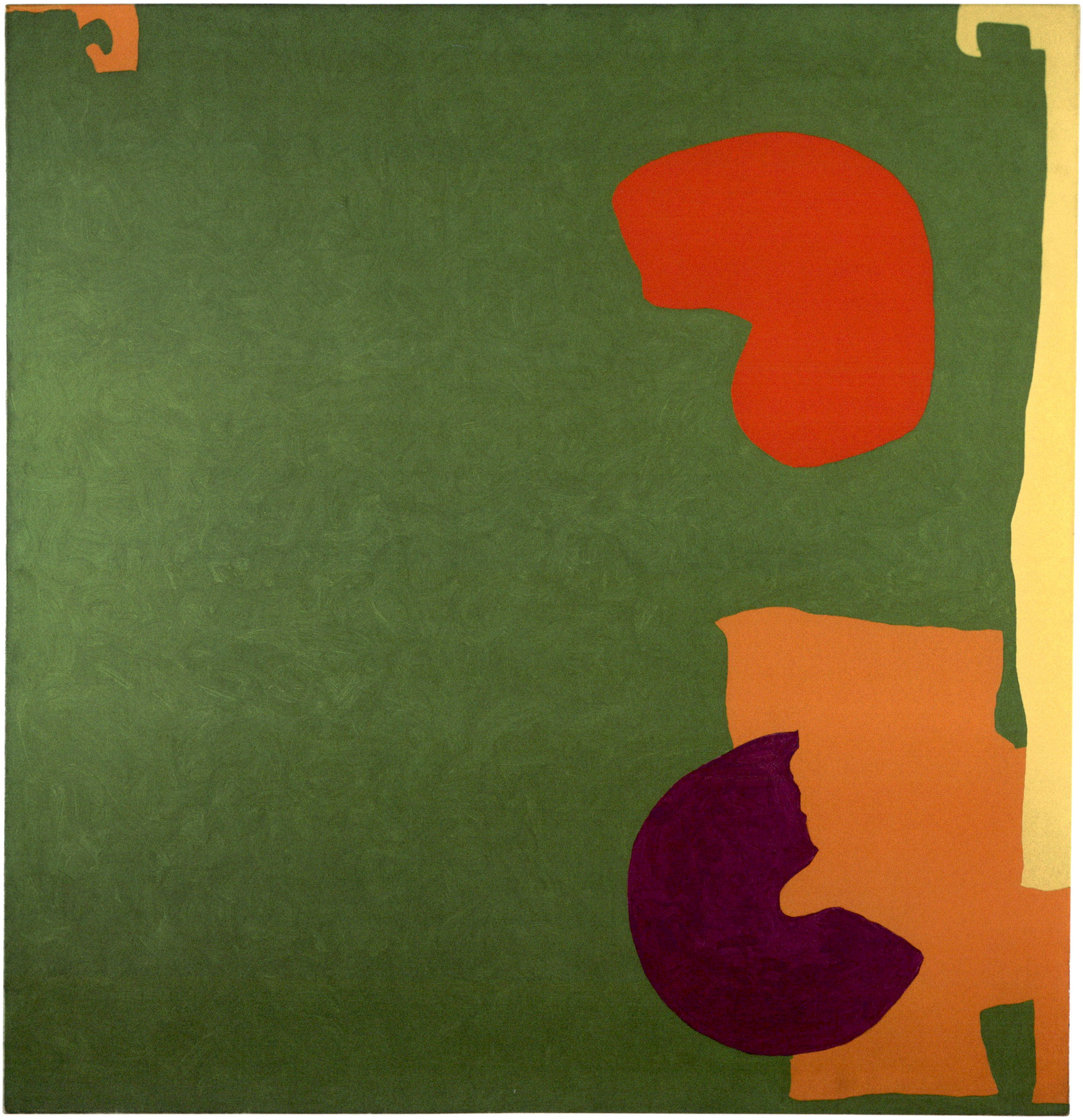

51 Square Green with Orange, Violet and Lemon: 1969
152.5 × 152.5

52 Small Orange with Deep Yellow, Lemon and Violet: 1969
76.2 × 101.6

Overleaf:
50 Cadmium with Violet, Scarlet, Emerald and Venetian: 1969 198 × 396

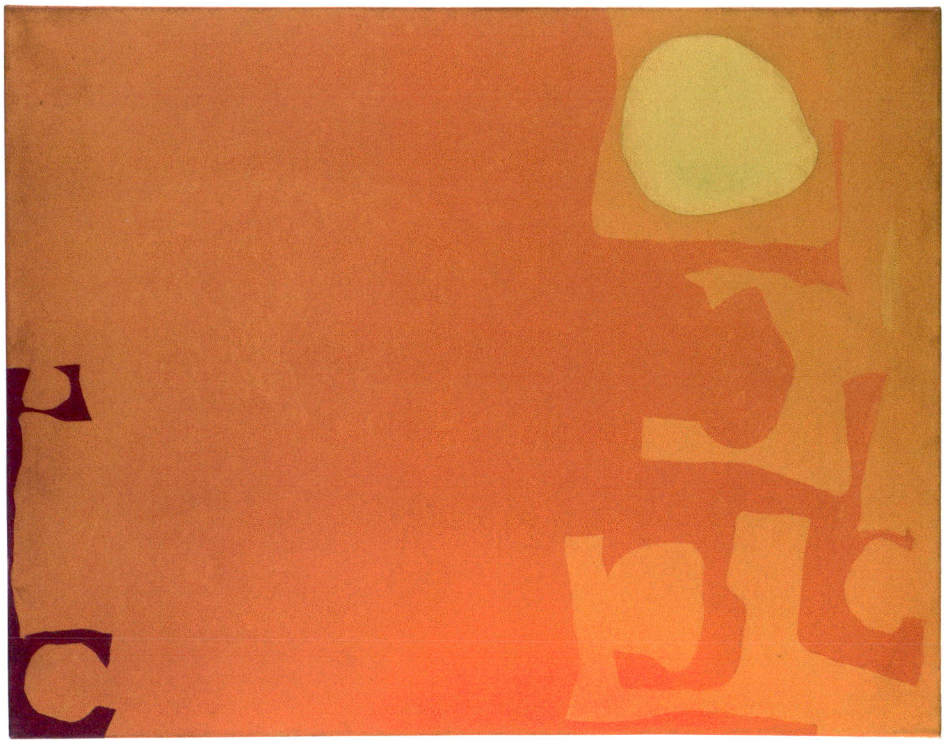

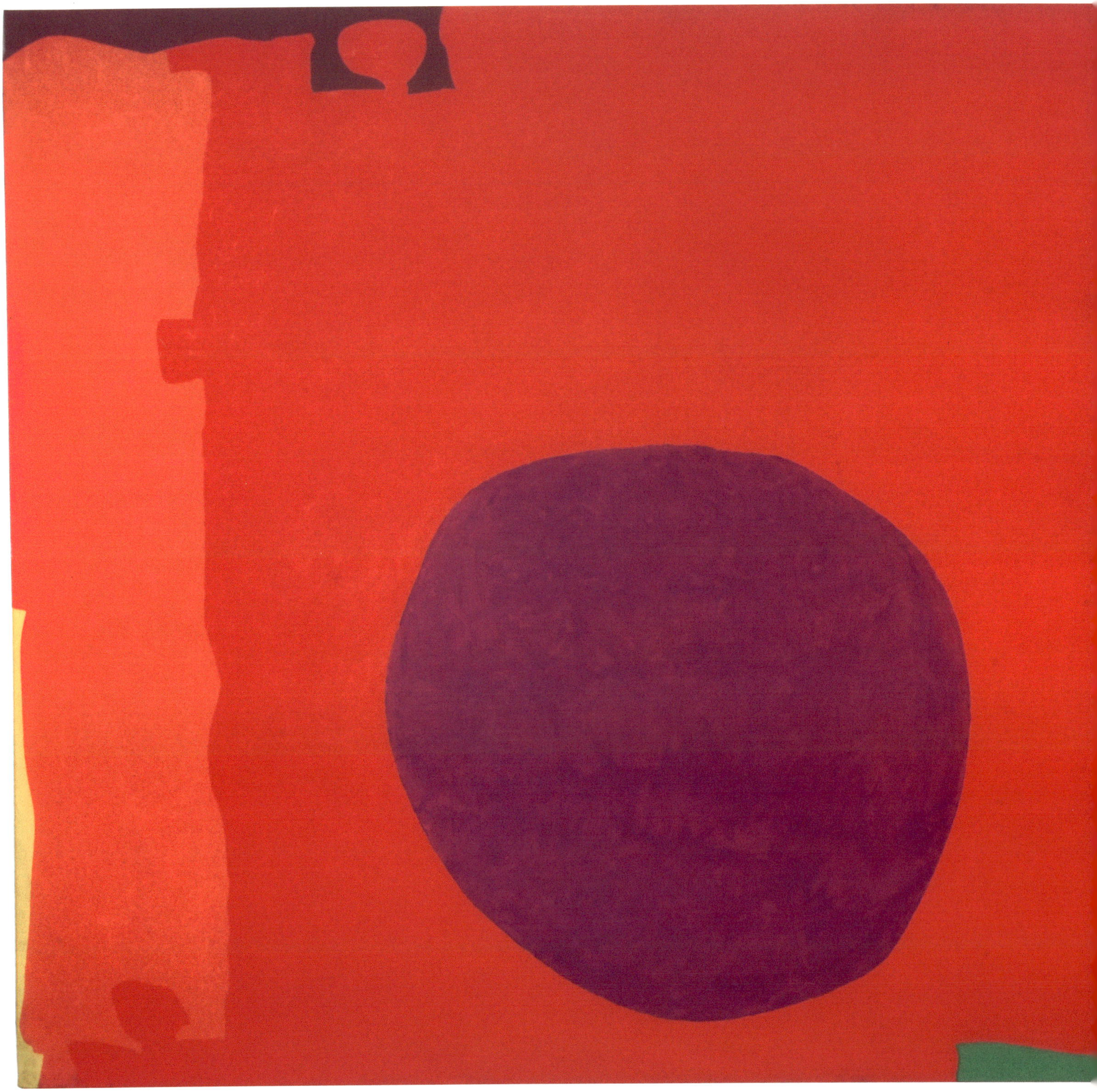

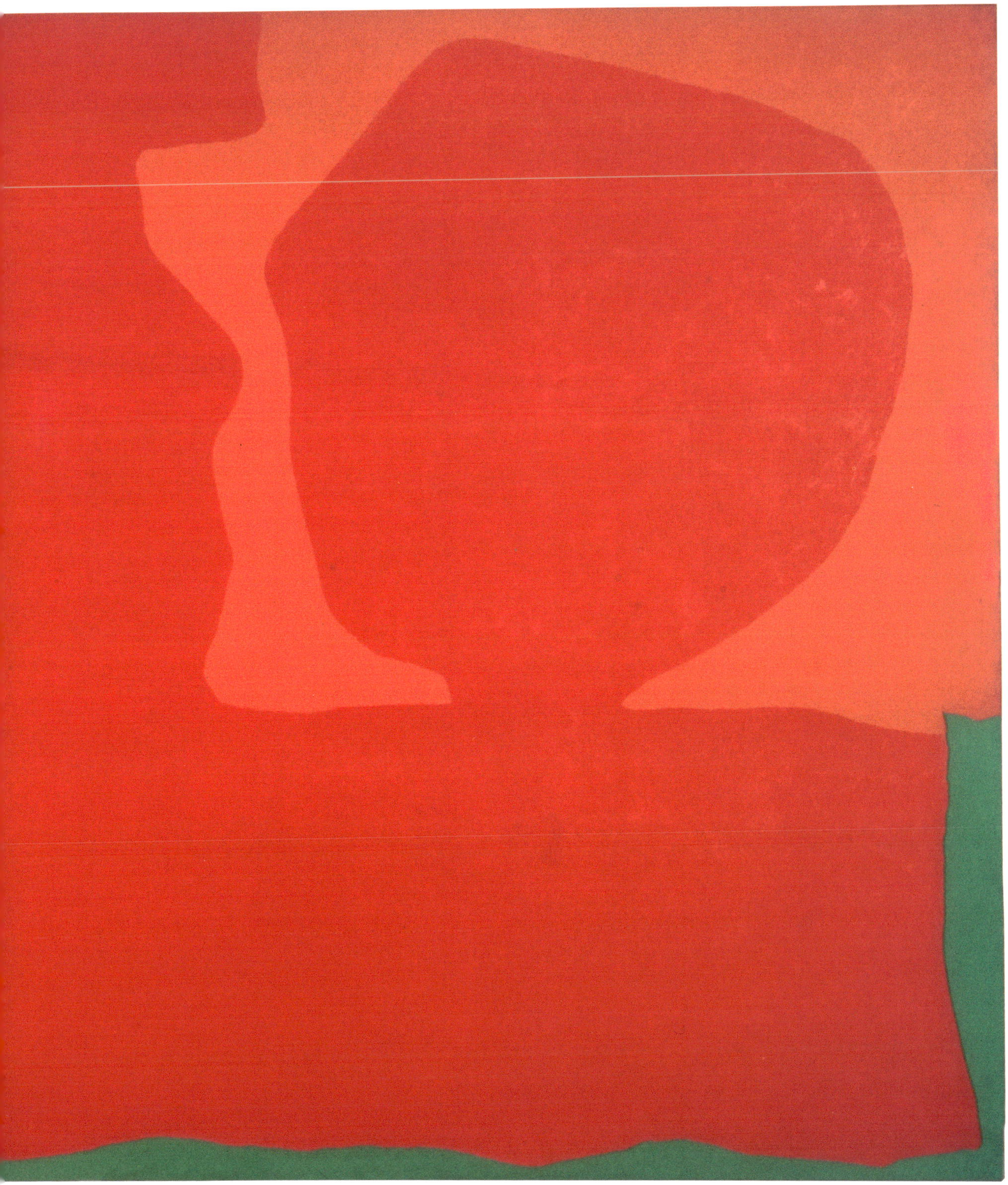

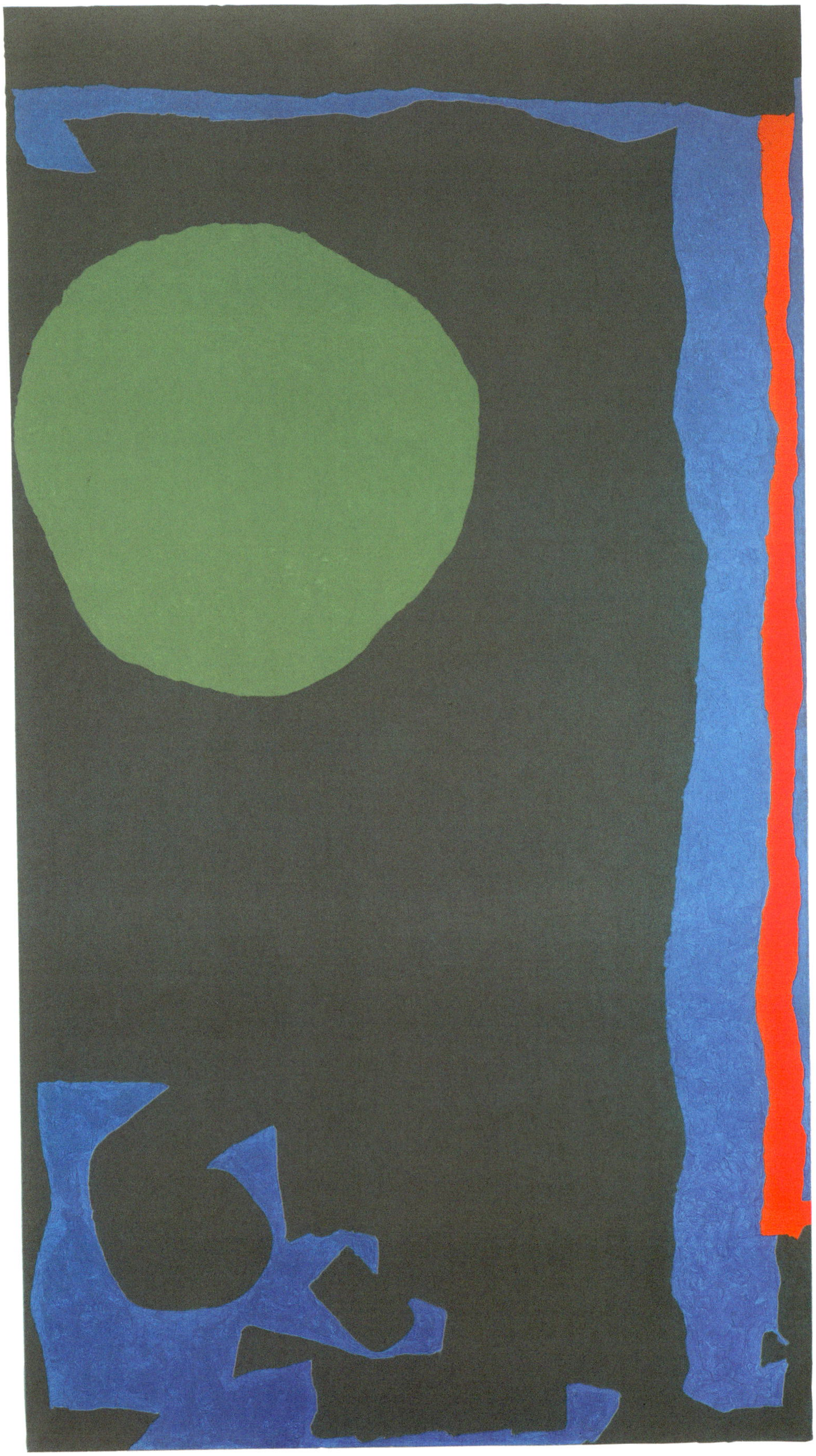

54 Rumbold Vertical Four: Green in Green with Blue and Red: September 1970 213.4 × 121.9

49 Orange in Deep Cadmium with Venetian: 1969 208.3 × 335.3

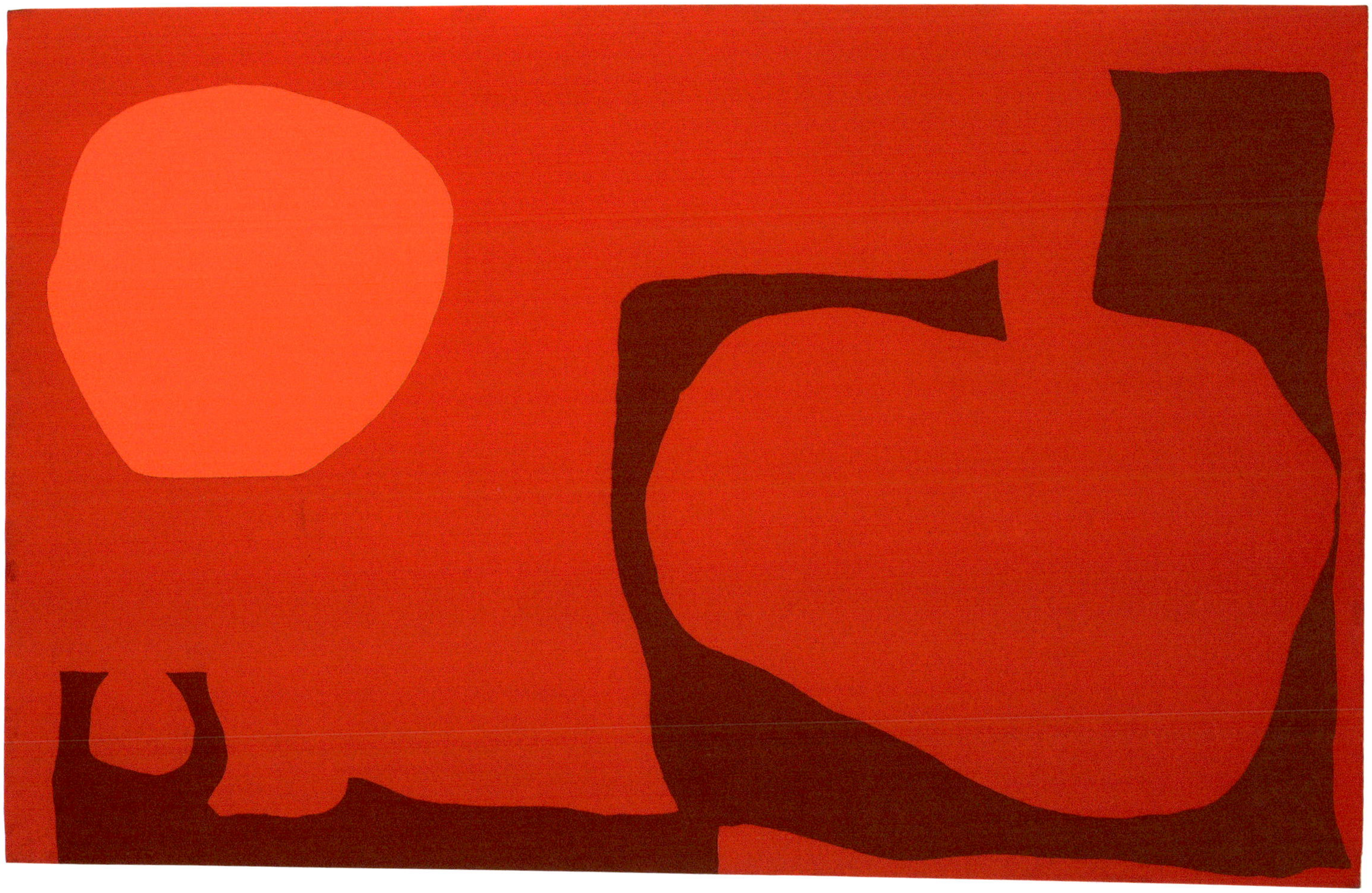

53 Rumbold Vertical One: Emerald in Reds: February **1970** 213.4 × 121.9

48 Square Red with Scarlet, Emerald and Orange: 1969 152.4 × 152.4

Overleaf
56 Big Cobalt Violet: May 1972 208.3 × 457

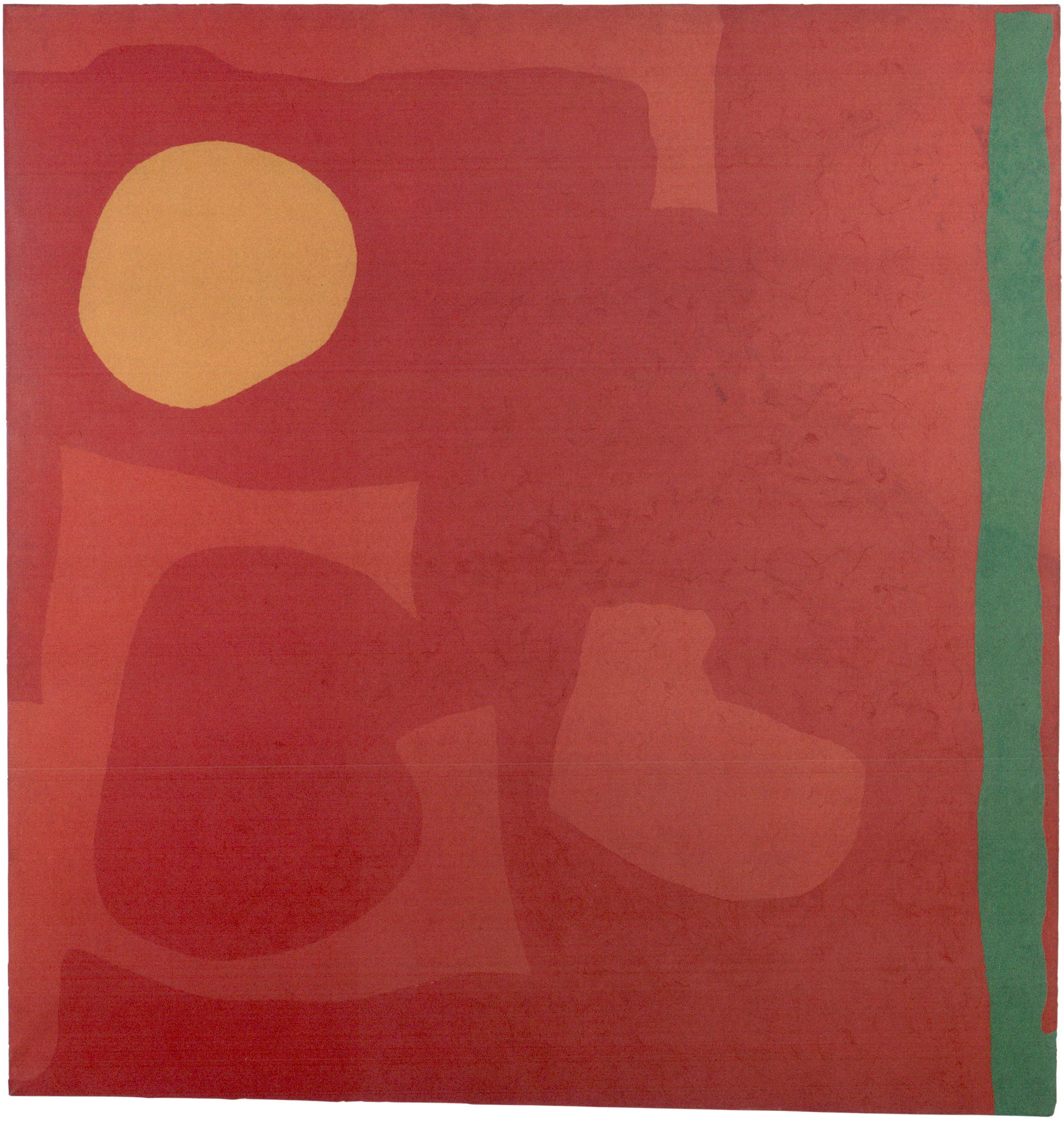

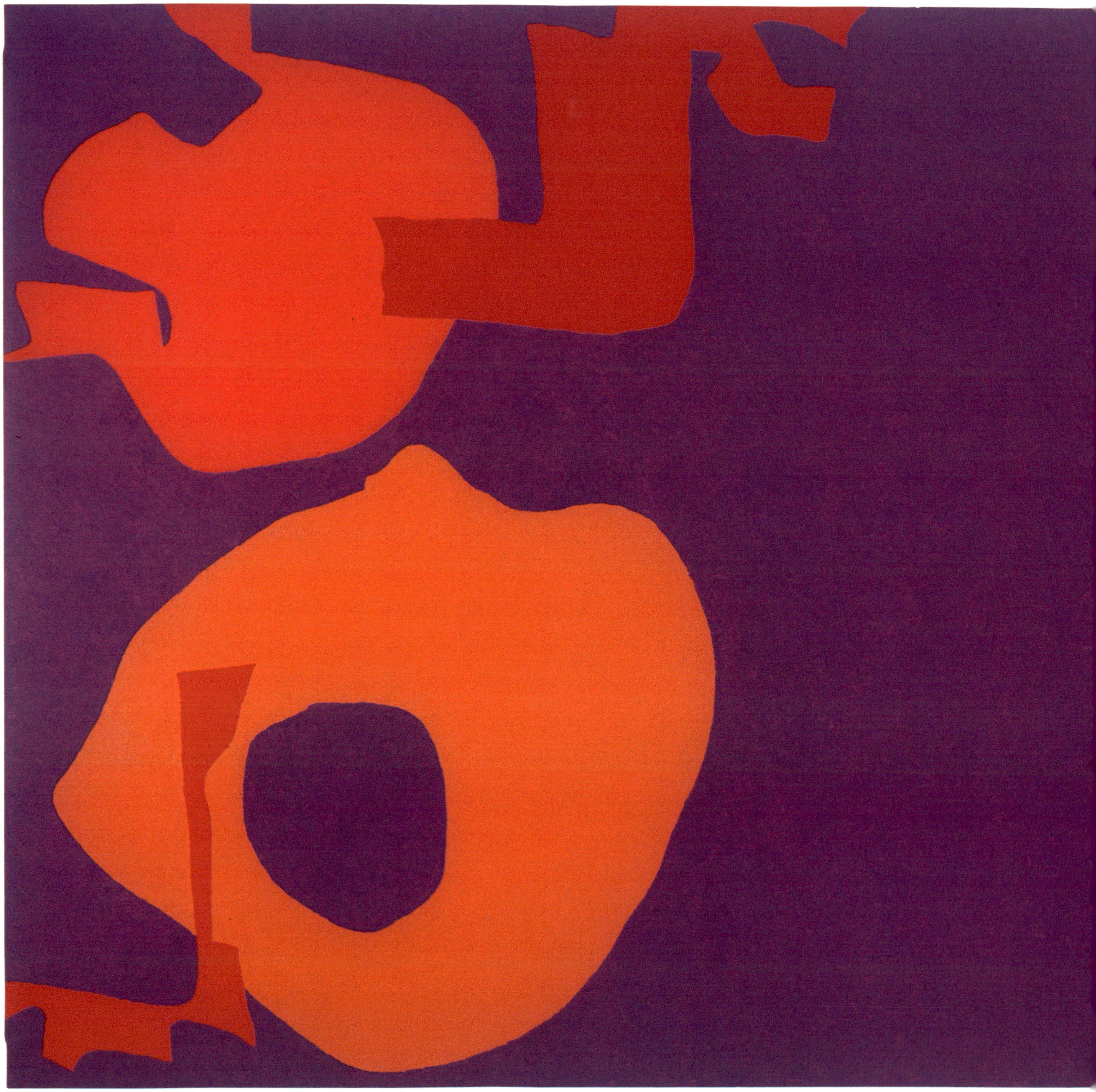

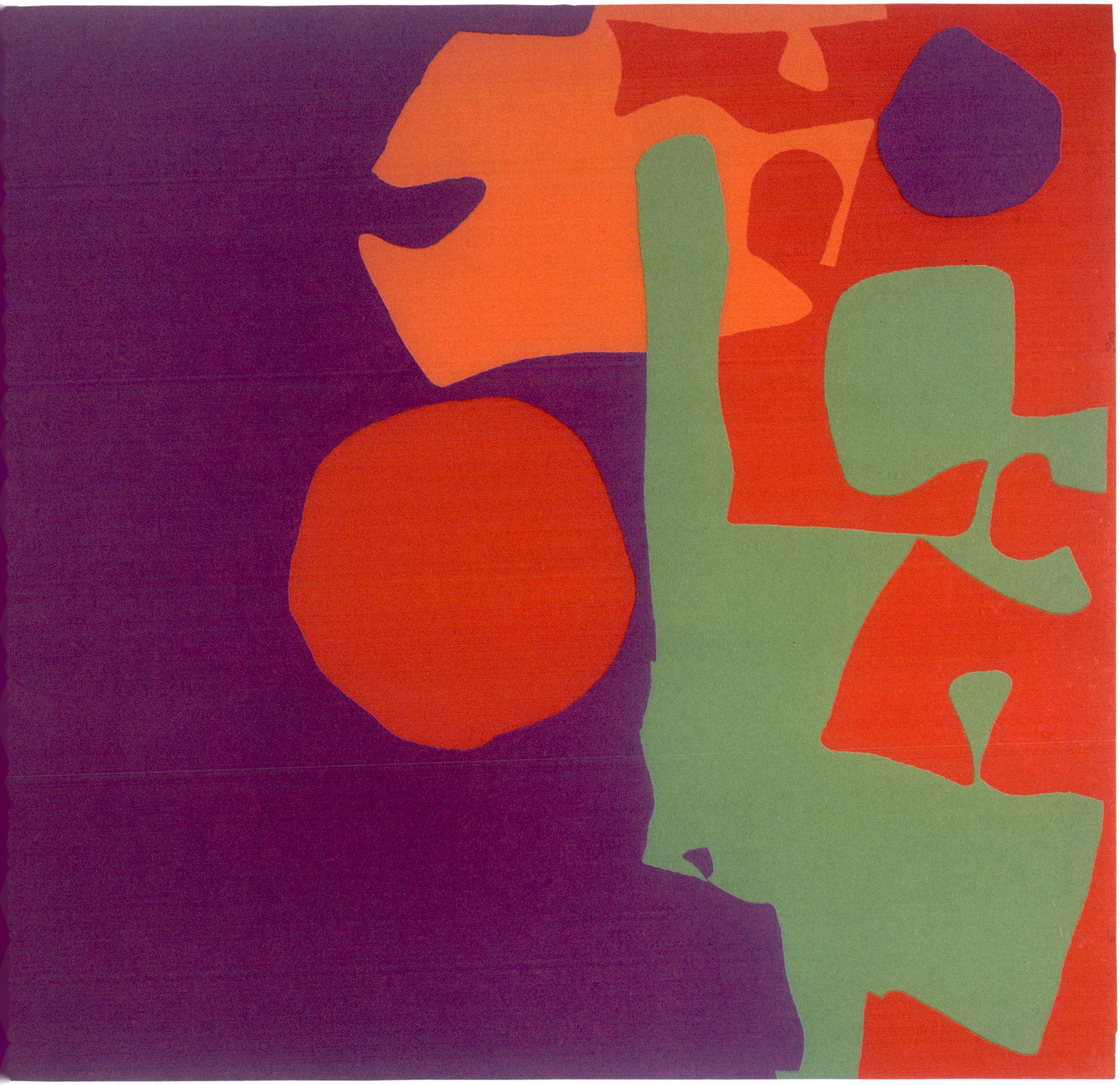

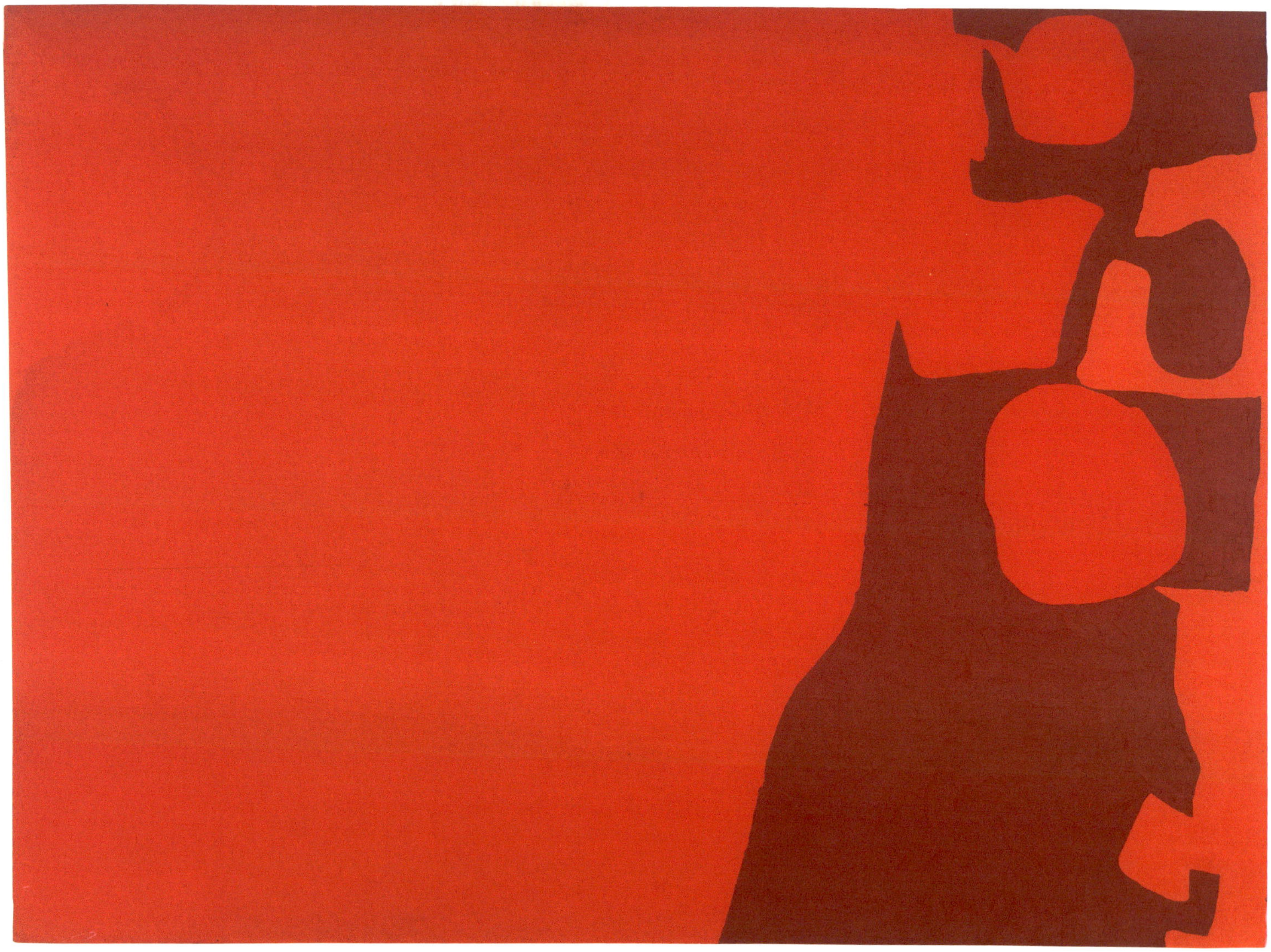

55 Dark Red, Scarlet and Venetian: February 1972
198 × 274.3

57 Scarlet, Emerald and Orange: July – September 1976
101.7 × 152.5

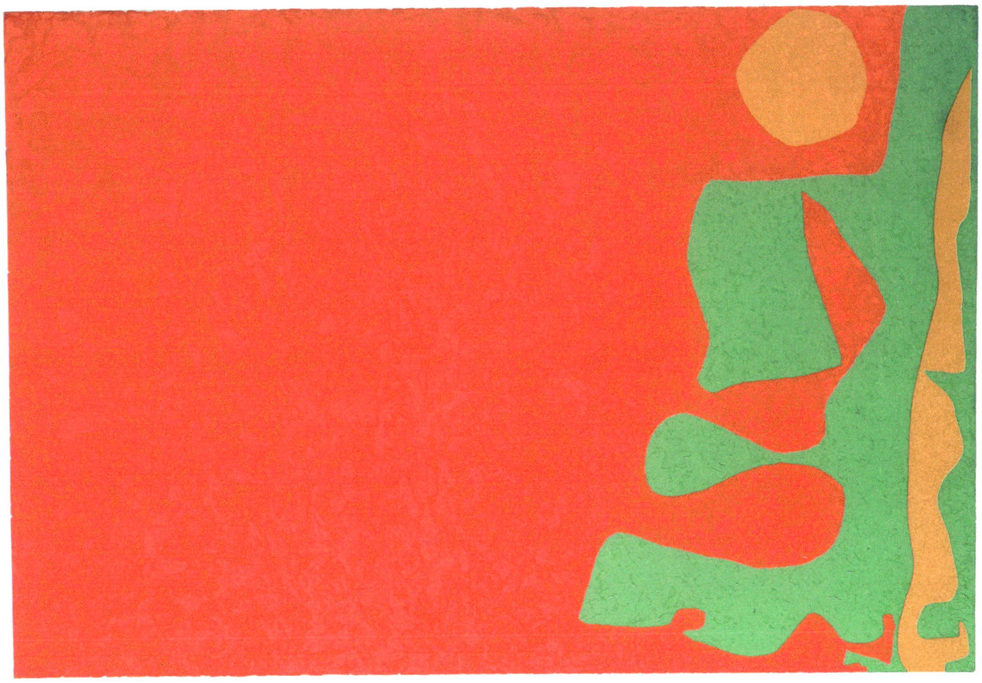

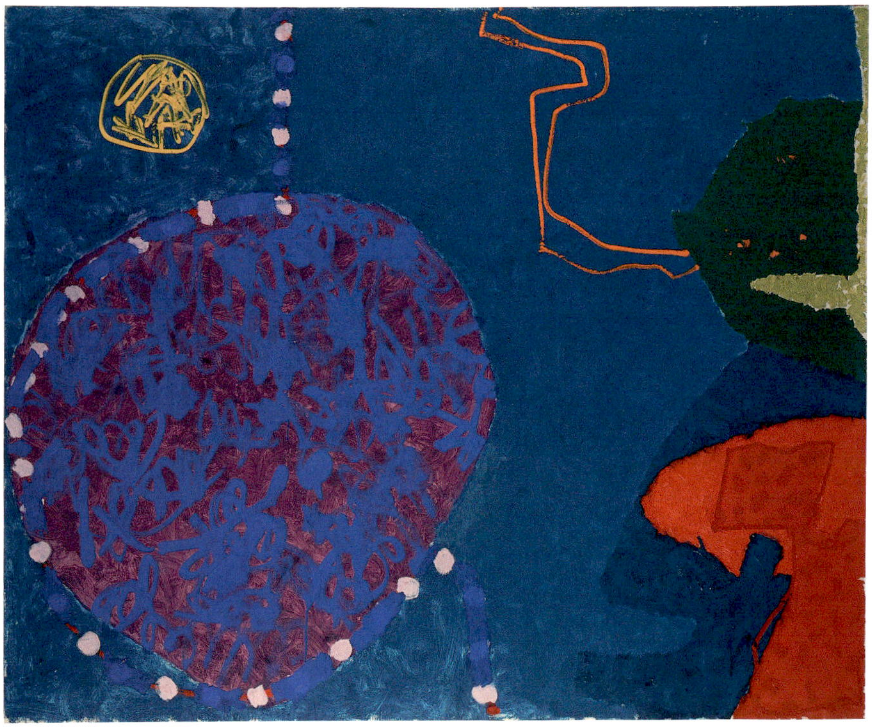

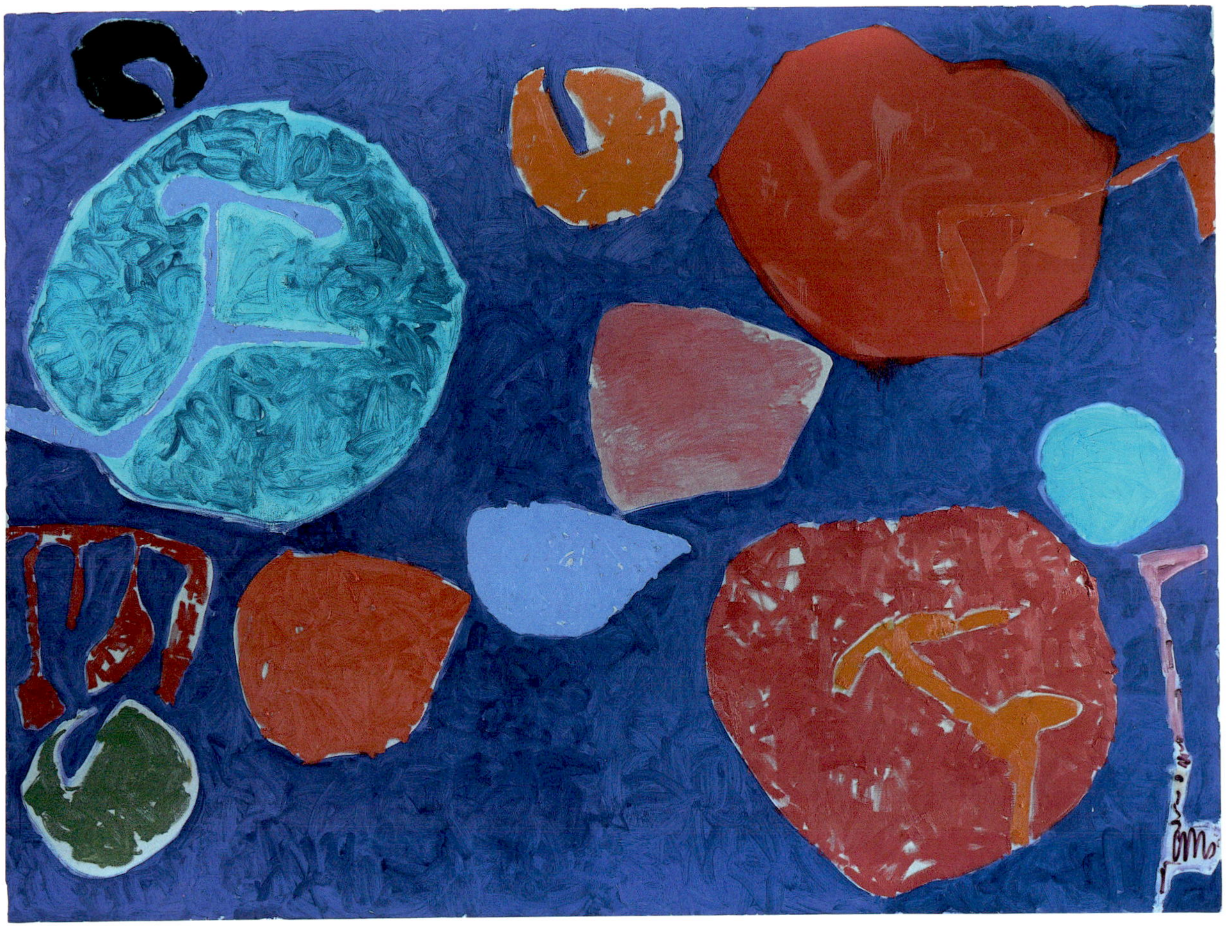

58 Scribbled Disc in Deep Ceruleum: February – May 1983 121.9 × 152.5

59 Afternoon Blue: July 1983 198 × 275

60 [R] Big Purple Garden Painting: July 1983 – June 1984 208.3 × 335.3

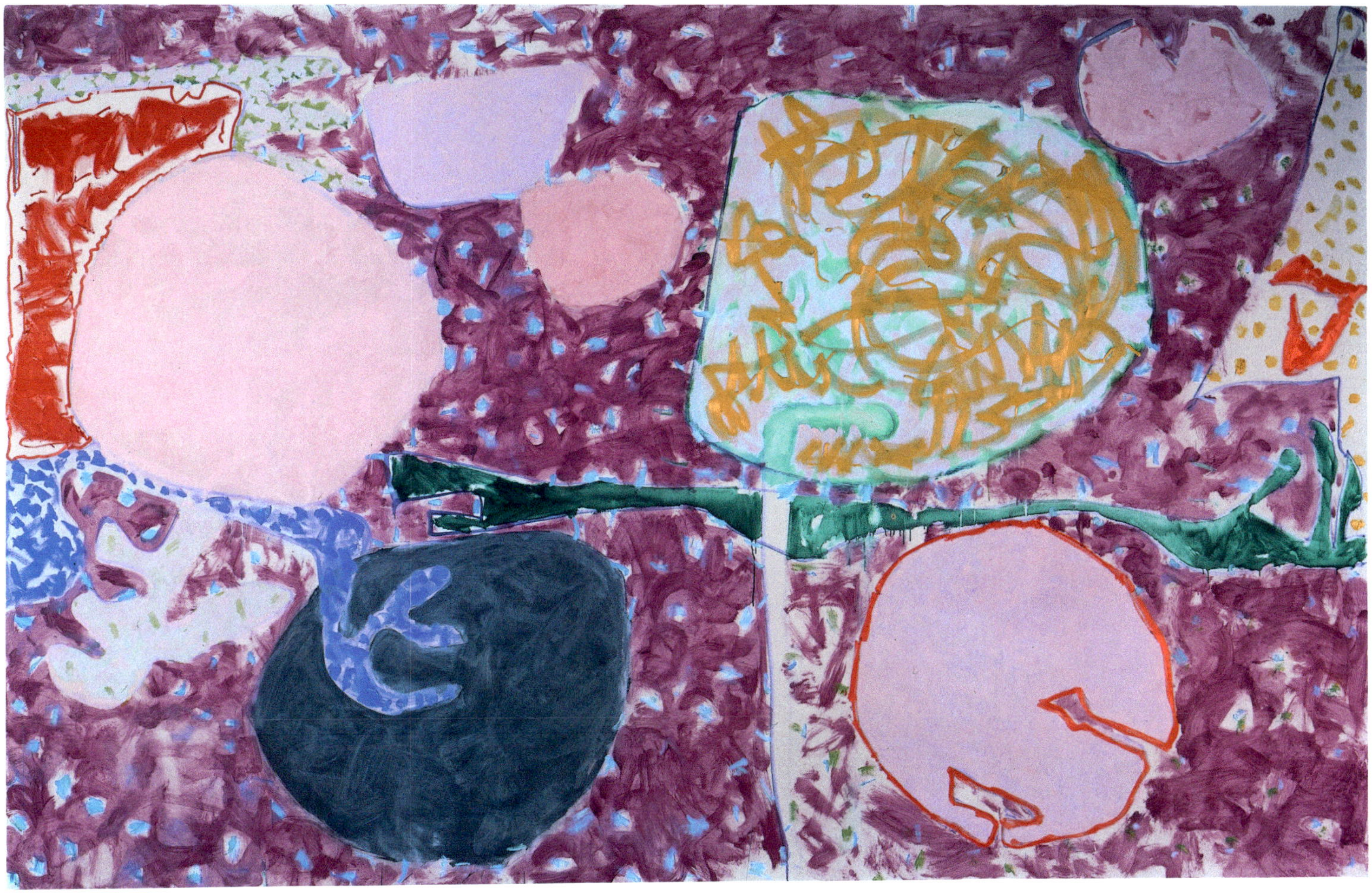

61 Red Garden Painting: June 3 – June 5: 1985 208.3 × 335.3

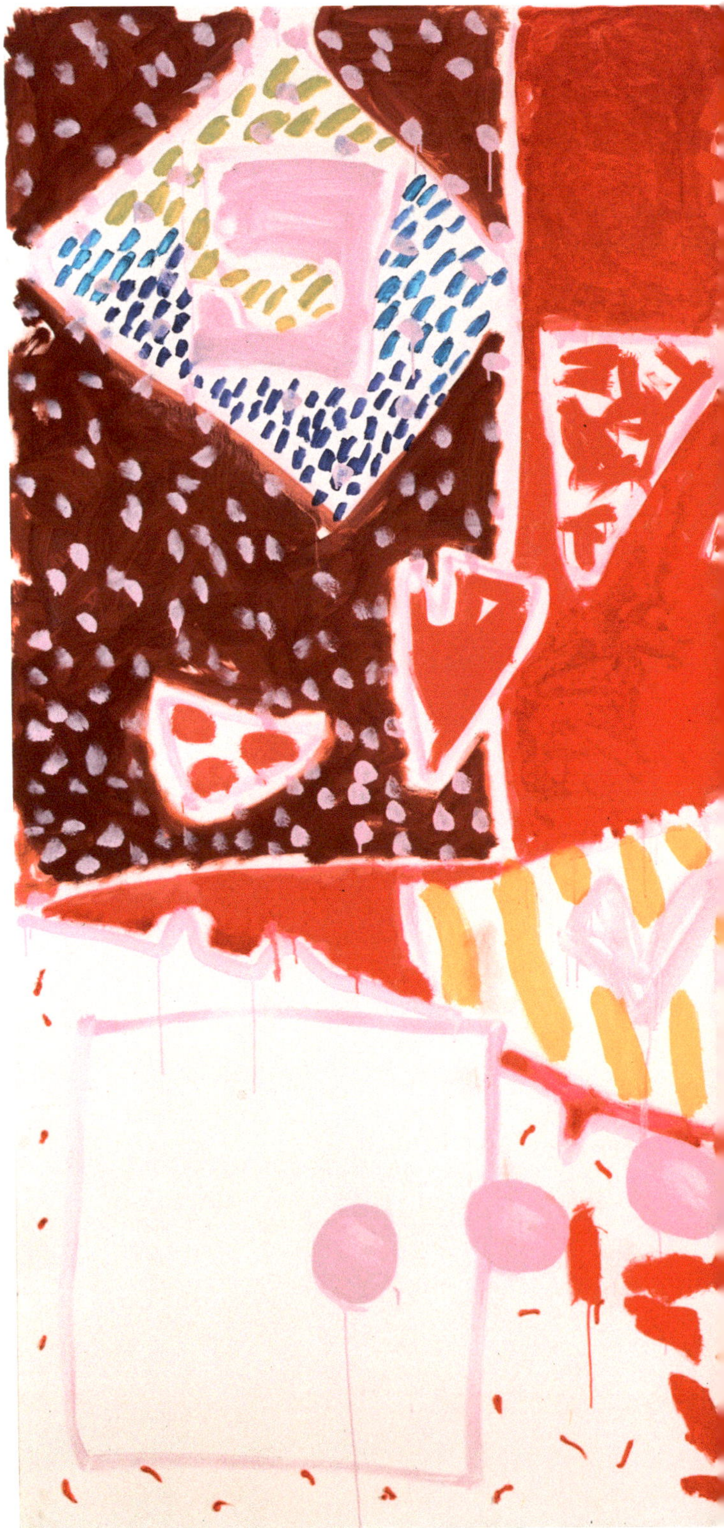

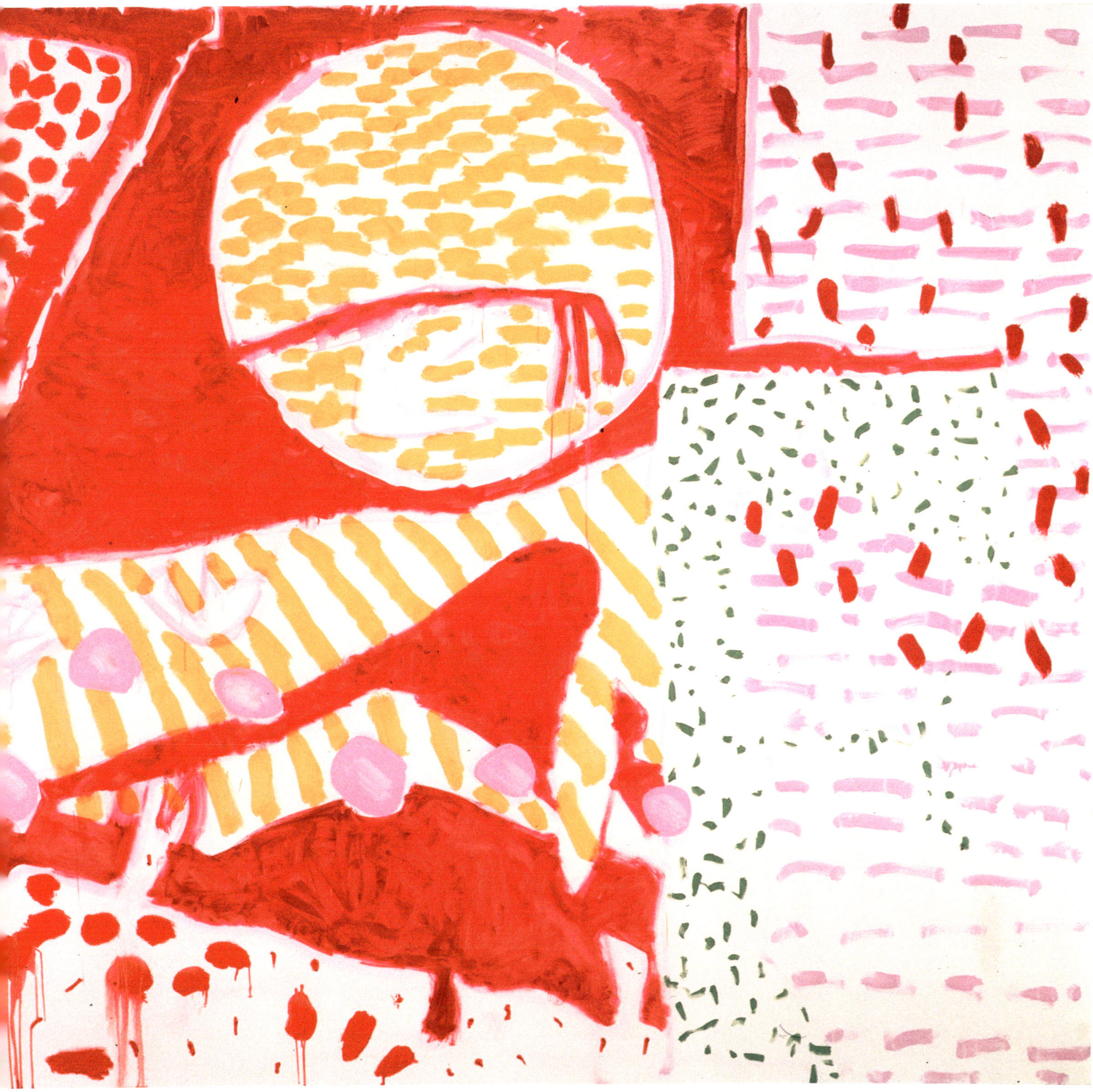

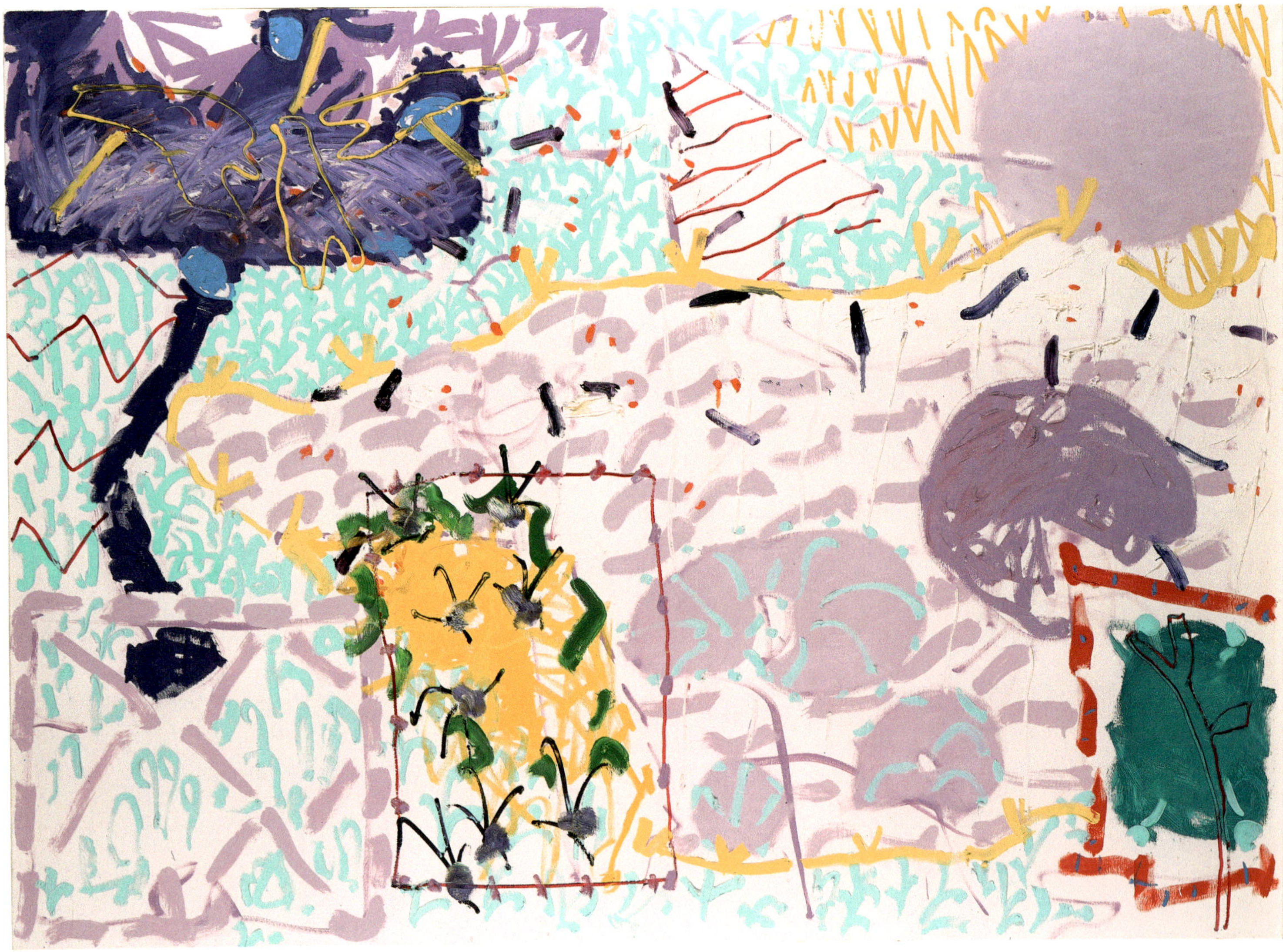

62 Sydney Garden Painting: December: 1989: II
152.4 × 213.4

63 Sydney Garden Painting: February: 1990: I
165.1 × 86.4

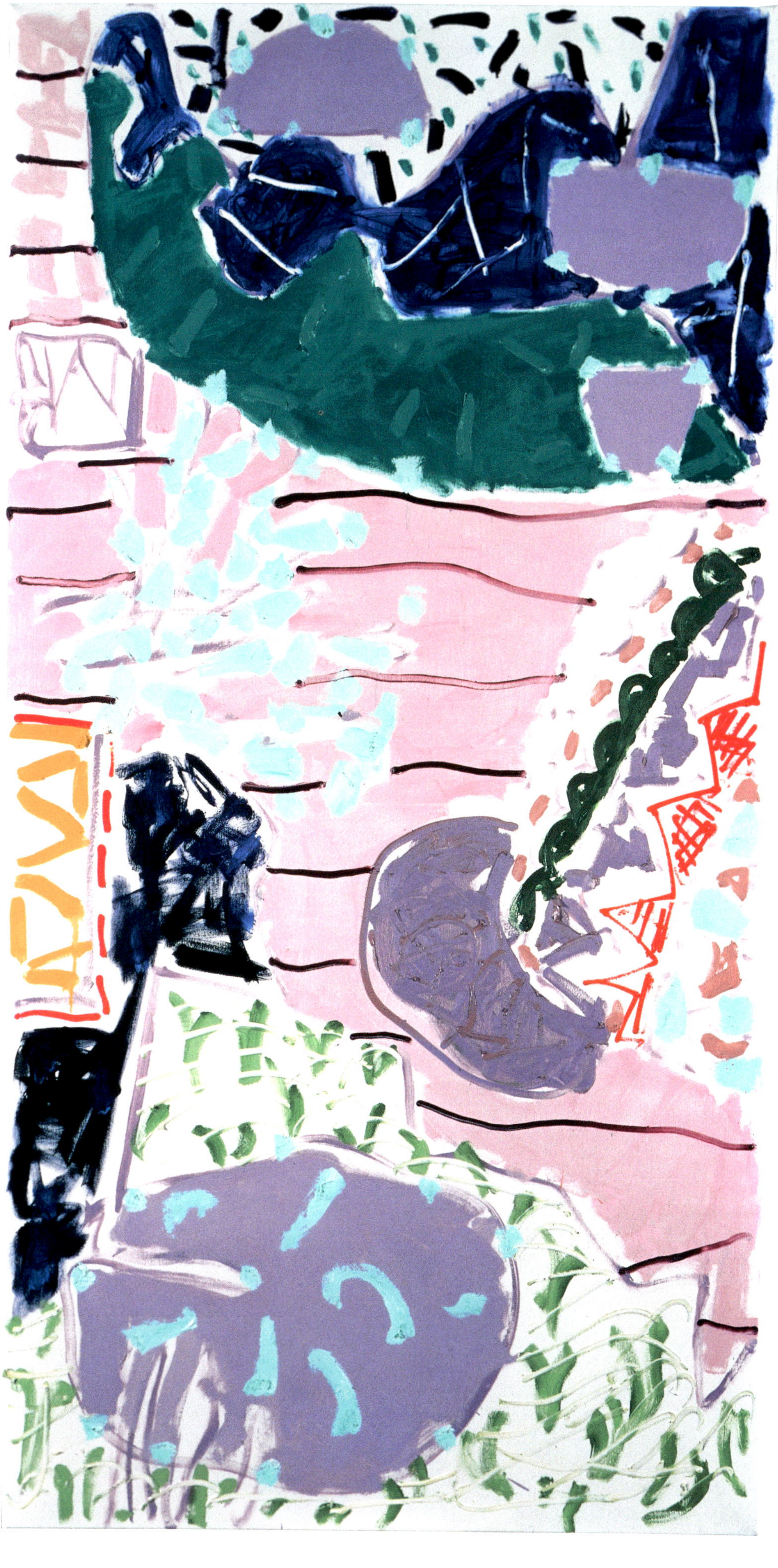

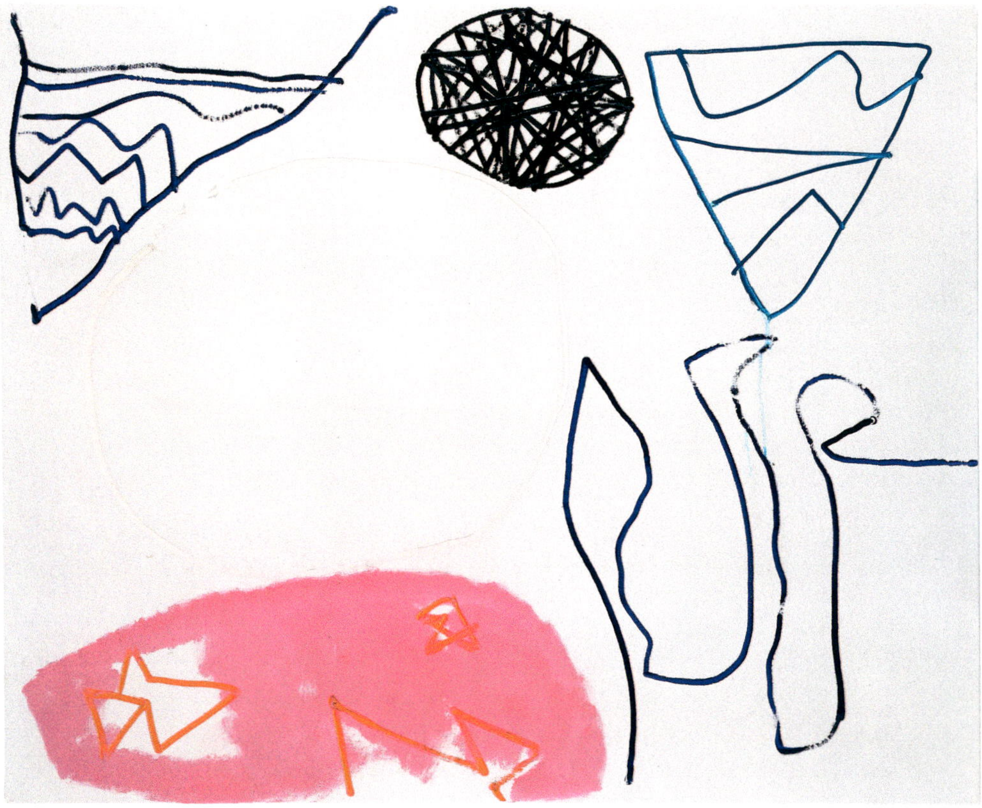

64 5 July: 1992 96.5 × 121.9

70 4 – 5 September: 1996 182.9 × 91.4

Overleaf
66 25 May – 18 June: 1994 198 × 396.2

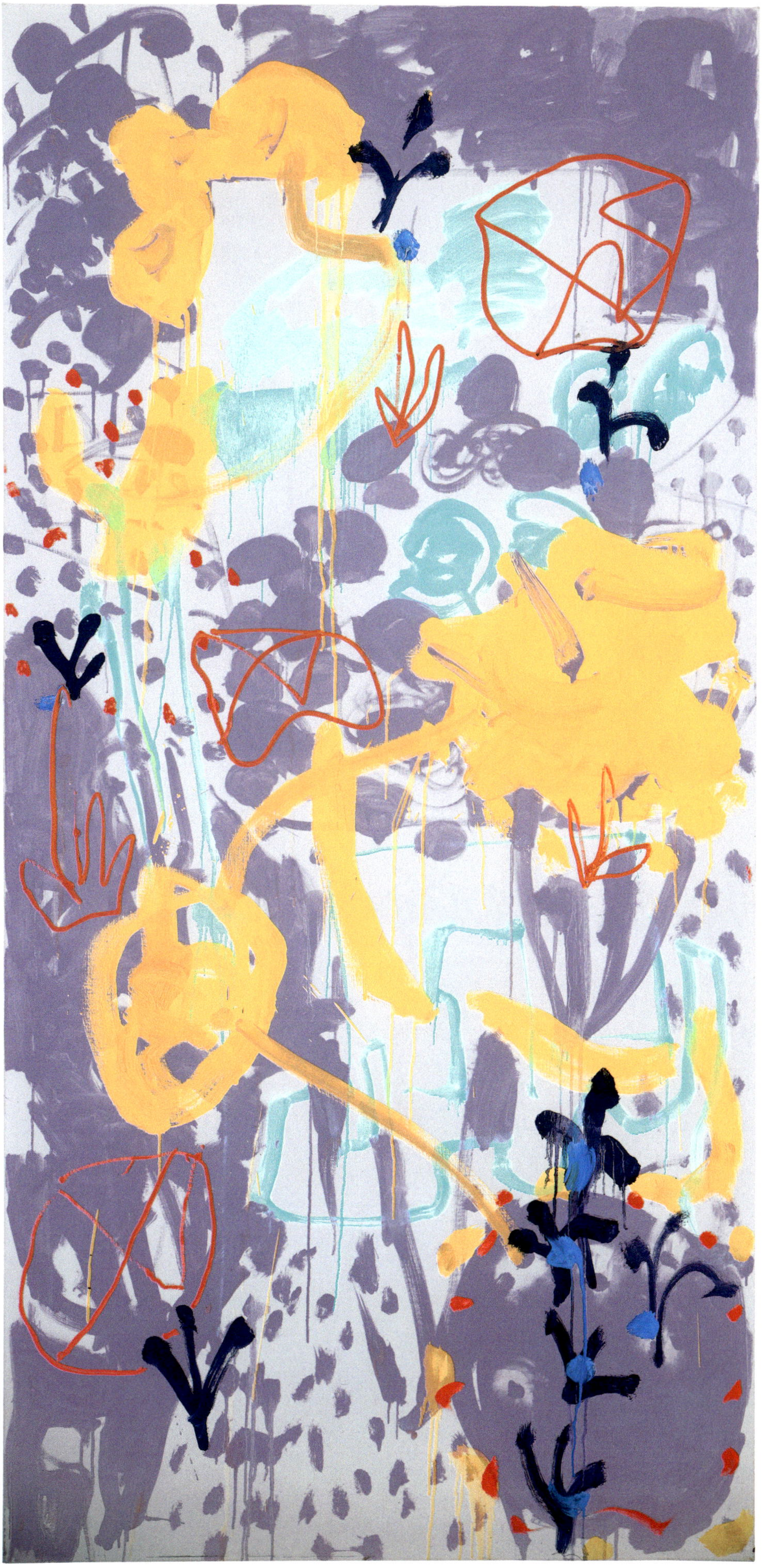

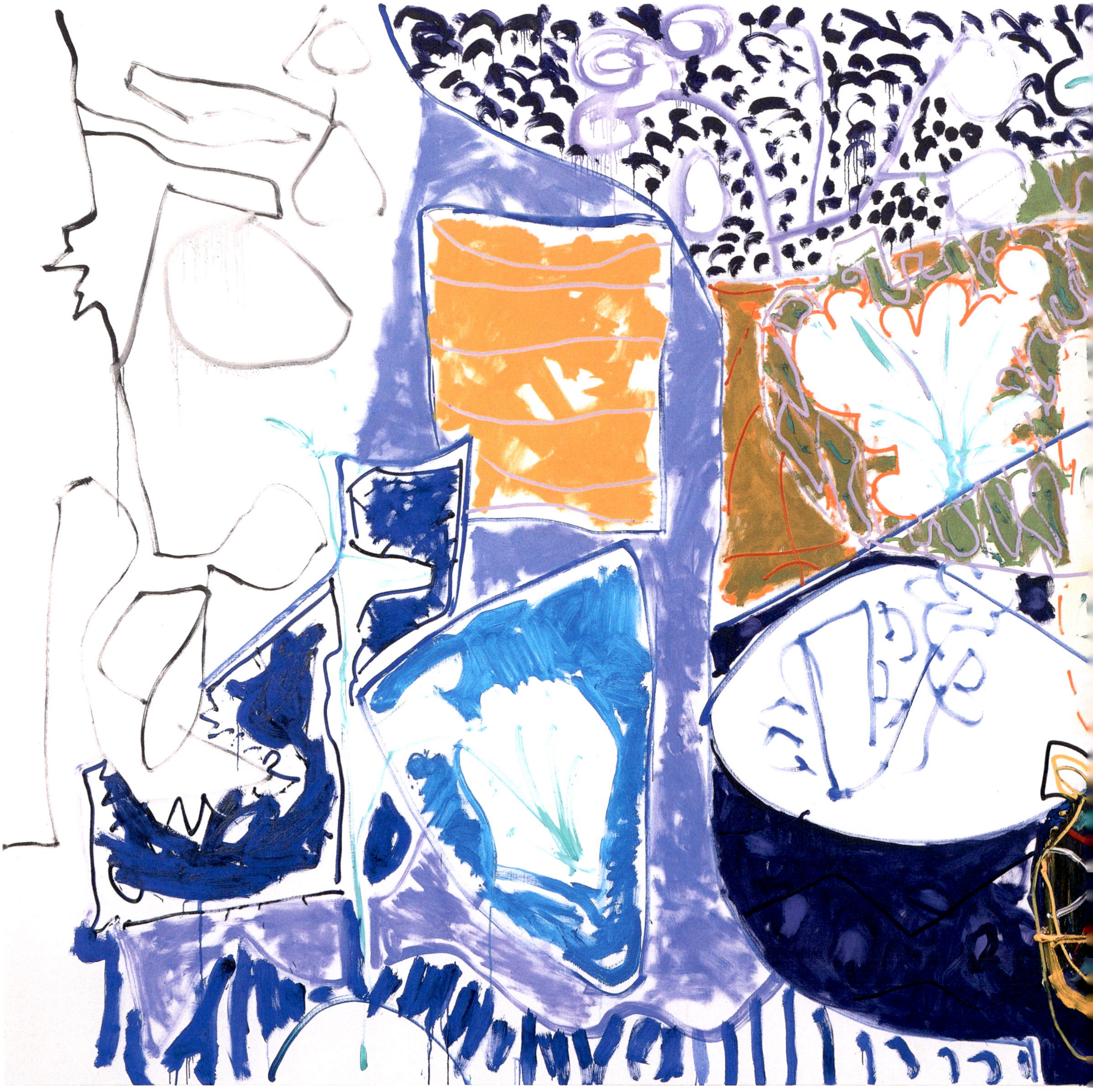

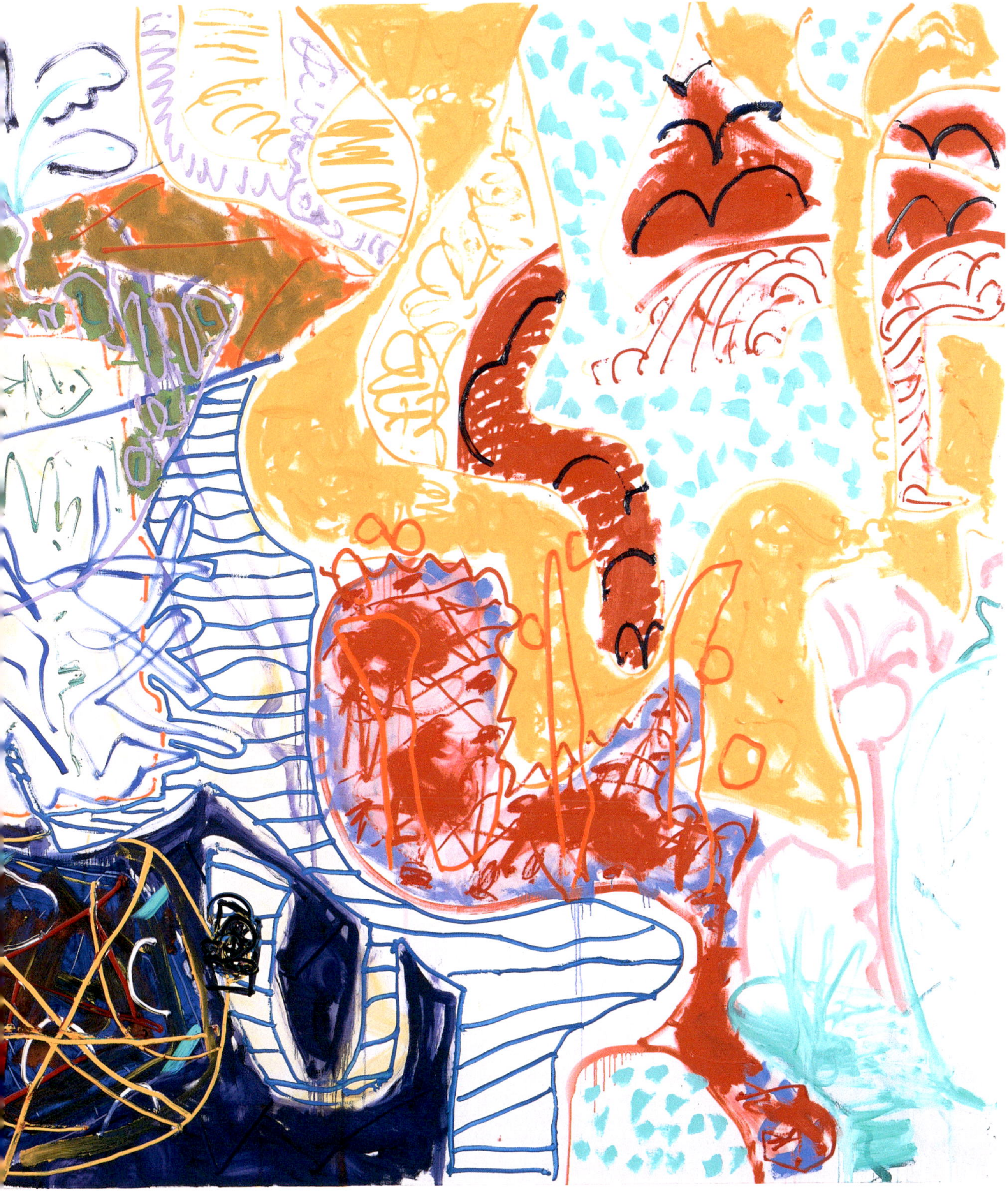

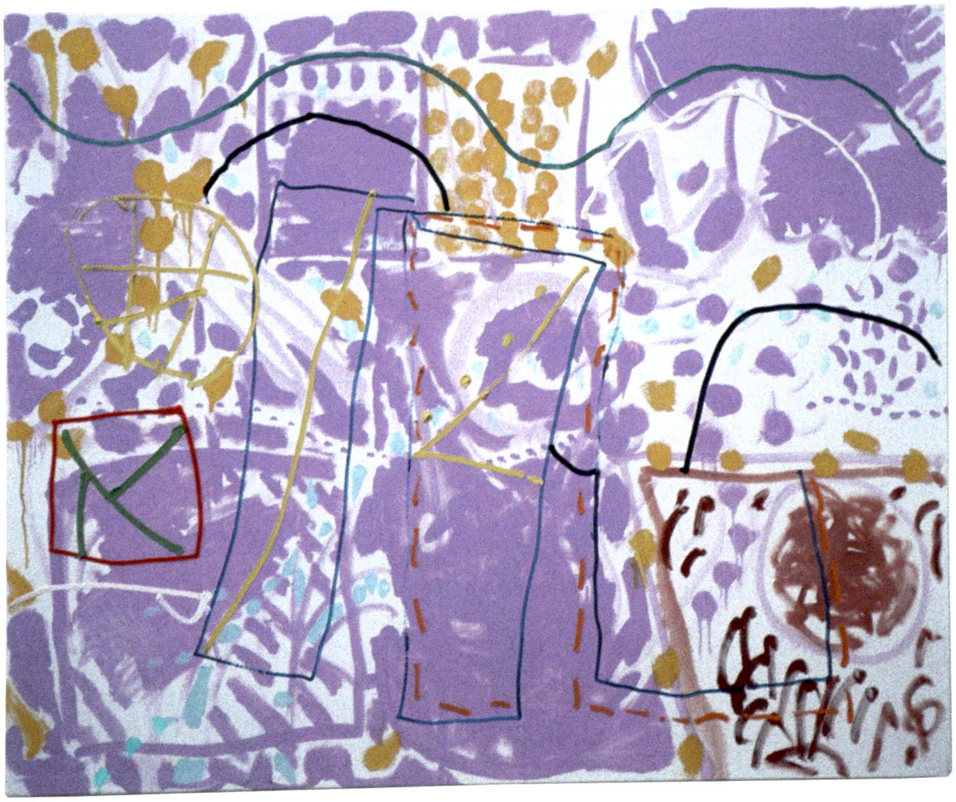

65 21 March: 1993 – 2 January: 1994 96.5 × 121.9

67 2 July – 3 July: 1994 198 × 274.3

Overleaf

68 19 July – 12 August: 1994 198 × 518

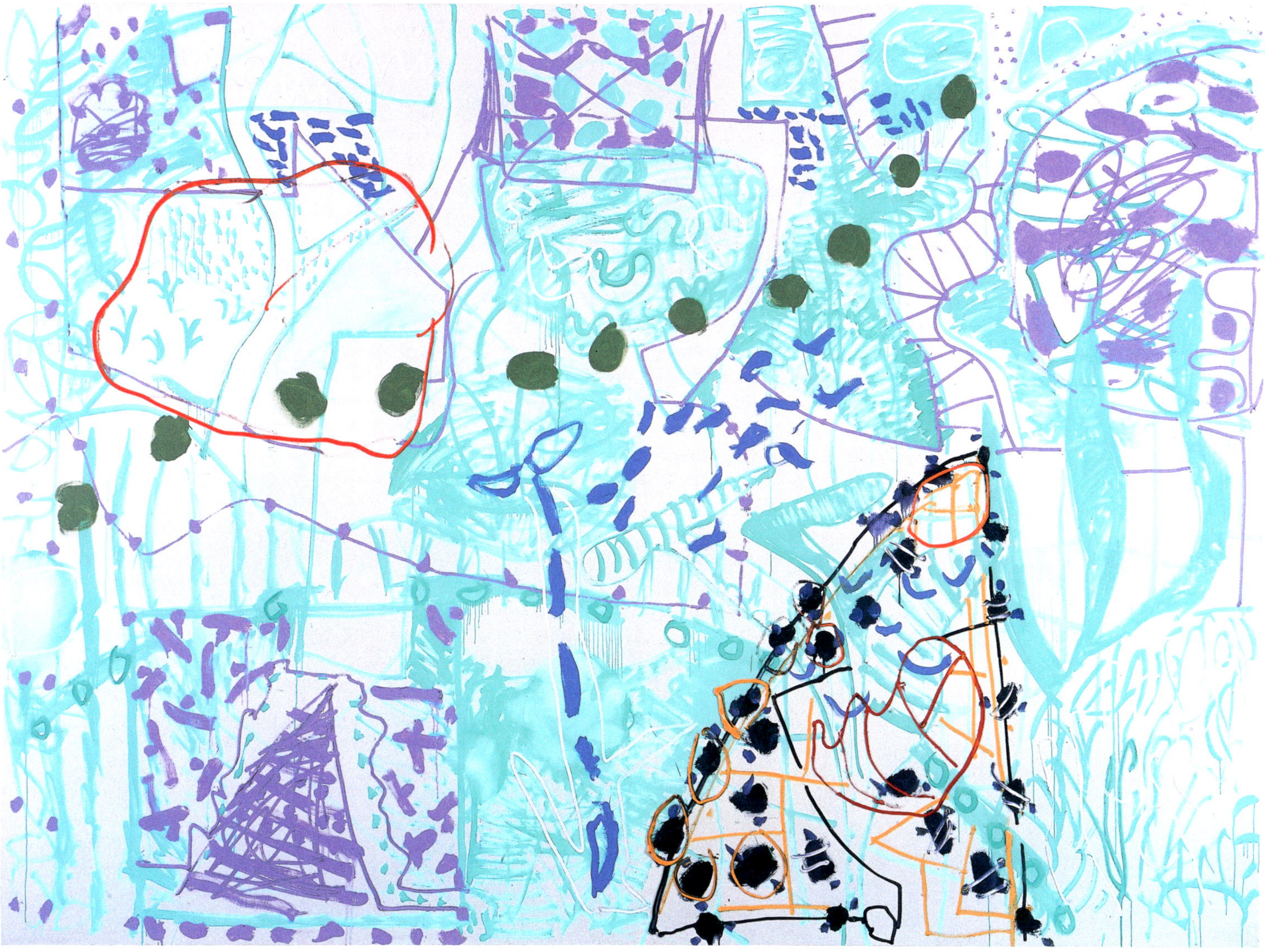

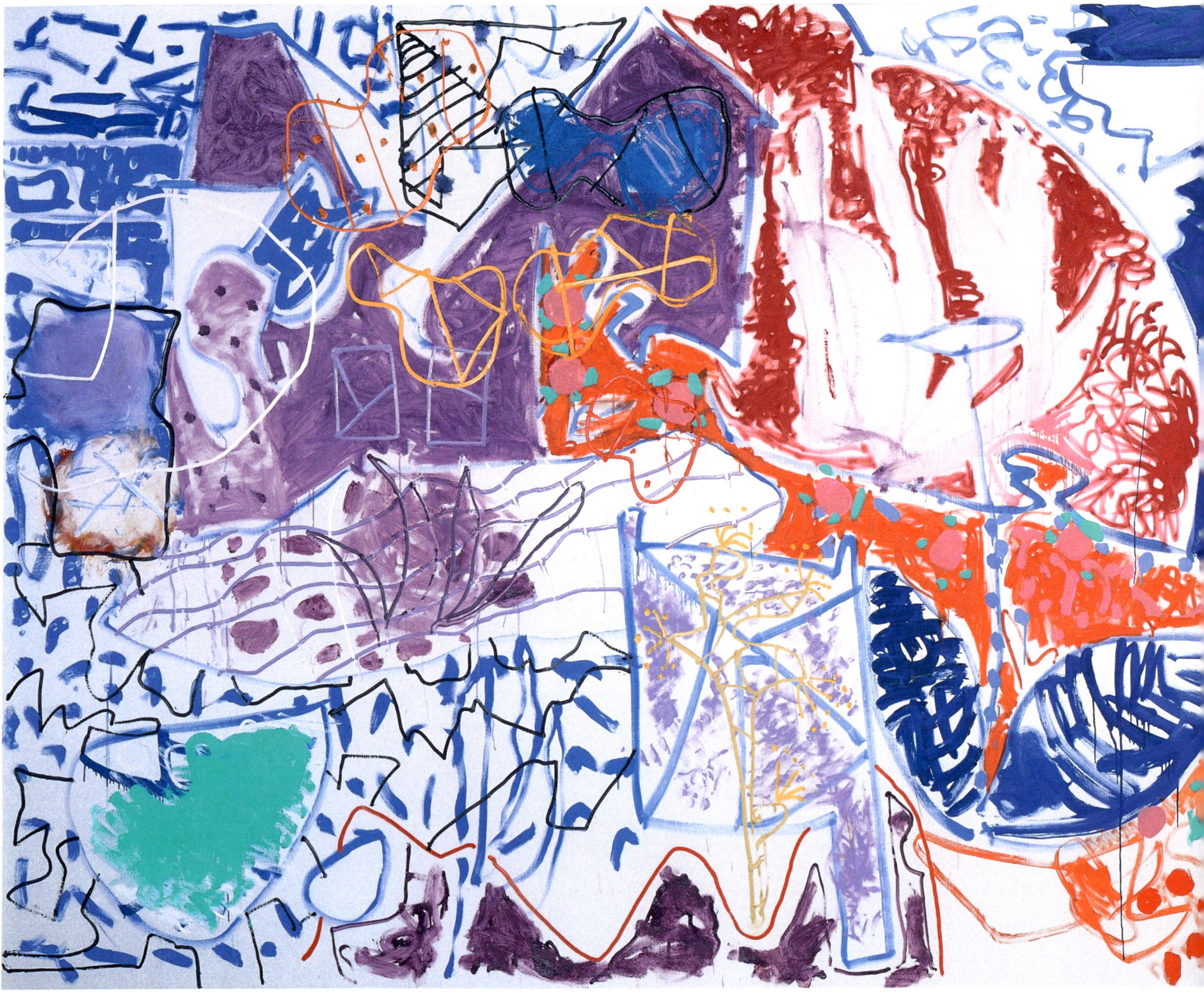

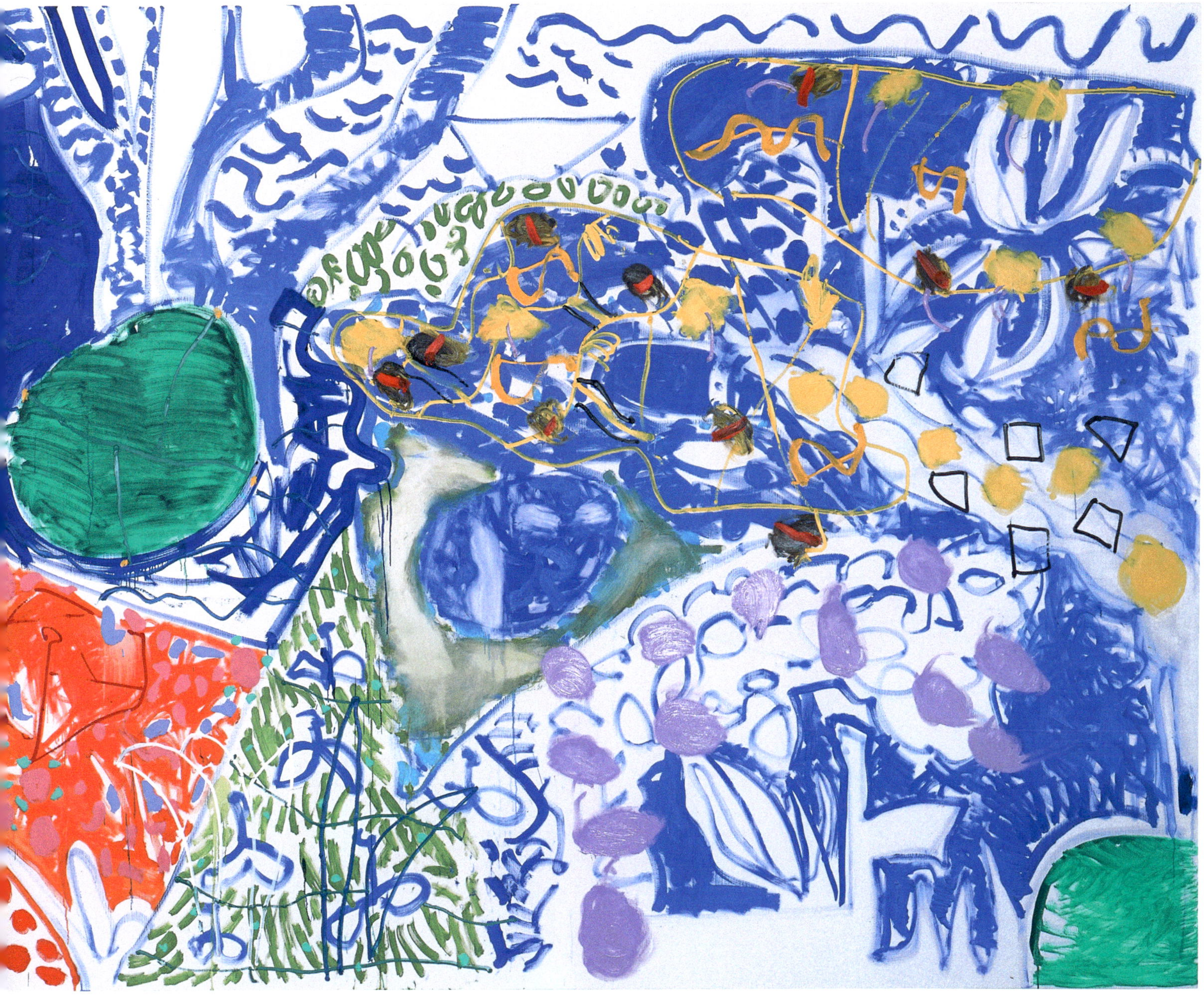

69 1 – 3 September: 1996 91.4 × 121.9

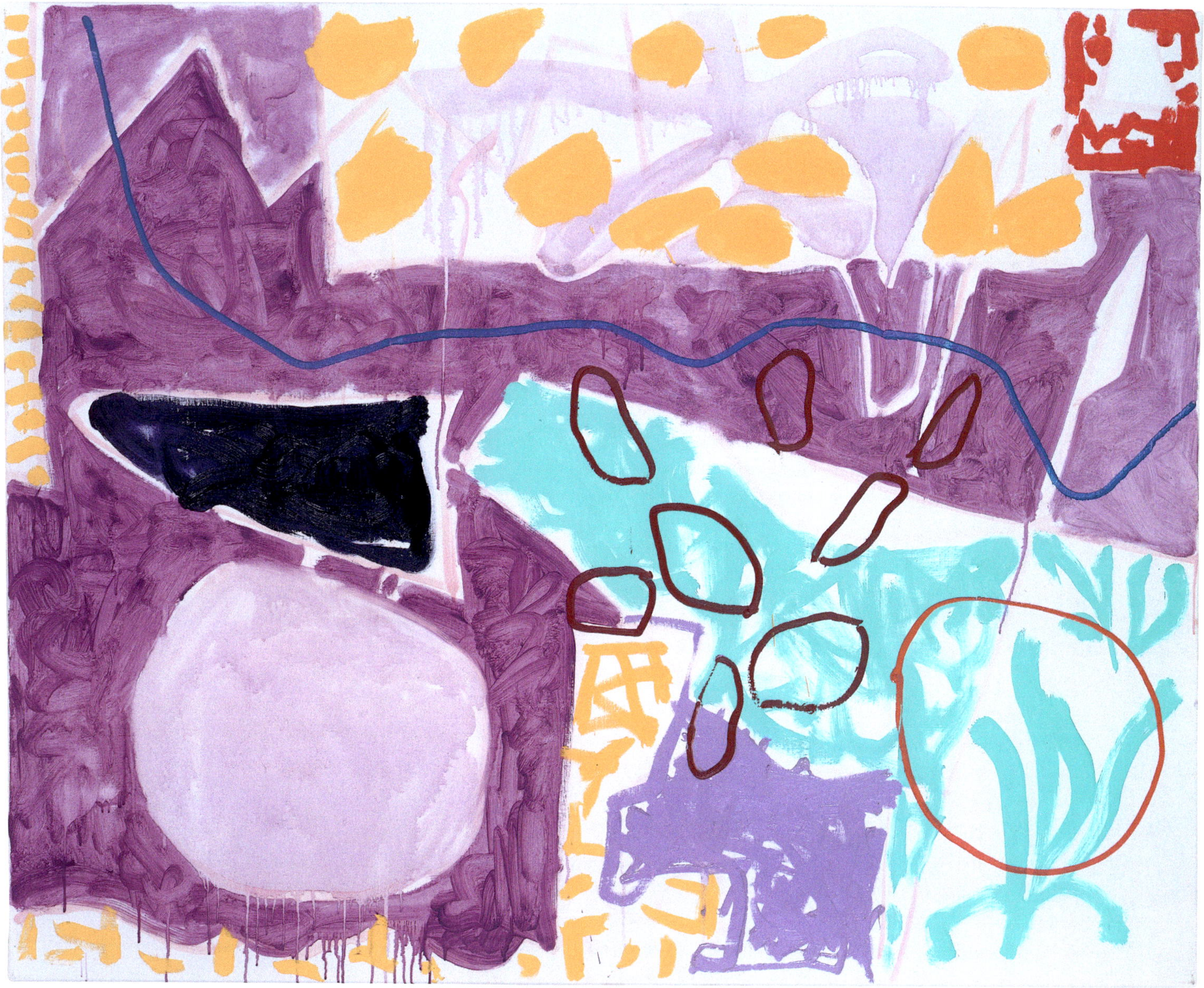

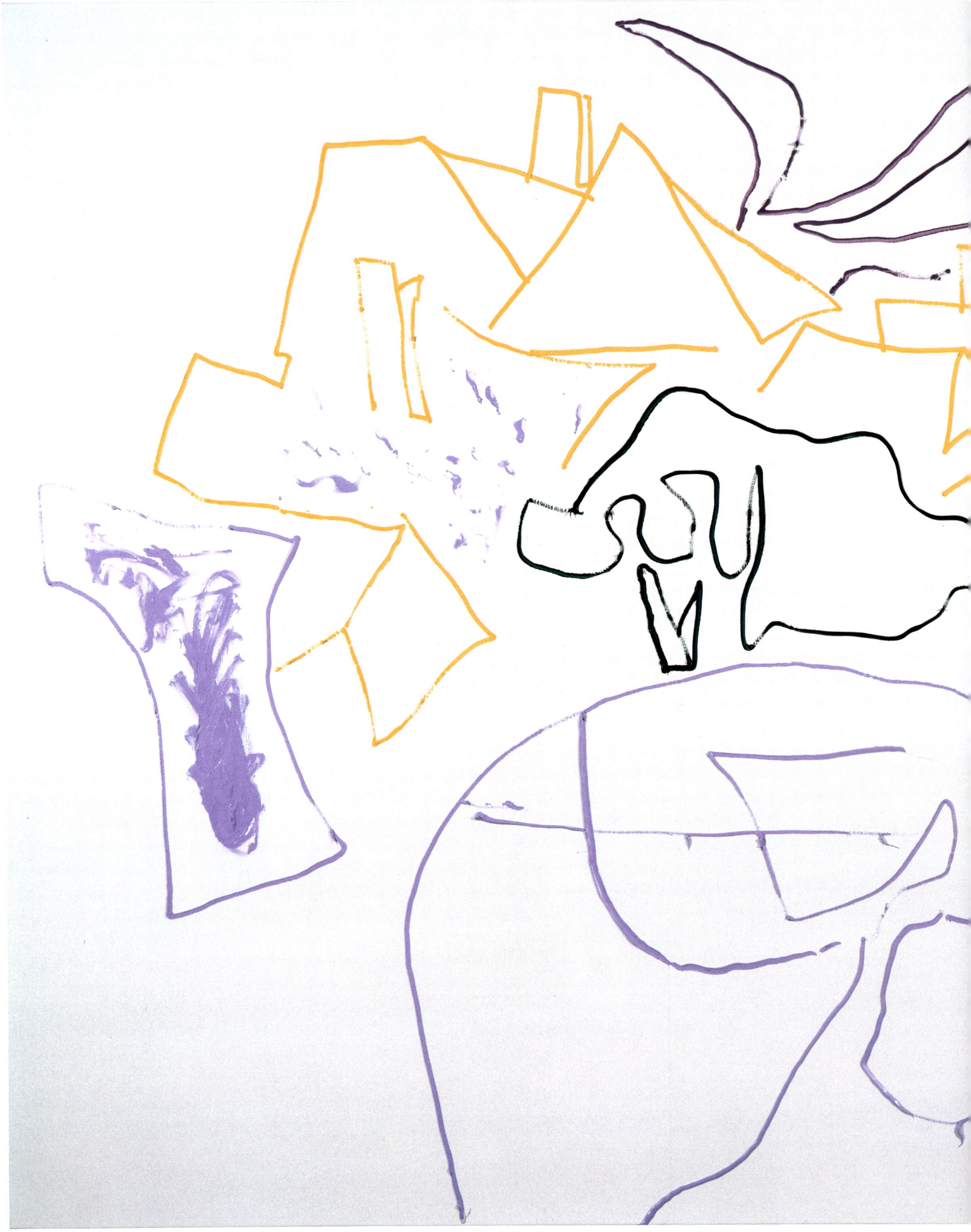

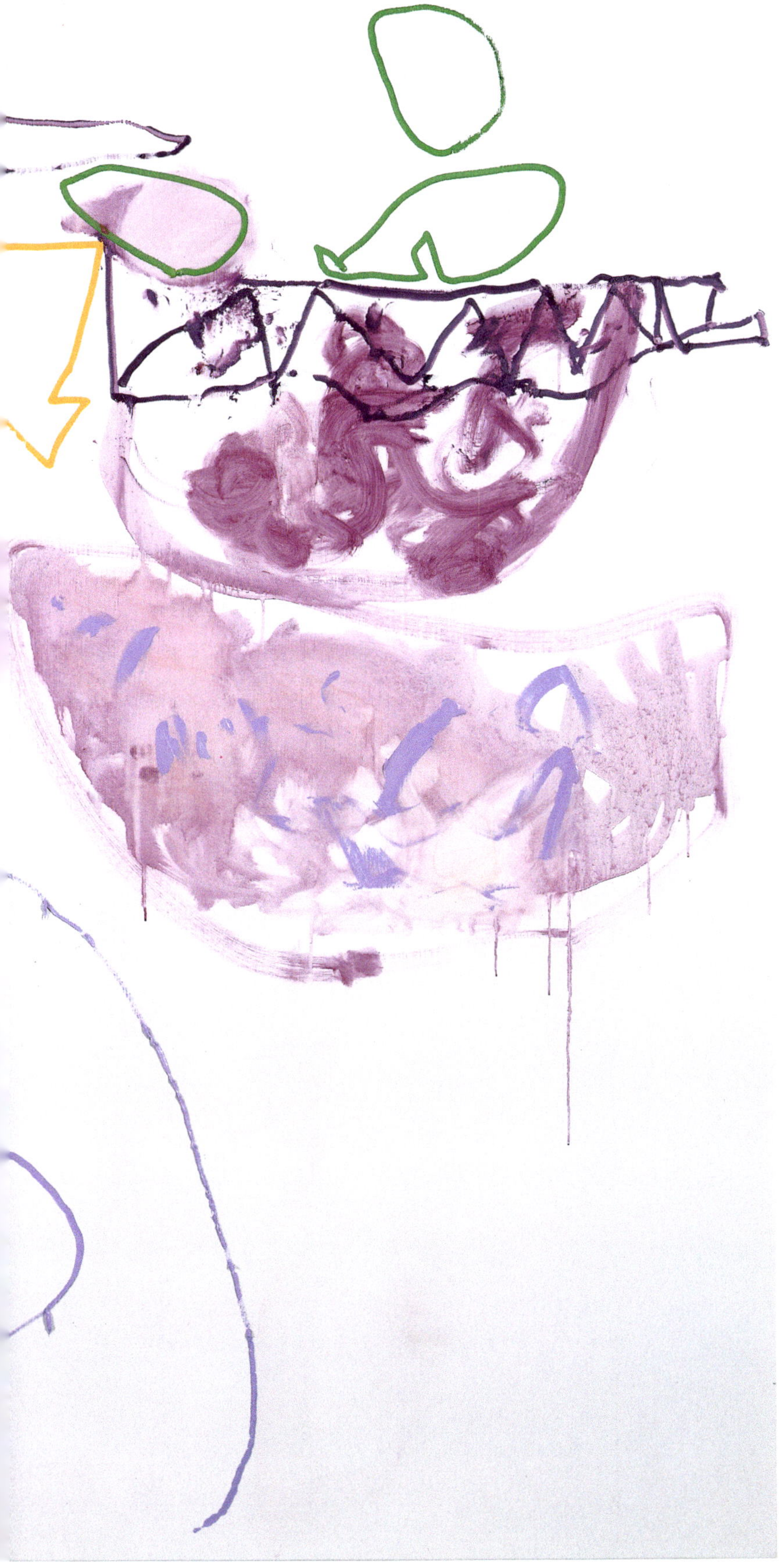

71 29 – 31 January: 1998 182 × 243.8

List of Works

The final selection for the exhibition will be made during the installation. There are therefore some works included in the catalogue that may not be in the exhibition.

Unless otherwise stated, works are oil on canvas.

Dimensions are given in centimetres, followed by inches in brackets, height before width.

1
Orchard, Lower Slaughter: 1936
41.3 × 55.2 (16¼ × 21 ¾)
Private Collection
[Illustrated on p.50]

2
Table, Window and Chair: 1937
76.2 × 50.8 (30 × 20)
Private Collection
[Illustrated on p.51]

3
Bogey's Bar (Woburn Place): February 1937
91.4 × 71.1 (36 × 28)
Private Collection
[Illustrated on p.50]

4
The Piano: 1943
Oil on paper 19 × 27.3 (7½ × 10¾)
Private Collection
[Illustrated on pp.52–3]

5
The Boats and the Iron Ladder: 1947
Oil on gesso wood panel
30.4 × 60.9 (12 × 24)
Private Collection
[Illustrated on p.54]

6
Still Life with Black Bananas: 1948
45.8 × 91 (18 × 35⅞)
John Evans
[Illustrated on p.57]

7
The Long Table with Fruit: 1949
45.8 × 91.4 (18 × 36)
Tate Gallery. Purchased 1994
[Illustrated on p.57]

8
Portrait of Herbert Read: 1950
76.2 × 63.5 (30 × 25)
National Portrait Gallery, London
[Illustrated on p.58]

9
Christmas Eve: 1951
182.9 × 304.8 (72 × 120)
Private Collection
[Illustrated on pp.60–1]

10
The Room at St Ives: 1952–1953
Oil on hardboard 121.9 × 182.8 (48 × 72)
Private Collection
[Illustrated on p.59]

11
Indigo Bay: 1952
45.1 × 121.9 (18 × 48)
Private Collection
[Illustrated on p.55]

12
Round White Table: St Ives: 1953–1954
91.4 × 45.8 (36 × 18)
Private Collection
[Illustrated on p.63]

13
The Red Table: 1954
101.6 × 127.6 (40 × 50)
Hatton Gallery, University of Newcastle
[Illustrated on p.63]

14
The White Table: 1955
71.1 × 91.4 (28 × 36)
Private Collection
[Illustrated on p.62]

15
Girl in Harbour Room: 1955
Oil on hardboard 121.9 × 182.8 (48 × 72)
Private Collection
[Illustrated on pp.64–5]

16
Azalea Garden: May 1956
152.4 × 127.6 (60 × 50)
Tate Gallery. Purchased 1980
[Illustrated on p.66]

17
Garden Painting: August 1956
127.6 × 91.5 (50 × 40)
Private Collection
[Illustrated on p.67]

18
Autumn Garden: 1956
182.9 × 91.5 (72 × 36)
Private Collection
[Illustrated on p.68]

19
Summer Painting: August 1956
182.9 × 91.5 (72 × 36)
Private Collection
[Illustrated on p.69]

20
Vertical Light: March 1957
55.9 × 121.9 (22 × 48)
Private Collection
[Illustrated on pp.70–1]

21
Scarlet, Lemon and Ultramarine: March 1957
61 × 182.9 (24 × 72)
Tate Gallery. Purchased 1967
[Illustrated on p.73]

22
Ochre Skies: April 1957
121.9 × 55.8 (48 × 22)
Private Collection
[Illustrated on p.74]

23
Yellow and Black: May 1957
91.4 × 121.9 (36 × 48)
Private Collection
[Illustrated on p.79]

24
Horizontal Stripe Painting: November 1957 – January 1958
274.3 × 152.4 (108 × 60)
Tate Gallery. Purchased 1972
[Illustrated on p.78]

25
Red Layers (with Blue and Yellow): 14 December 1957
182.9 × 91.5 (72 × 36)
Private Collection
[Illustrated on p.72]

26
Cadmium Scarlet: January 1958
182.9 × 106.6 (72 × 42)
Private Collection
[Illustrated on p.81]

27
Green and Mauve Horizontals: January 1958
121.9 × 55.9 (48 × 22)
Private Collection
[Illustrated on p.74]

28
Squares in Deep Cadmium: January 1958
182.9 × 106.6 (72 × 42)
Private Collection
[Illustrated on p.80]

29
Atmospheric Strata: February 1958
121.9 × 55.8 (48 × 22)
David Thomson
[Illustrated on p.75]

30
Lux Eterna: May – June 1958
182.9 × 91.4 (72 × 35⅞)
Private Collection
[Illustrated on p.77]

31
Brown Ground with Soft Red and Green: August 1958 – July 1959
152.4 × 213.4 (60 × 84)
Tate Gallery. Purchased 1974
[Illustrated on pp.84–5]

32
Grey and Yellow (with Circle): October 1958 – February 1959
152.4 × 121.9 (60 × 48)
David Thomson
[Illustrated on p.86]

33
Yellow Painting: October 1958 – May/June 1959
152.4 × 213.4 (60 × 84)
Private Collection
[Illustrated on pp.82–3]

34
Big Grey with Disc: June – September 1959
213.4 × 152.4 (84 × 60)
Waddington Galleries
[Illustrated on p.87]

35
Cadmium Painting with Soft Lemon Oblong: August 1959
213.4 × 152.4 (84 × 60)
David Thomson
[Illustrated on p.89]

36
Squares Floating in Brown (Emerald, Lemon, Violet): January 1960
76.2 × 101.6 (30 × 40)
Private Collection
[Illustrated on p.88]

37
White Painting (Pale Squares): 1961
96.5 × 121.9 (38 × 48)
David Thomson
[Illustrated on p.90]

38
Blue Painting: September 1961 – September 1962
121.9 × 182.9 (48 × 72)
David Thomson
[Illustrated on p.91]

39
Dull Green with White: December 1961
182.9 × 91.5 (72 × 36)
Private Collection
[Illustrated on p.92]

40
Orange (with Five): September 18 1962
121.9 × 152.4 (48 × 60)
David Thomson
[Illustrated on p.93]

41
Rectilinear Reds and Blues: 1963
152.4 × 182.9 (60 × 72)
Plymouth City Museum and Art Gallery
[Illustrated on p.96]

42
Fourteen Discs: July 20: 1963
152.4 × 121.9 (60 × 48)
Private Collection
[Illustrated on pp.94–5]

43
Two Vermilions, Orange and Red: September 1964
152.4 × 213.4 (60 × 84)
Waddington Galleries
[Illustrated on pp.98–9]

44
Yellow Painting with Four Discs: 1964
152.4 × 182.9 (60 × 72)
Fundacao Calouste Gulbenkian
[Illustrated on p.97]

45
Complicated Reds (Five Discs): March 1965
121.9 × 132.2 (48 × 52)
David Thomson
[Illustrated on p.100]

46
Yellows and Reds with Violet Edge: April 1965
152.4 × 167.6 (60 × 66)
Katharine Heron
[Illustrated on p.101]

47
Two Yellows and White: July 1966
121.9 × 152.9 (48 × 60)
David Thomson
[Illustrated on p.100]

48
Square Red with Scarlet, Emerald and Orange: 1969
152.4 × 152.4 (60 × 60)
Whitford Fine Art, London
[Illustrated on p.109]

49
Orange in Deep Cadmium with Venetian: 1969
208.3 × 335.3 (82 × 132)
David Thomson
[Illustrated on p.107]

50
Cadmium with Violet, Scarlet, Emerald, Lemon and Venetian: 1969
198 × 396 (78 × 156)
Tate Gallery. Presented by Lord McAlpine of West Green 1983
[Illustrated on pp.104–5]

51
Square Green with Orange, Violet and Lemon: 1969
152.5 × 152.5 (60 × 60)
David Thomson
[Illustrated on p.102]

52
Small Orange with Deep Yellow, Lemon and Violet: 1969
76.2 × 101.6 (30 × 40)
David Thomson
[Illustrated on p.103]

53
Rumbold Vertical One: Emerald in Reds: February 1970
213.4 × 121.9 (84 × 48)
Waddington Galleries
[Illustrated on p.108]

54
Rumbold Vertical Four: Green in Green with Blue and Red: September 1970
213.4 × 121.9 (84 × 48)
City of Aberdeen Art Gallery and Museums Collections
[Illustrated on p.106]

55
Dark Red, Scarlet and Venetian: February 1972
198 × 274.3 (78 × 108)
Waddington Galleries
[Illustrated on p.112]

56
Big Cobalt Violet: May 1972
208.3 × 457 (82 × 180)
David Thomson
[Illustrated on pp.110–11]

57
Scarlet, Emerald and Orange: July – September 1976
101.7 × 152.5 (40 × 60)
Tate Gallery Foundation. On loan to the Tate Gallery
[Illustrated on p.113]

58
Scribbled Disc in Deep Ceruleum: February – May 1983
121.9 × 152.5 (48 × 60)
David Thomson
[Illustrated on p.114]

59
Afternoon Blue: July 1983
198 × 275 (78 × 108 1/4)
David Thomson
[Illustrated on p.114]

60
Big Purple Garden Painting: July 1983 – June 1984
208.3 × 335.3 (82 × 132)
David Thomson
[Illustrated on p.115]

61
Red Garden Painting: June 3 – June 5: 1985
208.3 × 335.3 (83 × 132)
Waddington Galleries
[Illustrated on p.116–17]

62
Sydney Garden Painting: December: 1989: II
152.4 × 213.4 (60 × 84)
David Thomson
[Illustrated on p.118]

63
Sydney Garden Painting: February: 1990: I
165.1 × 86.4 (65 × 34)
David Thomson
[Illustrated on p.119]

64
5 July: 1992
96.5 × 121.9 (38 × 48)
David Thomson
[Illustrated on p.120]

65
21 March: 1993 – 2 January: 1994
96.5 × 121.9 (38 × 48)
Waddington Galleries
[Illustrated on p.124]

66
25 May – 18 June: 1994
198 × 396.2 (78 × 156)
Waddington Galleries
[Illustrated on pp.122–3]

67
2 July – 3 July: 1994
198 × 274.3 (78 × 108)
Waddington Galleries
[Illustrated on p.125]

68
19 July – 12 August: 1994
198 × 518 (78 × 204)
Waddington Galleries
[Illustrated on pp.126–7]

69
1–3 September: 1996
91.4 × 121.9 (36 × 48)
Waddington Galleries
[Illustrated on p.129]

70
4–5 September: 1996
182.9 × 91.4 (72 × 36)
Waddington Galleries
[Illustrated on p.121]

71
29 – 31 January: 1998
182 × 243.8 (72 × 96)
Waddington Galleries
[Illustrated on pp.130–1]

Selected Writings on Patrick Heron

Unless otherwise indicated, articles are reproduced here in the form in which they first appeared

On Patrick Heron's Striped Paintings

Alan Bowness

First published in 1968
in *Patrick Heron: A Retrospective Exhibition of Paintings 1957–66*, exhibition leaflet, Museum of Modern Art, Oxford

I can think of few more disconcerting pictures seen in England in the last twenty years than Patrick Heron's striped paintings of 1957. One must consider the circumstances in which they were first shown. It was at a curiously titled exhibition at the Redfern Gallery – *Metavisual Tachiste Abstract* – in April 1957. This was the year in the development of English painting when the abstract artists really began to make progress. It's hard to believe now, but not until the late fifties did abstract painting begin to be acceptable to artist and public alike, such was the strength of reactionary tendencies of the time, like the so-called 'social realism' of Bratby, Jack Smith and others, or David Bomberg's approach to realism that attracted such a fervent following.

So *Metavisual Tachiste Abstract* didn't get too warm a reception, and most of the critics, so far as I can remember, were more concerned with neologisms of nomenclature than with the paintings. It was, it must be admitted, something of a ragbag of an exhibition, which brought together almost everybody of consequence then painting abstract pictures, from embattled pioneers of some years standing like Nicholson and Pasmore, to very young painters like Ian Stephenson and Robyn Denny, not yet painting hard edge pictures. But the strength of the exhibition lay in what was later to be called the middle generation, and here the real outsiders of the early fifties like Davie and Hilton had been more recently joined as committed abstract painters by contemporaries such as William Scott, Bryan Wynter and Patrick Heron himself.

I have said that Heron's striped paintings were the most disconcerting in the exhibition. Certainly his conversion to abstraction attracted much comment at the time, most of it unfavourable. He had been too forthright an art critic for many people, and because he wrote art criticism his paintings were often dismissed as unserious and simply decorative. Heron had painted some abstract pictures in 1952, but the real change of style came in 1956. And when he did change he was accused somewhat paradoxically of both seeking originality for its own sake, and of slavishly copying the newly discovered American painters.

Matters were not improved when a large group of the striped paintings appeared at Heron's one man exhibition in February 1958 – his last at the Redfern Gallery. Virtually nothing was sold – which is why it has been relatively easy to bring most of the pictures together again for this exhibition at Oxford. Looking at them again ten years later one can understand why they were so upsetting. At that time qualities of paint texture and touch and expressive brushwork seemed to matter very much – indeed they were the things one looked for first in abstract painting. What was one to make of these parallel stripes of colour? Admittedly the structure reflects the movement of the painter's hand, and one could relate the brushstrokes to other pictures (including Heron's own garden paintings of 1956) which have a certain calligraphic quality. Yet this was all done with such lack of deliberate concern for texture and *matière*: the paint was so thin, and applied immediately to the canvas in a single stroke. All the artist seemed to be interested in was the relationship of these bands of colour echoing chords across or up and down the picture plane.

One should remember that these striped paintings were the first ever seen anywhere. We are now familiar with the idea from many sources, and in particular from the late pictures of Morris Louis, all done well after Heron's vertical bands, and just possibly (though not necessarily) dependent on them, as certain New York critics, magazines and dealers, had had photographs of Heron's work; and one influential American critic had actually seen such vertical stripe paintings as *Vertical Light: March 1957* [no.20] at Zennor in Cornwall before they were shown in London. Louis certainly painted some beautiful striped paintings, but, like too many American painters, he pursued a single idea in too ruthless and ultimately destructive a fashion.

Maybe it would have been better for Heron's international reputation had he gone on painting striped pictures from that day to this. He need scarcely have changed, and we would have read them in slightly different ways as the years passed, noticing at one point the quality of their edges, at another the form to ground relationship and so on. But Heron has never stood still – in fact his temperament compels him to look always for the contrary of what he is doing as a means of furthering his progress, or, if you like, to work from thesis to antithesis to synthesis in an everlasting sequence.

One can see this working itself out in the paintings of the last ten years – after the stripes, come paintings with an open ground of colour and elements floating in it, very complicated at first, but becoming extremely simple in 1961. However, the minute he achieves a kind of eloquent emptiness with isolated coloured shapes on a coloured ground, Heron seems to reject it as all too easy a solution, and we next find (in 1962) the ground itself being sliced up into different areas rather on the model of a Ben Nicholson. In turn this rigidity is rejected too, for a much looser construction where often a delicate balance is reached between form and ground so that the distinction disappears altogether.

It isn't easy to generalize, because of the variety of the pictures within the limits established by that challenging 1962 statement that 'of course it is obvious that colour is now the only direction in which painting can travel.' But there's no kind of programmatic quality about Heron's work, not even in the choice of colours. He doesn't consider physiological study of colour reaction as of particular consequence to the painter, preferring to regard anything as possible. And he tends to move from the sharply contrasting to the more monochromatic pictures without calculation, trusting a natural sensibility to guide him rather than any act of ratiocination.

Inevitably in such circumstances some paintings are more successful than others, just as some periods in the decade under review were much more productive. The very direct way the paintings are made allows no hesitation – the colour and line must be right straight away as no alteration is possible: the luminosity of the colour comes in part from its being laid in a single coat on a white ground. Of course painters don't necessarily improve as they become more skillful, but in Heron's case he does seem to me, unlike some of his contemporaries, to have gone on painting with conviction and certainly an increasing strength and beauty. That very unpopular stand which the vertical paintings represented in 1957 has been seen to be a central issue to the development of painting in our time.

Of course being right too early doesn't endear one to others who were later in seeing the light, and I don't feel that Heron has yet had his just recognition. The evidence for this is in his representation in public galleries – apart from the recently acquired vertical stripe painting, the Tate's choice has been of such uncharacteristic pictures that one suspects the whole point of Heron's art was either missed or rejected. And if some of the younger critics had longer memories they would realize that certain New Generation painters, much admired and rightly so, didn't spring up from nowhere.

But I don't want to end on this note, because the record will be put straight in time, and it's the paintings that count. And what we now see at Oxford are surely some of the most beautiful paintings done in England since the war, suffused with light and colour, and full of a positive life-enhancing quality so free and so refreshing. What better reminder at a time when we are soon to celebrate Matisse's centenary of the continuing validity of his dream of 'an art of balance, of purity and serenity, devoid of troubling and depressing subject matter . . .'

Patrick Heron: Recent Paintings and Selected Earlier Canvases

Alan Bowness

First published in 1972
as Introduction to *Patrick Heron: Recent Paintings and Selected Earlier Canvases*, exhibition catalogue, Whitechapel Art Gallery, London

One is told increasingly these days that painting is dead, overtaken by the rapidly developing new media that have proliferated in the twentieth century. But to a historian like myself this is a most improbable notion, for why should an activity that has been practised for millennia suddenly disappear in the 1970s? The fact is that painting remains, as it has always been, a difficult activity; that its tempo fluctuates, and we are passing through a period when the pace is slow. There is nothing particularly disturbing about this. The early twentieth century saw such a rapid development in the expressive language of painting once it had been freed from the task of representation, that it is hardly surprising if the rest of the century is needed to absorb these discoveries.

So I think we are wrong to look for the same kind of artist at work in the later part of the century that we found at the beginning, and perhaps the fact that we are expecting a certain pattern of artistic development can only have a deleterious effect upon the artist himself. If for example we take any of the great makers of modern art – Matisse or Picasso, Mondrian or Duchamp – we can point with exactitude to a brief historical moment when they produced a group of works that revolutionised art. It was a moment when they also established themselves as major artists, superior to their contemporaries, and the equal to great figures in the immediate past. Everything that follows such supreme moments must inevitably appear as a decline, or at best a repetition, a desperate maintaining of the standard set. In the nature of things you cannot do better, and whether one gives up altogether (Duchamp) or makes the practice of painting a compulsive obsession (Picasso) seems not to matter very much.

I have the suspicion that the grand gestures possible fifty and more years ago can't be made today. The revolutions of modern art have been institutionalised, so that we live in a state of permanent revolution where the word has lost its meaning. All the painter can do is to apprise the current situation, and act: which means, he must get on with his painting, however difficult and impossible this may seem. His field of action is likely to be circumscribed, which does not make it any less universal. The possibilities before him are certain to be restricted, which does not make them less worth investigating.

As far as the public is concerned, the painter of the later twentieth century is as likely to slowly impose his personality on his contemporaries as he is to suddenly break-through. That moment of break-through will continue to exist, as it must mark an essential stage in any artist's development. But I expect there to be a growing awareness about the stature of certain artists, a realisation that what may have seemed peripheral, even light-weight, in fact has a relevance and a fundamental seriousness which may surprise us.

It seems possible that this may be happening now in Patrick Heron's case. The evidence lies in the series of paintings made in the last three or four years. There was a fortuitous interruption in Heron's artistic development, when a serious accident in the summer of 1967 made it impossible for him to paint for a time. When he started again, he could work only on a small scale, and during 1968 painted little but gouaches. In retrospect, this was particularly valuable, because it resulted in an intensive period of research into compositional possibilities, and the emergence of certain new shapes and patterns. The rigidity of some of the earlier canvases disappeared before a fluency that was immediately obvious when Heron returned to the larger scale.

And of course the paintings are much bigger than before, partly in reaction against the time when only restricted work was possible. There is an excitement generated which I find very exhilarating, a boldness about the way these large areas are handled. The shapes of the canvases are not so different from what we have been accustomed to in Heron's work, but the scale is new, and this means that formerly congested elements in a composition can now expand and be stretched out across a wider arena. Space itself plays a larger part: in *Dark Red, Scarlet and Venetian: February 1972* [no.55] for example, everything is piled up on one side. In other pictures, things happen in the corners, or along the edges – busy areas that contrast with the open spaces elsewhere.

Colour remains the dominant interest, but there is less insistence on it than in the past, and clearly now composition, form, even line are equally the concern of the painter. There is no ground in the paintings: shapes are held suspended across the surface, colours are made to advance and recede in a constantly changing relationship. The meeting place of one coloured area with another has a new importance, and one is now aware that the edges form a line that twists and turns, describing a new kind of shape. Drawing assumes again that crucial rôle it played in Heron's very early work. Altogether there seems to me to be a much greater richness in the new pictures: they have gained in complexity without losing their directness and simplicity. They show a direction in which this kind of art can fruitfully move, at a moment when, as we have seen, there is a tendency to feel that all lines of progress have been tried and found exhausted.

This isn't the time or place for a retrospective of Patrick Heron's work, and the emphasis in the exhibition is firmly placed on the new paintings. But the Whitechapel Gallery is large, and there was room for more than just the most recent work. For several reasons I suggested to the artist that he show a group of paintings done in 1957–58. These have not been seen in London since they were first exhibited (and not all of them were). At that time they met with about as derisory a reception as any twentieth-century British artist has had to face. Bands of colour were not in 1957 the pictorial cliché they later became: on the contrary these were paintings of a remarkable originality and beauty as at least a few perceptive artists and critics were able to recognise. But in general the reaction was one of bewilderment, mixed with disappointment, that anyone with Heron's talents and reputation should suddenly move in this particular direction. In fact, it wasn't a sudden move – there had even been a brief proto-abstract period in 1952 – but it did certainly mark a decisive and historical shift from the French orientated earlier work to paintings that consciously reacted to the challenge that the new American painting represented.

At the time one was told that Heron was simply following Rothko. Now if this means that he was exceptionally quick to appreciate Rothko's quality and his importance, it is true, and there are indeed a few pictures which show the absorption of this influence. But the striped paintings of 1957 and the open paintings that immediately succeeded them are not really like Rothko at all, and the American paintings they do now recall are later in date. Speaking as someone who has known them from the time that they were painted, they seem to me to have got better year by year, assuming an authority that comes with age. I am inclined to claim now that Heron's paintings of 1957–58 are a major statement by a major British artist, and they occupy in the context of their time a situation analogous to William Scott's black and white pictures of 1954, or, to go further back into the past, Ben Nicholson's white reliefs of 1936.

It might be thought that this assessment of the striped paintings as Heron's break-through contradicts what was said at the beginning of this short introduction, and the design of the exhibition, setting the new work against a specially chosen group of early pictures, is in fact meant to test the very assumption made there. The artist runs the risk of being told that the new work is a falling-off, exactly as he was told in 1957–58. I don't believe this is true at all, but it seems a risk worth taking, even if only to be proved right long after the event. The two groups of painting must be essentially different in character, coming as they do at quite different stages in the artist's career. Certainly the early pictures do mark the artist's personal break-through, and this has given them a kind of talismanic quality that they will never lose. But I believe that Heron has the temperament and the intelligence to build on what he has achieved, without either rejecting it or diminishing it by repetition. He is exceptionally articulate about painting – as his own notes in this catalogue make very clear – and he understands better than anyone perhaps the social and historical situation in which the modern artist finds himself. (Thus the temptation to play the part of representative, which he does superlatively well, but which I think he should resist.)

An artist today faces a problem of survival; by this I do not mean that he should stretch a thin talent over a lifetime when everything has been said in a few years, but that he must, consciously or unconsciously, evolve an art that has in it the possibilities of fruitful and continuing development. Many of the best painters at work in England today are, like Heron, doing just this. It cannot be easy for them when they are expected to conform to the now outdated early twentieth century pattern of sudden emergence in a blaze of genius, followed by a long period of decline. I hope however that this exhibition will be seen to prove the contrary, and more generous, proposition.

Patrick Heron: The 1970s

James Faure Walker

First published in 1985
in *Patrick Heron*,
exhibition catalogue,
Barbican Art Gallery

What happens in a painting by Patrick Heron? What first comes to mind is a shimmering heat-haze of cobalt violet engulfing a lop-sided red disc. The disc is set low and somewhere to the left of the centre of the painting, and you register this shift of the centre of gravity – the disc's role is that of a visual touch-stone – all the time your eye explores the periphery. It functions like a magnet, but has a blunt time-worn look, like the flattened profile of a pebble, or a rock seen from far above so that only its contour and the eccentric wiggles of the coastline betray the work of a pounding sea. You are dimly aware of these analogies with natural forces – the shapes all look organic, shaped with the same rhythm – but what confronts you is too energetic for a landscape painting; the colour is hard and mineral in character. The sensation, even the stab of green, is unnaturally hot – the volatility of the red wobbling as it abuts the green, the drowsy radiance of the disc feeding into the violet. For a while this violet absorbs all your attention. Like the red it is very flat and unyielding – there are no apertures or punctures of white in the surface. But it isn't featureless, or opaque. The twisting squiggles of a small thumb-sized brush have whirled the cobalt pigment (which painters use for its grainy translucency) into knobbly ridges, and the varying thickness allows slight variations of density in the violet – like a musical vibrato sounding against the constant pitch of the red. Stepping back you sense this vibration as a subliminal murmur. You become preoccupied with more complicated wobbles and weavings – a deeper red fingering its way into the violet from the right, the green kidney-shape, an offshoot of the disc, that alternately looks like invader and invaded within its interlocking red. You compare the two reds, the way they appear more solid than the other colours though they are no thicker in texture – a smooth sheen runs across their surface, trembles at the edge.

Heron's paintings reached this state of maximum saturation in the seventies, and somehow as they crystallised into their now familiar configurations they grew more mobile. For over ten years he imposed a strict discipline on the way he painted. First, in the space of a few seconds, he would draw in the outlines of the shapes in Pentel. This would become the wobbling hard-edge, sharp or soft depending on whether the colours it divided were complementary or sympathetic. By the shapes it cut out and the way it sculpted its way around and across the surface it determined the possible structures – what kind of underlying rhythm, where the dominant masses would be. With the outline set – it wouldn't be altered – the act of painting consisted in deciding one by one what colour to paint the areas, and filling them in using colour straight from the tube laboriously brushed (with Zen-like absorption in the task) into place, right up to the edge, with small Japanese brushes. No area would be overpainted – the particular kind of brilliance he wanted depended on the pigment being tightly packed in with just one coat – and no white areas would be left unpainted or to function as white – white, like black and grey, was excluded from his palette. Throughout this period less than a dozen colours were used, none being mixed or reduced with white, though not all the colours were spectral – the rich earthiness of Venetian red, the colour of fertile soil, is a frequent foil for the pure reds of cadmiums, and dull oxide of chromium green sounds a solid base for lemon yellow. Few paintings contain more than five colours. What modulates and distorts the colour – apart from the way it is spread by the brush – is the inter-action of hue, the tightness of the edge, and the rhythmic pulse of the line this edge weaves about the surface.

Till the mid-sixties his paintings were more obviously open and luminous, genial rather than concentrated. Forms tended to merge rather than compete, and there wasn't this electric alertness. The paint was fluid, lightly dabbed or casually swept. Whether knitting an outline of a harbour window or distilling cool purities of hue from blending swathes of red and turquoise, everything depended on improvisation and reflex response to the configuration that formed in the liquid paint. Nothing was intentionally rigid, edges were indefinite, and an airy impressionistic effect was often achieved by juxtaposing line with floating colour patches, and letting the light of the white ground filter through the interstices. Stylistically, too, it was more open and relaxed, as if there was just one all-embracing world of painting – rather than a babble of competing voices – where sensibilities could meet and overlap. All the same, the phases of the fifties do look transitional and incomplete in comparison with what was to follow, and the kinship with Braque, Bonnard, Matisse, or even Scott and Rothko, is often a minor compensation when the structure is loose, the colour key undecided.

Here and there in Heron's earlier critical writings you catch a glimpse of some principle of pictorial structure or leitmotif that might not be fully realised in his own painting till twenty years later. There's a little sketch in *The Changing Forms of Art* of a typical Henry Moore profile, what Heron calls a 'semi-submerged crankshaft motif' with a Mexican square-round quality, like a fossil, or a sea-worn rock, that would fit straight into a seventies painting. The hard-worked texture of these paintings, the pigment rhythmically pressed into place like clay, comes to mind when reading the essay in the same volume on Bernard Leach, 'Submerged Rhythm' – Leach's 'intuitive apprehension of life', 'asymmetry of organic form', and total engrossment in abstract rhythm felt through handling and acknowledging inherent material properties. The pot's anatomy of foot, belly, shoulder, neck, mouth and lip, seems to describe Heron's geography.

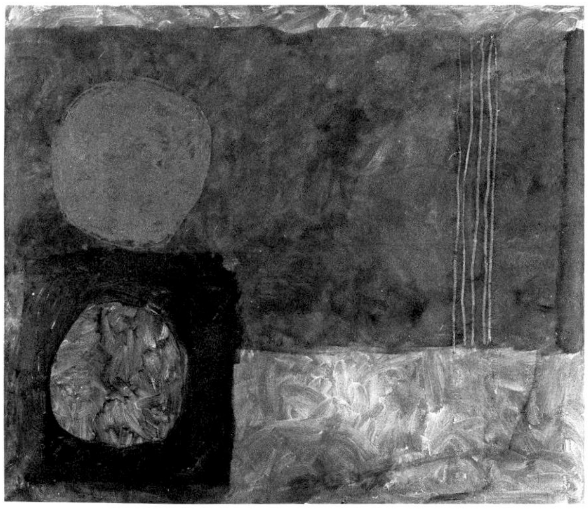

fig.20 **Blue November Painting: 1963** Oil on canvas 152.4 × 182.9 cm Basildon Arts Trust, Essex

Heron's disc and rectangle permutations are the descendants of Ben Nicholson's reliefs – and painted in the same studio in St Ives after Heron took it over in 1958. But Heron eliminated the empty framing areas and used the external edge of the canvas as though it were an internal form – he consistently made a point of the need to keep a painting as alive at the edge as at the centre, citing Bonnard as the master of this, and suggesting the absence of a gripping edge was a weakness in Pollock and de Kooning when he wrote on them in 1956. By the seventies Heron had fully absorbed the expansive scale and broad empty areas, lessons learnt from American painting, but his language was still more reminiscent of Nicholson's architecture, though distorted and flaunting colours that Nicholson's fastidious taste suppressed. Heron had been quite critical of Nicholson, contrasting his 'weak airy ghosts' with Braque's 'intense grip'; he commented on his hesitant, superficial rhythms which achieved only a 'brittle unity', a 'weak pulse', his 'chaste' profiles and 'coy waist-lines'; and was ambivalent as to whether the dilute colouring, 'the over-clean 'washedness' of the cool colours', could be excused because of the 'connection' that Nicholson insisted upon with the light and textures of 'Atlantic-blown' St Ives – when direct it could be 'too picturesque'.[1] By the seventies Heron's own airiness and lightness of touch had given way to a much firmer tread, the colour hot-blooded, the interpenetration of forms sometimes openly erotic, and he can speak with confidence of his own connection with the landscape – addressing an American audience in Texas in 1978 – 'I don't doubt for a moment that the enormously powerful rhythmic energies of the granite outcrops beneath my feet transmit certain rhythms straight up through the soles of my shoes every minute of the day.'[2]

Temperamentally Heron was closer to the intuitive lyricism of Ivon Hitchens, the paint fluid and spontaneously brushed, the colour full and pulsing with a plein air buoyancy. Heron's stripe paintings almost overlap with Hitchens' – those gliding shifts of hue, like a cloud passing overhead unseen. The first of Heron's organic geometry paintings to re-introduce a drawn line, Plymouth's *Rectilinear Reds and Blues: 1963* [no.41], is uncannily close in feel to Hitchens' 1937 *Coronation* – a coincidence no doubt, but suggestive of the affinities (they became close friends) that could emerge from a common source in Braque. Heron's book on Hitchens, also of 1955, rated him the major painter of his generation, the one who broke from the 'insular idiosyncrasies' of English painting with its weak formal sense and literary tastes, the one closest to 'the broader and more robust traditions of European art'. You can agree with this judgement on both counts, yet it is also true – and there are parallels with Heron's situation in the seventies when he became as attached to Penwith as to a modern painting mainstream – that Hitchens' self-reliance and affection for a small repertoire of local motifs left him an isolated figure, somewhat rigid and idiosyncratic in his endlessly repeated idiom. Describing Hitchens' painting he could have been describing his own wobbly hard-edge paintings – 'colour … the vibrant generator of space … that controlled vibrancy, that punch of the full saturation of colour'. And in listing Hitchens' occasional lapses – 'in the direction of fluidity of form … a failure to substantiate his surface forms … too animated for their three-dimensional, illusionistic content' – he might have been voicing doubts about what was facing him at the time in his own studio.

In the seventies his writings and lectures are clearly centred on his own work, and his analyses of how colour behaves can be obsessively descriptive. Except for the polemical forays against British subservience to American self-promotion, or perhaps because of that and because of withdrawing from the role of critic, his later writings are no longer so penetratingly critical; Heron no longer writes as a detached observer sniffing out weaknesses and strengths. But despite the exhaustive accounts of the effect of a square inch where lemon abuts orange, there are still discrepancies between what is being said and what actually happens in the paintings, and much that happens isn't – or cannot be – mentioned at all. The creator of the paintings, he speaks as if he were a third party, watching his hand reveal the contours, animate the surface with its scribble, as if the painting was in command; and of course this is what it feels like to be absorbed in a painting: it takes you outside of yourself, your identity dissolves into the painting so that you think of it as facing you, making demands. Heron describes the experience as becoming lost in the world of the visual, and his terms are optical rather than Jungian. Not that they shouldn't be, but arguably to see the visible world as a surface pattern of luminous colour-patches, as painters may have to, is also to detach yourself emotionally from it.

Necessarily Heron speaks of means rather than ends, of how one painting differs from another rather than about what is constant. But the persistence of his motifs, the constant disc, the interweavings of the rigid with the malleable, the vitalist undercurrents – sometimes too deliberate to carry an effective pulse – the qualities of light and good health he has made his own, all these invite some kind of imaginative interpretation even though it need not be spelled out. He signals his dedication to colour in bold major chords, and catalogue notes – significantly he develops the habit of quoting from his own writing at the same time as his pictorial vocabulary begins to solidify – but you could argue he overstates his case: that he isn't a colourist in the true sense but someone who uses colour in a special way, as quantifiable parcels of energy; the colour isn't transformed, it sits on the surface as visibly handled oil paint; it doesn't stain, smoulder, or blend with the canvas; it doesn't evaporate, melt, smoulder, glow, look sugary, succulent, sour, perfumed – it almost does but your attention is always brought back to the handling, the line, the tense edge feeling its way from soft to hard like an uncertain hand, to the optical ambiguities, the silhouette that becomes an opening, the embrace of shape with shape. My point isn't to contradict what Heron has said about the inseparability of shape and colour – and I would argue that he is an enormously accomplished colourist – but to suggest that his absorption in the optical behaviour of forms – which is the spectator's point of contact with the paintings – need not be understood as the whole story. You could follow every change of brush angle that announced the arrival of a new idiom, another step on the path towards the mature style; you could list formal principles that recur in the writings; you could track down every harbour-shape to a Wallis, every leaf to a Matisse cut-out; and you still might not grasp the aesthetic at the centre, the rationale informing the whole cell structure. You would not understand why expressionism and surrealism held no interest for him; why there was no place for struggle, anguish, darkness; why he couldn't be reconciled with values he saw as 'American' – though it has often been American recognition that he has most valued.

In 1975 seven recent paintings were shown at Waddington's. At the time you came to expect a certain orderliness from a Heron, and in fact the predictable variations on given forms were in danger of becoming clichés. But here the colour continents – in the familiar reds, greens, violets, tightly scribbled inside the one-minute doodle – seemed to be slipping out of place. The equilibrium was lost. The vertical edges of the canvases couldn't cope with a dominant diagonal and its ragged cavorting. In another there was no disc but an agitated cloud shape, like a Chinese pattern. Till then forms would remain in one plane if they touched – often they keep their distance from each other. Occasionally they would appear to overlap, but surreptitiously. Here the illusion of overlapping strips of green and red was pronounced. Heron had spoken of re-introducing complication, and in 1978 described 'the almost hallucinatory delights of the pure sensation we may have of the colour of colours'. Here shapes were wobbling and warping on your retina, floating and shredding into islands, propelled with a life of their own, nibbling at each other, pulsating with red-green flickers.

At the same time as that 1975 exhibition another was held close-by at the Rutland Gallery featuring paintings from 1956 to 1966, some never before having been seen in this country though exhibited in New York. On the whole these paintings were better received. For several painters they were a revelation.[3] And yet these were self-evidently formative works, embryonic versions of the distinctive hard-edge configurations. Here the colour was often pale and close-toned, more suggestively luminous, and various; the oblongs and circles were soft-edged and didn't spring so instantly into view; and the compositions weren't as schematic though Nicholson devices made several appearances. Each painting seemed to have been caught in the act of painting, taken by surprise by some juxtaposition of colour stirred about on the canvas – one reason the edges were blurry was that blocks of colour were expanded or contracted, swallowed up by engulfing fields, as the painting progressed. The facture was on the whole thin and easy-going, with different colours intermingling on the surface, with foggy opacities giving way to hues as clear and cool as morning light. Heron's feelings must have been mixed, as the enthusiastic response to these paintings – in which polemics played no part – was accompanied by a rejection of the more ambitious, but less instantly seductive, recent work. Some critics disliked the way the surface was worked, or the combination of wiggling shape and hard-edge; others recoiled from the shrill complementaries of saturated colour, finding them garish and brittle in comparison with the impressionistic oblongs. Not everyone responded that way, of course, but the juxtaposition did place a question-mark over the paintings of the seventies as a whole; unjustly, in my view, as prejudices against 'tight' painting were blinding people to their true qualities. At the time 'conceptualist' doctrines were in the ascendant and painters found themselves trapped in defensive enclaves, burnishing minimal surfaces or frantically spattering and sponging in pursuit of some ultimate painterliness. Heron's new work didn't look the way 'good painting' was supposed to look. It stimulated the wrong taste buds.

In retrospect the differences of idiom throughout Heron's career come to look less significant and it becomes puzzling to understand why contemporary taste could on occasion put up such a resistance. Heron's painting comes to look all of a piece, to breathe the same air in the same rhythm, to be naturally ebullient, fresh, alive with an innocent delight. Nowhere is this spontaneous delight more radiant than in the gouaches of the seventies, where nothing appears rehearsed, and barriers between segments momentarily breakdown and jets of pigment flow into each other. Painters who have thought better of their original 'Bric-a-Braque' or 'kindergarten colour' put-downs have come round to see how much understanding can be invested in Heron's apparent hedonistic simplicity. In 1958 artworld taste didn't know what to make of the stripe paintings at the Redfern Gallery, and in the seventies a Tate curator thought 1957 must be a mistake and put 1967 on the label. In the sixties there were ambitious hard-edge painters who found the St Ives middle generation too attached to Cornish romance, not sufficiently hard-headed and abstract – their measure came from New York. Yet in 1960, recalls Irving Sandler,[4] when Patrick Heron lectured at the Artists' Club in New York, the audience was surprised by the detached formalism of his talk; they were acclimatised to romantic rhetoric and it was rather unconventional to describe paintings in terms of flat surface pattern. Today, it seems, our view of Heron's work is still blocked by prejudice as critics take up new positions at odds with its values. For many students it is precisely the modest scale and the cosy romanticism of coastal imagery, however latent, that makes the St Ives painters a discovery – especially Lanyon's aerated whites and blues, and Hilton's disruptive drawing. Every abstraction is assumed to derive from emanations of local spirits (if it isn't a subjective map of the harbour) and – ironically – Heron tends to be too 'American'. Taste has once more retreated to the literary comforts of Englishness, the dreary introspection, secretive and mean in its forms, shy of the sunlight – those same 'insular idiosyncrasies' that frustrated Heron all those years ago. Not that this matters, because Heron's best paintings have a knack of always being refreshing – the fifties paintings don't have that crusty period look of many of his colleagues. At the Tate's *St Ives* exhibition it was Heron's *Big Cobalt Violet: May 1972* [no.56] that took my breath away, not just because as an optical sensation it was overpowering, a physical presence, not one triggered by association through images or gestural friction; it was because its determined ambitiousness set it free from the lingering diffidence that permeated through so much else there. It took painting into a different dimension.

This exhibition will provide an opportunity to get a comprehensive view of the paintings of the eighties, and to see to what extent the precarious stylistic rigidity of the seventies – which brought wonderful dividends before Heron found himself trapped – has been loosened. There are all the indications: the scribbling brush is louder, underpainting breaks through the surface, dabs of pink modulate a flat yellow, and his palette has opened up to include very pale tints. But much of the change is superficial. The new lyricism – which on occasion looks as if flourishes of brushwork are bobbing to the tunes of the School of Paris as they did in the early fifties – still keeps within the same contours, and the disc, sea and coastline/crank-shaft are still there. Speaking of these new paintings Heron mentioned being struck by the changes of mind and improvisation Matisse's *Bathers by a River* of 1916–17 betrayed when he saw it close-up in Chicago, how the mistakes showed; and he was also overwhelmed by the Bonnard show in Paris last year, the range of his yellows. He reached a point where he could no longer bring himself to fill in the final white of a painting; he had to scribble with his brush, deface the immaculate surface, escape from the prison of his method. The new paintings risk looking artfully unfinished, and the rebellious brushwork is kept under control by the overall schema, but their sense of adventure is undeniable. Snap judgements on new phases rely on previous preferences for this or that kind of surface treatment, and the oddness of some new and unlikely combination can initially be offputting. The new paintings work much more slowly on the eye, make it ask the questions, make it find a passageway through hedged-in textures – like wandering around a kitchen-garden without knowing what you are looking for. They are the most meditative paintings he has painted for a long time. Sometimes he seems to try and recall every phase of his development in the one painting – the self-conscious recollecting inhibiting the spontaneity. It's as if he wants the whole range of his sensibility to be contained within the one work. Previously each idiom has taken just one facet and exaggerated it so that it became irreconcilable with another side of his nature. Those gloriously awkward floods of competing colour-shapes of the seventies sealed out any airy lyricism – they were hermetic, closed organisms, nervy thoroughbreds. The new paintings may be a little more jerry-built and diffuse, but they will be a little more focused on the enduring problems of reconciling opposites, containing the serene and the agitated within a unified whole, and the balance may turn out to be quieter and a little more philosophical.

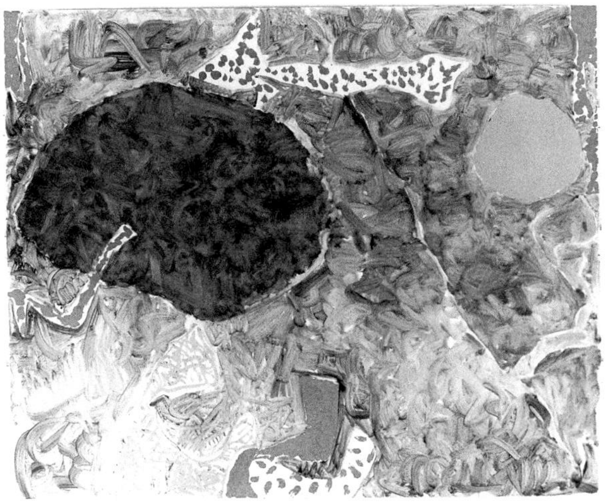

fig.21 **Manganese Blue with Spotted Red Arrow: June 1982**
Oil on canvas 121.9 × 152.4 cm
Private Collection

1 'Five Types of Abstraction – Ben Nicholson', *The Changing Forms of Art*, 1955, p.191.

2 'Brushwork is Spatial', *The Colour of Colour*, E. William Doty Lectures in Fine Arts, University of Texas at Austin, 1978, p.26.

3 Alan Gouk's 1982 essay on Heron (*Artscribe*, nos.34 and 35), itself a *tour de force* of critical writing, was first set in motion by seeing these paintings; and in the *Hayward Annual* exhibition chosen by John Hoyland (1980), a few Heron paintings of this period had an honorary place, looking remarkably calm.

4 Irving Sandler interviewed by James Faure Walker, *Artscribe*, no.33.

Recent Paintings

Alan Gouk

First published in 1985
in *Patrick Heron*, exhibition catalogue, Barbican Art Gallery

Always at the commencement of work that first innocence must be re-achieved; you must return to that unsophisticated spot where the angel discovered you when he brought you the first blinding message … if the angel deigns to come, it will be because you have convinced him, not with tears, but with your resolve to be always beginning; to be a beginner.
Rilke

An artist must recognise, when he is reasoning, that his picture is an artifice, but when he is painting, he should feel that he has copied nature.
Matisse

'Utter directness'[1] of attack, fluency of handling, the final design a genuine discovery as varying quantities of colour are adjusted to one another and to the shape of the canvas, – 'a sensuous subtlety of tone colour, a subtle asymmetry of shape, a varied tempo of working',[2] – these are the hall marks of Patrick Heron's best paintings of the '50s and '60s.

And though none of these in themselves guarantee that a work will rise above the hopeful norm, since the remedial spoonful of 'spontaneity' has become a contemporary 'disease',[3] what marks Heron's best paintings out is the extent to which the first and freshest impulses (to organise and arrange) become the unadorned pictorial means, the defining architectonic scaffold of the pictorial idea itself. Directness and the idea are one, economically stated, and discovered in the economy of stating it. (I am thinking of *Scarlet, Lemon and Ultramarine: March 1957* [no.21], *Vertical Light: March 1957* [no.20], or *Incandescent Skies (Yellow and Rose): December 1957*.)

Here, as in all the best things, happily arising as it were independently of the artist's volition like a fragrance from the surface of the work itself, there comes the disarmingly wayward visage of the really new.

These pictures, and others like them, have the exquisite frankness of some virgin and irrepressible power welling up innocent within the artist. The marks, the thoughts which they anticipate and register, the bringing together of intuitions of a possible new order of things, have the exhilaration of someone who has at last tumbled upon on his own subject.[4] Hence the perfect fitting of a sensuous at-homeness with the simplest uses of the means, and an open responsiveness to the morning beneficence which each day's sun throws upon experience, and a raising of feeling to the level of it.

The resonance of this experience can be felt as an afterglow influencing the colour and touch, the underlying rhythm of the design[5] of picture after picture for a good many years thereafter.

By the mid-sixties, a certain logic of decision began to put constraints on this favoured practice. What at first may have seemed to be an increasing boldness and clarity of outline, daring with colour, inadvertently was leading to a narrowing logic of painterly option in somewhat the following manner.

There was Heron's realisation that it was the drawn character of the frontier between colour areas which determined the apparent colour of the areas on either side of it. Allied to this, and partly as a consequence of it, was his commitment to an ever increasing frankness of hue, straight from the tube, allied to a once-only paint application directly to brilliant white priming, and with it, a sharper edge to the meeting of colours, a method which precluded adjustment and overpainting.

> *A colour is most intense when it is delimited; and the sharper the boundaries or frontiers or linear edges which delimit it are, the more intense that colour will be.*[6]

There was also a concern for a drawing-dance complication of the contours and interlocking of shapes themselves.

Now it may seem paradoxical to describe all this as a narrowing of possibility, but in terms of painterly fluency, what Heron was denying himself were all those surprising and predictable intermixings of colour, and interweavings of design on the canvas in the course of painting which often constitute the really innovative aspect for the artist himself, wherein 'he surprises himself by seeing, for the first time, a new rhythmical statement (in terms of his medium) which *embodies* his beloved subject-matter'.[7]

As Heron himself had written, in 1949: 'The quality of vitality in art is something very closely connected with risk, with pure daring. The artist who never feels, as he starts a new picture, that this time he is tempting madness to envelop him – such an artist is no artist at all'; and he continued 'It is one of the ecstasies of painting – this independence of the hand from the brain! The brain tells the hand 'Draw in that tree, or that jug, but only use one brushload'. Then the hand rushes in rapid circles, makes dashes and dots and sudden lines of unexpected severity or weight. And suddenly the painter sees the mess that his hand has made of the job he gave it and he finds it is marvellous; and that is the ecstasy. Indeed, he finds it is far better than anything he could have thought out in advance and thought out only *in his head*. So painting is thinking with one's hand; or with one's arm; in fact with one's whole body!'[8]

Elsewhere he wrote: 'from all this I conclude that, if one focuses the whole of one's conscious mind on one aspect of a creative problem, one's natural instinct will thus be freed to resolve things on another level and in its own terms. And I think this means, in relation to painting, that if the artist concentrates his mind upon his vision, his hand will take care of all those complex matters of design of which the finished painting primarily consists. One *cannot* consider a question of pictorial architecture in cold blood – one *cannot* measure one form against another, as a cold calculation of mere design. The result will always be a dead design. One can only record the pictorial configuration from the standpoint of one's vision, one's deepest feeling. And, as I've tried to suggest, one's vision may be felt before it is seen ... It is felt before it is seen – for the simple reason that it cannot be seen until one's hand has created it on canvas'.[9]

Heron had cut down the range of spontaneous action, had reduced these freedoms, to the received shock of seeing what would happen when he had committed himself to the choice of a particular colour for an area, and, when infilled, its chiming with its neighbours or in some cases, undoubtedly, not chiming with its neighbours, though not chiming may of course be only another way of chiming. 'Today's dissonance is tomorrow's assonance.'[10] And this method carried its own area of risk, its own unpredictability as the various gambles drew towards that ultimate gamble when the final white area had been painted in. But what of the long range interaction of colours at distances across surface? If no adjustments are allowed, it becomes a nerve-racking business fearing that it is impossible to be sure in advance one has made the right choice. Painting in fact became more of a strain, and a certain brittleness of design and paint application was its outward expression – a certain inward-looking wilfulness to the patterning of the brush-infilling which led up to these careful frontiers, which consequently did not have the rhythmic freedom of being brush-drawn laterally in broad movements related to the canvas as a whole, as formerly.

Heron was using so many reds, oranges, violets, yellows and greens, at such a pitch and of such equal temperature, that it is hard indeed to see them as one. Single colour areas tend to stamp themselves on the eye with such finality that they hang there like silhouetted lanterns on a string, scarves or tongues of flame, waving slightly in and out of depth, in a manner which calls to mind a Calder mobile; while the broader expanses of evenly-textured brush-writhing are strained to buckling to pull them back up onto the surface again. This is an inadvertent paradox of the somewhat feckless logic which was leading Heron by the nose in these paintings, or rather which the commitment to a particular chain of processes of painting was leading him.

The aim of the best painting now, from the time of *The Creation of the Sun, Moon and Planets*, to this, is nothing other than the representation of space; not empty space out there, not 'that vacuous background of neutral nothingness',[11] and not mechanically crossed, formula-flat, literal-extension space either; but tangible, particular, pressingly intimate space, inscaped space, charged with imagination and the artist's empathy with the spirit of place, with which he has identified his body, and all the contradictory pullings of his imagination working within his senses – vertiginous, irradiating, space with a cutting edge, sharp as a knife, stretching and spreading, expansive as a damask tablecloth, yet suddenly cut across like a shaft of daylight, containing fierceness, and the harsh brilliance of natural light and air; space as a rhythm of reconciliation, as the conscious artifices of picture-making come to terms with the involuntary promptings of the body.

How much of this formulation is owed to Heron himself, enthusiasts will know.

Space and light – real light. Every time one sees for the

first time a new Matisse painting, for instance, and often on re-seeing a familiar one, there is that sudden shock of surprise at how true and definitive is the chord of values encapsulated there; strangely changed by the transmutative workings of true art, but still a moment of nature (and of the artist), a surprising concordance between improbable elements, arising in the artist's feeling, out of feeling the object from a contemplative standpoint at a certain remove from the visual data. Consider *The Snail*, for instance. I had recently been having another look at the origins of Cubism, and went to the Tate to see the early Braques and Picassos. Wandering through the adjacent rooms, I was stopped in my tracks by *The Snail* of Matisse. I have been rather dead to this work for some time. It is perhaps only after steeping oneself in the artificial dinginess and the wilful complications of analytical Cubism that *The Snail*'s qualities reassert themselves through the iconic blankness it has acquired.

How sure Matisse's instincts were when he recoiled from the first intimation of Cubism, sensing that a re-complication and cerebration of the processes of painting were in the air. But this time it struck me with renewed force what it is that Matisse rings from the cutting edge of each of the gouache-saturated papers, as if each colour more than stands for, is charged with, has imbibed and re-presents a whole world of physical sensation even with these minimal means; no illusion of a third dimension, but somehow the evocation of great spaciousness, the quality in painting which has most to be desired before it can be felt and thence created.

There is no under-accounting the extent to which Matisse's long engagement with sculpture is sublimated into the placement of these papers, through this new entrancement with the sensation of scissors cutting into colour, and then the tangible pleasure of offering up these panes of the stuff of colour/substance/form for spatial ends – a very anti-cubist picture, for all its seeming affinity to synthetic Cubism. It differs markedly from the newly acquired Miró, which presents so emphatically a locked-out, somewhat Cubist influenced spaceless surface, or rather one whose space is almost literally that of the physically modulated scrub-brushed surface itself. Whereas, note how important are the openings of white around which the centrifugal design revolves in the Matisse. That such openings are in themselves shapes of positive pressure as well as of colour, is something which Heron has long known. It has been one of the strongest features of his own painting, at times amounting almost to an obsession. 'I believe absolutely in what I call the formal equality of all parts of the painting. To me, no section of the picture surface should be less of a shape than any other'. And his is not the artificial dinginess of studio intellected colour, or the artificial false brightness either. Anyone who doubts this has not taken into account the white brilliance of the natural light in which the paintings were painted, of which Heron has written so eloquently. Apropos of Ben Nicholson and St Ives he spoke of 'the white ocean-reflected light which almost bleaches things in its diffuse radiance'[12] and recently, describing the landscape visible directly in front of his Zennor home, he said 'the sea is then a gigantic mirror, brilliantly silver, and reflecting white light upwards. To have the rocks and the bushes illuminated from below, from a glittering reflector which is over 600 feet beneath one, and many miles wide – is a special experience'.[13]

The sometime stridency of Heron's colour is a seeking for some more elemental response to the spirit of place, the radiant brilliance of the light of the Cornish coast which has filled his entire living environment from 1956 onwards. Not a descriptive response, but a response in kind, in terms of the unique properties of pure pigment, purely applied to pure canvas. As de Staël said and as Heron must have noticed, 'the point when history becomes really thrilling is the moment when one grasps the Braques in the light in which they were painted – that kind of diffuse and violent light which the painting receives all the better for the ability to resist'.[14] The better the colour in a painting and the stronger the light, the better the painting stands up to it. This is a fact which most painters protect themselves against by one subterfuge or another.

The eye of a painter is an animal eye, operating according to an animal impulse. It selects from the visual spectacle only what it needs, according to an instinct for the new and different, the onward of painting, according to a sixth sense for the truly original, a nose for the correct demanded direction; and the pioneer is he who not only pushes his own painting forward, but who pushes forward the frontiers of painting itself. 'A common style is one which makes us exclaim, not "this is a man of genius using the language", but "this realises the genius of the language."' (T. S. Eliot).[15]

It is not a dramatic newness, being only in terms of true art but it can have startling consequences. In good painting now, the colour just sits there, right in and at the surface – anti-spatial in one way, in that nothing drops back into fictive depth – but utterly spatial in another. The whole image is space-creating, or space-sculpting, a space sculpted in terms of the purely pictorial. And the colour is fresh and real, redolent of real light as it falls on the unique qualities of the surface of objects. Colours drift away, and then drift back again, momentarily cutting disruptively into sight, peeling the surface away as a knife would an orange, then how right and necessary that tonic corrective is seen to be. There is an utterly fluent interchange of all the elements in the painting, a staccato visual dance finally resolving itself in harmony and calm. And so something surprisingly, unnervingly new is affirmed – a new vision of pictorial possibility, a new and altogether unexpected kind of unity.

This tonic corrective to the oh so knowing about painting, to the habituated expectations of educated good taste, would not exist without unrest being created at the same time; but a purely pictorial unrest. Since we all know what good painting looks like, a really new painting will inevitably trouble the eye in precisely that area where the eye is most engaged, but where it has come to expect rest, or where the brain has found itself a groove of, in effect, unseeing acceptance. That is the job of painting, working with and against the datum of continuous surface, being led to see that surface in a new way, to engage the eye, to extend it into areas where it has never been before, with the one question – can all this conceivably co-exist within the one image? is it whole? – to trouble the eye for a time, and then to return it to rest, the brain having left off wondering somewhere along the way. The unrest is part of the novelty at work. Which brings me to Heron's new paintings.

Heron has never been a painterly painter in one sense. He has always been uncomfortable with a built-up paint surface, cubist-derived sculptural effects of planar layering, or the 'tactile space' of painting as a kind of physical object. It was the more decorative aspect of Braque to which he was drawn. His painting has been uncompromisingly linear and flat even at its most fluent. Indeed it has been the speed and fluency of the drawing in his figurative work of the '50s that has been both his most original stroke, and his most problematical and awkward, to eyes nurtured on the subtle volumetric suggestiveness of the Parisian masters, Matisse, Braque, Picasso and Bonnard.

But beginning around 1980, the somewhat uncharacteristic meticulousness which had driven the paintings of the '70s began to be overtaken once more by the rebellious promptings of arm and hand.

It is the mark of a truly adventurous spirit that he throws his reputation into the balance with each new group of paintings; not yet another performance of self-assumed mastery, using one's accomplishment to charm and flourish, but a true beginning again. 'He has again and again put his whole art in question unbiased by his past achievement,' is how Roger Fry put it, speaking of Matisse.[16]

In one of the earliest, and one of the best, of the new paintings [fig.22], a lemon yellow scrub-brushed orb is surrounded by an *eau-de-nil* 'sea', comprised of a number of over-paintings (the new work is no longer all straight from the tube, nor all *alla prima*) in which one can subliminally discern the presence of some lemon striations and over which has been drawn, by squeezings from the tube, zig-zag lines of green. And straight away, by this device, which calls to mind Van Gogh, a whole area of the canvas irradiates with a single unified, pleasantly queasy sensation, like the ripples on the surface of a pond after a stone has been thrown. The *eau-de-nil* zone abuts abruptly against a very differently textured scribble-brushed shaft which cuts obliquely from top to bottom of the canvas, and hence is crowded to one side a cluster of sharper flatter shapes, scurrying and clawing, loosely tied by flecks and commas and wriggled squeezings.

Another early new work operates in a similar way; this time a cobalt violet (I nearly said violent) ball-of-fire is savagely contained within a sea of lime yellow, but the way in which both the ball and its surroundings are brush-painted, the one writhing inwardly up to its serrated edges, the other crazing open, with incisively directional dabs, allows the

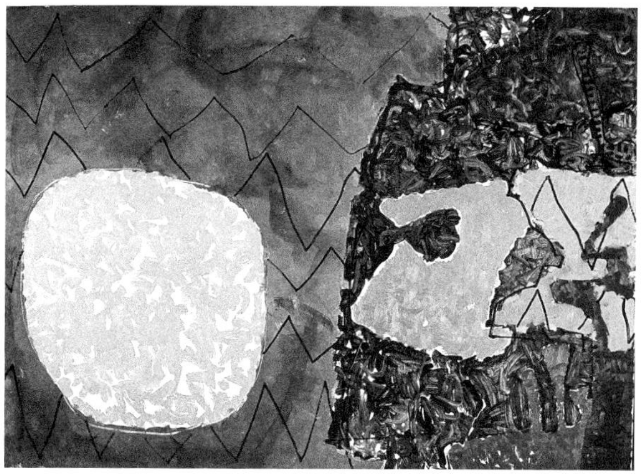

contained energy of the orb to spread its effect in a continuously pulsing wave right to the four edges of the canvas, carrying the slashed intervention of a pale violet finger, an orange scribbled dagger in the corner, and causing the scurrying Heifetz-fingered creatures at the right-hand corner to set a merry dance, rasping and sawing as in a devil's trill by Paganini.

In yet another, permanent rose tube-squeezings zip into the resilient tambourine-taut white priming in a sort of football lacing, while a sonorous rose-magenta surrounds it, a flurry of scarlet and a circled orange, to form a stark conspiracy. Heron has always been good at leaving such dramatically simple pictorial statements time to settle, to work on him, and dictate their finality to him, and sometimes these minimal intuitions turn out to be the best – I think back to *Dark Purple and Lemon in Orange: January 1962* [fig.23], or *Three Blues in Red: 1962*.

Pale Pink and Lemon Painting: November 1982 – May 28 1984 [fig.24] has two dovetailed zones, each surrounding a yellow disc. (One discovers this by analysis. It is not immediately evident, not the most salient relationship. One begins with an altogether more complex impression.) On the right, a frank and fluffy whitish pink bids fair to smother a lemon cup-wafer, while to the left, an ornamental blur of magenta and mauve, with a maze of scorings from the tube, stops short of a raw-white almond containing a loose flurry of cadmium yellow tube-and-brush twirling. Just when it begins to seem that the pink runs the risk of bleaching out too pale, avert one's eyes for an instant, and up it comes again, perfectly blushing at the discrete lemon wafer's sharply whispered suggestion, and a louder naughty importunity from a fluttering flaglet of deep red, almost too stark an intrusion, yet not, like an attempt to shape some notation for an as yet unformulated emotion which only the finished painting will provide. This very starkness, at once acutely specific as a shape and yet somehow imprecise as a sign, has the property of stirring multiple associations. I am again reminded of the bewildering muscular dance-pattern of the fingers of a violinist scurrying from string to string, or is it perhaps the rhythmic sawing of the bow, able both to caress at one instant, and to strike the next, bouncing across the strings with savage accent?

Meanwhile, this seeming discord is answered by

fig.22 **Lemon Disc in Sea Green with Zig-zags: July–December 1982** Oil on canvas 152.4 × 213.4 cm David Thomson

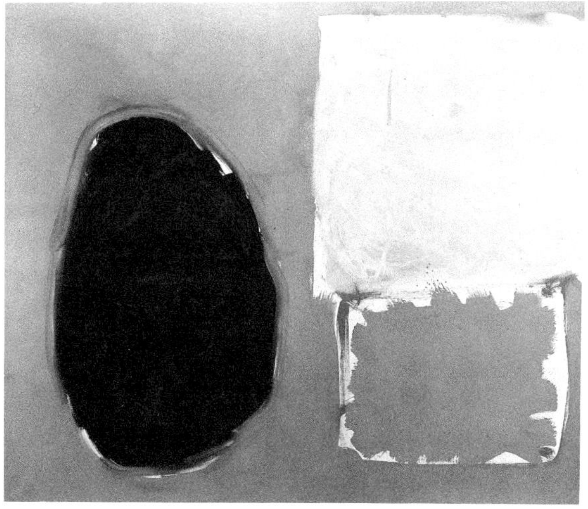

fig.23 **Dark Purple and Lemon in Orange: January 1962** Oil on canvas 152.4 × 182.8 cm Private Collection

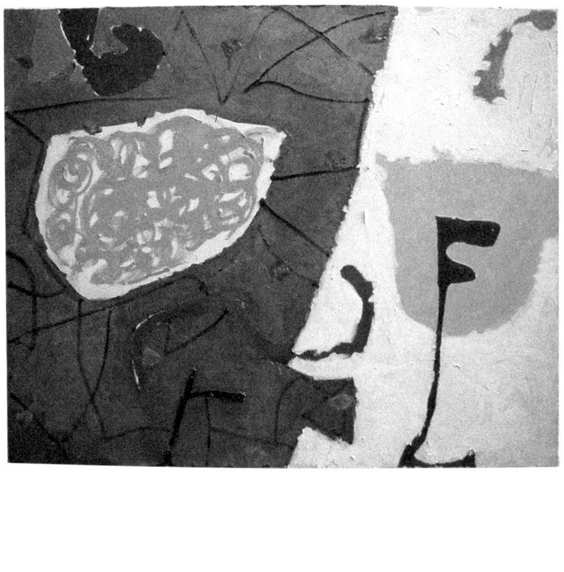

fig.24 **Pale Pink and Lemon Painting: November 1982 – May 28 1984** Oil on canvas 96.5 × 121.9 cm David Thomson

insinuations from the violet bloom which the left-hand softly hammers out on the drumskin of mauve spreading so sheer and yet so sumptuous right out to the canvas edges (as does the pink). And finally, continuously, instantaneously, there sit the monsoon rain-spots of cobalt blue, the quirky little twisted boomerang of scarlet, the two fleeting figures of orange and blue towards the left hand corner.

Can all these possibly cohabit in this little space without fractiousness? Of course they can. But as the series has developed, it is above all in the relaxation of their drawing that the newest pictures are remarkable, and this relaxation has allowed perhaps greater diversity of incident, variety of type of silhouette, and textural variety, than at any time in Heron's previous work.

The loosening enables great subtlety of transition between the various sub-worlds which are accommodated within the one image, and also a sudden sharpness at any desired point. Shapes are delimited just as clearly as ever, but the precise character of the wayward, wandering drawing does not tie them together, but rather, untied, the coloured areas, filled out velvety soft at one point, loosely scored and scraped with pungent accent in another, are freed to participate in a gently persuasive fusion of their own, like new morning mushrooms breaking through the grass-roots at dawn, or crocus buds opening to the pale light of spring. And all this has gradually brought an altogether more sophisticated and artistic measure of control. Intensity is no longer something which drives the artist in its hot pursuit. Heron has once more found his touch.

The first impression is likely to be, on seeing the largest of the new paintings, that they are somehow not finished; subtle enrichment, decorative splendour may be one thing as an aim, but surely these pictures are over-programmatic in its pursuit and as divided against themselves as were those that were unsuccessful amongst the pictures of the '70s, and ultimately for the same reasons? Some sub-sections of the picture seem not to reach each other at long range, but adumbrate a sub-world to the point where it detaches from the whole image. There are no doubt technical considerations which make translucency and opacity difficult to manage on the one surface where many overpaintings are involved, especially in a style as frankly decorative as Heron's has been becoming.

This is a fine line, one feels, which a more full-blooded painterliness might resolve, but Heron's strength as a painter is in getting it right early, with a swift certainty that exploits the taut membrane of silky-sheer whiteness, and the liquid gold of oil paint. (His gouaches have had a quite different feel to them, different edges, more soaked in than swept across.) It has, I am sure, been tempting to wish to see the oil paintings take on more of the qualities of the gouaches (and incidentally of the carpets) which have maintained a consistently high standard throughout the years, and have often been superior works of art to the oils.

But this is precisely the by now familiar kind of unity Heron's completely unforced intrigue is not going to give us. Little by little one begins to rise to the unique features of the unsteadying sensuosity on offer, and to see how pacific a unison that deliciously unfinished finishedness provides.

Apart from the inherent quality of his best paintings, Patrick Heron remains of vital importance to the onward of British painting for two reasons. He is our one contact with that moment at which British painting had the most unambiguous links with the continent, without that sense of an unbridgeable inferiority which causes most of our efforts to strain and distort the fundamental eloquence of the means with ponderous intent – that moment at which the objective world, unsullied by romantic fantasy, first met an English interpreter in this century to do justice to it. I am speaking of the confident Matthew Smith of the '20s and '30s. And secondly, because of the link with Matisse – feeling through colour. 'I feel through colour: it is thus through colour that my picture will always be organised' (Matisse):[19] not that his paintings are like Matisse's, or his feeling akin, (as I have suggested, St. Ives light has not the velvety lambency of Cap d'Antibes: Heron's light is more akin to the 'diffuse and violent' light of Braque, with his tonal northern harshness too); but this is his primary identification none the less, whence comes his extreme reliance on the first coup of colour, and a confidence in the capacity of decorative art to be sustainer of the highest ambition for painting, or as John Golding has recently so strikingly put it: 'it was Matisse more than any other artist who saw through to its ultimate conclusion the greatest lesson that

Gauguin had to teach, that it was possible to be a decorative artist and still remain within the avant-garde, or more strongly and more appositely, that it was possible to be a decorative painter, and simultaneously to be a high artist, even a revolutionary one.'[20]

If Heron is a deal more fallible and less subtle than Matisse in modulating this colour with tonal range and finesse, that subtlety is beginning to come in again. To do justice to the finer and more imponderable qualities of colour which are beginning to emerge in these new paintings, one needs to begin to think not so much of spectral colour, yellow, orange, red, violet, blue, green; more of unique qualities of substance, degrees of material quality and of the light that is reflected from them – gold, amber, olive, saffron, lime, mimosa, mustard, moonstone, milk-white, ivory, cream, silver, butter, pearl, donkey, suede, beige, tan, coffee, dove-grey, sepia, wine, aubergine, ruby, amethyst, sapphire; with these more sentient, earthy yet aerial qualities of colour which paint by some miracle can be led to evoke, he is coming more onto Matisse's ground than he has in a good number of years.

It strikes one more and more, as one looks at things the way Heron's art too would have us look, that what both Braque and Matisse succeed in rendering, from the vantage point of their relaxed, undemonstrative response to nature, is the sheer incongruity of the juxtapositions which nature throws upon the formalising fondnesses of man: the slanting pattern of window bars cast obliquely by the sun's rays in defiance of the architect's formal design, the amber luminosity of early evening sunlight, the sudden plunge into violet shade; yet when one really begins to identify the exact hue, it is the cast light that is silver-cool, the shadow turning olive-warm, and hard against this lattice, the utterly irregular distorting shadow of a subtly asymmetric leaf-form. What happens when one super-adds to this incongruity the fervour of a consummately artistic sensibility, savouring with slow emphasis the creative eloquence of brush moving on canvas, it is indeed hard to quantify. And one feels inevitably, as with any feature that one has tried to identify of such an artist's work, 'that they are parts of an infinitely richer process than we have hinted at by extracting them from the complex and naming them alone'[21]

1 Patrick Heron, *Ivon Hitchens*, Penguin Modern Painters, 1955, p.3.

2 Patrick Heron, 'Five Americans … at the Institute of Contemporary Arts', *Arts* (New York), May 1958.

3 Patrick Heron, 'The Guggenheim selection', *Arts* (New York), 1957.

4 Patrick Heron, 'Soutine', *The Changing Forms of Art*, 1955, p.148: 'no artist is really successful until he finds his *own subject*, a subject he can really identify himself with completely'.

5 Patrick Heron, 'Five Types of Abstraction – Ben Nicholson', *The Changing Forms of Art*, 1955, p.190:' Rhythm, one feels, should be a submerged force irresistibly unifying all the pictorial elements from behind, from underneath'.

6 'The Shape of Colour', text of the fifth Power lecture, reprinted *Studio International*, Feb. 1974; p.70.

7 Patrick Heron, 'Submerged Rhythm – A Potter's Aesthetic', *The Changing Forms of Art*, 1955; p.59.

8 Patrick Heron, 'The Necessity of Distortion in Painting', Lecture given at Leeds University, Oct. 1949; reprinted *The Changing Forms of Art*, 1955, pps.3–20; p.6 and p.12

9 Patrick Heron, 'Submerged Rhythm – A Potter's Aesthetic', *The Changing Forms of Art*, 1955, pp.60–61.

10 Patrick Heron in conversation with the author.

11 'The Shape of Colour', *Studio International*, February 1974; p.73.

12 Patrick Heron, 'Five Types of Abstraction – Ben Nicholson', *The Changing Forms of Art*, 1955, p.191.

13 'Heron's Nest', *Harpers & Queen*, August 1981.

14 Nicolas de Staël, in a letter to Denys Sutton, quoted in *Nicolas de Staël*, Tate Gallery 1981, p.14: 'Mais là où l'histoire devient passionante mais alors tout à fait passionante c'est au moment précis où l'on saisit les Braque dans la lumière ou ils ont été peints, cette espèce de lumière diffuse et violente que le tableau reçoit d'autant mieux qu'il a tout faitpour y résister avec toute l'abnégation que cela comporte …'

15 T.S. Eliot, 'What is a Classic? An Address delivered before the Virgil Society …', 1944, Faber & Faber, London 1945.

16 Roger Fry, *Henri-Matisse*, Editions des Chroniques du Jour, Paris; A. Zwemmer, London 1930.

17 Patrick Heron, *Ivon Hitchens*, 1955.

18 Patrick Heron, 'To an American Painter', *Magazine of Art* (New York), March 1949; reprinted *The Changing Forms of Art*, 1955; p.243.

19 Henri Matisse: 'Témoignage', in *Henri Matisse, Ecrits et Propos sur l'Art*, ed. Dominique Fourcade, Hermann, Paris 1972.

20 John Golding, *New York Review of Books*, January 1985.

21 'Five Types of Abstraction – Ben Nicholson', *The Changing Forms of Art*, 1955; p.187.

The Innocent Eye?

Peter Fuller

First published in 1985

This article first appeared in *Artscribe,* no.54, Sept./Oct. 1985. It is reproduced here as published in *Peter Fuller's Modern Painters: Reflections on British Art*, edited by John McDonald, Methuen, London 1993

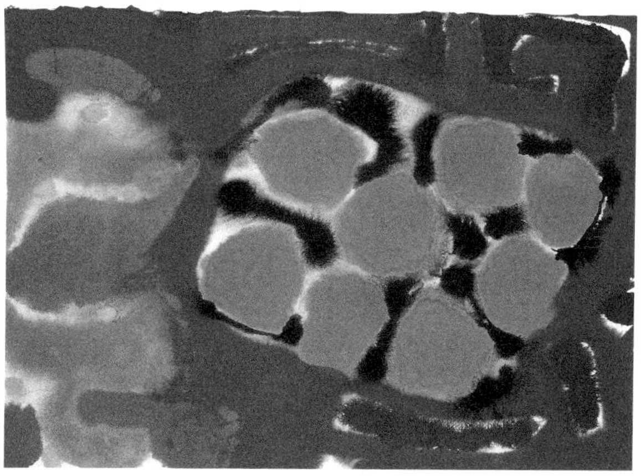

fig.25 **December 4: 1983: II**
Gouache on handmade paper
34.9 × 50.2 cm Private Collection

One of the paintings I most enjoyed in Patrick Heron's Retrospective at the Barbican in 1985 was *December 4: 1983: II* [fig.25], a small but extremely beautiful gouache, no bigger than 18 x 20 inches in an exhibition where some canvases were fifteen feet long.The forms in *December 4* are very fluid and the edges of colour areas generally fuzzy and indistinct. I doubt whether Heron would approve of the word, but the painting is vaguely 'biomorphic'. (Biomorph – 'Decorative form representing living object', *Concise Oxford Dictionary*.) It is suggestive of teeming life seen down a microscope after colour stains have been added.

And what colours! On the right of the picture, eight irregular, rose madderish, pink discs float in pools of deepening blues through which peep patches of white. These forms are insecurely contained by a branching, oval frame of red, which stretches across three quarters of the surface. On the far left are broken passages of green and illuminating spots of yellow. The picture gives rise to volatile sensations which are not easily pinned down in words. The meetings between the blue, the pink discs, and the surrounding red 'frame' are decisive. Often, these appear more as filigree or intricate tracery rather than as a line. We are a very long way from Heron's 'wobbly hard-edged' effects of the 1970s. The blue seems to drift on top of the pinks and reds, and yet its darkest points form recessive foci which tug back into illusory depths in the painting.

This ambiguity forms a visual trigger which tears the skin of the painting, sets everything in motion, and gives rise to enticing new illusions of space, or, to use a favourite phrase of Heron's, of colour as space. The discs seem to release their colour and light which not only flood out across the blues and reds, suffusing the entire surface with rose madderish tints; they also seem to billow forth in front of and behind the picture surface creating an engulfing illusion of coloured space. As one continues to watch, the blues reassert themselves, seeming to police the dissolving picture. The pink space retracts into the flat, floating discs where it is contained and held once more.

But I don't want to exaggerate the experience of a single, small picture. This was a fine exhibition, beautifully selected, and intelligently hung. It provided an excellent introduction to the 'changing forms' of Heron'a art from the 1930s until today.

[...] The earliest exhibit in this show is *Melon*, a printed silk of 1934, which Heron designed for his father's firm from his school sick bay [fig.9]. This scarf shows precocity in both colour and decorative sensibilities. These were to be hall-marks of all Heron's work. [...]

Although English landscape was to play such a decisive role in Heron's life, and art, his intuitive love of colour drew his eyes towards paintings produced on the other side of the Channel. There were many within the English art education system who admired the draughtsmanship of Degas, but this did not interest Heron. What he liked about French painting is perhaps summed up in something Cézanne once wrote in a letter to a friend: 'Shut your eyes.Wait, think of nothing. Now, open them ... One sees nothing but a great coloured undulation. What then? An irradiation and glory of colour. That is what a picture should give us, a warm harmony, an abyss in which the eye is lost, a secret germination, a coloured state of grace.'

Heron's earliest painting shows an impressionistic, or atmospheric, colour sense which perhaps owes something to the influence of Bonnard. This was soon to change. In 1943, with the world at war, Heron made repeated visits to the Redfern Gallery where he absorbed Matisse's *Red Studio*, which had been discovered in a Soho nightclub, and was on extended exhibition in the gallery. No single picture was to have a greater influence on him.

Much later, Heron was to explain, 'I dislike intensely the filmy, essentially unsubstantial, transparent, veil-like, revolving vapours of "colour".' He added that the sensation of space he valued was one generated by a plain, opaque surface placed at a measurable distance before his face. 'The contemplation of colour I refer to', he went on, 'is something which heightens my accurate awareness of my own physical position in relation to such surfaces, and to my actual, physical environment.' Heron also valued the way of dividing up the picture surface he perceived in Braque's work.

By the late 1940s, Heron's love of colour, joy in decorative forms, and intense responses to French, Post-Impressionist painting, especially Matisse and Braque, had come together in a style which was very much his own. Within the limits of this style, he produced a number of remarkable portraits, including one of T.S. Eliot (1949) which now hangs in the National Portrait Gallery [fig.15] and another of Herbert Read (1950) [no.8]. But many of his pictures at this time were explorations of the ambiguous relationship between depictions of indoor and outdoor space. Several were painted from the balcony window on those repeated visits to St Ives. Perhaps the most ambitious, and certainly the largest, work of these years, however, was *Christmas Eve: 1951* [no.9], a large canvas made for the Festival of Britain exhibition, which loosely refers to a scene in Heron's parents' home in Welwyn Garden City.

As Heron looked around him in the years following the second world war, he must have felt a sense of aesthetic isolation. Perhaps he saw precedents for some of his concerns in, say, Matthew Smith, or, more significantly, Ivon Hitchens. But neither geography, nor cultural tradition appeared to predispose the English to an art of colour, decorative form and visual pleasure. To Heron, England must have seemed to Heron to be addicted to its 'great-coat' weather, its puritanical traditions, and what he took to be its 'literary' and 'linear' occlusions of vision. (Later, he was to pronounce anathema on 'the besetting sin of the British – the eternal dependence upon line, and an illustrator's rather than a painter's drawing'.)

'The puritanical English,' he said, when looking back in 1978, 'the whole Euston Road ethic, you know, everything about the bloody English except Turner and Constable, really, had been against actual pleasure. Yet I have always thought that to call a painting decorative was one of the highest possible compliments, because it means that the painting is giving pleasure through every millimetre of the surface, that its formal dispositions are perfectly ordered and balanced.'

In 1945, Heron began a critical crusade which was intended to open a nation's eyes and warm its heart with aesthetic pleasures, in the uniquely bleak years of austerity, rationing and post-war 'reconstruction'. Heron's most influential articles were published in *The New English Weekly*, between 1945 and 1947, and in *The New Statesman and Nation*, from 1947 to 1950. Much as he may have

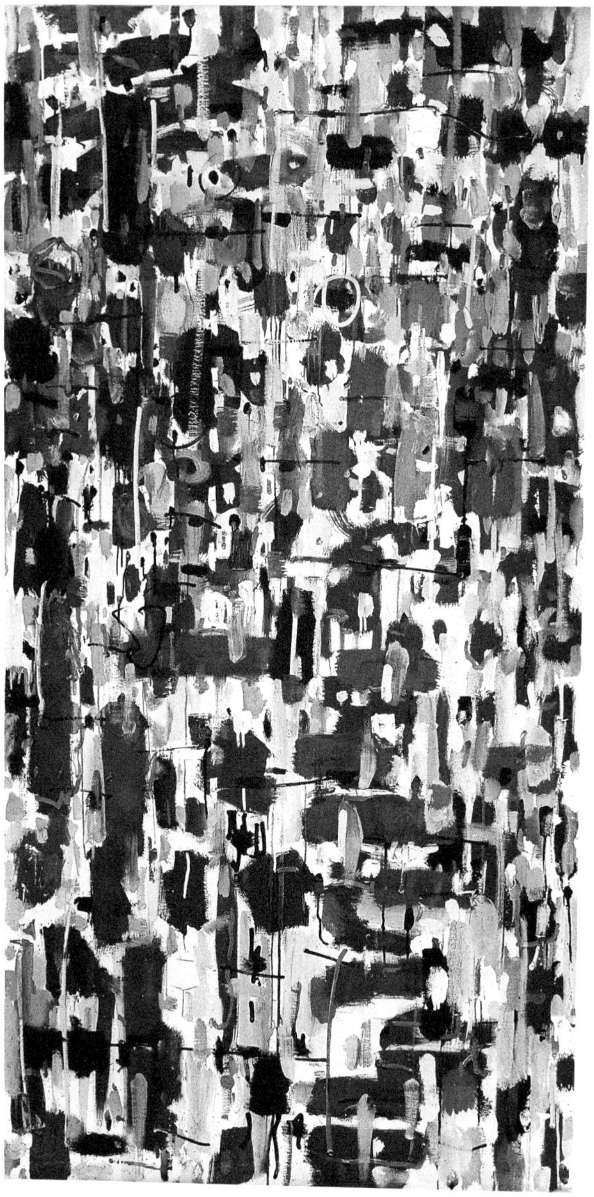

fig.26 **Camellia Garden: March 1956** Oil on canvas 182.9 × 91.5 cm Private Collection

despised English puritanism and English pedagogy, the English, it seems, were to be taught to learn to see in the dryest and most pedestrian manner. 'Criticism', Heron wrote in 1949, 'should sacrifice pleasantries of style for a ploddingly careful analysis of what is there on the canvases under review. Criticism should have more in common with science than with poetry, for it is the subject you are discussing that is important and not the thing you write about it.' Just as Heron came to believe that, 'concepts, and also symbols, are the enemy of painting, which has as its unique domain the realm of pure visual sensation', so he also believed that interpretations and 'any sort of verbal felicities' were the enemy of criticism, which he endeavoured to make 'as descriptive of the visual facts', that is, as formal, as he could.

Heron's criticism sprang out of very similar aesthetic beliefs to those which informed his painting. It is worth stressing at this point that, when working on a canvas, Heron made decisions about both colour and composition on the basis of imagination and intuition, rather than through reason, or scientific analysis. However, his critical position was one which excluded imagination and intuition, in both theory and practice. Heron was sacked from *The New Statesman* in 1950 on the grounds that, as the then editor put it, 'readers must have at least a *rest* from wrestling with the problems of new space'.

By the mid-1950s, Heron was clearly beginning to feel pinched by the self-imposed limitations of his chosen style of painting. A certain pleasing graphic facility often entered into his pictorial compositions at this time. Could he perhaps have perceived a resemblance between his own work and that of the quintessentially English 'linear' and 'literary' artist, John Piper? It was certainly there to be seen. Piper, too, had been influenced by French decorative traditions.

In 1956, Heron moved to Eagles Nest, Zennor, near St Ives, where he has lived ever since. He was searching for a more 'gestural' way of painting. Under the influences of the American artist Sam Francis, and of the light and life of the Cornish landscape, Heron moved sharply away from explicit figuration towards abstract organisations of patches of colour across the whole canvas surface. When they were shown in London, the resulting 'Garden' pictures were widely derided by critics as being 'Tachiste'. Today, this label seems inappropriate: not only are works like *Camellia Garden: March 1956* [fig.26] marked by that restrained taste and developed 'intelligence of feeling' which characterises all Heron's successful painting; their reference to the world of nature, beyond the canvas surface, appears self-evident. Though the colour may be based on memory, mood and reminiscences of flowers and light, rather than on the immediate perception of them, it is most decidedly not concocted 'studio colour' of London (or Paris). It was obviously more than a coincidence that Heron's decisive break with figuration coincided with the leaving of the metropolis to live in Cornwall.

For some time, Heron's sense of aesthetic isolation had been mitigated by the emergence of a so-called 'Middle Generation' of British artists, a good many of whom also lived in St Ives and shared at least some of his concerns. But, with the sad paling of the Parisian and Mediterranean suns, Heron had also been looking to America, and attending to the achievements of the Abstract Expressionists. He was one of their first articulate and informed advocates in Britain, although, from the beginning, he stressed weaknesses in their colour. In 1955, Heron began to write for the American magazine, *Arts*, to whose readers he introduced Peter Lanyon, Alan Davie, William Scott, Roger Hilton, Ivon Hitchens, Bryan Wynter, Terry Frost, and many others.

In 1956, the abstracted 'Garden' paintings began to be subjected to ever more pronounced vertical organisation, and a year later, Heron began a series of horizontal 'stripe' paintings. (A very beautiful example, *Green and Mauve Horizontals, January 1958* [no.27] was included in his retrospective.) In the 1970s these works were to become bones of contention in Heron's argument with the Americans over precedent. The crux of Heron's position was that, instead of having always been at the receiving end of ideas emanating from New York, several painters of his generation, himself included, had exerted 'crucial influence' upon New York painting from the late fifties onward. Heron established his case beyond any reasonable doubt – and it has never been answered. There have been those who have said that it just does not matter who did what first, but the truth always matters, in art, no less than in life. I would go further. I believe not only that Heron's stripe paintings preceded those of Morris Louis, but also that they are better, much better, in aesthetic terms.

Alongside the freshness and clarity of Heron's painting of 1956–8, there is a dowdy and depressing feel about even the best Morris Louis canvases. With few exceptions, Louis's paintings, today, have the look of last season's used and abused fashions. Heron was always a painter of superior sensibility, colour sense, and painterly intelligence. His work manifests a love of tradition, and a mastery of skills and techniques, which Louis's lacked. In the end, originality always shines out over second-hand novelty.

The greater sense of life in Heron's colour has to do with a certain replenishment from landscape and natural form, however much he may consciously have tried to resist this. Someone as visually sensitive as Heron could hardly not have been profoundly affected by his move to Cornwall, especially when that countryside was already redolent with childhood memories for him. Louis, on the other hand, really only produced Washington studio colour, plastic colour. Heron had an intuitive grasp of the importance of creating and crafting a surface (residues of his denied English puritanism perhaps?) through nuances of subtle brush-work which can imbue every square inch with the variety and feeling of a fully human touch. Louis poured his pigment out of buckets. Heron's oil paint is also a more versatile and enduring medium than the slick, filmy acrylics with which Louis worked. I have the gravest of doubts as to whether those first acrylics were truly fast: if they were, then Louis was an even worse colourist than I would otherwise have given him credit for. Quite probably, many of his works have physically deteriorated since the time they were made, but the many collectors who still shell out large sums for Louis's empty works are wasting their money. For a fraction of the price, they could buy a Patrick Heron which would not only antedate Louis's stripes by several years, but also be aesthetically superior, and, incidentally, a more conscientiously crafted object. They could also be sure – which they cannot when buying a Louis – that they were buying a painting which the artist himself acknowledged and approved of; one in which the artist, and no one else, had decided the crucial disposition of forms in relation to the canvas edge.

After his stripe paintings, Heron pursued his programme of 're-complicating the picture surface'; spending much of the 1960s creating canvases in which discs and irregular rectangular shapes float across vast fields of colour. 'Colour', he wrote in 1962, 'is both the subject and the means; the form and the content; the image and the meaning in my painting today.'

He also refused the central, symmetrical 'bunching' of his shapes which – like Louis's vulgar colours – appealed to banal and unsophisticated tastes. The compositional drawing in a Heron is, I believe, more independent of colour than he likes to suggest. This drawing surely must be finished in the first minutes, perhaps seconds, of creating a canvas; long before the full weight of the colour values can be assessed. Such drawing seems to be derived from an intuitive sense of balance, which, unlike repetitious, mechanical symmetry, can also be related to natural form. Even in black-and-white photographs, it is easy to perceive just such a 'balance' in the disposition of the rocks and boulders in the Cornish landscape.

In the 1970s, Heron went on to produce what he calls his 'wobbly hard-edged' paintings. In these, the colour surface has become more opaque and resistant than ever. Everything depends on the juxtaposition of one area of colour against, or within, another. In these works, Heron makes full use of his observation that the shape of an area of colour, as defined by its boundary line, greatly changes its value and the nature of the spatial illusions to which it gives rise. As he once put it, 'Complexity of the spatial illusion generated along the frontier where the two colours meet, is also enormously increased if the linear character of those frontiers is irregular, freely drawn, intuitively arrived at.' Although these works can appear exceptionally flat, and vigorously 'anti-atmospheric', they also give rise to intense, vibrating illusions of space which emanate out, both in front, and behind, the densely painted picture surfaces.

The sheer expanse of canvas covered in the mid- to late 1970s was daunting, but, occasionally, Heron did seem to be repeating himself. Perhaps Heron came to feel he was in danger of falling into American mannerisms. In any event, the 1980s saw another transformation in Heron's work. There is now a conspicuously greater freedom in his handling – a return to painterly gesture, rather than dependence on taut vibrancy. His colours are often softer and no longer necessarily fully-saturated. The great expanses are broken up, and there is more than a whisper of a return to Bonnard, whom he deserted for Matisse, so many years ago. The references to natural forms and colours, which were never entirely eliminated from Heron's work, even when his rhetoric was at its most radically abstract, now seem undisguised and undenied. I can only presume that Heron himself endorsed the reproduction of a full-page colour photograph of the rocks, shrubs and flowers in his garden at Eagles Nest towards the end of the Barbican catalogue.

Heron's life in art, hitherto, has shown an exceptional coherence, and a single-mindedness of direction. For all the manifest transformations in his painting, he has dedicated himself to a particular set of aesthetic beliefs which involve the affirmation of certain dimensions of painting and the refusal of others. As I intimated earlier, however, his actual *practice* of painting involves faculties and qualities unaccounted for in his criticism.

Heron has set down his underlying aesthetic argument on numerous occasions, but perhaps nowhere more succinctly than in an article of 1969:

> *Because painting is exclusively concerned with* the seen, *as distinct from the* known, *pictorial space and pictorial colour are virtually synonymous. That is to say, for the human eye there is no space without its colour; and no colour that does not create its own space. When you open your eyes, the texture of the entire visual field (which opening them reveals to you) consists of one thing; and that thing is* colour. *Variations in this colour texture (which sight reveals to us) are indications that* form *exists: but colour is there first, in that it is the medium through which form is communicated visually. And so, in manipulating colour, painting is organizing the very stuff of which sight or vision consists.*

Again, in 1973, he wrote that painting had as its unique domain the realm of pure visual sensation. 'Painting,' he argued, 'should start in that multicoloured and at first amorphous texture of coloured light which is what fills your vision, from eyelid to eyelid, when you open your eyes.' He added that the finished painting 'should also end in pure sensation of colour – having passed into the realm of the conceptual in the process, and come out again at the other side.'

For Heron, the fact that the world is revealed to sight exclusively through colour is the foundation stone of an aesthetic which maintains that painting ought to concern itself, first and last, with colour. The pleasure to be derived from 'visual sensation,' that is, the sensation of colour, and not lines, concepts, or symbols, constitutes painting's unique domain. His argument against the English tradition seems to be that because the English did not understand the primary importance of colour, they failed to grasp its exclusive claims over painting. Instead they fell into the traps of the linear, the literary, and the puritanical – or symbolic.

Given these beliefs it is easy enough to see why Heron separated himself from the harsh, deadening, linear empiricism of the Euston Road School; from almost all varieties of Neo-Romanticism – Samuel Palmer he saw as guilty of both 'writhing detail' and symbolism; and especially, of course, from Social and Socialist Realism. Heron saw John Berger's criticism as posing 'the main threat to major painting' in Britain. 'Colour', Heron wrote in 1962, 'is now the only direction in which painting can travel. Painting has still a continent left to explore, in the direction of colour (and in no other direction).'

One problem with Heron's line of argument, however, is that it simply does not follow from the fact that the visible world is revealed to us exclusively through colour, that colour is the only way of creating space within the illusions of a painting. There was, of course, much more to the great French painting, which Heron so loved, than 'pure sensation of colour'. Even if we had only Matisse's black-and-white drawings we would still recognise him as a great master of spatial depiction. Nor is the pursuit of a more depictive, and less decorative linearity than Matisse's *necessarily* destructive of colour sense. Euston Road, after all, is one thing, but Degas was quite another. For me, he is a colourist second to none – not even to Patrick Heron! And, as I have already implied, there is more to Heron's painting, too, than 'pure colour sensation'; his compositional sense is not a derivative of his response to colour, but is, in a real sense, independent of it. Lines, especially outlines, may be fictions, but drawing remains one of the vital means through which the painter can create illusions and make them live.

I suppose that if one man embodies those English aesthetic values which Heron feels his colour sense means he must reject, it must be John Ruskin. And yet it seems significant, that Ruskin's aesthetic was built on observations about colour almost identical to Heron's. Thus in *The Elements of Drawing*, Ruskin writes:

> *The perception of solid Form is entirely a matter of experience. We* see *nothing but flat colours; and it is only by a series of experiments that we find out that a stain of black or grey indicates the dark side of a solid substance, or that a faint hue indicates that the object in which it appears is far away. The whole technical power of painting depends on our recovery of what may be called the* innocence of the eye*; that is to say, of a sort of childish perception of these flat stains of colour, merely as such, without consciousness of what they signify, – as a blind man would see them if suddenly gifted with sight.*

In Ruskin's case, these insights did not lead to an automatic rejection of the 'linear', 'literary' and the symbolic. They were associated, rather, with a line even more 'writhing' than Palmer's, and a celebration of Pre-Raphaelitism – an aesthetic which, I imagine, Heron abhors.

The reason for this, of course, was that although Ruskin realised that the experience of art (and also of nature) began in sensation, he also recognised that it did not end there. Even now, if we no longer hope that the artist will reveal to us the presence of God in his world, we want something more from him or her than merely optical effects.

Our response, to, say Matisse's *Red Studio*, or Heron's *December 4*, clearly begins in simple visual sensation, which is more or less capable of accurate verbal description. But the full appreciation of such works of art, as much as the making of them, involves the imagination. Through the imagination, what began as a simple response of the senses enters into the whole terrain of feeling, differential value, (quite simply 'good' or 'not good') and High Sentiment. Simple optical sensations cannot reveal for us a work's place in relation to tradition, and its affiliations with other works. They will not help resolve vexed issues of precedent and originality. All of these matters, as Heron well knows, are legitimate components in our response to a work of art.

I believe Heron's best paintings are not to be valued on the grounds of visual sensation alone, but because, through the successful creation of such sensations, he stimulates significant affects, or feelings, in his viewers. He uses all his skill, knowledge, and sensibility, as one of the greatest living colourists, to re-create for us a fully adult version of that 'childish perception' to which Ruskin referred.

In her little book, *On Not Being Able to Paint*, Marion Milner, the English psychoanalyst, discussed her own recovery of the experience of colour. She writes:

> *Colour in painting had been a subject which for years I had been quite unable to think about. It was as if it had been so important that to think about it, to know just what one was trying to do with one's paints, had been to risk losing something; it seemed at first glance as if an experience so intimate and vital must be kept remote and safe from the cold white light of consciousness which might destroy its glories. In fact it was as if colour and the light of knowing were*

differences which must be kept firmly separate, just as objects had to be kept separated and not seen in their mutual effect upon each other.

Milner explained that when she finally risked not-knowing and gave herself up to colour, the common-sense world of objects separated by outline dissolved, and was transformed into 'a world of change, of continual development and process, one in which there was no sharp line between one state and the next, as there is no fixed boundary between twilight and darkness but only a gradual merging of the one into the other.' She insisted that this rediscovery, through colour, was not regressive. Rather, she associated it with the recovery of a spiritual, though secular, dimension in perception, or, as she put it, 'a re-emerging into a new division of the me-not-me, one in which there is more of the "me" in the "not-me", and more of the "not-me" in the "me".'

Through his best colour paintings, Heron intuitively offers us experiences of both fusion and separateness, of space and the material facts of the painted surface. He thereby recovers something of the lost 'innocence' of infantile perception, although his vision is anything but regressive. Heron's paintings elevate, even exult us, not simply because they provide pleasurable sensations, but because they suggest new kinds of integration between observer and observed, and indeed the whole world of nature, which cannot be revealed through logic, reason, nor even a conventional mode of seeing, which reads the world in terms of outlines and separate objects. This may not constitute the only direction for painting, but painting which ignores such a powerful means will certainly impoverish itself.

Chronology

(For detailed exhibition history, see Bibliography)

1920 Patrick Heron, son of Thomas Milner Heron and Eulalie 'Jack' Heron (née Davies), the first of four children (Michael, Joanna and Giles), born on 30 January at Headingley, Leeds, in Yorkshire. His father was a blouse manufacturer, pacifist, socialist, and leading member of the Leeds Arts Club: he was a reformer and an idealist. PH started drawing at the age of three; these drawings survive.

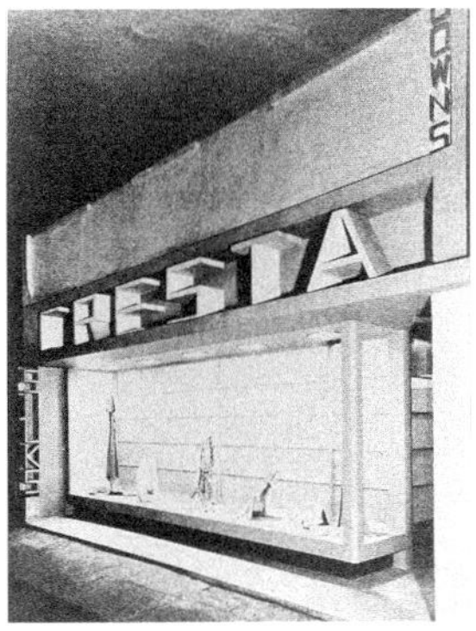

Wells Coates's first shop for Cresta Silks, Brompton Road, London 1929

1925 Heron family moved to West Cornwall, and Tom Heron took over management of Crysede Silks, a firm owned by his friend Alec Walker. The Herons lived first near Newlyn, then from late 1925 in a cottage at Lelant. PH attended first St Ia's School, St Ives, then Sunnycroft where fellow pupils included Will Arnold-Foster's son Mark, Peter Lanyon and Bernard Leach's daughters Eleanor and Jessamine.

1927–8 The Heron family spent five months living at Eagles Nest, a house above Zennor owned by Will Arnold-Forster, which PH was to buy in 1955. For the first time he drew and explored the Zennor landscape.

1928 The Herons moved to St Ives, above Porthmeor Beach. The pioneer modernist architect Wells Coates was invited by Tom Heron to modernise existing shops for Crysede.

1929 After a dispute between Tom Heron and Alec Walker, in September the Heron family moved to Welwyn Garden City, Hertfordshire. Tom Heron founded Cresta Silks, commissioning Wells Coates to design the factory and shops, Edward McKnight Kauffer to design notepaper and packing, and Paul Nash and Cedric Morris to design textiles, also Bruce Turner, a cubist artist friend from Leeds. PH first met his future wife, Delia Reiss, a fellow pupil at school. Her father, RL (Dick) Reiss, had been one of the founders of Welwyn Garden City.

1932 PH began to attend St George's School, Harpenden.

1933 Taken to National Gallery in London by the art and craft master at St George's, Ludvig van der Straeten (Vandy), to see work by Cézanne for first time. Immediately began to paint in Cézanne-influenced style.

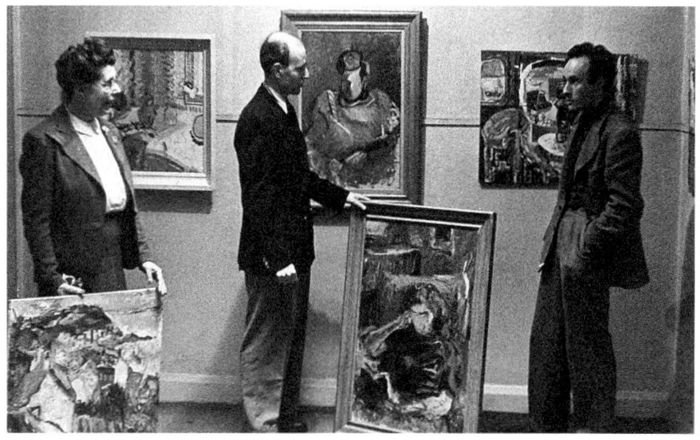

PH (right) at his first Redfern exhibition, 1947, with Dorothy Searle and Peter Cochrane

1934 Invited by Tom Heron to make designs for Cresta Silks. Continued to design for Cresta until 1951.

1937 Attended Slade School of Fine Art in London for two days a week from autumn for two years. Met Bryan Wynter who became close life-long friend.

1938 Revisited St Ives for first time. Toured West Penwith peninsula with Eleanor Leach and drew Zennor landscape.

1940–3 Registered as conscientious objector, and worked on chicken farm at Codicote, near Welwyn, then in Cambridge as labourer for Cambridgeshire War Agricultural Committee digging ditches and clearing fields. PH suffered from a weak chest from childhood, and after three years heavy labouring his health broke down completely. On medical advice he was exempted from further agricultural work.

1940–4 Stayed with his old Slade friend, Adrian Ryan, in his Tite Street studio in Chelsea on several occasions.

1941 Bought book of reproductions of twenty-four paintings by Matisse, selected by the artist himself, published by Braun et Cie, Paris, 1939.

1943 Visited St Ives. Saw Matisse's *The Red Studio* at the Redfern Gallery, London. Completed *The Piano*, which he later considered his first mature work.

1944–5 Worked for fourteen months from January 1944 at the Leach Pottery, St Ives (an approved work placement for a conscientious objector). Became friendly with Ben Nicholson, Barbara Hepworth, Adrian Stokes, Margaret Mellis, Naum Gabo, John Wells and Sven Berlin.

1945 Was asked to write art criticism by Philip Mairet, editor of *The New English Weekly*. First published article, written while still at Leach Pottery, was on Ben Nicholson. Married Delia Reiss in April and settled in the upper half of the house owned by his father-in-law, 53 Addison Avenue, Holland Park, London. Now free to become full-time painter. Spent the summer at Carbis Bay, St Ives.

1946 Saw Braque exhibition at the Tate, and wrote essay on Braque for *The New English Weekly*. Spent summer at Mousehole in Cornwall. Commissioned by Basil Taylor to give series of talks on contemporary art on the newly founded BBC Third Programme. Later invited to write series of talks on London art exhibitions for BBC Russian Service.

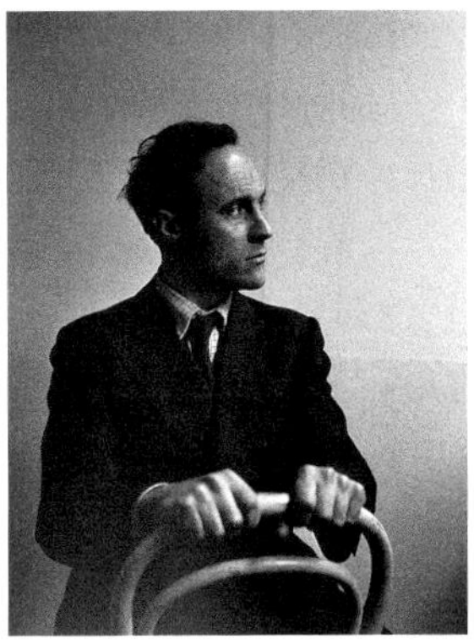

PH photographed for *Vogue* magazine, *c.*1947

1947 Began a series of portraits of T.S. Eliot (a close friend of Tom Heron). The final cubist version, painted in 1949, acquired by the National Portrait Gallery in 1966. Became art critic of *The New Statesman and Nation* at the unexpected invitation of Raymond Mortimer. (Continued as *New Statesman*'s art critic until 1950; contributed occasionally until 1955.) Birth of daughter Katharine (March). Spent summer at 3 St Andrew's Street, St Ives, a cottage on the sea wall, which the Heron family continued to rent annually until 1955. Visited North Wales in August. First London exhibition at Redfern Gallery in October. Wrote *Vlaminck Paintings, 1900–1945*.

1948 With Delia and Katharine, visited Provence and stayed with Francis Davison and Margaret Mellis at Château des Enfants, Cap d'Antibes, where they remained until early 1949, making visits to Nice and Arles. Attempted to visit Matisse at his villa, 'La Rêve', in Vence, but got no further than Lydia Delectorskaya on the doorstep.

1949 Visited Paris: saw Salon de Mai, and wrote about work of Pierre Soulages and other young French painters. Visited Braque in his Paris studio. Presented him with *The New English Weekly* article on himself. Birth of daughter Susanna (September).

1950 Painted portrait of Herbert Read; exhibited with Eliot portrait in third one-man show at Redfern Gallery (April–May). Read portrait acquired by the British Council. After Read's death this portrait was bought by Henry Moore and Barbara Hepworth and presented to the National Portrait Gallery in 1969.

1951 Visited Paris again, and also saw de Staël exhibition at the Mathiesen Gallery in London.

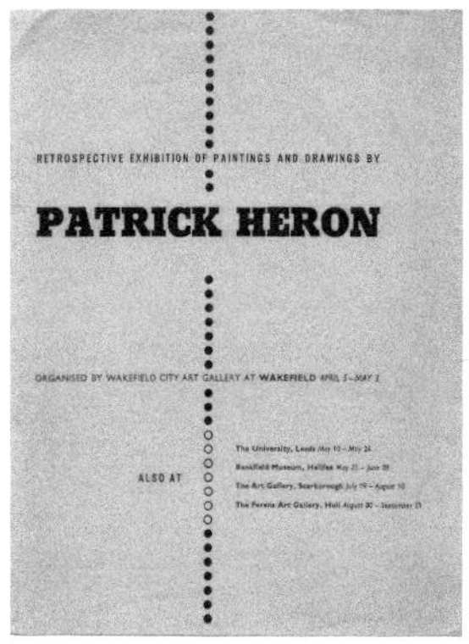

Cover of Wakefield City Art Gallery exhibition catalogue, 1952

1950s PH's writings admired by American art critic Clement Greenberg who sought him out in London in 1954. On his second visit to Britain, in 1959, Greenberg motored from Southampton, where he had landed, to Eagles Nest with his wife Jenny, to stay with the Heron family before visiting London. The friendship disintegrated after PH and Read disagreed as judges of the John Moores Liverpool Exhibition in 1965.

1952 Wakefield retrospective exhibition opened by Herbert Read (April). Gave lecture 'Submerged Rhythm' on Bernard Leach at the International Conference of Craftsman in Pottery and Textiles at Dartington Hall, Devon. Met Japanese potter Shoji Hamada. Visited Paris with William Scott to meet French painters, including de Staël and Soulages.

1953 Visited Italy with his brother Giles and Peter Lanyon. Made drawings of Assisi. Organised, wrote catalogue for and exhibited in *Space in Colour*, an exhibition of ten of his British contemporaries, at Hanover Gallery, London. Began teaching one day a week at Central School of Arts and Crafts, London (continued until 1956).

1953–4 Exhibited at Il Bienal de São Paulo, Brazil.

1955 Bought Eagles Nest from Mark Arnold-Forster. Began writing for *Arts Digest, New York* (later renamed *Arts (N.Y.)*), edited by Hilton Kramer. PH continued to be London correspondent of *Arts (N.Y.)* until 1958. *The Changing Forms of Art*, a selection of his criticism, published in UK by Routledge and Kegan Paul (US paperback edition published by Noonday Press, N.Y., 1958). When PH sent Braque a copy of *The Changing Forms of Art*, which included *The New English Weekly* Braque article, he received a letter from Braque in his own hand, (reproduced above right). Wrote *Ivon Hitchens* for Penguin Modern Painters.

1956 Saw, reviewed and highly praised American Abstract Expressionist painters from New York who occupied only one room of New York exhibition entitled *Modern Art in the United States* sent to the Tate Gallery by the Museum of Modern Art, New York. Moved to Eagles Nest in April. In June exhibited 'Tachiste garden paintings' at Redfern Gallery.

1957 'Stripe' paintings first exhibited in *Metavisual, Tachiste, Abstract*, a group exhibition at Redfern Gallery in April. (Exhibition title invented by Delia Heron.)

1958 At Ben Nicholson's suggestion, took over his studio at 5 Porthmeor Studios in St Ives (close to present Tate Gallery) when Nicholson emigrated to Switzerland. Last exhibition at Redfern Gallery, including many 'stripe paintings' (February). Resigned as London correspondent of *Arts (N.Y.)* and decided to take 'vow of silence' as writer on art. *Horizontal Stripe Painting: November 1957 – January 1958* installed in room at Bedford Square, London, offices of printers and publishers Lund Humphries, designed by Trevor Dannatt. Invited by Canon Collins to attend founding meeting of the Campaign for Nuclear Disarmament (CND). Made a series of stone-printed lithographs for Curwen Press.

1959 *Black Painting– Red, Brown, Olive: July 1959* awarded Grand Prize by International Jury from selection of twenty-five French and twenty-five British paintings at Second John Moores Liverpool Exhibition, Walker Art Gallery. Delia and PH visited Paris with John Wells and were entertained by Soulages.

1960s Opposition by PH to proposal to reopen a disused tin-mine at Carnelloe point, Zennor, caused him to begin the first of many campaigns to preserve the beauty of the ancient landscape of West Penwith, with its Bronze Age field patterns. These campaigns kept him away from painting, and brought him into disagreement with his friend Peter Lanyon, but he gained support from Henry Moore, Barbara Hepworth, General Sir Brian Horrocks, Edith Evans, Michael Tippett, Benjamin Britten, and many others. Other campaigns included ones for the protection of the local winding roads with their ancient walls and opposition to a proposed holiday village development at Penderleath, Towednack, in 1975.

1960 First New York show at Bertha Schaefer Gallery (April – May). First one-man show at Waddington Galleries (November – December).

1961 In pursuit of their passion to conserve the landscape, PH and Delia bought 165 acres of moorland adjacent to Eagles Nest. A plan by the Admiralty to use this land for a permanent troop-landing exercise area with marines, commandos and helicopters (officially christening the site 'The Zennor Troop Landing Area') caused him again to stop work. After two public enquiries the Admiralty withdrew.

1962 Second New York show at Bertha Schaefer Gallery in April. Visited Aix-en-Provence and saw Mont Saint-Victoire (Cézanne's favourite motif) for first time.

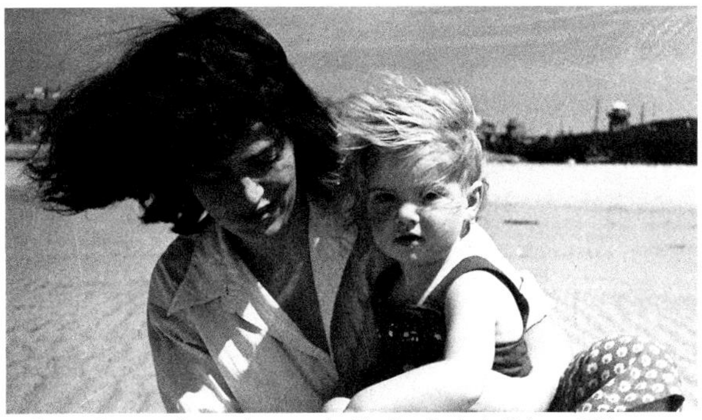

Delia and Susanna Heron photographed by Reg Butler in St Ives, 1951

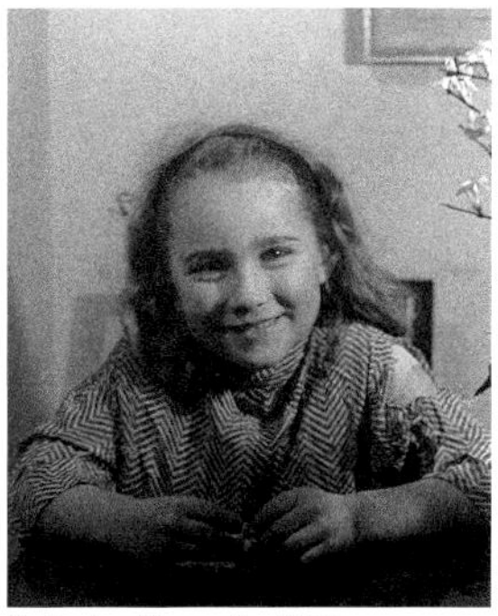

Katharine Heron, ?*c.*1953

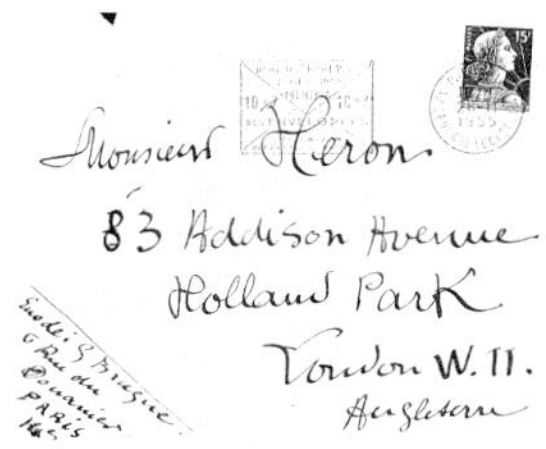

Monsieur Heron
83 Addison Avenue
Holland Park
London W.11.
Angleterre

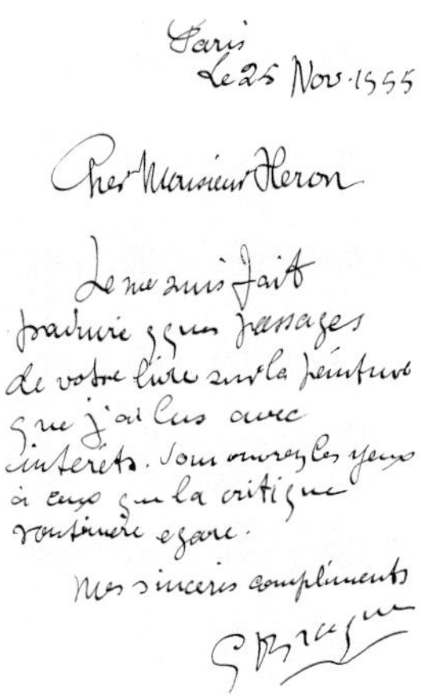

Paris
Le 25 Nov. 1955

Cher Monsieur Heron

Je me suis fait traduire quelques passages de votre livre sur la peinture que j'ai lus avec intérêt. Vous ouvrez les yeux à ceux que la critique routinière égare.

Mes sincères compliments
G Braque

Letter in French from Braque to PH, Paris, 25 Nov. 1955 [Dear Monsieur Heron. I have had translated certain passages of your book on painting, which I have read with interest. You open the eyes to those things which ordinary critics are unaware of. My sincere compliments G Braque']

1963 Exhibited at Galerie Charles Lienhard, Zurich (January), and wrote essay 'A Note on my Painting: 1962' for catalogue.

1965 Silver Medal at VIII Bienal de São Paulo, Brazil. Shared the British Pavilion with Victor Pasmore. Lectured in São Paulo, Brazilia, and Rio de Janiero. Visited Mexico. Accompanied Lilian Somerville, Director of Art, British Council, to Bienal. Third Bertha Schaefer exhibition in New York; Lilian Somerville attended private view.

1966 In December published first of series of articles in *Studio International* in which PH questioned the perceived ascendancy of American artists. He subsequently returned to the theme in 1968 and 1970 in *Studio International*; and in a three-hour lecture in December 1970 at the Institute of Contemporary Arts, London, entitled 'Symmetry in Painting: An Academic Formula' and in a very long article of fourteen thousand words, published over three days in *The Guardian* in October 1974.

1967 Invited by the Rose Skinner Gallery, Perth, to judge an all-Australia painting exhibition; lectured first in Perth and then in Sydney. While canoeing in Cornwall with Bryan Wynter broke leg and was disabled for a year. Concentrated on gouaches – an area of his work first explored in 1960.

1960s–1970s As external examiner at Leeds, Winchester and other art schools, PH came into close contact with both students and staff, and witnessed the amazing vitality generated in the late 1960s. He defended the independence and autonomy of the art schools, resisting their integration into the polytechnic system. The publication of his article 'Murder of the Art Schools' in *The Guardian* in 1971 precipitated an enormous correspondence in that newspaper over the next six months. It brought a response and offers of help from many teachers and students and also from Jo Grimond, former Leader of the Liberal Party, who organised a conference on the subject at Eliot College at the University of Kent in Canterbury in 1973. Also, at PH's suggestion, Grimond organised a visit to Mrs Thatcher, then Minister of Education. At the meeting PH and Jo Grimond were joined by Henry Moore, John Piper and others.

1968 Retrospective exhibition at the Museum of Modern Art, Oxford (May–June).

1969 'Colour in my Paintings' published in *Studio International* (December).

1972 At the invitation of the collectors, wrote 'Colour and Abstraction in the Drawings of Bonnard', an extended introduction to catalogue of exhibition of Bonnard drawings owned by Kyra Gerard and Alfred Ayrton, organised by Charles Terrasse for the American Federation of Arts. Exhibition toured to more than ten museums in the United States. Exhibition of large Heron canvases at Whitechapel Art Gallery, London.

1973 Exhibited large paintings, gouaches and prints at Bonython Gallery, Sydney. Delivered Power Lecture in Contemporary Art entitled 'The Shape of Colour', in Sydney, Brisbane, Canberra, Melbourne, Adelaide and Perth.

1977 Created CBE in New Year's Honours List.

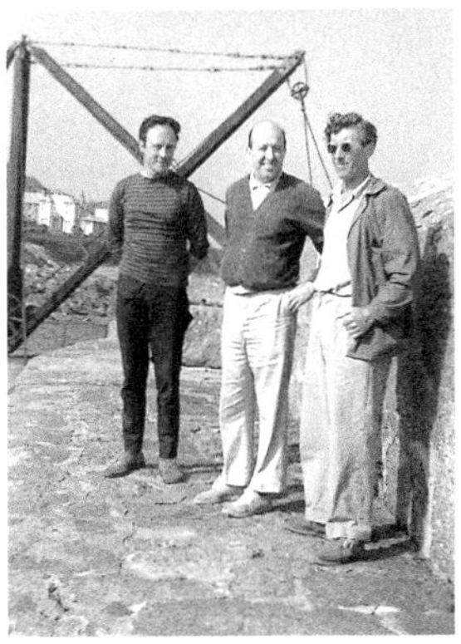

PH, Clement Greenburg and John Wells at Mousehole, September 1959

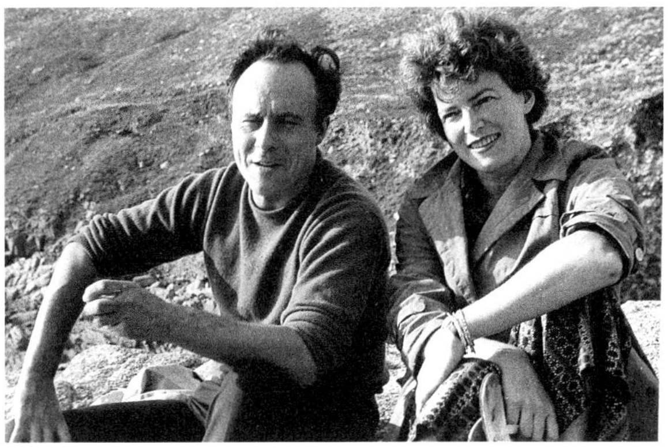

Patrick and Delia Heron photographed by F.E. McWilliam, *c.*1960

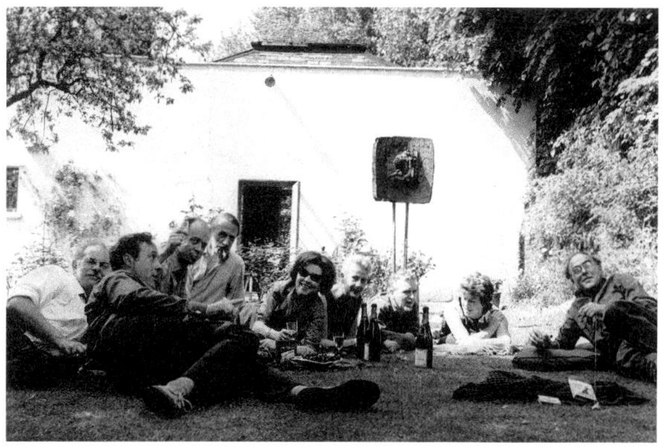

On the lawn in front of F.E. McWilliam's house: Left to right: Terry Frost, Patrick Heron, Bryan Wynter, F.E. McWilliam, Mary Scott, Beth McWilliam, Delia Heron, Roger Hilton, 1963

1978 At the invitation of Professor Kelly Fearing, delivered E. William Doty Lectures in Fine Arts at University of Texas at Austin, entitled 'The Colour of Colour'. Retrospective exhibition of work of previous twelve years at University of Texas at Austin Art Museum (March – May). PH and Delia made honorary citizens of Texas by order of the Secretary of State. PH and Delia toured USA. On return to England PH fell ill with pneumonia and worked little as a result. *The Shapes of Colour: 1943–1978*, book of screenprints, Kelpra Editions, Waddington and Tooths Graphics.

1979 Commissioned to design two carpets for foyer of Cavendish Hotel, London. Designed silk scarf to celebrate the opening of new galleries at the Tate. Delia died suddenly at Eagles Nest on 3 May. PH did little painting in the following year.

1980 Became Trustee of the Tate Gallery (until 1987). Visited Dordogne with Leslie Waddington and family.

1981 Commissioned to design tapestry for University of Galway, Eire. Commissioned by Harvey's of Bristol to design album cover for record of music by Shostakovich. Visited Venice with Leslie and Ferriel Waddington and family.

1982 Awarded Hon.D.Litt. by Exeter University. Visited Dordogne with Leslie Waddington and family.

1983 Television broadcast of BBC *Omnibus* programme 'Patrick Heron', directed by Colin Nears.

1985 Retrospective exhibition at Barbican Art Gallery, London (July – September). New works used the title *Garden Painting*, first used for the earlier but very different Tachiste paintings of 1965.

1986 Awarded Hon.D.Litt. by University of Kent at Canterbury, Chancellor Jo Grimond, whose portrait he painted for the Scottish National Portrait Gallery. Television broadcast of LWT *The South Bank Show* programme 'Patrick Heron', directed by John Read and presented by Melvin Bragg.

1987 Awarded Honorary Doctorate by Royal College of Art.

1988 Visited Russia on behalf of the Tate Gallery with Director Alan Bowness and Richard Rogers, Chairman of Trustees, and again in 1989 with the new Director Nicholas Serota, in order to borrow all the Russian-owned Matisses from the Hermitage Museum in Leningrad and the Pushkin Museum in Moscow, to be combined with American Matisses, for an exhibition at the Tate. This project was proposed by PH in October 1985 in his capacity as Chairman of the Exhibitions Sub-Committee at the Tate. It was subsequently thwarted, and the loans went instead to the Museum of Modern Art, New York, and to Paris. Monograph *Patrick Heron*, edited and with an introduction by Vivien Knight, published by John Taylor in association with Lund Humphries.

1989 Visited Japan and gave a lecture at the opening of the exhibition *St Ives* at the Setagaya Art Museum, Tokyo. Commissioned by the Royal Institute of British Architects (RIBA) to paint portrait of Michael Manser, past-President. Visited Sydney at the invitation of the Art Gallery of New South Wales, as artist-in-residence, as a guest of Lord McAlpine,

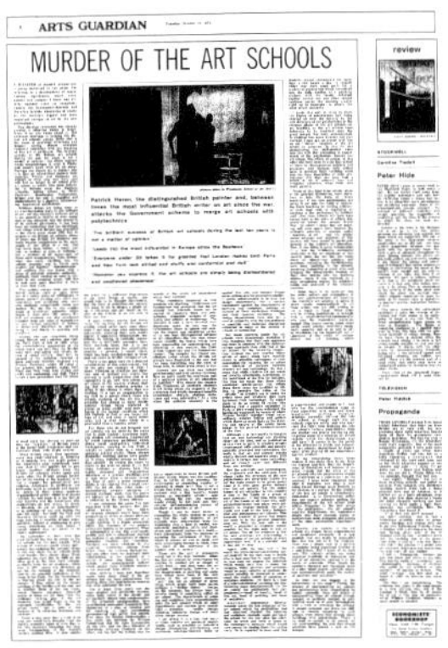
ARTS GUARDIAN

MURDER OF THE ART SCHOOLS

'Murder of the Art Schools', *The Guardian*, 12 Oct. 1971

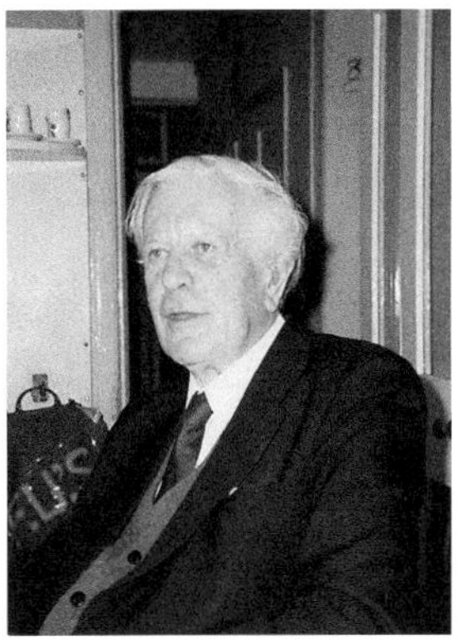
Jo Grimond at PH's flat in Chelsea *c.*1986

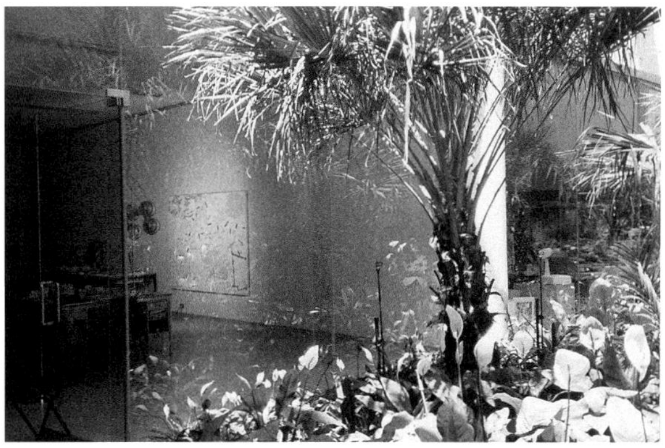
PH's studio at Art Gallery of New South Wales, 1989

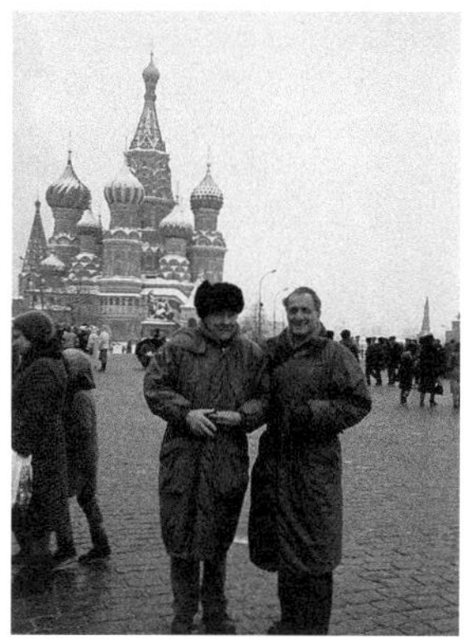
PH and Richard Rogers in Moscow, 1988

staying until February 1990. In these sixteen weeks he produced forty-six large gouaches and six large paintings. During his visit he held a large exhibition at the Art Gallery of New South Wales and also a one-man show at Rex Irwin Gallery. Made Hon.Ph.D., CNAA, Winchester School of Art.

1990–3 At the invitation of Sue Walker and Chris Pyatt of Victorian Tapestry Workshop, Melbourne, two tapestries made from Sydney gouaches.

1991 Travelled to New Zealand as visiting artist at the International Art Workshop at Teschamakers Conference Centre, near Omaru North Otago. With students he made vast canvas paintings which were temporarily fixed to the seventy foot walls in a disused limestone quarry, and to its floor.

1992 At the invitation of the architects, Eldred Evans and David Shalev, designed coloured glass window (with technical support from architect Julian Feary; manufactured by Wilhelm Derix) for Tate Gallery St Ives, which opened in June 1993. Made two visits to Wiesbaden, Germany, to supervise its production. Designed three silk banners, the largest sixty feet high, for Chelsea and Westminster Hospital; these were made by Cathy Merrow-Smith, with whom PH had collaborated on nine silk banners for the Tate Gallery shop in 1991 for the architect John Miller. At the invitation of Lord Palumbo, designed kneeler to surround circular Henry Moore altar at St Stephen Walbrook in the City of London. Made Honorary Fellow of RIBA.

1993 Wrote 'Late Matisse' for *Modern Painters,* for which he had earlier contributed an article 'Late Picasso' (1988).

1994 Exhibition of large new paintings at Camden Arts Centre, entitled *Big Paintings 1994* (September – November), also shown at Arnolfini in Bristol (January – February 1995). This exhibition toured to Preston and Llandudno. Wrote essay on Constable's drawings entitled 'Constable: Spatial Colour in the Drawings' for catalogue of exhibition at Dulwich Picture Gallery, London. The monograph *Patrick Heron,* written by Mel Gooding, published by Phaidon (272 pages).

1995 Commissioned by the National Portrait Gallery to paint portrait of A.S. Byatt. Painting unveiled April 1998.

1996 Essay 'Solid Space in Cézanne' published in *Modern Painters.* Selection of PH writings on art schools: *Patrick Heron on Art and Education,* published by Bretton Hall, Wakefield, to coincide with presentation of Honorary Fellowship of Bretton Hall, University of Leeds, and one-man show of gouaches (May). Exhibition of large paintings (from Camden exhibition) at Salander-O'Reilly Galleries, New York (November).

1996–8 Commissioned to design *Big Painting Sculpture*: site-specific outdoor installation at Stag Place, London, in collaboration with Julian Feary.

1998 *Painter as Critic – Patrick Heron: Selected Writings,* edited by Mel Gooding, published by Tate Gallery Publishing to coincide with the retrospective exhibition of paintings.

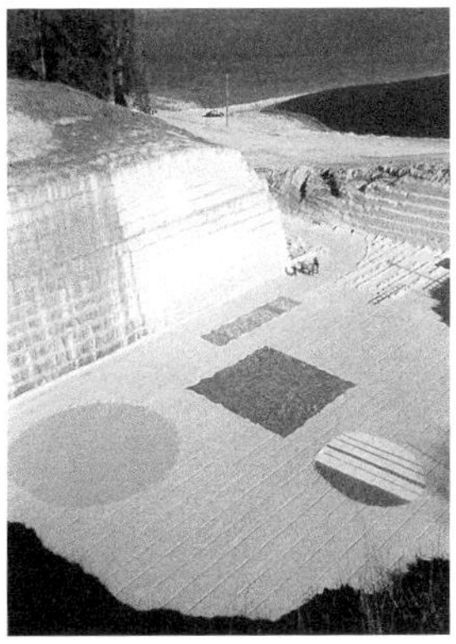

Quarry near Omaru, North Otago, New Zealand, 1991

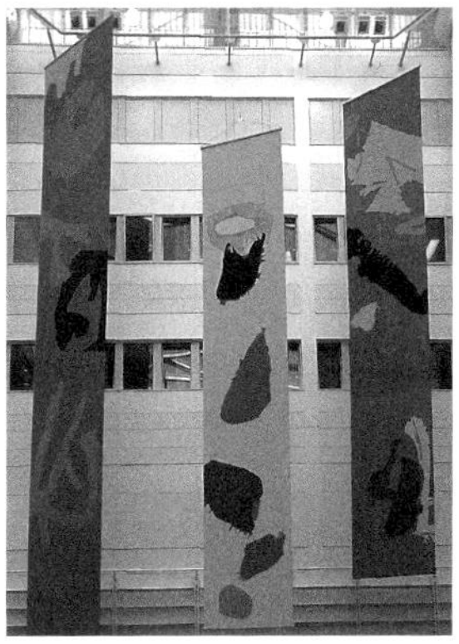

Banners at Chelsea and Westminster Hospital, 1992

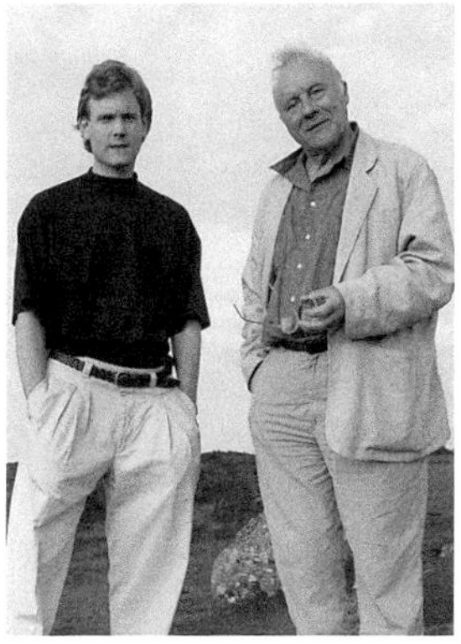

PH and David Thomson on the moors above Eagles Nest, *c.*1993

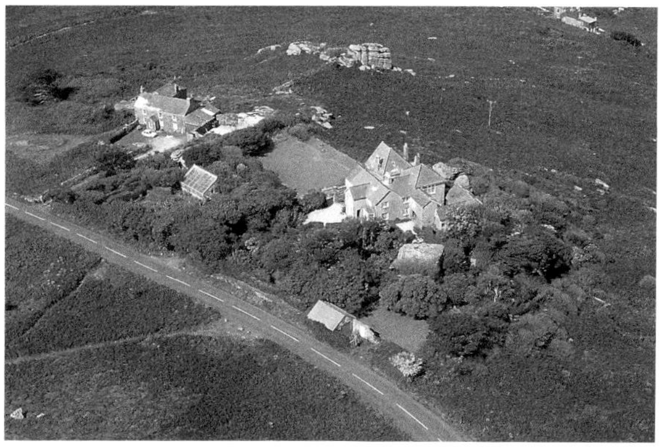

Aerial photograph by Frank Herholdt of Eagles Nest in the landscape, *c.*1993

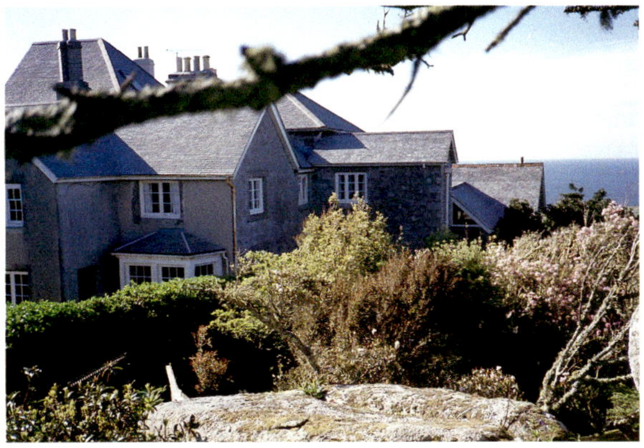
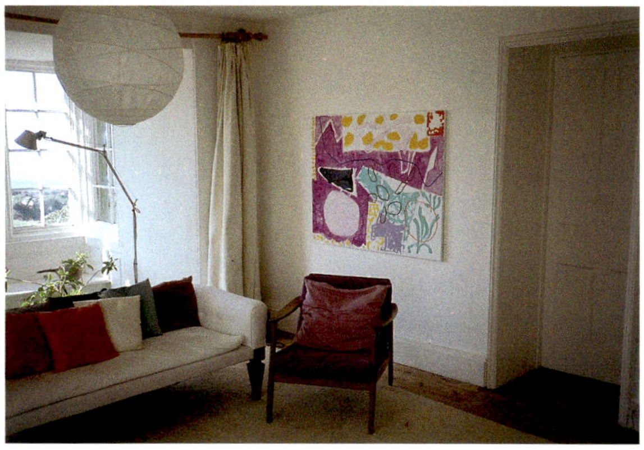
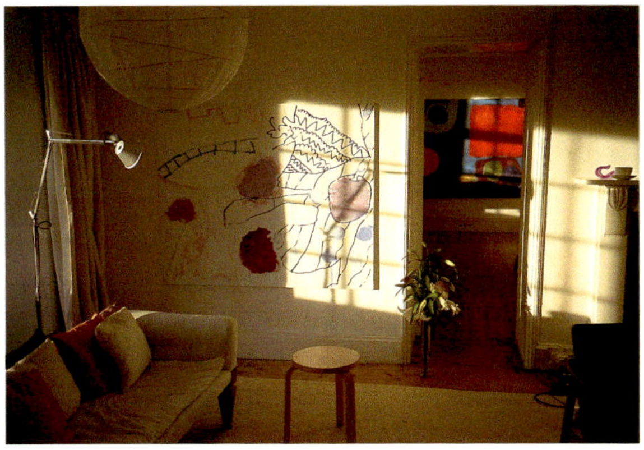
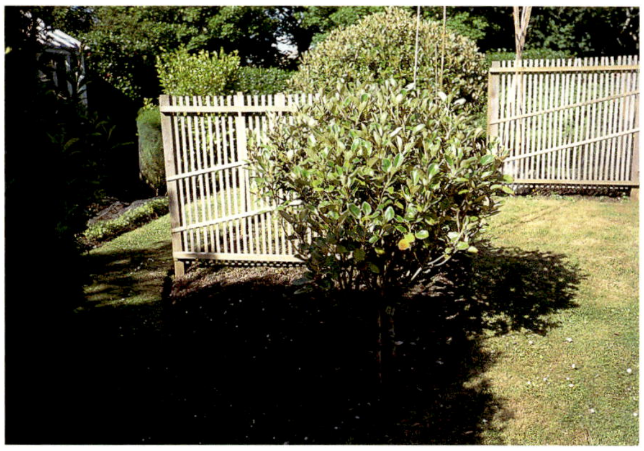
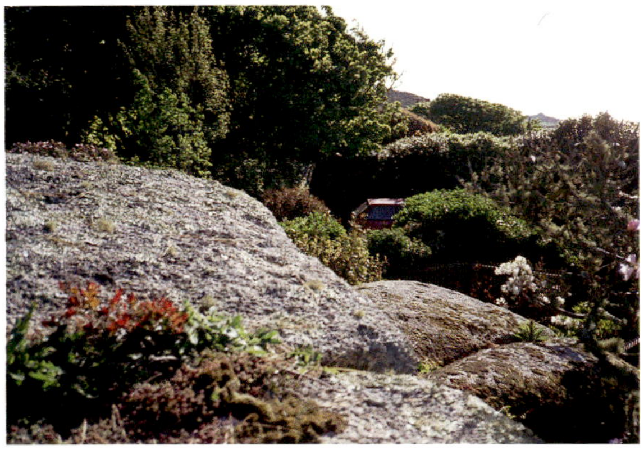
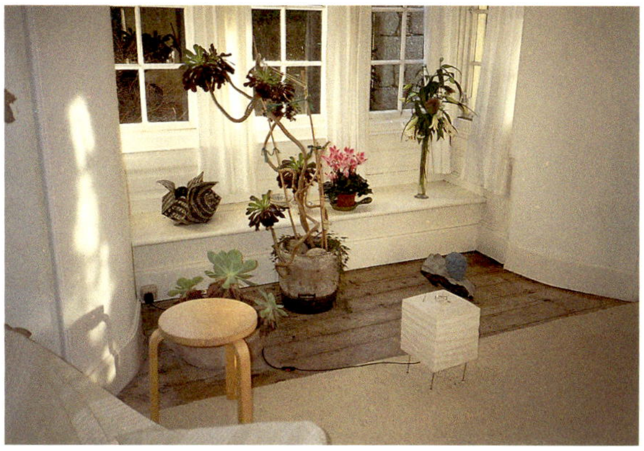
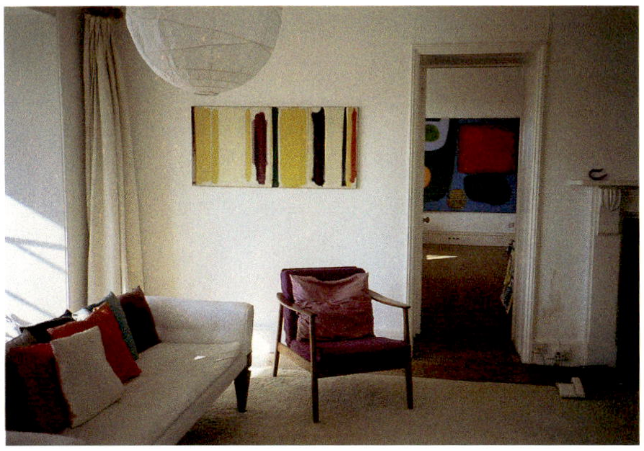
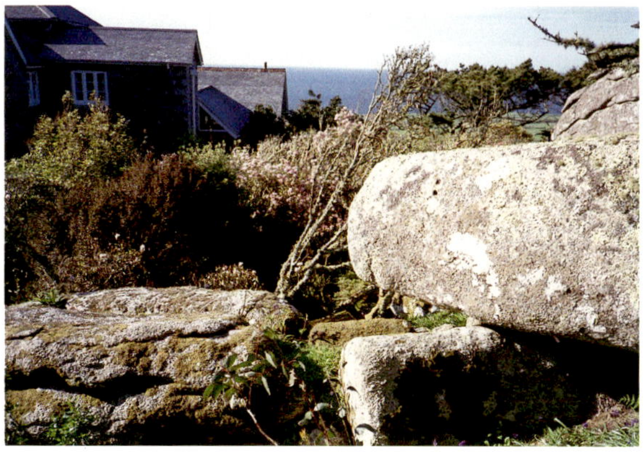

Photographs taken by Patrick Heron of Eagles Nest: the House and Garden

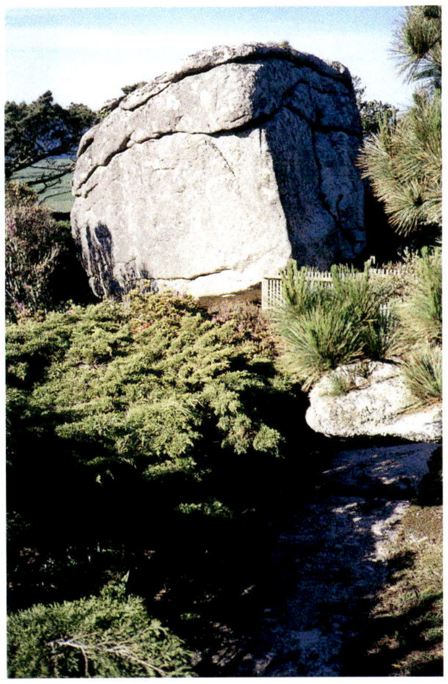
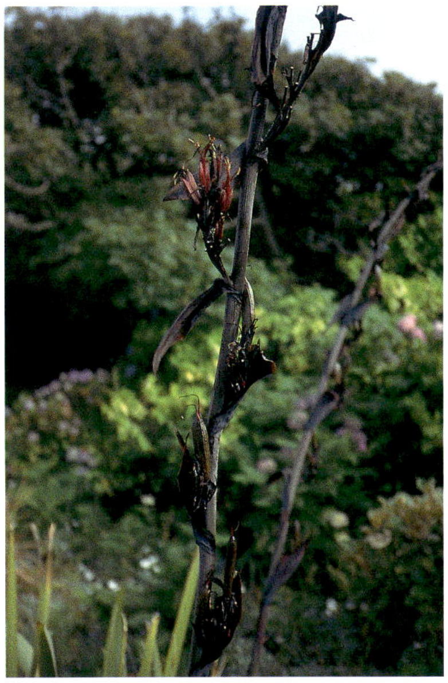
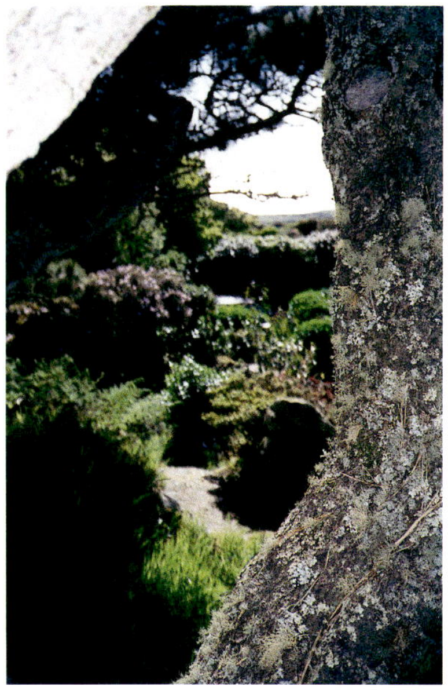
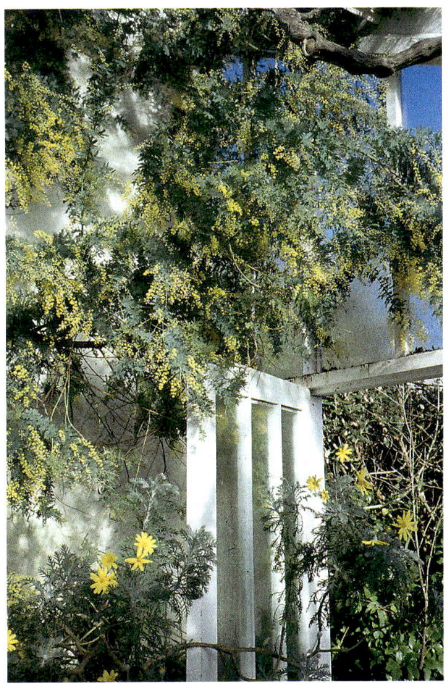
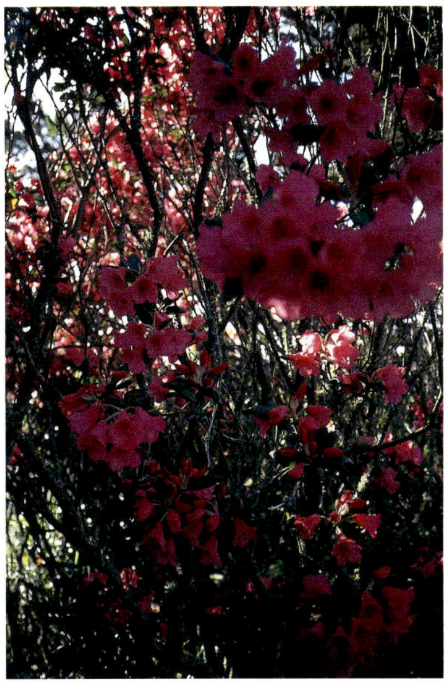
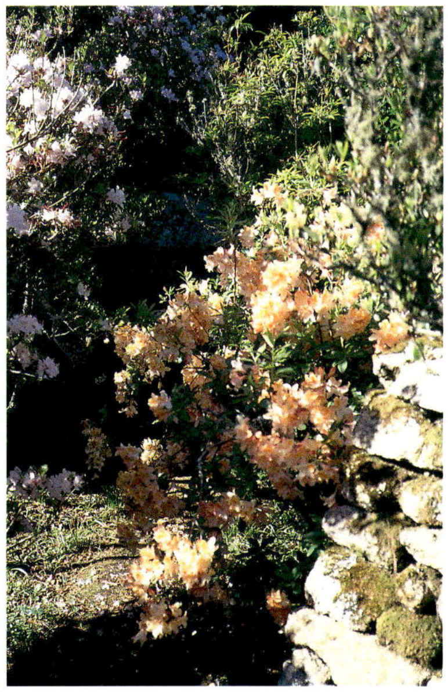
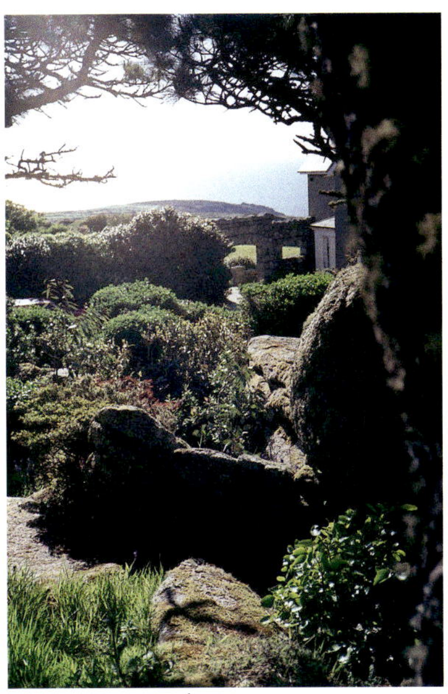
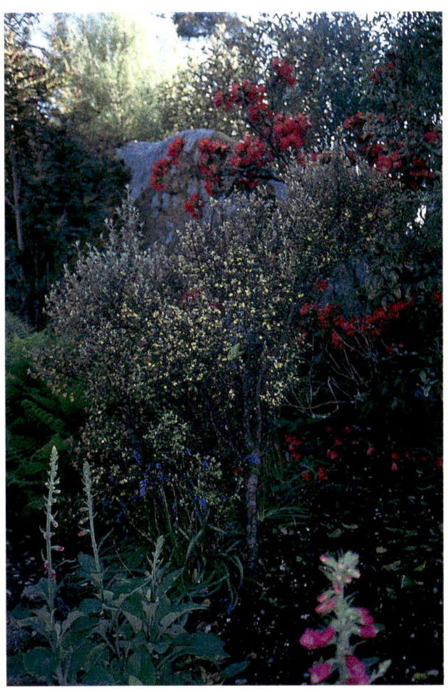
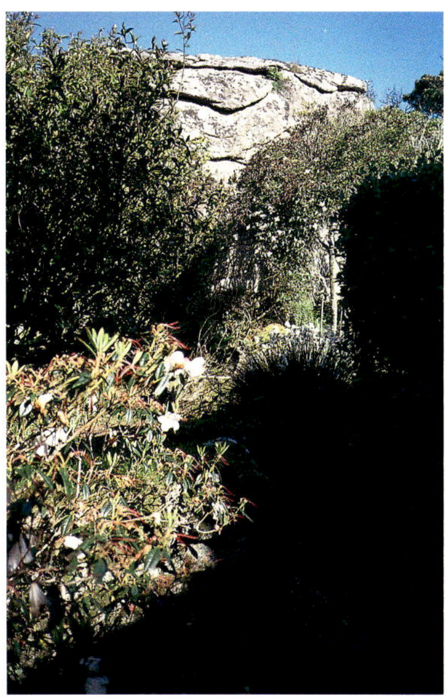

Bibliography

168

Compiled by Nicola Hunt of the Tate Gallery Library

The compiler gratefully acknowledges the use made of earlier bibliographic sources, particularly Mel Gooding's bibliography published in his 1994 monograph on Heron. Special thanks must go to Patrick Heron's assistant Janet Axten, who proofread the draft bibliography and provided many useful comments and invaluable first-hand additional information.

The bibliography is divided into six sections:

1 Selected writings by the artist
2 Solo exhibition catalogues
3 Selected group exhibition catalogues
4 Selected periodical and newspaper articles (including interviews)
5 Books and sections in books
6 Selected radio and television broadcasts, films and lectures

Section 5 is arranged in alphabetical order; all other sections are arranged chronologically. In sections 2 and 3 entries specify the number of works by Heron included in the exhibition. Section 2 chiefly includes catalogues of exhibitions in which Heron exhibited on his own, but also includes shows where Heron's work was exhibited, for example, on one whole floor or room of a gallery alongside other contemporary artists who also had their own individual exhibition space. For touring shows, not all variants of catalogues have been included, but an indication of the itinerary of the exhibition is given. Some publications containing statements by the artist appear in more than one section.

Items marked with an asterisk (*) have not been seen by the compiler, and the bibliographical data for these derives from secondary sources. Square brackets indicate information supplied from sources other than the item itself. Place of exhibition or publication is London, unless otherwise stated.

A comprehensive bibliography is available for consultation in the Tate Gallery Library.

1 Selected Writings by the Artist

Abbreviations for journal titles: *NEW* = *The New English Weekly*; *NSN* = *The New Statesman and Nation*.

1945

Ben Nicholson. *NEW*, 18 Oct. 1945, pp.6–7.

To Paris via Stockholm. *NEW*, 15 Nov. 1945, p.46.

1946

The art of the potter [letter]. *Time & Tide*, vol.27, pp.1261–2.

Picasso. *NEW*, 10 Jan. 1946, pp.124–5.

The Penguin Modern Painters. *NEW*, 7 Feb. 1946, p.164. Review of publication *Victor Pasmore* by Clive Bell.

Paul Klee 1879–1940. *NEW*, 21 Feb. 1946, pp.186–7.

Cézanne at the Tate. *NEW*, 30 May 1946, p.70.

Bernard Leach. *NEW*, 27 June, pp.109–10. Review of exh., Berkeley Galleries, 1946.

Braque. *NEW*, 4 July 1946, pp.118–19.

New sculpture (and sculptor's drawings). *NEW*, 31 Oct. 1946, pp.28–9. Review of Henry Moore show at Leicester Galleries, and Barbara Hepworth show at the Lefevre Gallery, London.

Pottery [book review of *The art of the potter* by W. B. Honey], *Time & Tide*, 23 Nov. 1946, p.1136.*

1947

Vlaminck paintings 1900–1945. London: Lindsay Drummond; Paris: Editions du Chène, 1947.*

Paul Nash 1889–1946 [part 1]. *NEW*, 13 Feb. 1947, pp.169–70.

Paul Nash 1889–1946 [part II]. *NEW*, 6 Mar. 1947, pp.180–1.

Bonnard, Vuillard, Sickert. *World Review*, June 1947, pp.48–54.*

M. Paulhan's Braque [book review of *Braque le patron* by Jean Paulhan]. *NEW*, 10 July 1947, p.115.

Views and reviews: the ethics of Mr. Herbert Read [book review of *Annals of Innocence and Experience* by Herbert Read]. *NEW*, 31 July 1947, pp.139–40.

At the Mayor Gallery. *NSN*, 11 Oct. 1947, pp.288–9.

Sutherland and Colquhoun. *NSN*, 25 Oct. 1947, p.328.

Matthew Smith, Craxton and Freud. *NSN*, 8 Nov. 1947, p.368.

Round the art galleries [letter to the editor]. *Listener*, 20 Nov. 1947, p.900.

The School of Paris. *NSN*, 22 Nov. 1947, p.48.

Pasmore at the Redfern. *NSN*, 6 Dec. 1947, p.448.

Van Gogh at the Tate. *NSN*, 27 Dec. 1947, pp.507–8.

1948

Introduction to exh. cat. *Engelsk Nutidskonst*, British Council, London (touring exh.) 1948, pp.9–13.

Artists in Cornwall. *NSN*, 17 Jan. 1948, pp.48–9.

The Redfern Gallery: Rouault's 'Guerre' and 'Miserere'. *NSN*, 24 Jan. 1948, p.71.

Marc Chagall at the Tate. *NEW*, 26 Feb. 1948, p.195.

Juan Gris [book review of *Juan Gris: his life and work* by Daniel Henry Kahnweiler, trans. Douglas Cooper]. *NSN*, 20 Mar. 1948, pp.239–40.

Paul Nash: a memorial exhibition at the Tate. *NSN*, 27 Mar. 1948, p.252.

Adrian Ryan. *NSN*, 17 Apr. 1948, p.313.

Barbara Hepworth, Lawrence Gowing. *NSN*, 24 Apr. 1948, p.333.

The Albertina/Augustus John. *NSN*, 15 May 1948, pp.393–4.

Courtauld exhibition at the Tate. *NSN*, 22 May 1948, p.413.

Sculpture in the Park. *NSN*, 29 May 1948, pp.433–4. Review of exh. in Battersea Park, 1948.

Graham Sutherland: Bryan Wynter. *NSN*, 12 June 1948, pp.477–8.

Standards in art criticism [letter to the editor]. *Listener*, 15 July 1948, p.99.

Round the galleries. *NSN*, 26 June 1948, pp.520–1. Includes reviews of Picasso at Zwemmers, Adler at Gimpel Fils and Vuillard at Wildenstein's.

Standards in art criticism. *Listener*, 29 July 1948, pp.165, 167.

August exhibitions. *NSN*, 14 Aug. 1948, p.132.

Jack B. Yeats. *NSN*, 21 Aug. 1948, pp.153–4.

Macbryde and Colquhoun. *NSN*, 4 Sept. 1948, pp.193–4.

The criticism of contemporaries. *NSN*, 2 Oct. 1948, pp.280–1.

Picasso: Trevelyan. *NSN*, 9 Oct. 1948, pp.302–3.

Three exhibitions. *NSN*, 23 Oct. 1948, pp.346–7. Review of work by Henry Moore and Ceri Richards.

Letter from London. *Magazine of Art (NY)*, Nov. 1948, pp.273, 277.*

Ivon Hitchens: Ben Nicholson. *NSN*, 20 Nov. 1948, p.438.

1949

The visual arts. *Architect's yearbook*, no.3, 1949, pp.20–31. (Article written in 1948).

John Minton. *NSN*, 12 Feb. 1949, p.151. Review of exh., Lefevre Gallery, 1949.

At the Redfern: Michael Rothenstein, Humphrey Spender. *NSN*, 19 Feb. 1949, p.180.

An exhibition. *NSN*, 5 Mar. 1949, p.226. Review of exh., Agnews, 1949, containing works by Duncan Grant, Vanessa Bell and Rodrigo Moynihan.

Contemporary American art: a note. *Magazine of Art (NY)*, Mar. 1949, p.102.*

Two galleries. *NSN*, 5 Mar. 1949, p.227. Review of exh. of French lithographs, Gimpel Fils, 1949.

Seven artists tell why they paint. *Picture Post*, 12 Mar., p.16.*

The galleries. *NSN*, 19 Mar. 1949, p.275. Review of Ivon Hitchens exh. at Leicester Galleries, and Raoul Dufy and Isabel Lambert exh. at the Hanover Gallery, 1949.

Frances Hodgkins. *NSN*, 26 Mar. 1949, pp.299–300.

The School of London. *NSN*, 9 Apr. 1949, p.351. Review of work by Robert Adams, Henry Moore and Wyndham Lewis [et al.].

[Bauchant, Klee and Lurcat]. *Art News and Review*, 9 Apr. 1949, p.5 (unsigned).*

Reality for the painter. *NSN*, 16 Apr. 1949, p.378. Review of work by Paul Klee, Jean Lurçat and André Bauchant.

Sutherland and Wood. *NSN*, 30 Apr. 1949, p.432.

Mr Wyndham Lewis. *NSN*, 7 May 1949, p.468.

Munich and Vienna I. *NSN*, 28 May 1949, pp.554–5.

Munich and Vienna II. *NSN*, 4 June 1949, p.584.

Degas at Roland, Browse and Delbanco's. *NSN*, 4 June 1949, p.585.

Massimo Campigli at the St. George's Gallery. *NSN*, 11 June 1949, p.612.

Picasso Lithographs, at the Hanover Gallery. *NSN*, 11 June 1949, p.612 (unsigned).

Paris: summer 1949. *NSN*, 16 July 1949, pp.67–8.

Salon de Mai Ve. *NSN*, 30 July 1949, pp.122–3. Review of work by Matisse, Manessier, Bazaine, Buffet [et al.].

William Townsend at Roland, Browse and Delbanco's. *NSN*, 6 Aug. 1949, p.148 (unsigned).

The summer exhibitions. *NSN*, 13 Aug. 1949, p.170. Reviews Reg Butler and also formation of Penwith Society.

Monsieur K's choice 1949. *NSN*, 3 Sept. 1949, p.244. Reviews Daniel Kahnweiler's choice of modern paintings.

Children's paintings. *NSN*, 17 Sept. 1949, pp.298–9.

Fame and promise: part II at the Leicester Galleries. *NSN*, 17 Sept. 1949, p.300 (unsigned).

James Pryde: 1866–1941. *NSN*, 1 Oct. 1949, p.355.

Adrian Ryan and Peter Lanyon. *NSN*, 15 Oct. 1949, pp.422–3.

Round the galleries. *NSN*, 29 Oct. 1949, pp.483–4. Includes review of work by Louis Le Brocquy, Lurcat and F.E. McWilliam.

Miss Clough and Miss McCannell. *NSN*, 5 Nov. 1949, pp.512–13.

The abstract Pasmore. *NSN*, 12 Nov. 1949, pp.574–8.

The new patron. *NSN*, 19 Nov. 1949, pp.579–80. Reviews the Arts Council and the British Council arts funding.

Francis Bacon. *NSN*, 3 Dec. 1949, pp.643–4.

1950

Colour photography: a painter's comment. *Penrose Annual*, 1950, pp.75–7.

English and French in 1950. *NSN*, 7 Jan. 1950, pp.9–10.

The Impressionists and Post-Impressionists at Burlington House. *Art News and Review*, 14 Jan. 1950, pp.3–4.

John Minton at Lefevre. *NSN*, 14 Jan. 1950, p.33 (unsigned).

The London Group, at the New Burlington. *NSN*, 14 Jan. 1950, p.33 (unsigned).

A perpetual colour. *NSN*, 21 Jan. 1950, p.63. Review of exh. of Howard Bliss Collection, Leicester Galleries, 1950.

Space in French landscape. *NSN*, 4 Feb. 1950, p.128.

The return of the image. *NSN*, 18 Feb. 1950, pp.187–8.

Fernand Léger. *NSN*, 25 Feb. 1950, p.215.

Julian Trevelyan and Aeply Replicas, at Gimpel Fils. *NSN*, 18 Mar. 1950, p.300.

New sculpture by Epstein, at the Leicester Galleries. *NSN*, 18 Mar. 1950, p.300.

London or Paris. *NSN*, 25 Mar. 1950, p.339.

Paintings by Roy de Maistre, at the Adams Gallery. *NSN*, 25 Mar. 1950, p.340.

Contemporary British sculpture. Central Office of Information for the British Council [written spring 1950]. Heron writes about Moore, Hepworth, Epstein, Gill and Gaudier-Brzeska.*

The private collector. *NSN*, 1 Apr. 1950, p.368. Review of Tate Gallery exh.

The poetry of measure [book review of *Art and science: a study of Alberti, Piero della Francesca and Giorgione* by Adrian Stokes]. *NSN*, 8 Apr. 1950, pp.410, 412.

French masters at the Marlborough Galleries. *NSN*, 8 Apr. 1950, p.402 (unsigned).*

Paintings by Mintchine, at Gimpel Fils. *NSN*, 22 Apr. 1950, p.457.

The French contemporaries. *NSN*, 29 Apr. 1950, p.484.

Lucian Freud at the Hanover Gallery. *NSN*, 29 Apr. 1950, pp.484, 486.

Peintre et sculpture actuélles *L'Age Nouveau* (Paris), May 1950, no.49/50, pp.109–17.*

Trends in contemporary British painting. *Listener*, 11 May 1950, pp.836–8. [Text of a Third Programme talk.]

Paintings by Peter Lanyon. *St. Ives Times*, 22 June 1951, p.6.*

Penwith Society's Third Exhibition: Pt 1. *St. Ives Times*, 7 July 1950, p.3.*

Penwith Society's Third Exhibition: Pt 2. *St. Ives Times*, 14 July 1950, p.2.*

The Biennale Exhibition in Venice [letter to the editor]. *Listener*, 3 Aug. 1950, p.166.

Picasso in Provence. *Art News and Review*, 2 Dec. 1950, p.2. Review of Picasso exh., New Burlington Galleries, 1950.

Victor Pasmore. *Art News and Review*, 30 Dec. 1950, p.4.

1951

'The critics' and Mr. Pasmore [letter to the editor]. *Listener*, 18 Jan. 1951, pp.106–7.

The changing jug. *Listener*, 25 Jan. 1951, pp.135–6. A Third Programme text discussing the recent work of Braque, Picasso and Matisse.

Some young British sculptors. *House and Garden*, Mar. 1951, p.69.*

The poetry of colour. *Art News and Review*, 21 Apr., 1951, p.3.

Introduction to *Barbara Hepworth: sculpture and drawings*, exh. cat., Wakefield City Art Gallery, 1951.

The sea-mists of the winter [letter to the editor]. *Listener*, 24 May 1951, p.840. Review of work by Wyndham Lewis.

Mobiles. *House and Garden*, June 1951, pp.38–41. Reviews Calder and Chadwick.

Hills and faces. *PS2 – Penwith Society Broadsheet 2*, summer 1951, pp.3–4.*

Pilot Read [book review of *Contemporary British art* by Herbert Read]. *NSN*, 6 Oct. 1951, pp.370, 372.

Picasso. *NSN*, 20 Oct. 1951, pp.432, 434.

Bonnard and visual reality. *NSN*, 24 Nov. 1951, pp.588–9.

1952

Note in exh. cat. *Abstract painting in England*. British Council, Jan. 1952.*

Wyndham Lewis the artist [book review of *The art of Wyndham Lewis* by C. Hanley Page]. *NSN*, 12 Jan. 1952, pp.43–4.

A master-potters' aesthetic [book review of '*A potter's portfolio*' by Bernard Leach]. *NSN*, 2 Feb. 1952, pp.130, 132.

Art's scientific credentials [book review of *The philosophy of modern art* by Herbert Read]. *NSN*, 29 Mar. 1952, pp.378, 380.

Ben Nicholson. *NSN*, 17 May 1952, p.584.

Ivon Hitchens. *NSN*, 14 June 1952, pp.701–2.

Paintings by Roger Hilton at Gimpel Fils. *NSN*, 28 June 1952, p.771.

The crafts in relation to contemporary art. In *The report of the International Conference of Craftsmen in Pottery & Textiles at Dartington Hall, Totnes, Devon*, July 17–27, 1952, pp.56–60.

The power of Paris. *NSN*, 19 July 1952, p.68.

The artist craftsman. *NSN*, 27 Sept. 1952, pp.346, 348.

Barbara Hepworth at the Lefevre. *NSN*, 18 Oct. 1952, p.450.

1953

Space in painting and architecture. *Architect's Yearbook*, no.5, Jan. 1953, pp.19–26.

Fruit or thorn? *NSN*, 24 Jan. 1953, p.92.

Paul Feiler, at the Redfern Gallery. *NSN*, 14 Feb. 1953, p.176.

Turner resurgent. *NSN*, 21 Feb. 1953, pp.204–5.

'Opposing forces': paintings by seven artists at the I.C.A. *NSN*, 21 Feb. 1953, p.206.

Introduction to exh. cat. *[James Cant]*, The Coffee House, Northumberland Avenue, Feb.–Mar. 1953.*

Three exhibitions. *NSN*, 7 Mar. 1953, pp.260–1. Review of exh. of work by Alan Reynolds and Jack Smith, and R.D.S. May's Collection, Gimpel Fils, 1953.

Mexico. *NSN*, 14 Mar. 1953, pp.292, 294. Review of exh. of Mexican art, Tate Gallery, Mar.–Apr. 1953.

Return to realism. *NSN*, 21 Mar. 1953, pp.341–2.

Artists and critics. *NSN*, 11 Apr. 1953, p.428.

Picasso in Rome. *NSN*, 16 May 1953, pp.576–7.

Introduction to exh. cat. *L'oeuvre graphique de Braque de 1910 à 1953*, Gimpel Fils, 1953.

Graham Sutherland. *NSN*, 6 June 1953, p.670. Review of exh., Tate Gallery, 1953.

William Scott. *NSN*, 20 June 1953, pp.730–1.

Braque. *NSN*, 27 June 1953, pp.772, 774.

Introduction to exh. cat. *Space in colour*, Hanover Gallery, July–Aug. 1953.

Matthew Smith. *NSN*, 19 Sept. 1953, p.313.

From Paris and Venice. *NSN*, 21 Nov. 1953, p.632.

1954

Discussion after John Berger's lecture *The thoery and practice of art in the Soviet Union. Journal of the Architectural Association*, Mar. 1954, pp.204–5.*

Peter Lanyon. *Art News and Review*, 6 Mar. 1954, p.7.

Henry Moore [letter]. *NSN*, 6 Mar. 1954, pp.288–9.

Henry Moore [letter]. *NSN*, 20 Mar. 1954, p.359.

Henry Moore [letter]. *NSN*, 3 Apr. 1954, p.439.

Patrick Hayman: a note. In exh. cat. *Patrick Hayman*, Gallery One, Nov. 1954.*

Artists missing from the Tate [letter]. *NSN*, 25 Dec. 1954, pp.855–6.

1955

The changing forms of art. London: Routledge & Kegan Paul, 1955 (paperback ed., New York: Noonday Press, 1958.).

Ivon Hitchens. Harmondsworth: Penguin Books, 1955.

Inspiration for the painter. *NSN*, 1 Jan. 1955, pp.6–7.

The Courbet exhibition in Paris [letter to the editor]. *Listener*, 17 Feb. 1955, p.299.

The Courbet exhibition in Paris. *Listener*, 3 Mar. 1955, p.387.

Space in colour: notes on nine British painters. *Arts Digest*, 15 Mar., pp.8–11.

Barbara Hepworth – carver. *Arts Digest*, 1 May 1955, pp.8–9.

London. *Arts Digest*, 1 July 1955, pp.23–4. Review of work by Picasso, Soulages and Mark Tobey.

London. *Arts (NY)*, Nov. 1955, pp.12, 14. Reviews the 'New Realism' and exhibitions of Ben Nicholson, Victor Pasmore and Piet Mondrian.

1956

London. *Arts (NY)*, Jan. 1956, pp.12–13, 62. Reviews work by Henry Moore, Germaine Richier and Stanley Spencer.

Henry Moore – pro and con. *Encounter 29*, Feb. 1956, pp.51–4.*

The painter. *Journal Forty Nine of the Society of Industrial Artists*, Feb. 1956, pp.7–9. [From the symposium 'The Seeing Eye'].

Peter Lanyon. *Arts (NY)*, Feb. 1956, pp.33–7.

Round the London galleries. *Listener*, 16 Feb. 1956, p.256.

The Americans at the Tate Gallery. *Arts (NY)*, Mar. 1956, pp.15–17.

London. *Arts (NY)*, Apr. 1956, pp.12–13. Review of Alan Davie, Terry Frost and Jackson Pollock.

London. *Arts (NY)*, May 1956, pp.12–13. Surveys modern British sculpture by William Gear, Robert Adams and F.E. McWilliam.

Nicolas de Staël: 1914–1955. *Listener*, 3 May 1956, p.560.

Introduction to exh. cat. *Ivon Hitchens*, Venice Biennale, Venice, June 1956, pp.7–8.

London. *Arts (NY)*, June 1956, pp.12–13. Review of works by Riopelle and Ceri Richards.

Introduction to exh. cat. *A selection of paintings by M. de Vlaminck*, Crane Calman Gallery, 1956. (Introduction extracted from an essay on Vlaminck first published in 1947.)

London. *Arts (NY)*, Aug. 1956, pp.11–12. Review of Renoir exh., Marlborough Galleries, 1956.

Is Cézanne still alive? *Arts (NY)*, Oct. 1956, pp.26–9.

Ivon Hitchens. *Quadrum*, no.2, Nov. 1956, pp.155–60.

London: John Wells and Bryan Wynter. *Arts (NY)*, Nov. 1956, pp.15, 73.

1957

Note in exh. cat. *Statements: a review of British abstract art in 1956*, ICA, 1957, p.7.

Braque at the Zenith. *Arts (NY)*, Feb. 1957, pp.34–5.

Profile – Ben Nicholson. *Observer*, 21 Apr. 1957, p.8 (unsigned).*

Introducing Roger Hilton. *Arts (NY)*, May 1957, pp.22–6.

London. *Arts (NY)*, June 1957, pp.17, 63. Reviews Tachisme, Karel Appel, Jean Dubuffet, Sam Francis, Paul Jenkins and Jean-Paul Riopelle.

London. *Arts (NY)*, Sept. 1957, pp.12–13. Reviews work by Wassily Kandinsky, Francis Bacon and Reg Butler [et al.].

London. *Arts (NY)*, Oct. 1957, pp.16–17, 64. Reviews work by Reg Butler, Terry Frost and Bryan Wynter.

London: [the Monet revival]. *Arts (NY)*, Nov. 1957, pp.20–1.

London. *Arts (NY)*, Dec. 1957, pp.14–15. Reviews work by Kenneth Armitage and William Scott.

1958

Braque [introduction and notes]. Faber Gallery, 1958.

London. *Arts (NY)*, Jan. 1958, pp.18–19. Chiefly reviews the work of eight American artists, but includes Terry Wynter and César.

Derain reconsidered. *Arts (NY)*, Jan. 1958, pp.26–9.

London. *Arts (NY)*, May 1958, pp.22–3. Reviews work by Pollock, de Kooning, Rothko, Still and Roger Hilton.

London. *Arts (NY)*, June 1958, pp.16–17. Examines Degas monotypes.

Mr Wells Coates – Mr Patrick Heron writes [obituary]. *Times*, 16 July 1958.*

London [Niarchos Collection]. *Arts (NY)*, Sept. 1958, pp.18–19, 62.

London. *Arts (NY)*, Oct. 1958, pp.20–1. Reviews work by Jean Dubuffet, Jean Fautrier, Serge Poliakoff, Terry Frost, Trevor Bell and Kate Nicholson.

Patrick Heron writes. *Architecture and Building*, Oct. 1958, p.397.*

Trevor Bell: a note. In exh. cat. *Trevor Bell paintings*, Waddington Galleries, Oct. 1958.*

1963

A note on my painting: 1962. Text in exh. cat. *Patrick Heron*, Galerie Charles Lienhard, Zurich, 1963.

1964

Mr Peter Lanyon, abstraction and the Cornish coast [obituary written with Alan Bowness]. *Times*, 2 Sept. 1964, p.13.

Introduction to exh. cat. *Exhibition of the work of B. S. Turner*, Leeds City Art Gallery, 1964, pp.3–8.

1966

Elizabeth Allen (Queen). Introduction to exh. cat. *First exhibition of patchwork pictures by Miss Elizabeth Allen (b.1883)*, Crane Kalman Gallery, 1966, pp.1–5.

Bonnard in 1966. Introduction to exh. cat. *Bonnard 1867–1947: drawings, gouaches, watercolours*, Victor Waddington, 1966.

Elizabeth Allen (Queen). *Studio International*, Nov. 1966, pp.250–1.*

The ascendancy of London in the sixties. *Studio International*, Dec. 1966, pp.280–1.

1967

Patrick Heron writes [letter]. *Studio International*, May 1967, pp.227–8.

1968

A kind of cultural imperialism? *Studio International*, Feb. 1968, pp.62–4.

Note in exh. cat. *Ben Nicholson*, Crane Kalman Gallery, July 1968.

1969

Denis Mitchell. Text in exh. cat. *Denis Mitchell*, Marjorie Parr Galleries, 1969, pp.3–4.

Colour in my paintings: 1969. *Studio International*, Dec. 1969, pp.204–5.

1970

Text in exh. cat. *Patrick Heron: recent paintings, gouaches, screenprints*, Gallery Caballa, Harrogate, 1970.

Space in colour, 1953; a note on my painting, 1962; colour in my painting, 1969. Statements in: Christopher de Marigny (ed.). *EM46, Patrick Heron: retrospective.* New York: E.S.M. Documentations, [1970?], pp.3, 5, 7.

Barnett Newman. *Studio International*, Sept. 1970, p.70.

Letters. *Art International*, 20 Sept. 1970, pp.79–80. Letter about 'Stripe' paintings issue.

Letter to the editor. *Times*, 7 Nov. 1970. [Charging for entry into art galleries].

Two cultures. *Studio International*, Dec. 1970, pp.240–8.

1971

Americanism, pro- and anti-. *Studio International*, Oct. 1971, pp.123–4.

Murder of the art schools. *Guardian*, 12 Oct. 1971, p.8.

All our Wednesdays [Z – Zennor]. *Sunday Times Magazine*, 12 Dec. 1971, pp.66, 68.

1972

Colour and abstraction in the drawings of Bonnard. Text in exh. cat. *Bonnard drawings 1893–1946*, American Federation of Arts, New York, 1972.

Notes on my painting: 1953–1972. Text in exh. cat. *Patrick Heron: recent painting and selected earlier canvases*, Whitechapel Art Gallery, 1972.

Matisse & Aragon [review of *Henri Matisse: a novel*, vols.1 and 2 by Louis Aragon, trans. Jean Stewart]. *New Statesman*, 1 Dec. 1972, pp.828–30.

1973

Crisis in the art schools: four crucial demands [letter]. *Guardian*, 16 Jan. 1973, p.12.*

Picasso – the end of an age. *Guardian*, 8 Apr. 1973, p.8.*

Introduction in exh. cat. *Patrick Heron: recent paintings*, Bonython Gallery, Paddington (N.S.W.), 1973.

Notes on my painting 1953–1972. Text in exh. cat. *Perception: the shape of colour II: Patrick Heron*, Midland Arts Centre, Birmingham, 1973.

1974

The shape of colour. *Studio International*, Feb. 1974, pp.65–75.

Art in danger. *Observer*, 25 Mar. 1974, p.10.*

The British influence on New York. *Guardian*, 10, 11, 12 Oct. 1974, pp.12, 10, 8–9 respectively.

1975

The shape of colour. Lecture published in: Bernard Smith (ed.). *Concerning contemporary art: the Power lectures 1968–1973.* Oxford: Clarendon Press, 1975, p.154–80.

Tony O'Malley. Text in exh. cat. *Tony O'Malley*, Arts Council of Northern Ireland Gallery, Belfast, 1975.

Mr Bryan Wynter: essays in kinetic art (obituary). *Times*, 13 Feb. 1975 (unsigned).*

Mr Roger Hilton (obituary). *Times*, 28 Feb. 1975.*

Hepworth: a singular passion (obituary). *Observer*, 25 May 1975, p.11.*

Bryan Wynter (obituary). *Studio International*, May/June 1975, pp.227–9.

Denny and St. Ives [letter]. *Studio International*, May/June 1975, pp.247–8.*

Bryan Wynter. Text in exh. cat. *Bryan Wynter*, Falmouth School of Art, 1975.

1976

Introduction to exh. cat. *Bryan Wynter 1915–1975: paintings, kinetics and works on paper*, Hayward Gallery, 1976, pp.4–6.

1977

On being beastly to British artists [letter]. *Guardian*, 28 July 1977, p.12.*

Crisis in British art [letter]. *Art monthly*, Sept. 1977, p.21.

1978

Notes on my painting 1953–1973; Writings on other painters. Text in exh. cat. *Paintings by Patrick Heron, 1965–1977*, University of Texas Art Museum, Austin (Texas), 1978.

The state of British art: [the multinational style]. *Studio International*, Feb. 1978, pp.101–2. This article is an edited transcript of a debate held at the ICA, 10–12 Feb. 1978. Heron took part in panel discussion no.3.

Introduction to exh. cat. *Norman 1874–1926 and Alethea Garstin 1894–1978: two Impressionists – father and daughter*, Penwith Gallery, St Ives, 1978, pp.4–16.

Alethea Garstin (obituary). *Times*, 7 Mar. 1978, p.18.*

1979

The colour of colour. Austin: College of Fine Arts, University of Texas at Austin, 1979. E. William Doty Lectures in Fine Arts, 3rd ser., 1978.

Patrick Heron: five statements on colour, 1953–1973. Text in exh. cat. *Patrick Heron: paintings 1950–55 and 1970–77*, Oriel Gallery, Cardiff, 1979.

Tom Heron: a biographical note. *Journal of the Decorative Arts Society 1890–1940*, no.4 1979, pp.34–5, 38–9.

A brush with purity – Ivon Hitchens (obituary). *Guardian*, 31 Aug. 1979, p.10.*

1980

Statements by Heron in: Christopher Butler. *After the wake: an essay on the contemporary avant-garde.* Oxford: Clarendon, 1980, p.128.

1981

Heron's Nest. *Harpers and Queen*, Aug. 1981, pp.104–5, 143.

Introduction to exh. cat.: *Bryan Wynter*, New Art Centre, 1981.

American art's opposing forces [letter]. *Guardian*, 12 Dec. 1981, p.8.

1982

Ben Nicholson O.M. 1894–1982 [obituary]. *Art Monthly*, no.54, Mar. 1982, p.2.

1984

Harbour window with two figures St Ives: July 1950; Azalea Garden: May 1956. A letter dated 27 Apr. 1983 reproduced in *The Tate Gallery 1980–82: illustrated catalogue of acquisitions*. London: Tate Gallery Publications, 1984, pp.129–30.

1985

A note on my gouaches. Accompanying text to exh. cat. *Patrick Heron gouaches*, Caledonian Club Theatre, Edinburgh, 1985.*

How the Tories develop Philistinism to a fine art. *Guardian*, 23 Dec. 1985, p.12.*

1986

Benighted stupidity: the art schools murdered. *Art Monthly*, no.92, Dec.1985/Jan.1986, p.2.

Francis Davison: a personal note. Text in exh. cat. *Francis Davison 1919–1984*, Redfern Gallery, 1986, p.13.

Blue cranes in the sky [Rogers' Lloyds Building]. *Architectural Review*, Oct. 1986, pp.57–8.

1987

Margaret Mellis: a personal note. Text in exh. cat. *Margaret Mellis: a retrospective exhibition 1940–1987: constructions in wood and paintings*, Redfern Gallery, 1987, pp.7–8.

Artists snubbed at art schools [letter]. *Observer*, 25 Jan. 1987.*

Painting is silent, *Art & Design*, vol.3, no.5/6, May/June 1987, pp.63–5.

Interchanges: British and American painting 1945–87. *Art & Design*, vol.3, no.9/10, Sept./Oct. 1987, pp.77–8. Text taken from a symposium organised at the Tate Gallery, by the British American Arts Association.

Into that world of light. *Sunday Times Magazine*, 1 Nov. 1987, pp.118–19.

1988

My painting now: 30 Aug 1987. Text in exh. cat. *Patrick Heron: garden gouaches 1983–1987*, Plymouth Arts Centre, Plymouth, 1988.

Selected writings by the artist in: Vivien Knight (ed.). *Patrick Heron*. London: John Taylor in association with Lund Humphries, 1988, pp.15–20, 21–38.

Defending modern painters [letter]. *Modern Painters*, vol.1, no.1, spring 1988, p.49.

Late Picasso. *Modern Painters*, vol.1, no.2, summer 1988, pp.6–10.

The lost portraits of a poet. *Guardian*, 24 Sept. 1988, p.34. The artist's account of his portrait studies of T.S. Eliot – one of which is now held by the National Portrait Gallery, London.

What was wrong with Gauguin? *Modern Painters*, vol.1, no.4, winter 1988/9, pp.7–11. Transcript of a BBC Radio 3 broadcast on 7 Apr. 1988.

Margaret Thatcher talks about Henry Moore [recalled by Patrick Heron]. *Modern Painters*, vol.1, no.4, winter 1988/9, pp.42–3.

1989

St. Ives and the landscape of the Lelant Peninsula, Cornwall: a personal impression. Essay in exh. cat. *[The bridge between the East and the West: St Ives, its climate and art]*, Hyogo Prefectural Museum of Modern Art, Kobe, 1989.

Introduction to exh. cat. *Prunella Clough: recent paintings 1980–1989*, Annely Juda Fine Art, 1989, pp.1–5.

Can Mark Rothko's work survive? *Modern Painters*, vol.2, no.2, summer 1989, pp.36–9.

Getting Braque upside down [review of book *Georges Braque* by Jean Leymarie]. *Modern Painters*, vol.2, no.2, summer 1989, pp.120–2.

1990

Remembering Gabo. Text in exh. cat. *Naum Gabo 1890–1977: centenary exhibition*, Annely Juda Fine Art, 1990, pp.25–6.

Conservation of intelligence. *Architecture Today 4*, Jan. 1990, pp.5, 8.*

Scott helped turn the tide in favour of abstract expressionists (obituary). *Sydney Morning Herald*, 13 Jan. 1990, p.66.*

The value of Fuller's elevation of rude argument: tribute to Peter Fuller. *Sunday Telegraph*, 6 May 1990, p.viii.*

The shape of a table. *Independent*, 2 Nov. 1990, p.27. Review of *Val d'Orcia* by Ben Nicholson.*

Short writings on Monet, Matisse, Bonnard and Hitchens in exh. cat. *Colour in modern painting*, Stoke-on-Trent City Museum and Art Gallery, 1990–1.

William Scott. *Modern Painters*, vol.3, no.4, winter 1990–1, pp.22–4.

1991

A note round the subject of 'the artist's role in relation to society' in: *Arts Council 46th annual report and accounts 1990–91*, pp.34–5.

Permanent home for Constable? [letter]. *Times*, 20 June, 1991, p.19.*

How blind bureaucracy is destroying Britain's art schools: the visual arts under attack. *Guardian*, 7 Nov. 1991, pp.25–6.

A note on the Sydney paintings. Text to accompany the exh. *Patrick Heron: Sydney paintings and gouaches 1989–1990*, Waddington Galleries, 1991.

1992

No minister, your'e no judge of art [letter]. *Independent*, 20 Jan. 1992, p.18.*

A painter speaks. *Building Design*, 29 May 1992, p.13.*

1993

Late Matisse. *Modern Painters*, vol.6, no.1, spring 1993, pp.10–19.

Ivon Hitchens at a hundred. Introduction in exh. cat. *Ivon Hitchens: a retrospective of paintings*, Waddington Galleries, 1993.

Braque prints. *World of Interiors*, Apr. 1993, p.126–7.*

West in the rising sun. *Guardian*, 22 June 1993, pp.2, 4–5.*

Designing the stained glass window. *Architects' Journal*, 23 June 1993, pp.32–3. The artist talks about his design for the window in the Tate Gallery St Ives building.

Statements by the artist in exh. cat. *Herbert Read: a British vision of world art*, Leeds City Art Galleries, Leeds, 1993–4. Includes a conversation between the artist and Benedict Read, pp.140–4.

1994

Constable: spatial colour in the drawings. Essay in exh. cat. *Constable, a master draughtsman*, Dulwich Picture Gallery, 1994, pp.45–50.

The artist's eye. *Art Review*, vol.46, Sept. 1994, p.36. Heron talks about his work *12 March – 30 March: 1994*.

Statements by the artist in article: *I love all images and hate all symbols* by Charles Hall, *Independent*, 20 Sept. 1994, p.28.

Sam Francis (obituary). *Independent*, Nov. 1994, p.16.*

The colour of colour. *Contemporary Art*, vol.2 no.4, winter 1994–5, pp.20–4 (a piece of text omitted).*

1995

Statements by the artist in: Tom Cross. *Painting the warmth of the sun: St Ives artists 1939–1975*. Rev. ed. Tiverton; Cambridge: Westcountry Books in association with the Lutterworth Press, 1995.

1996

Patrick Heron on art and education. West Bretton (Wakefield): University College, Bretton Hall, 1996. Preface by Patrick Heron. Contains selected writings by Heron from the past 40 years – the selection was made by the artist. The book cover is designed by Heron and is illustrated with new work throughout.

Is he the father of modern art ?. *Guardian*, 13 Jan. 1996, p.26. Article on Cézanne.*

Travelling exhibition 1975. Essay in: Brian Lynch (ed.). *Tony O'Malley*. Aldershot; Kilkenny: Scolar Press in association with Butler Gallery, 1996, pp.143–58.

Solid space in Cézanne. *Modern Painters*, vol.9, no.1, spring 1996, pp.16–24.

1997

Notes on Bonnard. Essay in exh. cat. *Pierre Bonnard, 1867–1947: landscapes*, Salander O'Reilly Galleries, New York, 1997, pp.4, 6, 8. Notes excerpted from Heron's essay 'Pierre Bonnard and abstraction', originally written in 1947.

Introduction to British Council exh. cat.: *Painting in the 50s*, Nicosia Arts Centre, Cyprus, May–July 1997.*

Please note that the artist has also written numerous articles on conservation and the environment which have not been mentioned above.

2 Solo Exhibition Catalogues

1947

Sigmund Politzer, Patrick Heron, Leon Zack. Redfern Gallery, 1947. [6]p. 32 works. Exhib. Oct. 1947.

1948

Paintings by Patrick Heron. St.Ives: G.R. Downing (Bookshop), 1948. [4]p. 10 works. Exhib. Sept. 1948.

Patrick Heron, Ian Fairweather. Redfern Gallery, 1948. 6p. 26 works. Exhib. Oct.–Nov. 1948.

1950

Patrick Heron. Redfern Gallery, 1950. [4]p. 27 works. Exhib. Apr.–May 1950.

1951

Patrick Heron, Humphrey Spender, Fred Uhlman, Graham Sutherland, Keith Vaughan, Marek Zulawski, Prunella Clough, Reginald Weston. Redfern Gallery, 1951. [8]p. 41 works. Exhib. Oct.–Nov. 1951.

1952

Retrospective exhibition of paintings and drawings by Patrick Heron. Wakefield City Art Gallery, 1952. [7]p. Introd. by Basil Taylor. 73 works. Exhib. Apr.–May 1952. Travelling to Leeds, Halifax, Scarborough, Nottingham, Hull until Sept. 1952.

Retrospective exhibition of paintings by Patrick Heron. Nottingham: Midland Group Gallery, 1952. 1 folded card. 36 works. Exhib. Nov. 1952.*

1954

Patrick Heron: new paintings. Redfern Gallery, 1954. [3]p. 30 works. Exhib. May–June 1954.

1955

Exhibition of paintings and drawings by Patrick Heron. Huddersfield: Simon Quinn Gallery, 1955. 1v. 21 works. Exhib. Feb.–Mar. 1955.*

1956

Patrick Heron, Mary Fedden, Robert MacGowan. Redfern Gallery, 1956. [6]p. 22 works (25 actually shown). Exhib. June 1956.

1958

[*Patrick Heron, Derwent Lees, Paul Olds and the abstract influence, 1910–1950*]. Redfern Gallery, 1958. [9]p. 27 works. Exhib. [Feb.–Mar.] 1958.

1960

Patrick Heron. New York: Bertha Schaefer Gallery, 1960. [6]p. (folded). 15 works. Exhib. Apr.–May 1960.

Patrick Heron. Waddington Galleries, 1960. [6]p. 26 works. Exhib. Nov.–Dec. 1960.

1962

Patrick Heron. New York: Bertha Schaefer Gallery, 1962. [6]p. (folded). 17 works. Exhib. Apr. 1962.

1963

Patrick Heron. Zurich: Galerie Charles Lienhard, 1963. [12]p. Text by J. P. Hodin. 'A note on my painting: 1962' by the artist. 23 works. Exhib. Jan. 1963.

Patrick Heron. Waddington Galleries, 1963. [11]p. 27 works. Exhib. Feb.–Mar. 1963.

1964

Patrick Heron. Waddington Galleries, 1964. 1 folded card [2]p. 30 works. Exhib. Nov.–Dec. 1964.

1965

Patrick Heron, Bryan Wynter: paintings. Edinburgh: Hume Tower, 1965. [10]p. 9 works. Exhib. Aug.–Sept. 1965.

VIII Bienal de São Paulo, Gra Bretanha 1965: Victor Pasmore, Patrick Heron / exh. organised by the British Council. [London]: [British Council], 1965. [23]p. Text by Alan Bowness and Herbert Read. Parallel text in Portuguese/Spanish/English. 15 works. Exhib. 1965. Travelling to Rio de Janeiro, Buenos Aires, Santiago (Chile) and Caracas through into 1966.

1967

Patrick Heron: gouaches. Dublin: Dawson Gallery, 1967. [6]p. (Folded). 18 works. Exhib. Feb.–Mar. 1967.

Patrick Heron: recent paintings. Waddington Galleries, 1967. 1 card. Exhib. May 1967.

Patrick Heron: retrospective. Edinburgh: Richard Demarco Gallery, 1967. [15]p. Introd. by Robert Hughes. 84 works. Exhib. June–July 1967.

1968

Patrick Heron. Oxford: Bear Lane Gallery, 1968. 1 folded card [2]p. 24 works. Exhib. May–June 1968.

Patrick Heron: a retrospective exhibition of paintings 1957–66. Oxford: Museum of Modern Art. [8]p. (folded). Text by Alan Bowness. 46 works. Exhib. May–June 1968.

Patrick Heron: gouaches. Waddington Galleries, 1968. 1 card. Exhib. July 1968.

Patrick Heron: gouaches. Leeds: Park Square Gallery, 1968. 1 sheet. 15 works. Exhib. Oct.1968.

1970

[Patrick Heron]. Montreal: Waddington Fine Arts, 1970. 1v. Exhib. 1970.*

[Patrick Heron]. Toronto: Mazelow Gallery, 1970. 1v. Exhib. 1970.*

[Patrick Heron]. Sydney: Rudy Komon Gallery, 1970. 1v. Exhib. travelling around Australia during 1970.*

Patrick Heron: recent paintings. Waddington Galleries, 1970. 4p. 4 works. Exhib. Jan.–Feb. 1970.

Patrick Heron: recent paintings, gouaches, screenprints. Harrogate: Gallery Caballa. [8]p. folded. Text and statements by the artist. 12 works. Exhib. Aug. 1970.

1971

Exhibition of paintings by Patrick Heron. Exeter: Devonshire House, University of Exeter, 1971. 7p. 15 works (screenprints). Exhib. Nov. 1971.*

1972

Patrick Heron: recent paintings and selected earlier canvases. Whitechapel Art Gallery, 1972. [28]p. Introd. by Alan Bowness; essay by the artist. 37 works. Exhib. June–July 1972.

1973

Patrick Heron: recent paintings. Paddington (N.S.W.): Bonython Gallery, 1973. [17]p. Introd. by Heron. 21 works. Exhib. June–July 1973.

Patrick Heron. Birmingham: Compendium Galleries, 1973. 1 card. Exhib. July 1973.

Patrick Heron: graphics. Waddington Galleries, 1973. 1 card. Exhib. Nov.–Dec. 1973.*

Perception: the shape of colour II: Patrick Heron. Birmingham: Midland Arts Centre, 1973. [12]p. Text by Heron. 10 works. Exhib. Nov.–Dec. 1973.

1974

[Patrick Heron]. Perth (W. Australia): Skinner Galleries, 1974. 1v. Exhib. 1974.*

[Prints on Prince Street]. New York: Prince Street Gallery, 1974. 1v. Exhib.1974.*

1975

Patrick Heron: paintings 1971–1975. Waddington Galleries, 1975. [15]p. 6 works. Exhib. May 1975.

Patrick Heron: paintings 1958–1966. Rutland Gallery, 1975. [6]p. (Folded). 23 works. Exhib. May 1975.

1977

Terry Frost et Patrick Heron. Paris: Galerie Le Balcon des Arts, 1977. 4p. (folded). Exhib. June–Aug. 1977.*

1978

Paintings by Patrick Heron, 1965–1977. Austin: University of Texas Art Museum, 1978. 71p., [15 leaves of plates]. Introd. by Kelly Fearing; a further introd. by Alan Bowness; essays by R. C. Kenedy and the artist. 69 works. Exhib. Mar.–May 1978.

[Patrick Heron: graphics]. Vermont: Bennington College, 1978. 1v. Exhib. 1978.*

1979

Patrick Heron: paintings 1950–55 and 1970–77. Waddington Galleries, 1979. [15]p. 14 works. Exhib. Feb.–Mar. 1979.

Patrick Heron: paintings 1950–55 and 1970–77 = peintiadau 1950–55 a 1970–77. Cardiff: Welsh Arts Council, 1979. [13]p. Introd. by Isabel Hitchman; statements by the artist. English and Welsh text. 19 works. Exhib. Apr. 1979.

1981

Patrick Heron: paintings. Riverside Studios, 1981. [2] leaves. 21 works. Exhib. Sept.–Oct. 1981.

1983

Patrick Heron at Waddington Galleries. Waddington Galleries, 1983. 1 card (folded). Exhib. Sept.–Oct. 1983.

1984

Patrick Heron: recent paintings, gouaches and drawings. Kendal: Abbott Hall Gallery, 1984. 7p. Introd. by M.E. Burkett. 29 works. Exhib. Feb.–Apr. 1984.

1985

[Patrick Heron: gouaches]. Edinburgh: Caledonian Club Theatre, 1985. 1v. Accompanying text by the artist. Exhib. 1985.*

Patrick Heron: paintings, drawings & gouaches. Manchester: Castlefield Gallery, 1985. 4p. (folded card). Exhib. Feb–Mar. 1985.*

Patrick Heron: paintings, drawings & gouaches. Harrogate: Arcade Gallery, 1985. 1 sheet. 21 works. Exhib. Apr.–May 1985.

Patrick Heron. Barbican Art Gallery, 1985. 56p. Essays by Vivien Knight, James Faure Walker and Alan Gouk. 66 works. Exhib. July–Sept. 1985.

Patrick Heron from Eagles Nest: paintings and drawings, 1925–1985. Newlyn: Newlyn Art Gallery, 1985. [4]p. (2 sheets). 49 works. Exhib. Sept.–Oct. 1985.

1986

Hitchens & Heron. New Grafton Gallery, 1986. 4p. (folded card). 14 works. Exhib. Feb–Mar. 1986.

Patrick Heron. Sunderland: Northern Centre for Contemporary Art, 1986. 1 folded leaflet. Includes a note by James Faure Walker. Exhib. July–Aug. 1986.

1987

Jo Grimond portraits and garden gouaches. Waddington Galleries, 1987. 1 card. Exhib. Mar. 1987.*

1988

Patrick Heron. Oxford: Oxford Gallery, 1988. 1 sheet. 15 works. Exhib. Feb.–Mar. 1988.

Patrick Heron: garden gouaches 1983–1987. Plymouth: Plymouth Arts Centre, 1988. [5] leaves, 1 card. Includes statements by the artist. 12 works. Exhib. July–Sept. 1988.

1989

Patrick Heron exhibition. St. Helier: Jersey Arts Centre, 1989. 4p. (folded). 11 works. Exhib. Apr. 1989.*

Patrick Heron: gouaches 1961–1989. Waddington Galleries, 1989. 40p. 36 works. Exhib. 26 Apr.–20 May 1989.

1990

Patrick Heron: recent paintings: artist in residence, November–January 1989–90. Sydney: Art Gallery of New South Wales, 1990. 2p. card Exhib. Jan. 1990.*

Patrick Heron: works completed during the artist's residency at the Art Gallery of NSW. Woollahra: Rex Irwin, 1990. 2p, (1 card and 1p. list) 22 works. Exhib. Apr. 1990.*

1991

Patrick Heron: Sydney paintings and gouaches 1989–1990. Waddington Galleries, 1991. 36p. 12 works. Exhib. Mar.–Apr. 1991.

1992

Patrick Heron: new paintings, 1988–1992. Waddington Galleries, 1992. 36p. 12 works. Exhib. Sept. 1992.

1994

Patrick Heron. Cambridge: Bodilly Galleries, 1994. 1 sheet. 17 works. Exhib. Sept.–Oct. 1994.

Patrick Heron: [big paintings 1994]. Camden Arts Centre, 1994. 13p. Text by Mel Gooding. 11 works. Exhib. Sept.–Nov. 1994. 1994. Travelling to Bristol, Arnolfini Gallery Jan.–Feb. 1995.

1995

Patrick Heron recent gouaches. Oxford: Oxford Gallery, 1995. 2p. card. Exhib. Mar.–Apr. 1995.*

Patrick Heron: big paintings. Preston: Harris Museum & Art Gallery, 1995. 2p. card Exhib. Apr.–May 1995.*

Patrick Heron: big paintings. Llandudno: Oriel Mostyn, 1995. 2p. card. Exhib. June 1995.*

Patrick Heron and Denis Mitchell. Aldeburgh: Aldeburgh Cinema Gallery, 1985. 4p (folded card). 9 works. Exhib. June 1995.*

From the artist's studio: paintings by Patrick Heron. Milngavie: Lillie Art Gallery, 1995. 15p. 16 works. Exhib. Apr. 1995. Travelling to Maclaurin Art Gallery, Ayr in June 1995.*

Patrick Heron. Kilkenny: Butler Gallery, Kilkenny Castle, 1995. (Kilkenny Arts Week brochure) Exhib. Aug.–Oct. 1995.*

Patrick Heron: Colin Lanceley. Sydney: Sherman Galleries, 1995. 6p. (folded card). Essay by Terence Measham. Exhib. Aug.–Sept. 1995.*

1996

Patrick Heron. Wakefield: Bretton Hall, 1996. 1 card, (in conjunction with conferment of Honorary Fellowship). Exhib. Apr.–May 1996.*

Patrick Heron. New York: Salander-O'Reilly Galleries, 1996. [16]p. Introd. by Lawrence B. Salander; essay by Mel Gooding. 9 works. Exhib. Nov. 1996.

3 Selected Group Exhibition Catalogues

1947

Summer exhibition. Redfern Gallery, 1947. 15p. 4 works. Exhib. July–Sept. 1947.

1949

Summer exhibition. Redfern Gallery, 1949. [13]p. 2 works. Exhib. June–Oct. 1949.

Exhibition of contemporary paintings and drawings. Derby: Museum and Art Gallery, 1949. 4p. (folded sheet). 2 works. Exhib. Nov.–Dec. 1949.*

Original French and English lithographs and monotypes in colour. Redfern Gallery, 1949. 10p. Foreword by Philip James. 6 works. Exhib. Dec. 1949.

1950

Contemporary English painting: Adrian Ryan, Bryan Wynter, Patrick Heron, R.W. Treffgarne, Paul Feiler. Bristol: City Art Gallery, 1950. [7]p. Introd. by J. Wood Palmer. 20 works. Exhib. Feb.–Mar. 1950.

Aspects of British art. ICA, 1951. [4]p. (folded sheet). Introd. by Peter Watson. 1 work. Exhib. Dec. 1950 – Jan. 1951.

Fifteen contemporary British painters. Leeds: City Art Gallery, 1950. 12p. 6 works. Exhib. Dec. 1950 – Jan. 1951.*

1951

Sixty paintings for '51: the Arts Council Festival of Britain. Arts Council, 1951. [55]p. Foreword by Philip James. 1 work. Touring exhib. 1951.

21 modern British painters: an exhibition organized by the British Council in conjunction with the Vancouver Art Gallery, 1951. Vancouver: Vancouver Art Gallery, 1951. 17, [10]p. Introd. by Doris Shadbolt. 2 works. Exhib. 1951. Travelling to Seattle, San Jose, San Francisco, Salt Lake City and Portland, Ohio.

Exhibition of works by fifteen artists & craftsmen from around Saint Ives. Heal's Mansard Gallery, 1951. 10p. 5 works. Exhib. Jan.–Feb. 1951. (Cat. printed by Guido Morris, St Ives).*

Penwith Society of Arts in Cornwall: Festival of Britain 1951. St Ives: Penwith Society of Arts in Cornwall, 1951. [4]p. 3 works. Exhib. Penwith Galleries, St Ives, summer 1951.

Penwith Summer Exhibition 1951. St Ives: Penwith Society of Arts in Cornwall, 1951. 6p. 3 works. Exhib. Penwith Galleries, St Ives, summer 1951. (Typescript of the Society's Festival of Britain catalogue, 1951).

1952

Seventeen collectors: an exhibition of paintings and sculpture from the private collections of members of the Executive Committee of the Contemporary Art Society. Tate Gallery, 1952. [20]p. Foreword by Colin Anderson. 2 works. Exhib. Mar.–Apr. 1952.

1953

20th century form: painting, sculpture and architecture. Whitechapel Art Gallery, 1953. 16p. Introd. by Bryan Robertson, Trevor Dannatt. 1 work. Exhib. Apr.–May 1953.

International water color exhibition: seventeenth biennial. New York: Brooklyn Museum, 1953. [20]p. 3 works. Exhib. May–June 1953.

Exhibition of contemporary British paintings. Redfern Gallery, 1953. [5]p. 3 works. Exhib. May–July 1953.

Space in colour: Hitchens, Scott, Pasmore, Frost, Vaughan, Hilton, Lanyon, Heron, Johnstone, Davie. Hanover Gallery, 1953. [6]p. Text by Patrick Heron. Exh. devised by Patrick Heron. 4 works. Exhib. July–Aug. 1953.

Gra-Bretanha: esposiçao de obras de Moore, Richard, Evans, Scott, Gear, Heron. [Lund Humphries], 1953. [7]p. Introd. by Herbert Read. Organised by the British Council for the 2nd Bienal of the Museu de Arte Moderna, São Paulo 1953–4. English and Portuguese text. 12 works. Exhib. 1953–4.

II Bienal do Museu de Arte Moderna de São Paulo: catálogo geral. São Paulo: Museu de Arte Moderna de São Paulo, 1953. 346p., [63]p of plates. Introd. to section on Great Britain by Herbert Read. Portuguese text. 12 works. Exhib. Dec. 1953 – Feb. 1954.

Tio Engelske målare. British Council, 1953. 15, [10]p. Introd. by Michael Middleton. Swedish text. 5 works. Exhib. 1953–4. Travelling to Gothenburg, Stockholm and Malmö.

1954

British painting & sculpture 1954. Whitechapel Art Gallery, 1954. [15]p. Foreword by Bryan Robertson. 1 work. Exhib. Sept.–Oct. 1954.

Romantic abstraction: paintings by leading British artists. Huddersfield: Simon Quinn Gallery, 1954. 3p. (folded card). 3 works. Exhib. Oct.–Nov. 1954.*

1955

Exhibition of abstract design by thirteen artists in collaboration with Portia Prints. Craftman's Market and Picture Gallery, Heal & Son, 1955. 7p. 3 works. Exhib. Mar. 1955.

[*Six painters from Cornwall: Peter Lanyon, Patrick Heron, John Wells, Terry Frost, David Haughton, Bryan Wynter*]. [Montreal]: [Museum of Fine Art], 1955. [8]p. Introd. by Norman Levine. 6 works. Travelling to Vancouver, Hamilton, Toronto, London (Ont.) and Winnipeg. Exhib. 1955–6.

1956

Ten years of English landscape painting: 1945–1955. Institute of Contemporary Arts, 1956. 3p. (folded card). Introd. by Andrew Forge. 2 works. Exhib. Jan.–Feb. 1956.*

The seasons. Tate Gallery, 1956. 11p. Organised by the Contemporary Art Society. Foreword by Raymond Mortimer. 1 work. Exhib. Mar.–Apr. 1956.*

Britisk kunst, 1900–1955: malerier og skulptur. Copenhagen: Kunstforeningen i Kobenhavn, 1956. 15p. Introd. by Herbert Read. Danish text. 3 works. Exhib. Apr. 1956.

Summer exhibition. Redfern Gallery, 1956. [13]p. 3 works. Exhib. July–Sept. 1956.

Critic's choice: 1956 selection by Herbert Read: Ben Nicholson, Victor Pasmore, William Scott, Terry Frost, Patrick Heron, Alan Davie, Peter Kinley. Arthur Tooth & Sons, 1956. [22]p. Introd. by Herbert Read. 3 works. Exhib. Sept.–Oct. 1956.

Vision and reality: an exhibition of contemporary painting and sculpture. Wakefield: City Art Gallery, 1956. 11p. Introd. by Helen Kapp. 9 works. Exhib. Sept.–Oct. 1956.*

Recent abstract painting. Manchester: Whitworth Art Gallery, 1956. [6]p. Introd. by Paul A. Chew. 2 works. Exhib. Dec. 1956.

1957

[*Exhibition 57*]. St Ives: Penwith Society of Arts in Cornwall. [3] leaves. 3 works. Exhib. St. Ives, Penwith Galleries, 1957.

New exhibition, 1957. St Ives: Penwith Society of Arts in Cornwall, 1957. 1 sheet. 3 works. Exhib. St Ives, Penwith Galleries, 1957.

Statements: a review of British abstract art in 1956. Institute of Contemporary Arts, 1957. [13]p. 1 work. Introductory notes by Lawrence Alloway; statement by the artist. Exhib. Jan.–Feb. 1957.

Spring 57. St Ives: Penwith Society of Arts in Cornwall, 1957. [4] leaves. 3 works. Exhib. at Penwith Galleries, spring 1957.

Metavisual, tachiste, abstract: painting in England. Redfern Gallery,

1957. [63]p. Preface by Denys Sutton. 12 works. Exhib. Apr.–May 1957. Toured to Liège in May 1957.

Summer 57. St Ives: Penwith Society of Arts in Cornwall, 1957. [8]p. 4 works. Exhib. St Ives, Penwith Galleries, summer 1957.

La peinture britannique contemporaine. Paris: Salle Balzac, 1957. 16p. Collection chosen by Eric Newton. French and English text. 2 works. Exhib. Oct. 1957.

The John Moores Liverpool Exhibition [1]. Liverpool: Walker Art Gallery, 1957. 20p. 1 work. Exhib. Nov. 1957 – Jan. 1958.

The Penwith Society of Arts in Cornwall: a selection of paintings, drawings, sculpture & pottery. Arts Council, 1957. [5]p. 4 works. Exhib. Newcastle-upon-Tyne, Laing Art Gallery, Nov.–Dec. 1957. Travelling to Hull, Leicester, Birmingham, Bolton, Cambridge, until Nov. 1958.

Dimensions: British abstract art 1948–1957. O'Hana Gallery, 1957. [12]p. Exh. arranged by Lawrence Alloway. Additional research by Toni del Renzo. 1 work. Exhib. Dec. 1957.

Contemporary British painting / selected from the Collection of the British Council by Colin MacIness, Michael Middleton, Nan Youngman. British Council, 1957. 19p. Introd. by Michael Middleton. 2 works. Touring exhib. 1957–8.

1958

British abstract painting. Auckland: Auckland City Art Gallery, 1958. 15p. Preface by Denys Sutton. 3 works. Exhib. 1958.

Spring Exhibition St. Ives: Penwith Society of Arts in Cornwall, spring 1958. [77] leaves. 1 work. Exhib. St Ives, Penwith Galleries, spring 1958.

Abstract Impressionism: an exhibition of recent paintings / arranged by Lawrence Alloway and Harold Cohen. Cambridge: Arts Council Gallery, 1958. [11]p. Text by Lawrence Alloway. 1 work. Exhib. Apr.–May 1958. Travelling to Newcastle and London until June 1958.

The Guggenheim Painting Award 1958: British section. Whitechapel Art Gallery, 1958. 3 leaves. 1 work. Exhib. May–June 1958.

The religious theme: an exhibition of painting and sculpture organised by the Comtemporary Art Society. Tate Gallery, 1958. [12]p. Introd. by Robert Speaght. 1 work. Exhib. July–Aug. 1958.

Summer Exhibition. St Ives: Penwith Society of Arts in Cornwall, 1958. [4] leaves. 3 works. Exhib. St Ives, Penwith Galleries, summer 1958.

Five Cornwall artists: Terry Frost, Patrick Heron, Peter Lanyon, John Wells, Bryan Wynter. Oxford: Bear Lane Gallery, 1958. 4p. Introd. by Herbert Read. 4 works. Exhib. Nov. 1958.*

1959

Second Summer Exhibition. St. Ives: Penwith Society of Arts in Cornwall, [1959?]. [4]p. (1 folded sheet). 2 works. Exhib. St Ives, Penwith Galleries, [1959?].

Heron, Wynter, Frost, Hilton: four English middle generation painters. Waddington Galleries, 1959. [10]p. Introd. by Alan Bowness. Exhib. May 1959.

7 British painters of today: Davie, Frost, Heron, Hilton, Pasmore, Richards, Vaughan. Cardiff: National Museum of Wales, 1959. 27p. Introd. by P.J. Barlow. Foreword by Philip Jones. 7 works. Exhib. July 1959. Touring to Aberystwyth and Swansea 1959.*

10th Anniversary Exhibition. St Ives: Penwith Society of Arts in Cornwall, 1959. [3] leaves. 2 works. Exhib. autumn 1959.

The John Moores Liverpool Exhibition, 1959. Liverpool: Walker Art Gallery, 1960. 20p. Preface by W.R. Maylor. 1 work. Exhib. Nov. 1959 – Jan. 1960.

1960

English painting of the 20th century. Johannesburg: Lawrence Adler Galleries, 1960. [12]p. ill. Exh. by arrangement with Piccadilly Gallery, London. 1 work. Exhib. Apr. 1960.

The British Guggenheim Award Paintings. Royal Society of Painters in Watercolours, 1960. [8]p. 1 work. Exhib. Royal Watercolour Society Galleries, Apr.–May 1960.

Artists from the Waddington Galleries. Nottingham: Nottingham University Art Gallery, 1960. [10]p. 2 works. Exhib. May 1960.

Penwith Society of Arts tenth anniversary exhibition. Arts Council, 1960. 12p. Introd. by Herbert Read. Note by Alan Bowness. 2 works. Exhib. Jan.–July 1960. Touring to Middlesborough, Nottingham, Cirencester, Eastbourne, Norwich, Newport and Liverpool.*

Northern artists. Manchester: City Art Gallery, 1960. 26p. Organised by the Arts Council of Great Britain. Introd. by J. Wood Palmer. 4 works. Exhib. July–Dec. 1960. Touring to Sheffield, Newcastle, Bolton, Bradford and Carlisle.*

Aspects: Frost, Heath, Heron, Hilton, Scott, Vaughan, Wells, Wynter: an exhibition of various media on paper. Waddington Galleries, 1960. [9]p. 5 works. Exhib. Oct.–Nov. 1960.

1961

New painting 58–61. Arts Council Collection, 1961. [12]p. Introd. by Alan Bowness. 1 work. Exhib. 1961–3. Travelling to Liverpool, Lincoln, Luton, Nottingham and Bradford until Jan. 1963.

21st International Watercolor Biennial: Germany, Great Britain, United States. New York: Brooklyn Museum, 1961. [16]p. Text by Hertha Wegener. 2 works. Exhib. 1961.

Summer Exhibition 1961. Redfern Gallery, 1961. 19p. 1 work. Exhib. June–Aug. 1961.

Middle roads: four British abstract painters: Adrian Heath, Patrick Heron, Roger Hilton, Bryan Wynter. Manchester: City Art Gallery, 1961. 7p. Introd. by A. C. Sewter. 6 works. Exhib. June–July 1961.*

House Exhibition 1961. Waddington Galleries, 1961. [2] leaves. 2 works. Exhib. Aug. 1961.

The 1961 Pittsburgh International Exhibition of Contemporary Painting and Sculpture. Pittsburgh: Department of Fine Arts, Carnegie Institute, 1961. [88]p. Introd. By Gordon Bailey Washburn. 1 work. Exhib. Oct. 1961 – Jan. 1962.

Exhibition of contemporary painting. Norwich: Castle Museum, 1961. 2p. (card). 4 works. Exhib. Dec. 1961.*

1962

Arte Britânica na século XX. Lisbon: Fundaçao Calouste Gulbenkian, 1962. [73]p. Introd. by John Russell. Portuguese text. 2 works. Exhib. 1962. Travelling to Coimbra and Porto.

Six painters: Hitchens, Hilton, Heron, Frost, Wells, Mackenzie. Waddington Galleries, 1962. [12]p. 4 works. Exhib. Jan. 1962.

British art today / an exhibition organised by the San Francisco Museum of Art for the occasion of London Week in San Francisco. San Francisco: San Francisco Museum of Art, 1962. [65]p. Introd. by Lawrence Alloway. 2 works. Exhib. Nov.–Dec. 1962. Travelling to Dallas and Santa Barbara until Apr. 1963.

1963

Contemporary British painting: la peinture contemporaine britannique. British Council, 1963. [38]p. Introd. by David Thompson. Parallel English/French text. 4 works. Exhib. touring around Canada during 1963.

20th century French and English drawings and watercolours. Redfern Gallery, 1963. 23, [12]p. ill. 2 works. Exhib. Feb.–Mar. 1963.

British painting in the Sixties. Tate Gallery, 1963. [37]p. Introd. by John Sainsbury, Bryan Robertson, Alan Bowness and Lord Croft. 3 works. Exhib. June 1963. (Exhib. split into two parts; part 1 at the Tate Gallery, and part 2 at the Whitechapel Art Gallery, London).

1964

Recent acquisitions of the Contemporary Art Society. Arts Council Gallery, 1964. 6p. (1 folded sheet). Foreword by Whitney Straight. 1 work. Exhib. 1964.

Painting & sculpture of a decade: 54–64. Tate Gallery, 1964. 276p. Introductory notes by Alan Bowness, Lawrence Gowing and Philip James. Organised by the Calouste Gulbenkian Foundation. 1 work. Exhib. Apr.–June 1964.

Twentieth century French and English paintings, drawings, watercolours. Redfern Gallery, 1964. [45]p. 1 work. Exhib. June–Sept. 1964.

1965

Frost, Heron, Hilton, Wynter. Waddington Galleries, 1965. [10]p. 6 works. Exhib. June 1965.

VIII Bienal de São Paulo: catálogo. [Sao Paulo]: [Museu de Arte Moderna], 1965. 464p, [133]p. of plates. Text accompanying British section on Heron by Alan Bowness. Portuguese text. 15 works. Exhib. Sept.–Nov. 1965.

1967

The Penwith Society of Arts: Spring Exhibition 1967. St Ives: Penwith Society of Arts in Cornwall, 1967. [6]p. (1 folded card). 1 work. Exhib. St Ives, Penwith Galleries, Mar.–June 1967.

Patrick Heron, Ceri Richards. Oslo: Kunstnernes Hus, 1967. [18]p. Introd. by Oistein Thurmann-Nielsen. 25 works. Exhib. Oct.–Nov. 1967.

Recent British painting: Peter Stuyvesant Foundation Collection. Tate Gallery, 1967. 159p. Introd. by Alan Bowness. Exhib. Nov.–Dec. 1967.

1968

Painting 64–67. Arts Council, 1968. [23]p. Introd. by John Russell. 1 work. Touring exh. 1968.

Works on paper. Waddington Galleries, 1968. [1 card]. Exhib. Mar.–Apr. 1968.

Britische Kunst heute. Hamburg: Kunstverein Hamburg. [15]p., 52 plates. Introd. by Hans Platte. German text. 2 works. Exhib. Mar.–May 1968.

1969

Works on paper: a selection of works from the exhibition. Waddington Galleries, 1969. [25]p. 1 work. Exhib. Feb.–Mar. 1969.

Penwith Gallery: [Spring 1969]. St Ives: Penwith Society of Arts in Cornwall, 1969. [4]p. 2 works. Exhib. St Ives, Penwith Galleries, Feb.–May 1969.

Penwith Gallery: [Autumn 1969]. St Ives: Penwith Society of Arts in Cornwall, 1969. [4]p. 1 work. Exhib. St Ives, Penwith Galleries, July–Oct. 1969.

1970

Festival Exhibition. Leeds: Park Square Gallery, 1970. [2] leaves. 1 work. Exhib. Apr.–May 1970.

Kelpra prints. Hayward Gallery, 1970. [31]p. Introd. by Ronald Alley. 2 works. Exhib. June–July 1970.

British painting and sculpture 1960–1970 / an exhibition organized by the Tate Gallery and the British Council. Tate Gallery, 1970. 124p. Introd. by Edward Lucie-Smith. 2 works. Exhib. Washington, National Gallery of Art, Nov. 1970 – Jan. 1971.

1972

Decade: painting, sculpture and drawing in Britain 1940–49. Whitechapel Art Gallery, 1972. 51p. Introd. by Alan Bowness. 2 works. Exhib. Nov. 1972. Travelling to Southampton, Manchester, Carlisle, Durham, Bradford, and Aberdeen until June 1973.

1973

Europalia 73, Great Britain: [Moore to Gilbert & George: modern British Art from the Tate Gallery]. Brussels: Palais des Beaux-Arts, 1973. 215p. Introd. by Paul Hooreman. Parallel Dutch/French/English text. Exhib. Sept.–Oct. 1973.

The Biennale of Sydney (1st). Sydney: Sydney Opera House, 1973. [52]p. Introd. by Harry Nicholson. 1 work. Exhib. Nov. 1973.

1974

Tony O'Malley / St. Ives retrospective 1940–1974. St Ives: Wills Lane Gallery, 1974. [2]p. 3 works. Exhib. 1974.

St. Ives retrospective 1970–1974. St Ives: Wills Lane Gallery, 1974. [2]p. 3 works. Exhib. 1974.

Penwith Gallery: [Spring 1974]. St Ives: Penwith Society of Arts in Cornwall, 1974. [4]p. 2 works. Exhib. St Ives, Penwith Galleries, Apr.–June 1974.

Some significant British artists 1950–1970. Rutland Gallery, 1974. [22]p. Introd. by Lou Klepac. 2 works. Exhib. May 1974.

British painting '74. Arts Council, 1974. [251]p. Introd. by Andrew Forge. 1 work. Exhib. Sept.–Nov. 1974.

1975

British painting 1900–1960. Sheffield: Mappin Art Gallery, 1975. [78]p. Foreword by Frank Constantine. 1 work. Exhib. Nov. 1975 – Feb. 1976. Touring to Aberdeen Art Gallery, Jan.–Feb. 1976.

1976

Penwith Gallery: [Spring 1976]. St Ives: Penwith Society of Arts in Cornwall, 1976. [4]p. 4 works. Exhib. St Ives, Penwith Galleries, Apr.–June 1976.

John Moores Liverpool Exhibition 10. Liverpool: Walker Art Gallery, 1976. [24]p 1 work. Exhib. May–Aug. 1976.

Penwith Gallery: [Summer Exhibition]. St Ives: Penwith Society of Arts in Cornwall, 1976. [4]p. 4 works. Exhib. St Ives, Penwith Galleries, July–Sept. 1976.

Sixth exhibition: [pictures by Victor Ambrus, pictures by Patrick Heron, jewellery by Susanna Heron, textiles by Carol Packard]. Farnham: New Ashgate Gallery, 1976. 6p. (folded). Exhib. Sept.–Oct. 1976.

1977

Penwith Gallery: [Spring Exhibition]. St Ives: Penwith Society of Arts in Cornwall, 1977. [4]p. 3 works. Exhib. St Ives, Penwith Galleries, Mar.–June 1977.*

Penwith Gallery: [Summer Exhibition]. St Ives: Penwith Society of Arts in Cornwall, 1977. [4]p. 1 work. Exhib. St Ives, Penwith Galleries, June–Aug. 1977.

British painting 1952–1977. Royal Academy of Arts, 1977. 129p. Introd. by Frederick Gore. 1 work. Exhib. Sept.–Nov. 1977.

Cornwall 1945–1955. New Art Centre, 1977. [23]p. Introd. by David Brown. 6 works. Exhib. Nov.–Dec. 1977.

Drawings and watercolours of distinction. Victor Waddington, 1977. [23]p. 2 works. Exhib. Nov.–Dec. 1977.

1978

25 from 51: paintings from the Festival of Britain. Sheffield: Mappin Art Gallery, 1978. 38p. Introd. by James Hamilton, Exhib. May–Aug. 1978. Touring to City Museum & Art Gallery, Birmingham.*

Penwith Gallery: [Autumn 1978]. St Ives: Penwith Society of Arts in Cornwall, 1978. [4]p. 2 works. Exhib. St Ives, Penwith Galleries, Sept.–Oct. 1978.

1979

Colour 1950–1978. Durham: DLI Museum & Arts Centre, 1979. 12p. Introd. by Nerys A. Johnson. Exhib. Jan.–Mar. 1979.

Penwith Gallery: [Autumn 1979]. St Ives: Penwith Society of Arts in Cornwall, 1979. [4]p. 1 work. Exhib. Sept.–Nov. 1979.

1980

Leeds' painting: 20th century British art from Leeds City Art Gallery. [Arts Council], 1980. [45]p. Introd. by Miranda Strickland-Constable. 1 work. Exhib. Bath: Victoria Art Gallery, May–June 1980. Travelling to Huddersfield, Coventry, Preston, Barnsley, Lincoln, Bolton, until Mar. 1981.

Modern British abstracts: paintings and sculpture on loan from the collections of Mr. Alistair McAlpine and the Arts Council of Great Britain. Glasgow: Art Gallery & Museum, 1980. 20p. 2 works. Exhib. Mar.–May 1980.*

Hayward Annual 1980: contemporary painting and sculpture / selected by John Hoyland. Hayward Gallery, 1980. 62p. Introd. by Hoyland, 1 work. Exhib. Aug.–Oct. 1980.

1982

The sea, St Ives and the seeing eye: St Ives Festival Exhibition. St Ives: Penwith Galleries, 1982. [5]p. Introd. by Roy Ray. 1 work. Exhib. Sept.–Oct. 1982.

1983

The Granada Collection: recent British paintings and drawings. Manchester: Whitworth Art Gallery, 1983. 44p. Introd. by Robin Vousden. 1 work. Exhib. Jan.–Feb. 1983.

Pintura británica contemporánea. Madrid: Museo Municipal, 1983. 196p. Introd. by Mercedes Agulló y Cobo. Spanish text. 2 works. Exhib. Apr.–May 1983.

1984

British artists' books 1970–1983. Atlantis Paper Company, 1984. 45p. Introd. by Michael Heseltine. Essay by Silvie Turner and Ian Tyson. 1 work. Exhib. Atlantis Gallery, Mar.–Apr. 1984.

Capital painting: pictures from corporate collections in the City of London. Barbican Art Gallery, 1984. 63p. Introd. by Paul Atterbury. 1 work. Exhib. Apr.–June 1984.

English contrasts: peintres et sculpteurs Anglais 1950–1960 / textes de Bryan Robertson. Paris: Artcurial, 1984. 63p. French text. 1 work. Exhib. Sept.–Nov. 1984.

1985

Printmakers at the Royal College of Art. [s.n.], [1985?]. [234]p. Introd. by Alistair Grant. 2 works. Exhib. Barbican Art Gallery, [1985?].

St Ives 1939–64: twenty five years of painting, sculpture and pottery. Rev. ed. Tate Gallery, 1996. 248p. Includes essays by David Lewis and Oliver Watson. 10 works. Exhib. Feb.–Apr. 1985.

Aspects of modern British art II, 1910 to 1965. Ascot: Austin/Desmond Fine Art, 1985. 28p. 3 works. Exhib. Apr.–May 1985.

1986

Forty years of modern art 1945–1985. Tate Gallery, 1986. 120p. Introd. by Ronald Alley. 1 work. Exhib. Feb.–Apr. 1986.

Side by side: contemporary British and Malaysian art, 1986. Kuala Lumpar: National Art Gallery, 1986. [66]p. Introds. by Syed Ahmad Jamal and Mary Rose Beaumont. 4 works. Exhib. Sept.–Oct. 1986.*

134th Annual Exhibition. Bristol: Royal West of England Academy, 1986. [57]p. 2 works. Exhib. Nov.–Dec. 1986.

1987

2D/3D: art and craft made and designed for the twentieth century. Newcastle-upon-Tyne: Laing Art Gallery, 1987. 72p. Introd. by John Millard, Tony Knipe. Exhib. Jan.–Mar. 1987.

British art in the 20th century: the modern movement / ed. Susan Compton with contributions by Dawn Ades [et al.]. Royal Academy; Munich: Prestel, *c.*1986. 457p. Introd. by Frederick Gore. 1 work. Exhib. Royal Academy, Jan.–Apr. 1987.

John Moores Liverpool Exhibition 15. Liverpool: Walker Art Gallery, 1987. [75]p. 1 work. Exhib. Jan.–Apr. 1987.

British and European paintings and drawings. Redfern Gallery, 1987. [15]p. 1 work. Exhib. Mar.–Apr. 1987.

Looking West: landscapes of West Cornwall from the 1880s to the present day. Newlyn: Art Gallery, 1987. 24p. ill. 2 works. Exhib. Sept.–Nov. 1987. Touring to the Royal College of Art, London.*

Charles Causley: a tribute from the artists – 1987. Exeter: New Library, Exeter University, 1987. 36p. Foreword by Ronald Tamplin. 2 works. Exhib. Oct.–Dec. 1987.*

1988

Spring Exhibition 1988: an exhibition of British and European paintings, drawings and sculpture. Redfern Gallery, 1988. [20]p. 2 works. Exhib. Mar.–Apr. 1988.

St Ives exhibition. New Art Centre, 1988. [2] leaves. 1 work. Exhib. Sept.–Oct. 1988.

100 years of art in Britain: an exhibition to celebrate the centenary of Leeds City Art Gallery. Leeds: Leeds City Art Gallery, 1988. 123p. Introd. by Frances Spalding. Exhib. Oct. 1988 – Jan. 1989.

A selection of post-war British abstract art. Austin/Desmond Fine Art, 1988. 44p. Introd. by Margaret Garlake. 3 works. Exhib. Nov.1988.

The presence of painting: aspects of British abstraction 1957–1988. Sheffield: Mappin Art Gallery, 1988. 63p. Introd. by Michael Tooby. 4 works. Exhib. Nov. 1988 – Jan. 1989. Travelling to Newcastle-upon-Tyne and Birmingham until May 1989.

Eleven artists: paintings and sculpture. Francis Graham-Dixon Gallery, 1989. [3] leaves. 1 work. Exhib. Dec. 1988 – Jan. 1989.

1989

A century of art in Cornwall 1889–1989: an exhibition to celebrate the centenary of Cornwall County Council. Truro: Truro County Hall. 24p. 1 work. Introd. by James Halkes. Exhib. 1989.*

Spring Exhibition 1989: 20th century British paintings, watercolours, drawings and ceramics. Redfern Gallery, 1989. 30p. 2 works Exhib. Feb.–Mar. 1989.

[The bridge between the East and the West: St Ives, its climate and art]. Tokyo: Japan Association of Art Museums, 1989. 176p. Preface by Alan Bowness. Includes essay extract by Patrick Heron. Japanese and English text. 6 works. Exhib. Kobe, Hyogo Prefectural Museum of Modern Art, Apr.–May 1989.

[St Ives 1920–1989]. Bath: Beaux Arts, 1989. [4] leaves. 2 works. Exhib. May–June 1989.

The modern British artist as printmaker: the post-war years. Austin/Desmond Contemporary Books. [40]p. 2 works. Exhib. June 1989.

From prism to paintbox: colour thoery and practice in modern British paintings. Mold (Clwyd): Oriel Gallery, 1989. 32p. Researched and selected by Roy Osborne. Exhib. 21 Oct. – 3 Dec. 1989. Travelling to Warrington and Barnsley until Feb. 1990.

Picturing people: British figurative art since 1945. British Council, 1989. 207p. Introd. by Norbert Lynton. 1 work. Exhib. 1989–90. Touring exh. travelling to Kuala Lumpar, Hong Kong and Singapore until May 1990.

1990

Festival of Fifty-one: [painting and sculpture of 1951 from the Arts Council Collection]. South Bank Centre, 1990. [8]p. (folded). 1 work. Exhib. 1990.

Colour in modern painting. Stoke-on-Trent: City Museum and Art Gallery, 1990. [6]p. (folded). Introd. by Ian Vines. Includes writings on Monet, Matisse, Bonnard and Ivon Hitchens by Patrick Heron. 3 works Exhib. Nov. 1990–Jan. 1991.

1992

The new patrons: twentieth century art from corporate collections. Christie's, 1992. [74]p. 1 work. [Organised by the National Art Collections Fund]. Exhib. Jan. 1992.*

The poetic trace: aspects of British abstraction since 1945. New York: Adelson Galleries, 1992. [43]p. Essay by Mel Gooding. 1 work. Exhib. May–June 1992.

Artists from Cornwall. Bristol: Royal West of England Academy, 1992. 48p. Introd. by Tom Cross. 2 works. Exhib. June–Aug. 1992.

New beginnings: post-war British art from the collection of Ken Powell / Alastair Grieve. Edinburgh: Scottish National Gallery of Modern Art, 1993. 64p. Introd. by Keith Hartley. 2 works. Exhib. Nov. 1992 – Jan. 1993.

1993

Tate Gallery St Ives, Barbara Hepworth Museum and Sculpture Garden: opening displays: an illustrated companion / Michael Tooby. Tate Gallery, 1993. 92p. 5 works. Exhib. St Ives, Tate Gallery St Ives, 1993.

St. Ives. Montpelier Studio, 1993. [8]p. ill. Text by Tom Cross. 1 work. Exhib. June–July 1993.

Herbert Read: a British vision of world art / edited by Benedict Read and David Thistlewood ; with a foreword by Sir Alan Bowness, and contributions by Robert Burstow [et al.]. Leeds: Leeds City Art Galleries, 1993. 182p. Includes statements by the artist. 4 works. Exhib. Nov. 1993 – Feb. 1994.

1994

British abstract art: part 1, painting. Flowers East, 1994. [38]p. Introd. by Bryan Robertson. 1 work. Exhib. Aug.–Sept. 1994.

National Westminster Bank Contemporary Art Collection at the Royal West of England Academy, Bristol. Bristol: Royal West of England Academy, 1994. 24p. Introd. by Lord Alexander of Weedon. 1 work. Exhib. Sept.–Oct. 1994.

1995

3 ways: an exhibition of contemporary British painting. Cape Town, South African National Gallery, 1995. [15]p, 2p. (1 folded sheet). Introd. by Marilyn Martin. 1 work. Exhib. Jan.–Mar. 1995.

From here. Waddington Galleries/Karsten Schubert, 1995. 53p. Introd. by Andrew Wilson. 1 work. Exhib. Mar.–Apr. 1995.

Colour and nature: Patrick Heron and Bridget Riley. Norwich: Norwich Castle Museum, 1995. [7]p. Introd. by Andrew Moore. 10 works. Exhib. Mar.–June 1995.

Post–war to Pop. Whitford Fine Art, 1995. [8]p. (folded). 1 work. Exhib. Sept.–Oct. 1995.

The urban scene: paintings, drawings and prints by 20th [century] British artists. 4 New Burlington Street, 1995. [8]p., [16 col. postcards]. Exhib. organised by James Huntingdon-Whiteley. 1 work. Exhib. Nov.–Dec. 1995.

1996

Colourful language. Curwen Gallery, 1996. [10]p. (folded) Curated by Paul Ryan. 1 work. Exhib. May–June 1996.

Artists of fame and promise. Beaux Arts, 1996. [6]p. (folded). Exhib. June–Sept. 1996.

Catalogue eight [modern prints]. Gordon Cooke, 1996. [78]p. 1 work. Exhib. autumn 1996.

1997

Annual exhibition: Royal Scottish Society of Painters in Watercolours. Edinburgh: Royal Scottish Academy Galleries, 1997. 79p. ill. 3 works. Exhib. Jan.–Feb. 1997.*

A ilha do Tesouro = Treasure Island. Lisbon: Fundaçao Calouste Gulbenkian, 1997. 279p. Essays by Alan Bowness, Richard Cork, Gill Hedley, Andrew Renton and Bryan Robertson and Richard Shone. Portuguese and English text. 6 works. Exhib. Feb.–Mar. 1997.*

British art: a selection from Waddington Galleries. Waddington Galleries, 1997. [76]p. 3 works. Exhib. Foire Internationale d'Art Contemporain, Paris, Oct. 1997. Travelling to Tokyo, Cologne, Miami and Maastricht until Mar. 1998.

The English Arts & Crafts Movement and Hamada Shoji. Mashiko: Ceramic Art Centre, 1997. 185p. Essays by Nagata Ken'ichi, Margot Coatts and Timothy Wilcox. Japanese and English text. 1 work. Exhib. Oct. 1997 – Sept. 1998.*

1998

Terry Frost, Barbara Hepworth, Patrick Heron, Roger Hilton, Peter Lanyon, William Scott. Beaux Arts, 1998. [23]p. 3 works. Exhib. Feb. 1998.

Twentieth century British art from Sickert to Hirst. Spink-Leger Pictures, 1998. [144]p. Statements by the artist. 4 works. Exhib. Apr. 1998.

4 Selected Periodical and Newspaper Articles

1947

Cora J. Gordon. London commentary. *Studio*, Oct. 1947. Review of Heron exh., Redfern Gallery, 1947.*

Hugh Gordon Porteus. Redfern Gallery. *NEW*, 23 Oct. 1947, pp.15–16. Review of exh., Redfern Gallery, 1947.

1948

Young painters' exhibition at the Crypt. *St. Ives Times*, 6 Aug. 1948. Review of 3rd Crypt Exhibition, St Ives, 1948.

Exhibition of modern art. *St. Ives Times*, 10 Sept. 1948, p.6. Review of Heron exh., Downing's Bookshop, St Ives, 1948.*

N.A.D.W. Around the galleries. *Punch*, 10 Nov. 1948. Review of Heron exh., Redfern Gallery, 1948.*

Robert Melville. Picture books. *NSN*, 4 Dec. 1948. Review of *Vlaminck*, introduction by Heron, published by Lindsay Drummond.*

1949

Robert Vrinat. Début de saison artistique à Londres. *L'Age Nouveau, Paris*, Jan. 1949, no.33, p.115. Review of Heron exh., Redfern Gallery, 1948.*

1950

Basil Taylor. Patrick Heron. *NSN*, 6 May 1950, p.514.

David Sylvester. Patrick Heron. *Art News & Review*, 6 May 1950, p.3. Review of Heron exh., Redfern Gallery, 1950.

Nevile Wallis. At the galleries: painter's progress. *Observer*, 14 May 1950. Review of exh., Redfern Gallery, 1950.

Michael H. Middleton. Art. *Spectator*, 19 May 1950, p.682. Review of exh., Redfern Gallery, 1950.

1951

John Berger. *The arts and entertainment: Brobdingnag. NSN*, 30 June 1951. Review of *Sixty paintings for '51* exh., R.B.A. Galleries, 1951.*

1952

David Sylvester. Paintings by Patrick Heron. *Manchester Guardian*, 4 Apr. 1952.*

A.D.W. Patrick Heron's paintings: exhibition opened by Professor Read. *Wakefield Express*, 10 Apr. 1952. Article on Heron exh., Wakefield City Art Gallery, 1952.*

David Sylvester. Portrait of the artist no.85: Patrick Heron. *Art News & Review*, 3 May 1952, pp.1–2.

1953

Space and colour: an exhibition and its thesis. *Times*, 20 July 1953, p.11. Review of *Space in Colour* exh., Hanover Gallery, 1953.*

Basil Taylor. Space in colour. *Times*, 26 July 1953. Review of *Space in Colour* exh., Hanover Gallery, 1953.*

1954

Nevile Wallis. At home. *Observer*, 16 May 1954. Review of Heron exh., Redfern Gallery, 1954.

John Berger. The gourmet, the shepherd and the critic. *NSN*, 22 May 1954, p.660. Review of exh., Redfern Gallery, 1954.*

1955

Alan Bowness. Form and content. *Observer*, 11 Sept. 1955, p.11. Review of *The changing forms of art* by Heron.*

J. Ry. Art forms. *Manchester Guardian*, 13 Sept. 1955, p.4. review of *The changing forms of art.**

T. W. Earp. A key to modern art. *Telegraph*, 16 Sept. 1955. Review of *The changing forms of art.**

Quentin Bell. A painter's criticism. *NSN*, 22 Oct. 1955, pp.515–16. Review of *The changing forms of art.**

Gerald McSweeney. Trends in painting. *Books & Bookmen*, Nov. 1955. Review of *The changing forms of art.**

Anthony Thwaites. The English sensibility. *Kunstwerk*, 1955/6, vol.5, no.9, pp.55–6. Review of *The changing forms of art.**

1956

The Penguin Modern Painters. *Times Literary Supplement*, 17 Feb. 1956. Review of *Ivon Hitchens* by Heron, Penguin, 1955.*

Hilton Kramer. The changing forms of art. *Arts (N.Y.)*, May 1956, p.45. Review of *The changing forms of art.* Also a review of *Ivon Hitchens.**

Basil Taylor. Contemporary arts: crystals of sculpture. *Spectator*, 15 June 1956. Review of Heron exh., Redfern Gallery, 1956.*

Space in colour: Mr. Patrick Heron's new pictures. *Times*, 19 June 1956. Review of exh., Redfern Gallery, 1956.

Lawrence Alloway. Painting now: Tooth's Gallery. *Art News and Review*, 29 Sept. 1956. Review of *Critic's choice* exh. at Tooth's Gallery, 1956.*

Robert Melville. Action painting, New York – Paris – London. *Ark*, no.18, Nov. 1956, pp.30–3.

1958

Stephen Bone. Coloured stripes and Cubist art: Redfern exhibitions. *Manchester Guardian*, 26 Feb. 1958.

Andrew Forge. Round the London galleries. *Listener*, 27 Mar. 1958, p.548. Review of Heron exh., Redfern Gallery, 1958.

1959

Alan Bowness. Middle Generation. *Art News and Review*, 9 May 1959, pp.6–7. Review of *Four English Middle Generation Painters* exh. at Waddington Galleries, 1959.

John Russell. Heron aloft. *Sunday Times*, 13 Dec. 1959.

1960

Alan Bowness. John Moores Liverpool Exhibition. *Arts Magazine*, Jan. 1960, pp.16–17.

Carlyle Burrows. Near Eastern arts: Sloan, Heron show: Heron has debut. *New York Herald Tribune*, 17 Apr. 1960, section 4, p.6. Review of Heron exh., Bertha Schaefer Gallery, New York, 1960.*

Stuart Preston. The art cauldron: an English modern. *New York Times*, 17 Apr. 1960.

Stuart Preston. [Review of exh., Bertha Schaefer Gallery, New York, 1960]. *New York Post*, 17 Apr. 1960

George Dennison. Month in review. *Arts (NY)*, vol.34, no.7, Apr. 1960, pp.50–1. Review of exh., Bertha Schaefer Gallery, New York, 1960.

Keith Sutton. Round the London art galleries. *Listener*, 1 Dec. 1960, p.985. Review of Heron exh., Waddington Galleries, 1960.

Bryan Robertson. With or without politics. *New Statesman*, 10 Dec. 1960. Review of exh., Waddington Galleries, 1960.

1961

J.P. Hodin. Patrick Heron. *Quadrum*, 11, 1961, pp.146–7. French text.

Keith Roberts. For small collectors. *Time and Tide*, 16 Mar. 1961. Review of Heron exh., Bear Lane Gallery, Oxford, 1961.*

1963

Nevile Wallis. Heron's flight. *Observer*, 3 Mar. 1963. Review of Heron exh., Waddington Galleries, 1963.

Helen Lambert. U.K.'s Patrick Heron, U.S.'s Paul Jenkins. *New York Herald*

Helen Lambert. U.K.'s Patrick Heron, U.S.'s Paul Jenkins. *New York Herald and Tribune*, 6 Mar. 1963.*

David Storey. Towards colour. *New Statesman*, 8 Mar. 1963, pp.353–4. Review of Heron exh., Waddington Galleries, 1963.

Norbert Lynton. London letter. *Art International*, 25 Apr. 1963, pp.65–6.

1964

Max Kozloff. British painting today: an American view. *Encounter*, Jan. 1964, pp.39–42. Review of *British painting in the Sixties* exh. at the Tate and Whitechapel galleries, 1963.*

Nevile Wallis. The colony at St Ives. *Spectator*, 24 July 1964, pp.110–11.

1967

John Russell. Art. *Sunday Times*, 7 May 1967. Review of Heron exh., Waddington Galleries, 1967.

Bryan Robertson. Underlining the difference. *Sunday Times Weekly Review*, 7 May 1967, p.47. Review of exh., Waddington Galleries, 1967.*

Robert Hughes. Colour standing up alone. *Observer Review*, 14 May 1967. Review of exh., Waddington Galleries, 1967, p.25.

Guy Brett. Circles and squares. *Times*, 26 May 1967, p.8. Review of exh., Waddington Galleries, 1967.*

Alan Bowness. The American invasion and the British response. *Studio International*, June 1967, pp.285–93.

Ronald Alley. Patrick Heron: the development of a painter. *Studio International*, July/Aug. 1967, pp.18–25.

1968

Derek Grigs. Patrick Heron at Oxford. *Guardian*, 10 June 1968. Review of Heron exh,. Bear Lane Gallery, Oxford, 1968.*

1969

Richard Ormond. Patrick Heron's 'Portrait of Sir Herbert Read', 1950 (National Portrait Gallery). *Burlington Magazine*, Oct. 1969, p.618.

1971

Hilton Kramer. The American juggernaut. *Studio International*, Feb. 1971, pp.44–5.

1972

Michael McNay. Heron's nest. *Guardian*, 21 June 1972, p.8.[Review of Heron exh., Whitechapel Art Gallery, 1972.

Edward Lucie-Smith. A show to be seen. *Sunday Times*, 25 June 1972, p.37. Review of exh., Whitechapel Art Gallery, 1972.*

Hilary Spurling. East end flame thrower. *Observer*, 25 June 1972, p.28. Review of exh., Whitechapel Art Gallery, 1972

Richard Cork. When 1,000 words are better than a picture. *Evening Standard*, 29 June 1972, p.29.*

Hilton Kramer. Patrick Heron's art on view in London, *New York Times*, 11 July 1972, p.24. Review of exh., Whitechapel Art Gallery, 1972.*

Robert Melville. Birth of the stripe. *New Statesman*, 14 July 1972, pp.66–7. Review of exh., Whitechapel Art Gallery, 1972.

1973

Lenore Nicklin. The interlocking artist. *Sydney Morning Herald*, 15 June 1973.

Laurie Thomas. Stirred by a wobbly hard-edger. *Australian*, 16 June 1973.

Daniel Thomas. Artist's passion for colour. *Sydney Morning Herald*, 21 June 1973.

Sandra McGrath. Colour is the medium and the message. *Australian*, 23 June 1973.

Nancy Borlase. Brilliant use of color, form. *The Bulletin (Sydney)*, 30 June 1973.

Patrick McCaughey. Déjà vu paintings are the real thing. *The Age, Melbourne*, 4 July 1973. Written when Heron delivered the John Power Lecture at Queensland University, 1973.*

Donald Brook. Victims of a US hardsell? *Nation Review (Sydney)*, 6 July 1973, p.1182.

Stephanie Britton. Flaws in a lecture. *The News, Adelaide*, 13 July 1973. Written when Heron delivered the John Power Lecture at the Art Gallery South Australia, 1973.*

1976

Patrick Heron interviewed by James Faure Walker & Brandon Taylor. *Artscribe*, no.2, spring 1976, pp.2–5.

1977

James Burr. From canvas to casting. *Apollo*, Dec. 1977, p.514. Review of exh., Waddington & Tooth Galleries, 1977.

1978

Charlotte Moser. Heron: the unwitting father of Abstract Expressionism? *Houston Chronicle*, 16 Apr. 1978, p.24. Review of Heron exh. at the University of Texas at Austin Art Museum, 1978.*

1979

Brandon Taylor. Abstract colour painting in England: the case of Patrick Heron. *Artlog 4*, [1979].*

Bernard Denvir. Defiant diffidence: un certain art anglais. *Art and Artists*, vol.13, no.12, Apr. 1979, p.15–19.

Caryll Faraldi. Upfront. *Observer Magazine*, 6 May 1979. Review of Heron's woven carpet design for Cavendish Hotel.

1980

Brandon Taylor. Abstract colour painting in England: the case of Patrick Heron. *Art History*, vol.3, no.1, Mar. 1980, pp.115–27.

1981

Peter Davies. St. Ives: the creative emergence in Cornwall 1940–1960. *The Fine Art Letter*, vol.3, May 1981, pp.3–5.

John Russell Taylor. High flying Heron. *Times Preview*. 4 Sept. 1981, pp.6–7. Review of Heron exh., Riverside Studios, 1981.

Mel Gooding. Patrick Heron. *Arts Review*, 25 Sept. 1981, p.416. Review of exh., Riverside Studios, 1981.

Peter Fuller. Patrick Heron. *Art Monthly*, no.50, Oct. 1981, pp.8–9. Review of exh., Riverside Studios, 1981.

James Faure Walker. Erica Daborn at AIR, Patrick Heron at Riverside, Patrick Jones at Nicola Jacobs, Dubuffet at Waddington's. *Artscribe* no.31, Oct. 1981, pp.54–6.

1982

Adrian Lewis. British avant garde painting 1945–1956: Pt I. *Artscribe*, no.34, Mar. 1982, pp.17–33.

Alan Gouk. Patrick Heron I. *Artscribe*, no.34, Mar. 1982, pp.40–54.

Hilton Kramer. British abstract painting: Ignored it? We adored it! *New York Observer*, 25 May 1982, pp.1, 23. Review of Adelson Gallery exh. and symposium, New York, 1982.*

Adrian Lewis. British avant garde painting 1945–1956: Pt II. *Artscribe*, no.35, June 1982, pp.16–31.

Alan Gouk. Patrick Heron II. *Artscribe*, no.35, June 1982, pp.32–43.

1983

Beatrice Phillpotts. Patrick Heron. *Arts Review*, 16 Sept. 1983, p.508. Review of Heron exh., Waddington Galleries, London 1983.

Margaret Garlake. Patrick Heron at Waddingtons. *Art Monthly*, no.70, Oct. 1983, p.19.

S. Bradshaw. Patrick Heron at Waddington. *Artscribe*, no.43, Oct. 1983, pp.51–2. Review of exh., Waddington Galleries, 1983.

1984

Irene McManus. Patrick Heron. *Guardian*, 12 Apr., 1984, p.10. Review of exh., Abbot Hall Art Gallery, Kendal, 1984.

1985

Peter Fuller. St. Ives at the Tate. *Artscribe*, no.53, May–June 1985, pp.47–50. Review of *St Ives* exh. at the Tate Gallery, 1985.

Sarah Jane Checkland. Sharp eye on the painter's craft. *Times*, 6 July 1985, p.18. An interview in which Heron talks to Checkland about his abstracted approach to painting.

Nicholas Usherwood. Quiet face of reaction. *Sunday Times*, 14 July 1985, p.41. Review of Heron exh., Barbican Art Gallery, 1985.*

Giles Auty. Prisoner of theory. *Spectator*, 20 July 1985, pp.34–5.

William Feaver. Zing and buzz. *Observer Review*, 21 July 1985, p.21. Review of exh., Barbican Art Gallery, 1985.

John Russell Taylor. Healthy rebuff for thoughts of school. *Times*, 23 July 1985, p.15. Review of exh., Barbican Art Gallery, 1985.

Michael McNay. Star with the stripes. *Guardian*, 23 July 1985, p.11. Review of exh., Barbican Art Gallery, 1985.

John Spurling. Cornish cricket. *New Statesman*, 26 July 1985, pp.34–8. Review of exh., Barbican Art Gallery,

Review of exh., Barbican Art Gallery, 1985.

Mary Rose Beaumont. Patrick Heron, *Arts Review*, 2 Aug. 1985, p.393. Review of exh., Barbican Art Gallery, 1985.

Richard Cork. Serene. *Listener*, 29 Aug. 1985, pp.33–4.

Peter Fuller. The innocent eye? *Artscribe*, no.54, Sept./Oct. 1985, pp.40–4. Review of exh., Barbican Art Gallery, 1985.

Caroline Collier. The drama of colour, *Arts Review*, 10 Oct. p.453.

1986

W.E. Johnson. Patrick Heron, Ian Bottle. *Arts Review*, 1 Aug. 1986, p.426. Review of Heron and Bottle exhibitions at Northern Centre for Contemporary Art, Sunderland, 1986.

Laurence Marks. Artist resigns over merger. *Observer*, 21 Dec. 1986, p.3.

1987

Giles Auty. Unfamiliar ground. *Spectator*, 14 Mar. 1987, pp.41–2.

1988

Frances Spalding. The coastlines of colour. *Times Literary Supplement*, 13 May 1988, p.537. Review of *Patrick Heron*, ed. Vivien Knight.

Simon Parker. Comeback for abstract art. *Western Morning News*, 4 July 1988, p.7. Review of Heron exh., Plymouth Arts Centre, 1988.*

David Cohen. Patrick Heron. *Modern Painters*, vol.1, no.2, summer 1988, pp.94–5.

John Furse. Patrick Heron: gouaches. *Arts Review*, 12 and 26 Aug. 1988, p.579. Review of exh., Plymouth Arts Centre, 1988.

1989

Giles Auty. Cornish connections. *Spectator*, 6 May 1989, p.33.

Ena Kendall. Room of my own. *Observer Magazine*, 28 May 1989, p.63. Interview with the artist.

Peter Fuller. Britain and America: a special relationship? *Modern Painters*, vol.2, no.2, summer 1989, pp.4–5.

David Lillington. Patrick Heron. *Artscribe*, no.77, Sept./Oct. 1989, pp.10–12.

Peter Cochrane. Reprieve from the handbag-wielding warrior. *Sydney Morning Herald*, 26 Dec. 1989. Interview with the artist.*

1990

John McDonald. One man against the U.S. onslaught. *Sydney Morning Herald*, 13 Jan. 1990, p.6.*

1991

Peter Crookston. A childhood: Patrick Heron. *Times*, 5 Jan. 1991, p.46.

Tim Hilton. Bouquet from down under. *Guardian*, 27 Mar. 1991, p.36. Review of Heron exh., Waddington Galleries, 1991.

Andrew Wilson. Late Herons, early Hockneys. *Galleries*, Apr. 1991. Review of exh., Waddington Galleries, 1991.*

David Lillington. Colour code. *Time Out*, 3–10 Apr. 1991, p.40. Review of exh., Waddington Galleries, 1991.

Marina Vaizey. A map of the modern. *Sunday Times*, 7 Apr. 1991. Review of exh., Waddington Galleries, 1991.*

David Cohen. Patrick Heron: the courage of conviction. *Artline*, vol.5, no.6, winter 1991–2, pp.16–17.

1992

Tim Hilton. Everything in the garden is lovely. *Guardian*, 10 Sept. 1992, p.29.

Giles Auty. Limbos of theory. *Spectator*, 19 Sept. 1992, p.47.

Sue Hubbard. Patrick Heron. *Time Out*, 23–30 Sept. 1992, p.51. Review of exh., Waddington Gallery, 1992.

My best teacher: Patrick Heron talks to Susan Thomas. *Times Educational Supplement*, 25 Sept. 1992, p.3. Interview with the artist.

Andrew Wilson. Patrick Heron. *Art Monthly*, no.160, Oct. 1992, p.23.

David Cohen. William Gear and Patrick Heron. *Modern Painters*, vol.5, no.3, autumn 1992, pp.95–7.

1993

Famous artist designs new Tate window. *Royal Cornwall Gazette*, 28 Jan. 1993. Review of Heron's design for coloured glass window at Tate Gallery St Ives.

Elspeth Moncrieff. Museum openings: the St. Ives Tate. *Apollo*, vol.137, no.373, Mar. 1993, pp.178–9.

Ian Mayes. The Heron has landed. *Guardian*, 27 Mar. 1993. Review of Heron's design for coloured glass window at Tate Gallery St Ives.*

Angela Lambert. On a coast of many colours: the Angela Lambert interview. *Independent*, 27 July 1993, p.16.

1994

Rachel Barnes. A brilliant career. *Guardian*, 17 Sept. 1994, p.30.

Charles Hall. I love all images and hate all symbols. *Independent*, 20 Sept. 1994, p.28.

Jonathan Glancey. Colour sensitive. *Independent Magazine*, 24 Sept. 1994, pp.28–33.

Martin Gayford. An artists owns up. *Daily Telegraph*, 26 Sept. 1994, p.21.

William Packer. The flame of modernism still burns in St. Ives. *Financial Times*, 2 Oct. 1994, p.22.

Simon Morley. The artist as critic. *Art Monthly (U.K.)*, no.181, Nov. 1994, pp.12–15.

Michael McNay. Behind the lines. *Guardian*, 2 Dec. 1994, pp.14–15. Review of book *Patrick Heron* by Mel Gooding.

John McEwan. Enshrining living painters. *Sunday Telegraph*, 4 Dec. 1994, p.11. Review of *Patrick Heron* by Mel Gooding.*

1995

Patrick Heron: Big paintings. *Venue*, 3–17 Feb. 1995. Review of Heron exh., Arnolfini, Bristol, 1995.

Clare Henry. The old master of riot in pure colour. *Glasgow Herald*, 10 Apr. 1995. Review of exh., Milngavie, Lillie Gallery, 1995.

A.S. Byatt. My favourite place in the Westcountry. *Western Morning News*, 22 Apr. 1995.

David Cohen. Heron & Hodgkin. *Art Line International*, autumn 1995, vol.6, no.3, pp.32–5.*

Samuel Walsh. Patrick Heron. *CIRCA* (Belfast/Dublin), winter 1995, no.74. Review of Heron exh., Butler Gallery, Kilkenny, 1995.*

Simon Morley. Patrick Heron by Mel Gooding. *Contemporary Art*, winter 1995/6, vol.3, no.1, pp.88–89. Review of *Patrick Heron* by Mel Gooding.*

1996

Patrick Heron, artist: the Country Life interview. *Country Life*, 7 Mar. 1996, pp.64–5. The artist interviewed by Michael Hall about his creative and campaigning life.

Leaving a mark. *Art Review*, vol. 48, May 1996, pp.28, 30. Rachel Barnes talks to the artist about St Ives, art, and Mark Rothko.

J. Bower Bell. Patrick Heron. *Review Art (New York)*, 15 Nov. 1996, p.30. Review of Heron exh. at Salander-O'Reilly Galleries, New York, 1996.*

1997

Frank Ruhrmund. A champion of colour: a view from the Eagle's Nest of 'an artist of extraordinary energies.' *Western Morning News*, 28 Feb. 1997, p.36.

Paul Barker. Observations. *New Statesman*, 4 Apr. 1997, p.54. (Part of the article is an interview with Heron.)

1998

Martin Gayford. Winners and dogs, *Spectator*, 3 Jan. 1998. Some detail of the forthcoming Heron exh., Tate Gallery, 1998.

Tim Hilton. A capital idea for the regions: exhibitions, *Independent on Sunday*, 4 Jan. 1998, p.21. Compares forthcoming exhibitions around the UK for 1998.

5

Books and Sections in Books

Alley, Ronald. *Patrick Heron: the development of a painter.* [S.l.]: [s.n.], 1967. (Reprinted from *Studio International*, July/Aug. 1967).

Butler, Christopher. *After the wake: an essay on the contemporary avant-garde.* Oxford: Clarendon Press, 1980, p.128.

Cross, Tom. *Painting the warmth of the sun: St Ives artists 1939–1945.* Rev. ed. Tiverton ; Cambridge: Westcountry Books in association with the Lutterworth Press, 1995. Originally published: Penzance: Alison Hodge; Guildford: Lutterworth Press, 1984.

Eighty from the eighties: the Peninsula voice interviews. Penzance: Rainyday Publications, 1993, p.[56].

Gooding, Mel. *Patrick Heron.* Phaidon, 1994.

[*Interview with Patrick Heron at Zennor, Cornwall, Mar. 1980*]. Arts Video, Eaton House Publishers, [1980]. (Item consists of 2 video cassettes – 30 mins. each).

Knight, Vivien (ed.). *Patrick Heron.* John Taylor in association with Lund Humphries, 1988.

Lucie-Smith, Edward. *Movements in art since 1945: issues and concepts.* 3rd rev. and expanded ed. Thames and Hudson, 1995, pp.47–8.

Meneely, Edward and Christopher de Marigny (eds.). *EM46 Documentations, Patrick Heron: retrospective.* New York: E.S.M., [1970?].

Nairne, Sandy. American type painting. In: Nicholas Serota [et al.]. *Views from abroad: European perspectives on American art 3: American realities.* New York: Whitney Museum of American Art, 1997, p.36.

Patrick Heron: in conversation with Michael McNay: abstraction and intimations of landscape. Lecon Arts, [1987]. (Artists talking). (Item presented as 24 slides and 1 sound cassette).

Read, Herbert. *A concise history of modern painting.* Thames & Hudson, 1959, p.81.

Robertson, Bryan with John Russell and Lord Snowdon. *Private view.* Nelson, 1965.

Spalding, Frances. *British art since 1900.* Thames & Hudson, 1986 (reprinted 1994). pp.172, 184–9.

The 20th-century art book. Phaidon, 1996, p.200.

6

Selected Radio and Television Broadcasts, Films and Lectures

Broadcast items are included whether or not a transcript or recording exists.

1947

Two modern British landscape painters: Paul Nash and Graham Sutherland, BBC World Service (Russian broadcast), 1947.

A Cubist's creed, BBC Third Programme broadcast, 10 Apr. 1947.

Nicholson and Soutine, BBC Third programme broadcast, May 1947.

Sickert and Keene, BBC Third Programme broadcast, 12 June 1947.

Christopher Wood: painter of the Atlantic Seaboard, BBC World Service (Russian broadcast), 30 Aug. 1947.

Turner and Constable, BBC Third Programme broadcast, 26 Sept. 1947.

Smith, Craxton and Freud, BBC Third Programme broadcast, 4 Nov. 1947.

1948

Art review, BBC World Service (Russian broadcast), 3 Jan. 1948. Heron talks about Henry Moore and Matthew Smith.

Van Gogh, Pasmore & Colquhoun, BBC World Service (Russian broadcast), Feb. 1948.

Paul Nash and some Cornish painters, BBC World Service (Russian broadcast), Mar. 1948.

Art review: September exhibition: Jack B. Yeats, BBC World Service (Russian broadcast), 12 Oct. 1948.

1949

A note on the Modern Movement in painting and architecture, talk at the Royal Institute of British Architects, 2 Sept. 1949.

The necessity of distortion in painting, lecture at Leeds University, 24 Oct. 1949 (published in *The changing forms of art*).

1950

Trends in modern British painting, BBC Third Programme broadcast, 28

1950

Trends in modern British painting, BBC Third Programme broadcast, 28 Apr. 1950.

Matthew Smith and Barbara Hepworth, BBC Italian service broadcast, 12 July 1950.

1951

The changing jug, BBC Third Programme broadcast, Jan. 1951 (published in the *Listener*, 25 Jan. 1951).

Keith Vaughan, lecture at the Institute of Contemporary Arts, 24 Oct. 1951.

1952

Pottery and painting, lecture at Dartington Hall, Totnes for the International Conference of Craftsmen in Pottery & Textiles, 17–27 July 1952 (produced in a set of lecture papers by selected speakers, 1954).

1955

Reply to Renato Guttuso, lecture at the Italian Institute, London, 21 Mar. 1955. The discussion was entitled 'Some aspects of contemporary painting' and was under the chairmanship of Ernst Gombrich.

1970

Symmetry in painting: an academic formula, lecture at the Institute of Contemporary Arts, Dec. 1970.

1971

Colour in my painting, lecture at the Gardner Centre for the Arts, University of Sussex, 11 Mar. 1971.

Art for all: abstraction, London Weekend Television broadcast, 31 Oct. 1971. Heron interviewed by Trewin Copplestone.

1972

Review: long live the Whitechapel, BBC2 film, 16 June 1972. Shows the artist in his studio with uncompleted canvases in colour.

1973

The shape of colour, the 5th Power Lecture in Contemporary Art, 1973, delivered in Sydney, Brisbane, Canberra, Melbourne, Adelaide and Perth. (Published in *Studio International*, Feb. 1974, and in *Concerning contemporary art: the Power lectures 1968–73*, Clarendon Press, Oxford, 1974).

1981

Picasso, BBC World Service, Sept. 1981. Heron interviewed by John Pickford.

1983

Patrick Heron, BBC television 'Omnibus' film, 13 Mar. 1983.

1985

Painting the warmth of the sun, TSW production for Channel 4, 7/8/9 Apr. 1985.

Kaleidoscope, BBC Radio 4 broadcast, 11 July 1985. Produced by Carol Moore. Heron interviewed at the time of his exh. at the Barbican Art Gallery, London.

1986

South Bank Show: Patrick Heron, London Weekend Television, 9 Feb. 1986.

BBC2 television broadcast, autumn 1986. Interview on art schools.

Rothko symposium: Interchanges, Heron takes part in panel discussion alongside Grace Hartigan and Bryan Robertson. Symposium introduced by Sir Paul Wright and Irving Sandler, Tate Gallery, 27 June 1987.

1988

The late great Picasso?, Heron takes part in panel discussion along with Chris Green, Peter Fuller and John Nash [et al.], Tate Gallery, 12 July 1988.

Kaleidoscope – William Scott, BBC Radio 4 broadcast, 27 Sept. 1988.

1992

The visual arts under attack, lecture at Charleston Farmhouse, 20 May 1992. [Given during the 1992 Charleston Festival.]

The Late Show – Matisse, BBC2 television broadcast, 2 Dec. 1992.

Kaleidoscope – Peter Lanyon, BBC Radio 4 broadcast, 15 Dec. 1992.

1993

Braque, lecture at the Tate Gallery, 7 May 1993.

Drawing in painting, lecture at the Tate Gallery London for the Patrons on British Art, 3 Nov. 1993.

The Silver Knight, BBC Radio 3 broadcast, 12 Nov. 1993. The artist talks about Herbert Read.

Margaret Mellis: a life, Anglia TV, 22 Nov. 1993.

1994

Picasso v. Matisse, BBC2 television broadcast, 'The Late Show', 16 Feb. 1994.

Ben Nicholson: a portrait with landscape, BBC Radio 3 broadcast, 8 Apr. 1994.

Making the Big Paintings: 1994, lecture at Kingston University (Surrey), 23 Nov. 1994. [5th Stanley Picker Memorial lecture].

1995

BBC Radio 2 interview, 20 Jan. 1995. Heron interviewed by Tony Staveacre during *Big Paintings* exh. at Arnolfini, Bristol.

Hidden hands, Channel 4 television broadcast, 29 Oct. 1995. Discussion about the C.I.A. and modern art. This programme was number 2 in the series. Produced by Frances Stonor for Fulmar Films.

1996

Kaleidoscope, BBC Radio 4, 24 Jan. 1996. Heron talks about Christopher Wood.

1997

Kaleidoscope, BBC Radio 4, 24 Jan. 1997. Heron talks about Georges Braque.

State of the arts: 1 – Public & Private, BBC Radio 4, 9 Aug. 1997. Presented by Jonathan Glancey.

Sentimental journey, BBC Radio 4, 2 Feb. 1997. Janet Street-Porter recalls her time in Cornwall and Eagles Nest in particular. (Repeated on 25 Nov. 1997).

1998

Centurions – Matisse, BBC Radio 3, 15 Mar. 1998. Talk about Matisse's *The Red Studio*. Produced by Hannah Andrassy.

Lenders

Aberdeen, City of Aberdeen Art Gallery and Museums Collections no.54

John Evans no.6

Katharine Heron no.46

Lisbon, Fundaçao Calouste Gulbenkian no.44

London, National Portrait Gallery no.8

London, Tate Gallery nos.7, 16, 21, 24, 31, 50,

London, Tate Gallery Foundation no.57

London, Waddington Galleries nos.34, 43, 53, 55, 61, 65, 66, 67, 68, 69, 70, 71

London, Whitford Fine Art no.48

Newcastle upon Tyne, Hatton Gallery, University of Newcastle no.13

Plymouth City Museum and Art Gallery no.41

Private Collection nos.1, 2, 3, 4, 5, 9, 10, 11, 12, 14, 15, 17, 18, 19, 20, 22, 23, 25, 26, 27, 28, 30, 33, 36, 39, 42

David Thomson nos.29, 32, 35, 37, 38, 40, 45, 47, 49, 51, 52, 56, 58, 59, 60, 62, 63, 64

Photographic Credits

City of Aberdeen Art Gallery and Museum Collections

Bob Berry

CAM José de A. Perdigão

David Clarke

Prudence Cuming Associates

Julian Feary

Susanna Heron

Patrick Heron

David Lambert

National Portrait Gallery, London

Hatton Gallery, University of Newcastle

The Museum of Modern Art, New York

Plymouth City Museum and Art Gallery

John Riddy

Salander-O'Reilly Galleries, New York

Sotheby's London

Tate Gallery Photographic Department

Waddington Galleries, London
John Webb

Whitford Fine Art, London

Andrew Wilson

The Tate Gallery Exhibition Team

Head of Exhibitions
Ruth Rattenbury

Senior Exhibitions Officer
Sarah Tinsley

Exhibitions Assistant
Ben Tufnell

Exhibitions Graphics
Philip Miles

Exhibitions Registrar
Stephen Dunn

Head of Art Handling
Jim Grundy

Senior Art Handler
Rick Forbes

Paintings Conservators
Mary Bustin
Rica Jones

Press and Marketing
Kate Burvill
Catherine Holden

Index

For list of works in the colour plate section, see p.132–3.
When titles begin with a date in figures, this is indexed as if the date were spelt out.

F

G

H

I

J

K

M

N

O

P

R

S

T

Ways of Giving

The Tate Gallery attracts funds from the private sector to support its programme of activities in London, Liverpool and St Ives. Support is raised from the business community, individuals, trusts and foundations, and includes sponsorships, donations, bequests and gifts of works of art. The Tate Gallery is an exempt charity; the Museums & Galleries Act 1992 added the Tate Gallery to the list of exempt charities defined in the 1960 Charities Act.

Donations

There are a variety of ways through which you can make a donation to the Tate Gallery.

Donations All donations, however small, will be gratefully received and acknowledged by the Tate Gallery.

Covenants A Deed of Covenant, which must be taken out for a minimum of four years, will enable the Tate Gallery to claim back tax on your charitable donation. For example, a covenant for £100 per annum will allow the Gallery to claim a further £30 at present tax rates.

Gift-Aid For individuals and companies wishing to make donations of £250 and above, Gift-Aid allows the gallery to claim back tax on your charitable donation. In addition, if you are a higher rate taxpayer you will be able to claim tax relief on the donation. A Gift-Aid form and explanatory leaflet can be sent to you if you require further information.

Bequests You may wish to remember the Tate Gallery in your will or make a specific donation In Memoriam. A bequest may take the form of either a specific cash sum, a residual proportion of your estate or a specific item of property, such as a work of art. Certain tax advantages can be obtained by making a legacy in favour of the Tate Gallery. Please check with the Tate Gallery when you draw up your will that it is able to accept your bequest.

American Fund for the Tate Gallery The American Fund was formed in 1986 to facilitate gifts of works of art, donations and bequests to the Tate Gallery from the United States residents. It receives full tax exempt status from the IRS.

Individual Membership Programmes

Friends

Friends share in the life of the Gallery and contribute towards the purchase of important works of art for the Tate. Privileges include free unlimited entry with a guest to exhibitions; *tate: the art magazine*; private views and special events; 'Late at the Tate' evening openings; exclusive Friends Room. Annual rates range from £22 to £65. Tate Friends Liverpool and Tate Friends St Ives oVer local events programmes and full membership of the Friends in London.

The Friends of the Tate Gallery are supported by Tate & Lyle PLC.

Further details on the Friends in London, Liverpool and St Ives may be obtained from:

Membership Office, Tate Gallery,
Millbank, London SW1P 4RG
Tel: 0171-887 8752

Patrons and Fellows

Fellows support the acquisition of works of art for the British and Modern Collections of the Tate Gallery. Privileges include invitations to Tate Gallery receptions, curatorial talks and behind-the-scene tours, complimentary catalogues and Joint or Family membership of the Friends. Annual membership ranges from £100 to £500.

Patrons of British Art support British painting and sculpture from the Elizabethan period through to the early twentieth century in the Tate Gallery's collection. They encourage knowledge and awareness of British art by providing an opportunity to study Britain's cultural heritage.

Patrons of New Art support contemporary art in the Tate Gallery's collection. They promote a lively and informed interest in contemporary art and are associated with the Turner Prize, one of the most prestigious awards for the visual arts.

Privileges for both groups include invitations to Tate Gallery receptions, an opportunity to sit on the Patrons' executive and acquisitions committees, special events including visits to private and corporate collections and complimentary catalogues of Tate Gallery exhibitions.

Annual membership of the Patrons ranges from £350 to £750, and funds the purchase of works of art for the Tate Gallery's collection.

Further details on the Patrons may be obtained from:

Membership Office, Tate Gallery,
Millbank, London SW1P 4RG
Tel: 0171-887 8752

Corporate Membership Programme

Membership of the Tate Gallery's Corporate Membership Programme offers companies outstanding value-for-money and provides opportunities for every employee to enjoy a closer knowledge of the Gallery, its collection and exhibitions.

Membership benefits are specifically geared to business needs and include private views for company employees, free and discounted admission to exhibitions, discount in the Gallery shop, out-of-hours Gallery visits, behind-the-scenes tours, exclusive use of the Gallery for corporate entertainment, invitations to VIP events, copies of Gallery literature and acknowledgment in Gallery publications.

Tate Gallery Corporate Members

Partners

The British Petroleum Company plc

Ernst & Young

Freshfields

Glaxo Wellcome plc

Manpower PLC

Prudential

Unilever

Associates

Alliance & Leicester plc

American Express

BUPA

Channel Four Television

Credit Suisse First Boston

De La Rue plc

Digital Equipment Group Limited

Drivers Jonas

Global Asset Management

Goldman Sachs International

Lazard Brothers & Co Limited

Linklaters

Merrill Lynch

Morgan Stanley Dean Witter

NatWest Group

Nomura International plc

Nycomed Amersham plc

Robert Fleming & Co. Limited

Schroder Investment Management

Simmons & Simmons

The EMI Group

Union Bank of Switzerland

Corporate Sponsorship

The Tate Gallery works closely with sponsors to ensure that their business interests are well served, and has a reputation for developing imaginative fund-raising initiatives. Sponsorships can range from a few thousand pounds to considerable investment in long-term programmes; small businesses as well as multi-national corporations have benefited from the high profile and prestige of Tate Gallery sponsorship.

Opportunities available at Tate Gallery London, Liverpool and St Ives include exhibitions (some also tour the UK), education, conservation and research programmes, audience development, visitor access to the Collection and special events. Sponsorship benefits include national and regional publicity, targeted marketing to niche audiences, exclusive corporate entertainment, employee benefits and acknowledgment in Tate Gallery publications.

Tate Gallery London:
Principal Corporate Sponsors
(alphabetical order)

The British Petroleum Company plc
1990–2000, *New Displays*
1998–2000, Campaign for the Creation of the Tate Gallery of British Art

Channel Four Television
1991–9, *The Turner Prize*

Ernst & Young
1996, *Cézanne**
1998, *Bonnard*

J.P. Morgan & Co. Incorporated
1995, *Willem de Kooning**

Magnox Electric plc
1995–8, *The Magnox Electric Turner Scholarships*
1997, *Turner's Watercolour Explorations*
1998, *Turner and the Scientists*

Pearson plc
1992–5, Elizabethan Curator Post
1995, *Dynasties: Painting in Tudor and Jacobean England 1530–1630*

Prudential
1996, *Grand Tour*
1997, *The Age of Rossetti, Burne-Jones and Watts: Symbolism in Britain 1860–1910*

Tate & Lyle PLC
1991–2000, Friends Marketing Programme
1997, *Henry Tate's Gift*

Volkswagen
1991–6, The Volkswagen Turner Scholarships

Tate Gallery London: Corporate Sponsors
(alphabetical order)

Akeler Developments PLC
1997–8, Art Now Programme

AT&T
1997, *Piet Mondrian*

Beck's
1995, *Rites of Passage*

The British Printing Company Ltd
1994–5, sponsorship in kind

The Government of Canada and The Canadian High Commission, London
1995, *Rites of Passage*
1995, *Art Now – Genèvieve Cadieux*

CDT Design Ltd
1995–6, *Art Now*

Classic FM
1995–6, Regional tour of David Hockney's 'Mr and Mrs Clark and Percy' (in kind)

Clifton Nurseries
1991–5, Christmas Tree (in kind)

Coutts Group
1998, *Per Kirkeby*

Coutts Contemporary Art Foundation
1997, *Luciano Fabro*

Danish Contemporary Art Foundation
1998, *Per Kirkeby*

The German Government
1997, *Lovis Corinth*

The Guardian
1995, *Rites of Passage* (in kind)

Glaxo Wellcome plc
1997, *Turner on the Loire*

Häagen-Dazs Fresh Cream Ice Cream
1995–6, *Art Now*

The Hiscox Group
1995–6, Friends Room

HUGO BOSS
1997, *Ellsworth Kelly*

Pro Helvetia
1995, *Through Switzerland with Turner*
1997, *Art Now – Beat Streuli*

Romulus Construction Limited
1996, Bill Woodrow: *Fools' Gold*

Spink-Leger Pictures
1997, *Francis Towne*

Swiss National Tourist Office
1995, *Through Switzerland with Turner*

Tarmac Group plc*
1995–9, Paintings Conservation

The EMI Group
1997, *Centre Stage* education project

TSB Group plc
1992–5, *William Blake* display series
1995, Paintings Conservation

Tate Gallery of Modern Art: Corporate Sponsors
(alphabetical order)

Ernst & Young
1995, *Tate Gallery of Modern Art: Selecting an Architect*
1997–2000, Tate Gallery of Modern Art Visitor Centre

Tate Gallery Liverpool: Corporate Sponsors
(alphabetical order)

Girobank plc
1995, *Primary Cooking* Education booklet

Ian Short Partnership
1995, *Testing the Water*

The Littlewoods Organisation plc
1992–5, *New Realities*

MOMART plc
1991–5, The Momart Fellowship

Royal Liver Assurance
1995, *Making It*

Tate & Lyle PLC
1995, Tate Friends Liverpool membership leaflet

Tate Gallery St Ives: Corporate
(alphabetical order)

Barclays Bank PLC*
1995, *Porthmeor Beach: 'A Century of Images'*

Marks & Spencer
1998, Education Events and Workshops

Northcliffe Newspapers in Education*
1995–7, Education Programme

*denotes a sponsorship in the arts, recognised by an award under the Government's 'Pairing Scheme' administered by the Association for Business Sponsorship of the Arts.

Tate Gallery Founding Benefactors
(date order)

Sir Henry Tate
Sir Joseph Duveen
Lord Duveen
The Clore Foundation
Heritage Lottery Fund

Tate Gallery Principal Benefactors
(alphabetical order)

American Fund for the Tate Gallery
The Annenberg Foundation
Calouste Gulbenkian Foundation
Friends of the Tate Gallery
The Henry Moore Foundation
The Kreitman Foundation
Sir Edwin and Lady Manton
National Art Collections Fund
National Heritage Memorial Fund
The Nomura Securities Co., Ltd
Patrons of New Art
Dr Mortimer and Theresa Sackler Foundation
St Ives Tate Action Group
The Wolfson Foundation and Family Charitable Trust

Tate Gallery Benefactors
(alphabetical order)

The Baring Foundation
Bernard Sunley Charitable Foundation
Gilbert and Janet de Botton
Mr and Mrs James Brice
Mr Edwin C.Cohen
The Eleanor Rathbone Charitable Trust
Esmée Fairbairn Charitable Trust
Foundation for Sport and the Arts
GABO TRUST for Sculpture Conservation
GEC Plessey Telecommunications
The Getty Grant Program
Granada Group plc
The Paul Hamlyn Foundation
Horace W. Goldsmith Foundation
John Hughes
The John S.Cohen Foundation
The John Ellerman Foundation
John Lewis Partnership
John Lyon's Charity
The Leverhulme Trust
Museums and Galleries Improvement Fund
Ocean Group plc (P.H. Holt Trust)
Patrons of British Art
Peter Moores Foundation
The Pilgrim Trust
Mr John Ritblat
The Sainsbury Family Charitable Trusts
Samsung Foundation of Culture
The Stanley Foundation Limited
Save and Prosper Educational Trust
SRU Limited
Weinberg Foundation

Tate Gallery Donors
(alphabetical order)

London

Professor Abbott
The Andy Warhol Foundation for the Visual Arts, Inc
The Fagus Anstruther Memorial Trust
Lord Attenborough CBE
The Austin and Hope Pilkington Charitable Trust
BAA plc
Friends of Nancy Balfour OBE
Balmuir Holdings
The Hon. Robin Baring
B.A.T. Industries plc
Nancy Bateman Charitable Trust
Mr Tom Bendhem
Mr Alexander Bernstein
David and Janice Blackburn
Michael and Marcia Blakenham
George and Mary Bloch
Miss Mary Boone
Frances and John Bowes
The Britwell Trust
Mr and Mrs Donald L. Bryant, Jr
Mrs Melva Bucksbaum
Mr and Mrs Neville Burston
Card Aid
Carlsberg Brewery
Mr Vincent Carrozza
Mrs Beryl Carpenter
Cazenove & Co Charitable Trust
Charlotte Bonham Carter Charitable Trust
Christie, Manson & Woods Ltd
The Claire Hunter Charitable Trust
The Clothworkers Foundation
Mrs Elisabeth Collins
Mr R.N.Collins
Mr Christopher Cone
Giles and Sonia Coode-Adams
Mrs Dagny Corcoran
C.T. Bowring (Charitable Trust) Ltd
Cognac Courvoisier
Mr Edwin Cox
Paula Cussi
Gordon and Marilyn Darling
Antony d'Offay Gallery
Mr and Mrs Kenneth Dayton
Mr Damon and The Hon. Mrs de Laszlo
Baron and Baroness Elie de Rothschild
Madame Gustava de Rothschild
The Leopold de Rothschild Charitable Trust
Baroness Liliane de Rothschild
Deutsche Bank AG
Miss W.A. Donner
Mr Paul Dupee
Mrs Maurice Dwek
Elephant Trust
Eli Broad Family Foundation
Elizabeth Arden Ltd
The Essick Foundation
European Arts Festival
Evelyn, Lady Downshire's Trust Fund
Roberto Fainello Art Advisers Ltd
First Boston Corporation
Mr and Mrs Donald G. Fisher
The Flow Foundation
Foreign & Colonial Management Limited
Miss Kate Ganz
Mr Henry Geldzahler
Ms Laure Genillard
Mr and Mrs David Gilmour
The German Government
Goethe Institut
Jack Goldhill
Sir Nicholas and Lady Goodison Charitable Settlement
David and Maggi Gordon
Mr William Govett
Mr and Mrs Richard Grogan
Gytha Trust
Mr and Mrs Rupert Hambro
Miriam and Peter Haas
Mrs Sue Hammerson
Harry Kweller Charitable Trust
The Hon. Lady Hastings
The Hedley Foundation
Hereford Salon
Mr and Mrs Michael Heseltine
Mr Rupert Heseltine
Mr Robert Hornton
Hurry Armour Trust
Idlewild Trust
The Italian Government
Lord and Lady Jacobs
Mrs Gabrielle Keiller
James and Clare Kirkman Trust
Knapping Fund
Mr and Mrs Richard Knight
Mr and Mrs Jan Krugier
The Kirby Laing Foundation
The Lauder Foundation-Leonard and Evelyn Lauder Fund
The Leche Trust
Robert Lehman Foundation, Inc
The Helena and Kenneth Levy Bequest
Mr and Mrs Gilbert Lloyd
Mr and Mrs George Loudon

Mr and Mrs Lawrence Lowenthal
Mail on Sunday
Mr Alexander Marchessini
The Mayor Gallery
Midland Bank Artscard
Mr and Mrs Robert Mnuchin
Mr and Mrs Peter Nahum
Mr and Mrs Philip Niarchos
Fondation Nestlé pour l'Art
Dr Andreas Papadakis
The Paradina Trust
Mr William Pegrum
Philips Fine Art Auctioneers
The Earl of Plymouth
Old Possum's Practical Trust
The Hon. Mrs Olga Polizzi
Paul Nash Trust
Peter Samuel Charitable Trust
Mr Jean Pigozzi
Ptarmigan Trust
Sir Gordon Reece
Reed International P.L.C.
Richard Green Fine Paintings
Mrs Jill Ritblat
Rothschild Bank AG
Kathy and Keith Sachs
Mrs Jean Sainsbury
Salander-O'Reilly Galleries LLC
The Hon. Simon Sainsbury
Sebastian de Ferranti Trust
Schroder Charity Trust
Mr and Mrs D M Shalit
Ms Dasha Shenkman
South Square Trust
Mr A. Speelman
Standard Chartered Bank
The Swan Trust
Sir Adrian and Lady Judith Swire
Mr and Mrs Louis A. Tanner
Mrs Barbara Thomas
Time-Life International Ltd
The 29th May 1961 Charitable Trust
Lady Juliet Townsend
Laura and Barry Townsley
The Triangle Trust
U.K. Charity Lotteries Ltd
Mrs Anne Uribe-Mosquera
Visiting Arts
Mr and Mrs Leslie Waddington
Waley-Cohen Charitable Trust
Mr Mark Weiss
Weltkunst Foundation
Mrs Alexandra Williams
Graham and Nina Williams
Willis Faber plc
Mr Andrew Wilton
Thomas and Odette Worrell
The Worshipful Company of Goldsmiths
The Worshipful Company of Grocers
Mrs Jayne Wrightsman
and those donors who wish to remain anonymous

Friends Benefactors and Life Members 1958–1998

The André Bernheim Charitable Trust
Dr and Mrs David Cohen
Mrs Isobel Dalziel
Mr and Mrs Charles Dickinson
Lady Gosling
Miranda, Countess of Iveagh
Lord and Lady Jacobs
Mr and Mrs A.G.W. Lang
Sir Sydney and Lady Lipworth
The Sir Jack Lyons Charitable Trust
Mr Michael Rose
Lieutenant Commander and Mrs Shilling
Mrs Jack Steinberg
Mr John B. Sunley
Mr and Mrs Terry Willson

Tate Gallery of Modern Art

Arthur Andersen (pro-bono)
The Annenberg Foundation
Lord and Lady Attenborough
The Baring Foundation
David and Janice Blackburn
Mr and Mrs Anthony Bloom
Mr and Mrs John Botts
Frances and John Bowes
Mr and Mrs James Brice
Donald L. Bryant Jr Family
Mrs Melva Bucksbaum
Monsieur Alain Camu
Mr Edwin C. Cohen
The John S. Cohen Foundation
Gilbert de Botton
Sir Harry and Lady Djanogly
The Drapers' Company
English Heritage
English Partnerships
Ernst & Young
Esmée Fairbairn Charitable Trust
The Worshipful Company of Fishmongers
The Foundation for Sport and the Arts
Friends of the Tate Gallery
The Worshipful Company of Goldsmiths
Noam and Geraldine Gottesman
GJW Government Relations (pro-bono)
The Worshipful Company of Haberdashers
Hanover Acceptances Limited
André and Rosalie Hoffmann
Horace W. Goldsmith Foundation
Lord and Lady Jacobs
Irene and Hyman Kreitman
Mr and Mrs George Loudon
McKinseys & Co (pro-bono)
The Mercers' Company
The Millennium Commission
The Monument Trust
Mr and Mrs M.D. Moross
Guy and Marion Naggar
The Paul Hamlyn Foundation
The Quercus Trust
The Rayne Foundation
The Dr Mortimer and Theresa Sackler Foundation
The Salters' Company
Belle Shenkman Estate
Simmons & Simmons
London Borough of Southwark
The Starr Foundation
Sir Dennis and Lady Stevenson
Miss M.F. Stevenson
Mr and Mrs Ian Stoutzker
Mr John Studzinski
David and Linda Supino
Laura and Barry Townsley
Townsley & Co
The 29th May 1961 Charitable Trust
The Vintners' Company
Robert and Felicity Waley-Cohen
The Weston Foundation
Graham and Nina Williams
Poju and Anita Zabludowicz
and those donors who wish to remain anonymous

Tate Gallery of Modern Art: Collections Benefactor

Janet Wolfson de Botton

Tate Gallery of British Art

The Annenberg Foundation
Sir Harry and Lady Djanogly
The Dulverton Trust
Maurice and Janet Dwek
Friends of the Tate Gallery
Heritage Lottery Fund
Lloyds TSB Foundation for England and Wales
Sir Edwin and Lady Manton
The P.F. Charitable Trust
The Polizzi Charitable Trust
Mrs Coral Samuel CBE
Tate Gallery Centenary Gala
The Trusthouse Charitable Foundation
The Duke of Westminster OBE TD DL
and those donors who wish to remain anonymous

Tate Gallery Liverpool

ABSA
Arrowcroft Group Limited
Arts Council of Great Britain
The Australian Bicentennial Authority
Barclays Bank plc
The Baring Foundation
BASF
Solomon and Isabel Blankstone Charitable Trust
Boddingtons plc
British Alcan Aluminium plc
The British Council
British Gas
British Telecom plc
Calouste Gulbenkian Foundation
Coopers & Lybrand
Mr and Mrs Henry Cotton
Cultural Relations Committee
David M Robinson Jewellery
Deloitte Haskins & Sells
D'Oyly Carte Charitable Trust
The John Ellerman Foundation
English Estates
The Esmée Fairbairn Charitable Trust
European Arts Festival
European Regional Development Fund
The Foundation for Sport and the Arts
GPT Ltd
The Granada Foundation
Granada Television
The Henry Moore Sculpture Trust
Heritage Lottery Fund
Mr John Heyman
Higsons Brewery plc
Ian Short Partnership
IBM United Kingdom Trust
Ibstock Building Products Ltd
ICI Chemicals & Polymers Limited
The John Lewis Partnership
The John S. Cohen Foundation
The Laura Ashley Foundation
The Littlewoods Organisation
Liverpool Council for Voluntary Services
Liverpool John Moores University
Mr & Mrs Jack Lyons
Manchester Airport plc
Manor Charitable Trust
Merseyside Development Corporation
Mobil Oil Company Ltd
Momart plc
The Henry Moore Foundation
The Moores Family Charitable Foundation
The Nigel Moores Family Charitable Trust
New Moorgate Trust Fund
NSK Bearings Europe Ltd
Ocean Group plc (P.H. Holt Trust)
P & P Micro Distributors Ltd
Parkman Consulting Engineers
The Pilgrim Trust
Pilkington plc
Pioneer High Fidelity (GB) Ltd
Eleanor Rathbone Charitable Trust
Royal Insurance (UK) Ltd
Royal Liver Assurance
RTZ Chemicals Ltd
Sainsbury Family Charitable Trusts
Samsung Electronics
Save & Prosper Educational Trust
Scottish & Newcastle Breweries
Stanley Thomas Johnson Foundation
The Summerfield Charitable Trust
Bernard Sunley Charitable Foundation
Friends of the Tate Gallery
Tate Friends Liverpool
Trinity International
Trustee Savings Bank Foundation
Unilever
United Biscuits (UK) Limited
United Utilities plc
The University of Liverpool
Vernons Organisation Ltd
Visiting Arts
Volkswagen
Whitbread & Company plc
The Wolfson Foundation
and those donors who wish to remain anonymous